corporeal

DANCING KNOWLEDGE, CULTURE AND POWER

"A tour de force ... Foster has collected sparkling,
interesting, individual essays on topics ranging from tango
to the history of hysteria and puts them in play with each
other to create a substantial and provocative discourse."
Janelle Reinelt, University of California, Davis.

"This forward-looking collection of essays ... breaks new
ground in exploring the relationship between moving
bodies and cultural meanings."
Joseph Roach, Tulane University.

The contributors look at bodies engaged in practices as
varied as pageantry, physical education, festivals and
exhibitions, tourism, and social and theatrical dance. They
succeed in bringing these bodies to life with all the
political, gendered, racial, and aesthetic resonances of
which bodily motion is capable. Dance is used in this
volume as a theoretical framework to assist the reader in
understanding the body's permanent transience, and in the
task of transposing its movements into words and its
choreography into theory.

These are groundbreaking essays that work to resurrect
bodies in all their cultural significance. They move bodies
across disciplinary boundaries, and encourage the
rethinking of knowledge categories by illuminating the
body's role in the production of narrative, the construction
of collectivity, and the articulation of the unconscious.

Corporealities is an important and exciting
development in dance studies. As a bridge to other
disciplines that have neglected dance for too long, it
demands to be read by all who have an interest in cultural
studies, gender or performance.

Susan Leigh Foster is Professor of Dance at the
University of California, Riverside and is the author of
Reading Dancing (1986).

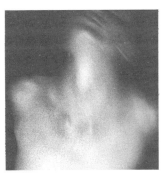

corporealities

edited by
SUSAN LEIGH FOSTER

DANCING KNOWLEDGE,
CULTURE
AND POWER

ROUTLEDGE
London and New York

First published 1996
by Routledge
11 New Fetter Lane, London EC4P 4EE

Simultaneously published in the USA and Canada
by Routledge
29 West 35th Street, New York, NY 10001

Typeset in Bell Gothic by Solidus (Bristol) Limited

Printed and bound in Great Britain

Text design by Secondary Modern

British Library Cataloguing in Publication Data
A catalogue record for this book is available from the British
Library

Library of Congress Cataloguing in Publication Data
A catalogue record for this book has been requested

ISBN 0-415-12138-8 (hbk)
ISBN 0-415-12139-6 (pbk)

CONTENTS

LIST OF ILLUSTRATIONS

CONTRIBUTORS' BIOGRAPHIES

SUSAN LEIGH FOSTER, choreographer, dancer, and writer, is Professor of Dance at the University of California, Riverside. She is author of *Reading Dancing: Bodies and Subjects in Contemporary American Choreography* and *Storying Bodies: Ballet's Choreography of Narrative and Gender*, and editor of *Choreographing History*.

MARK FRANKO, Associate Professor of Theater Arts at the University of California, Santa Cruz, is author of *The Dancing Body in Renaissance Choreography, Dance as Text: Ideologies of the Baroque Body*, and *Dancing Modernism, Performing Politics*.

HEIDI GILPIN is Assistant Professor in the Department of Dance at the University of California, Riverside. She works as a dramaturg for William Forsythe and the Frankfurt Ballet and directs the Institute for New Dramaturgy in Amsterdam and Los Angeles. Her work focuses on the interdisciplinary terrain created by scholars and artists working in the areas of performance, technology, architecture, and critical theory.

LENA HAMMERGREN is a Research Fellow and Director of Dance Studies Division, Theater and Film Studies, Stockholm University. She is currently at work on a book on modern dance in Sweden with emphasis on historiographical and feminist issues.

RANDY MARTIN teaches in the Department of Social Science at the Pratt Institute. He is author of *Performance as Political Act: The Embodied Self* and *Socialist Ensembles: Theater and State in Cuba and Nicaragua*, and co-editor of *New Studies in the Politics and Culture of U.S. Communism*.

SALLY ANN NESS, author of *Body, Movement, and Culture: Kinesthetic and Visual Symbolism in a Philippine Community*, is a cultural anthropologist, specializing in peoples and cultures of Southeast Asia, interpretive ethnography, and the analysis of human movement. She is an Associate Professor in Dance at the University of California, Riverside.

PEGGY PHELAN is Chair of the Department of Performance Studies, Tisch School of the Arts, New York University. She is the author of *Unmarked: The Politics of Performance*, and co-editor with Lynda Hart of *Acting Out: Feminist Performances*.

NANCY LEE CHALFA RUYTER is Associate Professor of Dance at the University of California, Irvine. Her publications include *Reformers and Visionaries; The Americanization of the Art of Dance* and articles on the Delsarte System, nineteenth-century Yugoslav dance, and dance in Hispanic cultures. She is currently at work on a book that addresses the relation of the Delsarte system to development of modern dance.

MARTA E. SAVIGLIANO is an Associate Professor of Dance at the University of California, Riverside. She is the author of *Political Economy of Passion: Tango, Exoticism, and Decolonization*. Her interests revolve around the critical re-appropriation of Marxist, feminist and postculturalist theories for the study of representations and performances of subaltern moving bodies.

LINDA J. TOMKO is a historian, dancer and reconstructor of period dance. She is Assistant Professor of Dance at the University of California, Riverside, and focuses her research on women and dance in the early twentieth-century United States. She also directs the Baroque dance troupe *Les Menus Plaisirs* and is a faculty member of the annual Stanford University Summer Workshop in Baroque Dance and Music.

ACKNOWLEDGMENTS

This volume of essays issues from a two-year initiative entitled "Choreographing History" sponsored by the University of California Humanities Research Institute. The unprecedented support from the Institute enabled intensive focus on and discussion of the work presented in this volume. Contributors to *Corporealities* met weekly for a period of five months to engage with one another and invited guests in dialogue that constructed an interdisciplinary context for dance studies and a bodily presence within cultural studies. As part of that dialogue, versions of these essays were read and commented on by all members of the group.

For their support and guidance throughout this project, we wish to acknowledge Christena L. Schlundt, Professor Emerita in the Department of Dance at the University of California, Riverside; Mark Rose, Director of the University of California Humanities Research Institute and the staff of the Institute; and Brian Copenhaver, Dean of the College of Humanities and Social Sciences at the University of California, Riverside.

INTRODUCTION

Corporealities seeks to vivify the study of bodies through a consideration of bodily reality, not as natural or absolute given but as a tangible and substantial category of cultural experience. The essays in this volume refuse to let bodies be used merely as vehicles or instruments for the expression of something else. They acknowledge that bodies always gesture towards other fields of meaning, but at the same time instantiate both physical mobility and articulability. Bodies do not only pass meaning along, or pass it along in their uniquely responsive way. They develop choreographies of signs through which they discourse: they run (or lurch, or bound, or feint, or meander...) from premise to conclusion; they turn (or pivot, or twist...) through the process of reasoning; they confer with (or rub up against, or bump into...) one another in narrating their own physical fate. In approaching physicality as a site of meaning-making, these essays lend greater precision to our understanding of the reality of embodiment. They also illuminate the corporeal play that is vital to cultural production and to theoretical formulations of cultural process. Talk about the body has become really real. Surely it was always everywhere, but now it moves in intellectual circles. In theory, it has become incorporated. Bodies moving about. Thinking, writing, speaking is now more fully inflected with this corporeality. But how to know this? To have knowledge of it? The fragile suspension bridge that once seemed the lone crossing between mind and body now appears as a super-highway. It is by this design that the traffic flows. Inscription in motion. Choreography. That is what this volume is about. Choreography is psychic. It is critical. Historicizing. It is deployed here as a thinking tool, a mental physic. Not just to think through dance, which many of the essays do, but to rethink how disciplines do their work. Ethnography, historiography, dialectical materialism, psychoanalysis, hermeneutics. Each of these critical procedures is subjected to choreographic revision. As writings on how bodies get inscribed through cultural practices, and where they don't, these choreographic operations can perform for that broader interest in the body that still awaits development in language.

These essays summon up bodies engaged in practices as diverse as pageantry, physical education, festivals and exhibitions, tourism, social and theatrical dance, and postcolonial and psychoanalytic encounters. They bring these bodies to life, quivering with all the political, gendered, social, racial, sexual, and aesthetic resonances of which bodily motion is capable. Their ability to flesh out bodily motion – the body's spatial, temporal, and tensile qualities, the patterns of shape and rhythm it constructs alone and alongside other bodies – lends a new exactitude to the widespread use of body as a critical term in contemporary theory.[2010] At the same time, the diverse methodological approaches employed in these essays expand the registers of cultural significance in which the body perforce participates.

Recent scholarly focus on the body grows out of anthropological and historical interest in non-documented human endeavors and from the complementary interest taken within literary studies towards non-written texts. It equally results from the feminist problematization of gender, a concept that repeatedly forces an interrogation of the relationship between biological and cultural bodily constructions. Bodily subjection, disciplining, appropriation, colonization, mobilization, and agency have also occupied the center of crucial theoretical debates gathered loosely under the rubric of body politics. Yet, too often, these scholarly inquiries into body have treated it as a mute event passed over hastily on the way to more concrete data or more abstract concepts. The essays in this volume, even as they draw on cross-disciplinary theoretical developments – studies of text, gender, and power – generated within these disciplines that have enabled the body to emerge as an area of inquiry, give the body greater depth, a more powerful valence, than it has yet achieved in most scholarly treatments of it.

Dancing wends its way through these texts as a consistent and unifying thematic. In some it serves as the primary subject under analysis, while in others it works as a metaphorical framework that generates the analysis. Much like the body, dancing has been celebrated for its evanescence and for the speechlessness it produces as a response in those who witness it. Or else it has been pinned down by the dates, places, and names that surface readily in its wake. These more accessible traces documenting the fact that dancing occurred, like measurements conducted on the body, do not probe the significance of dancing. History - what does that word mean? Sometimes it's used as a feeble synonym for the past, for all that happened prior to a thing's nowness. Sometimes it connotes the present-in--the-making. Sometimes it stands for longstanding authentications. Sometimes it flexes as a rubric, embracing biography, chronology, all the kinds of works for which dance writers have claimed the name history. Seldom is it invoked to signal its professional or academic conception: the study of change or process through time. Why should we now worry new meanings for "history?" Why trouble dance thinkings that have long deferred (re)defini-

[2010] *Fragments of bodies – texts that have long been haunting historians with their elusiveness. What if we think ourselves the heirs to ancient methods of remembering the body and its movements and of methods of deconstructing corporeal similitudes? As we use all five senses to sniff, touch, crawl, think, leap, peek, write, fantasize, mutter about, and listen our way through the history of bodies, we perform our knowledge of dance. A knowledge that is a curious collection of mental pictures derived from sense impressions, but with a time element added. For these images are memories and they come from both the past and the present. What is this text, except for being the last of an immense number of fictional footnotes to an imagined essay? This page performs a marginality taking precedence over centrality. Perhaps a vision of a day when dominating orders are reversed within the academic disciplines and everybody choreographs their histories.*

tions? You could say that the body compels us. Postmodern performances of bodies; cross-discipline fascination with the body as
discourse; theoretical de-stabilizations of the grounds and identities in which bodies have moved. Long absent from analysis, the
body looms open – open to theorizing, historicizing, interpretation. It's this present that for dance demands a past to be wrought
through the makings of histories. Dance must consider its constructions, its changes through time, its presents. Yet dancing, as a cultural
practice that cultivates disciplined and creative bodies, as a representational practice
that explores rigorously strategies for developing bodily signification, as a cultural
endeavor through which cultural change is both registered and accomplished, provides
a rich resource for any study of embodiment.

These essays, written at the intersection of dance studies and cultural studies of the
body, demonstrate dance's contribution to the study of meaning-filled physicality. They
treat choreography as a theorization of relationships between body and self, gender,
desire, individuality, community, and nationality. They show how the crafting of moving
bodies into a dance reflects a theoretical stance towards identity in all its registers. At
the same time, these essays, by incorporating developments in feminist, anthropological, textual, and political studies of body, bring to dance studies new stagings of
dance's cultural practice.

Body in this volume thus provides the critical bridge among disciplinary and political
interests. It stretches in multiple directions, collecting with a powerful sweep of its arm
distinct methodological and theoretical orientations, instantiating the interstices among
distinct perspectives and providing an anatomy for dialogue among them.

In imbuing bodies with corpo-realities, these essays necessarily theorize the project
of writing about body as well. From the beginning then, the body is capable
of being scripted, of being written. In that writing, the body's
movements become the source of interpretations and judgments –
moral, aesthetic, philosophical, empathetic. Freud, not an addict
in his impulse to reference the Scriptures, reaches for this reassurance near the end of *Beyond the Pleasure Principle*. Freud is
casting his eye back over what he has written, fears it is not a bold
step forward but only a stutter step, a tentative walk on thin ice,
a speculation on "the beyond" that he can only write from the position of historian. Limping from the energy he has spent wrestling
the two opposing drives, the death drive (Thanatos) and the life
drive (Eros), into some more or less coherent choreography, Freud
attempts to salvage his effort by reminding himself (and us) that

the Bible tells us it is not a sin to limp. He reminds us that "it is written." In this gesture he reveals that his work, in addition to pacifying the opposing energies of Thanatos and Eros, also must contend with the opposing hope of writing – to fix, to make permanent, to secure – and the restless movements which define the unconscious – movements which unfix and make consciousness itself tentative and insecure. Freud tracks the movements of the unconscious as they do the work of repression, he follows the trace of that which has disappeared from consciousness. In this regard, Freud's work precedes our own – to write about dance is to fix and make secure the thing that reveals itself *as* it disappears.

Dance studies has long recognized as a central and critical problematic the techniques of research and representation necessary to write about dancing. Following the lead of dance studies, these essays grapple with the ephemerality of the moving-body-object and the equally non-substantial history of its habits, routines, inclinations, and accomplishments. They persevere in the arduous task of traducing movement into words, bodily phrasing into syntactical structure, and movement quality into metaphor. And they give body, positionality, and motional directionality to their own authorial voices. This reflexive double-bodiedness in writing about the body permits that writing to perform alongside those third bodies which are its referents. **For the Kaluli people of Papua New Guinea, history — the *taking of account* of the various collective conflicts and actual individual tragedies of social life — is conceived of as a kind of dancing. For the Pintupi people of Western Australia, history is a traveling dancer whose record is inscribed in the landscape as a fabric of power, a terrain composed of namings and beings left in its wake, a visible realm rendered out of a prefigured eternal reality. Dancing, for the Apache, is a means of achieving lucidity. It allows an apprehension of the "makingness" of the present. The authors of these essays met to have a dance with History. We met to unseat History, to turn it on its heels and "have a go" with it. We met to write to life what has been written to death. We are trying to deal with History somewhat differently from the historians of (T)he (P)ast — those writers who were themselves more like statues than like dancers. Some of us promenade History, some trade bows and curtseys with it, some join in its waltzes, some its tangos, some partner its more acrobatic moves. We have turned ourselves (in)to writing to dance with this figure, to achieve a lucid rendering of its realms.**

These essays work to resurrect bodies in all their fulsome cultural significance, but they also move bodies across disciplinary and theoretical boundaries so as to enable a rethinking of previously stable categories of knowledge. **What would it mean for writing to perform its own utterance? Hopefully, not to become the icon of its own meaning, introducing a new realm of the visual as signifier. But probably, still, to introduce bodies into writing, to uncover how bodies write, corpo-realize writing. No mirror reflection, that; no easy mimesis. Hopefully not one more formalization, another reduction of something to itself as a medium, but a recognition in *physis* or *graphe*, of bodies whose writing is bound to challenge but also profoundly to alter the discipline – the human sciences – such as they are not disposed to incorporate it.** As they examine the body's role in the production of narrative, in the construction of collectivity, in the articulation of the unconscious, in the generation of postcoloniality, and in the economies of gender and expression, they contour new relations between history and memory, the aesthetic and the political, the social and the individual. These new kinds of epistemic relations enable a reorientation within existing disciplines, and they also inspire unconventional formulations of human agency that promise to move us past current modes of academic and political stasis.

These essays evoke realms of physical concreteness and interdisciplinary connectedness. The eloquence and passion of their evocation rests upon their collective and mutually supporting presence.

> Siesta time,
> peak of heat and dust;
> swollen dreams,
> smack of dryness,
> tight skins longing for a sting
> of water.
>
> A scorpion writes,
> balancing on her tail,
> the perfect calligraphy of dreams,
> wet recordings encoding secrecy,
> Awake,
> at the margins of dreams.
> Blind and awake,
> and the sun in the middle.

What would dreaming be like in a siesta, dreaming of noon meeting moon mirroring sun, warming up the cold, forging the circle . . . Despiertos, sleeping open-eyed, and the secrets – but not all – start spilling out, crawling out, in confusion (day or night?) shared against our will but following our desires. The scorpion scribbles. A conclusion, an introduction, an inclusion, a commitment at the very end. No more space for further communion, for more love, for less distress or mistrust. Writing from a field of fantasy, blurring, to leave the burning sign of a "non-existent" field. On her tail. The poisoning mixture has a dash of the discourse of the hysteric and drops of the discourse of the analyst, to taste. What if our object of desire were mobile, let us say, movement; the split subject pretending/attempting to be a master of change (displacement, condensation), signifiers never coinciding with signifieds. What if the analysts of embodied ephemeral fantasies fall in love, can not help but pursue the knowledge of that which changes unpredictably, the revolution with-out a vanguard. "Urgent readings," "desperate writings," notates the scorpion, balancing on her tail. [illegible] Longing for a less stiff tool with which to write, a tail capable of curling in and out, in waves, dropping down softly, at the side. Satisfied. Giving up nothing. Risking ambition, multiplied.

Each essay gives writing a different body, some of whose gestures reiterate or vary those made in other essays. The essays have been arranged here, like ten chapters in an experimental novel, so as to suggest multiple meandering paths that the reader's body could traverse in engaging them. If read in the order presented, they invite the reader, first, to settle back into the plush and familiar chair of the ballet's auditorium, only to be shaken from it by the unorthodox interpretations of beauty, virtuosity, and sexuality presented on-stage. Bumping into choreographers, critics, and other viewers, the reader then travels across the stage of modernism, and out into one of its exhibition parks where buildings and bodies comingle in such a way as to elucidate their mutual concerns. Pulled back into the drawing room, site of modernism's hidden, feminine, bodily labor, the reader confronts the slippages among comportment, exercise, elocution, and art. Then, situated in a similar room, the reader witnesses the infusion into the psychic space of memory, and its repressive and transformative maneuvers, of the concrete and mundane movements of daily life. Voyaging across the landscape that memory provides, the reader is asked to revel in and take inspiration from the fugitive nature of any performance. Traveling to the ethnographic field and then to the historical archive, the reader winds, hurtles, and backtracks, or zooms along trajectories that attempt to account for the pasts and presents that make up the interpretation and representation of past movement. Sitting back in the auditorium, but this time on the edge of the seat, the reader is invited to project onto the dancing body over-abun-dances of relevant meanings. Finally, in a fantastical theater, the reader is swept along in the ironic gesturing towards an operatic tradition that stages the multiple positionings of power.

Or the reader's travels could be narrated as an account of the bodies encountered in the texts: the monstrous body of the ballerina-as-phallus; the equally cyborgian choreographer–critic–historian; the strolling *flâneuse* whose casual walk thinly disguises the acuteness of her vision; the map-maker who charts the transitions from statue to pose to movement; the dissected and still performative bodies of patient and psychoanalyst; the shadow of a body, symbol of its perpetual disappearance; the tourist whose body is replete with bodies she moved alongside; the body that sutures individual to communal embodiments of American girlhood; the African-American, gay male body that bears the weight and commands the respect that his labor entails; the parodic entrepreneur who orchestrates the ensemble of chorus, soloists, and choreocritic in their grand spectacle.

Still other accounts might focus on the methodological moves made in each essay, the interdisciplinary spaces they mark out, or the performances of their own subject matter that they undertake. But such summaries presume a stillness for the reader's body that violates the spirit of our collective choreography. They also direct attention away from the impact of the volume as a whole, whose combined gestures say far more than any single body's motion could.

Susan Foster, Mark Franko, Heidi Gilpin, Lena Hammergren,
Randy Martin, Sally Ness, Peggy Phelan, Nancy Ruyter,
Marta Savigliano, Linda Tomko

Irvine, California
May 1993

The ballerina's phallic pointe

SUSAN LEIGH FOSTER

Pliant, quivering with responsiveness, ready to be guided anywhere, she inclines towards him, leaving one leg behind, ever erect, a strong reminder of her desire. As he promenades around the single pointe on which she balances, the leg lifts higher and higher. They pause at the moment her breast bone appears about to break. Arms in a wide V connect to his supporting lunge. The leg, a full 180 degrees vertical, looms behind them, white-pink, utterly smooth, charged with a straining, vibrant vitality.

Then, she floats impetuously away from him. His gaze following her, his arm gestures a pathetic desire. As the music builds to its climax, she reaches the corner and turns back towards him. The emollient rush of her body into his outstretched arms results in yet another stiffening: she holds decorously rigid as he lifts and swirls her in a circle above his head. Her delicate tensility allows her to dwell there high in space, a proud ornament, a revolving bowsprit.

If we have seen it once, we have seen it a thousand times, this generic sequence that resembles *pas des deux* in *Swan Lake, Jewels, The Ballet of the Red Guard*, that can be found in the repertories of the National Ballets of Canada, Taiwan, South Africa, Cuba, the Philippines, Australia, Argentina, Mexico, Brazil.... We have interpreted this phrasing of two bodies as a sequence of abstract referents, a culmination in the striving towards physical refinement and purification that originated in Renaissance European court codes of bodily civility.[1] These bodies celebrate a breathtaking physical accomplishment. They dance out an ethereal realm of perpetually vanishing perfect forms.

But they are also desiring bodies, bodies that turn away from and rush back towards one another, bodies that touch one another, that strive together delicately and fervently in front of other bodies who, from their anonymous location in a darkened auditorium, desire them as well. And they are gendered bodies. Even when costumed in the most unisex unitards, *she* wears pointe shoes, and *he* wears ballet slippers. *She* elaborates a vast range of intricate coordinations for legs, feet, arms, and head, while *he* launches into the air, defying gravity in a hundred different positions. *She* extends while *he* supports. *She* resides in front and *he* remains in back. *She* looks forward as *he* looks at her. *She* touches his arms, hands, and shoulders, whereas *he* touches her arms and hands and also her waist, thighs, buttocks, and armpits.[2]

And these two bodies, because of their distinctly gendered behavior, dance out a specific kind of relationship between masculine and feminine.[3] They do more than create an alert, assertive, solicitous manliness and a gracious, agile, vibrant womanliness. Their repeated rushes of desire – the horizontal attraction of bodies, the vertical fusion of bodies – do more than create unified sculptural wholes that emblematize the perfect union of male and female roles. *He* and *she* do not participate equally in their choreographic coming together. *She* and *he* do not carry equal valence. *She* is persistently put forward, the object of his adoration. *She* never reaches out and grabs him but is only ever impelled towards him, arms streaming behind in order to signal her possession by a greater force. *He* longs for her and moves with alacrity to support her from behind or at her side, yet he dances as though *she* were a dream, an hallucination he can long for but only momentarily handle. *She* is the registering of *his* desire. *She* is attraction itself which *he* presents for all the world to see.

The world sees more and more of her as ballet, taken up by former colonies in the Pacific and Latin America, and also in China and Japan spreads across the globe.[4] Strong contendent for a universal standard of physical achievement in dance, ballet, with its pedagogical orderliness and clear criteria for excellence, promises a homogenizing medium for the expression of cultural difference. It offers a global aesthetic whose universal claims enable each community to particularize itself while at the same time assuring each community's access to the status of a world player of the form. Annual Ballet Olympics, by conflating distinctions between sport and art, extend an invitation to all to participate in this single aesthetic enterprise. Video, a medium well-suited to the documentation of ballet's aesthetic ideals – extended bodily lines and clear shapes – transports images of balletic bodies around the world. This First World export contains in its historical repertoire numerous images of the hitherto exotic populations that are now adapting its aesthetic as their tradition. Yet in the abstraction of contemporary ballet, little residue remains of the foreign Exotics – the colorful, sensuous settings, or the tempestuous, irresistible women and aggressive, voracious villains – that moved the nineteenth-century ballet plots forward through their combination of evil and sexual impulses. Today's ballet, a sanitized geometry, emphasizes physical discipline and dedication. Rather than offering a travelogue through real and imaginary worlds as it did in the nineteenth century, contemporary ballet provides a seemingly neutral *techne* through which intensities of cultural or psychological ambience can be projected.

In these landscapes of virtuosity, both *her* and *his* bodies bear the marks of colonization and colonial contact. They stand against indigenous forms of dancing as bodies estranged. The sheer excitement of their physical endeavor, however, galvanizes viewers in proud and enthusiastic response. Both *he* and *she* dare to accomplish so much and dare to mask the effort necessary to make their bodily shapings, rhythmic phrasings, and complex exchanges of weight appear so effervescent. Both *she* and *he* sweat to make the choreographer's vision manifest just as they erase their faces of the tension inherent in their exertion and modulate the energy through their limbs so as to render their labor effortless in appearance. Perspiration marks slowly appearing around armpits, groins, abdomens, or backs only make the masking of their effort more miraculously convincing.

But if these two dancing bodies share a dedication to artisanal perfection, they do not enjoy equal visibility. In their joint striving, they construct two unequivalent forms of presence. *He* fades away behind or beneath *her* in their duets, becoming an indispensable assistant, the necessary backdrop against which *she* sparkles. And even though *he* asserts a compelling presence in his solos when the full power of his aerial dexterity is revealed, in the end, even in their bows, he remains upstage, orchestrating, enabling *her* performance, but also channeling all attention towards her. *She*, like a divining rod, trembling, erect, responsive, which *he* handles, also channels the energy of all the eyes focused upon *her*, yet even as *she* commands the audience's gaze, *she* achieves no tangible or enduring identity. *Her* personhood is eclipsed by the attention *she* receives, by the need for her to dance in front of everyone. Just as *he* conveys her, *she* conveys desire. *She* exists as a demonstration of that which is desired but is not real. *Her* body flames with the charged wantings of so many eyes, yet like a flame it has no substance. *She* is, in a word, the phallus, and *he* embodies the forces that pursue, guide, and manipulate it.[5]

Now this is a naughty thing to propose. Why revile the delicate and flexible grace, the superb celebration of feminine physicality that these women display by connecting it to the sexual politics of the phallus? Why not give male and female dancers an egalitarian future, regardless of their past, at the moment where ballet enters the late twentieth-century global stage? The answer rests on the series of gendered bodies developed historically within the ballet tradition over the past two hundred years.[6] Whether visible in reworked versions of the classical masterpieces – *Giselle, Swan Lake, Coppelia,* etc. – or merely in the vocabulary and style of the dancing, the weight of these past bodies presses too hard upon contemporary ballet to allow a nongendered reception of its meaning, or even to allow for the dismissal of gendered content as a superfluous formal feature analogous in impact only to that of an irrelevant cliché.

At this moment of ballet's global visibility, the labor of historicizing its gendered meaning is more crucial than ever. The ballerina-as-phallus provokes an analysis of the performance of both feminine and masculine desire. It forces an inquiry into the classical routing of the female viewer's attention: either she must look through the eyes of the male dancer at his partner in order actively to assert attraction, or she must empathize passively with the ballerina as an object of male desire. Both these mappings of her participation as viewer are subtended by a masculine logic that traffics women to sustain various forms of male hegemony.[7] The ballerina-as-phallus likewise problematizes the male viewer's gaze: his point of identification on-stage is an effeminate man, a man in tights, through whom he must pass on his way to the object of fascination, or on whom he can focus within a homosexual counter-reading of the performance.[8] The global context of ballet performance, the remarkable homogeneity of ballet productions regardless of cultural context, and the prevalence of ballet technique as a form of physical training, regardless of the aesthetics of the choreographic tradition – modern dance, jazz, experimental or ethnic – mandate a consideration of all these gendered identities.

But there is also a promise in the naughtiness of the ballerina-phallus, the promise that all monsters afford, to forge from the cataclysmic energy of their aberrant parts a new identity that meets the political and aesthetic exigencies of the moment.[9] The ballerina is, after all, gulp, magnetically magical. An object of revulsion while under feminist scrutiny, she nonetheless enchants us. Perhaps, via the ballerina-as-phallus, her power can reconfigure so as to sustain her charisma even as she begins to determine her own fate. Perhaps the ballerina-as-phallus can even reclaim for ballet, long viewed as a neutral parade of geometrized forms, a certain sensual and even sexual potency. But first, the ballerina-as-phallus must be fleshed out, provided an origin, a history, and an anatomy.

Sometime early in the middle of the nineteenth century, in Paris, city host to the most lavish and sustained achievements in theatrical dance of any European capital, choreographic and narrative elements congealed so as to form that distinct genre of spectacle, known as the Romantic ballet, whose imprint haunts the aesthetics of contemporary ballet performance.[10] Two ballets from this period, *La Sylphide* (1832) and *Giselle* (1841) survive in the repertories of many ballet companies and retain immense popularity. More significantly, the Romantic ballet celebrated the principle of distinct vocabularies for male and female dancers – the dainty and complex footwork, the *developés* of the leg and extended balances for women and the high leaps, jumps with beats, and multiple pirouettes for men. It rationalized the new technique of pointe work which added a strenuous precariousness to the female dancer's performance. And it encouraged new conventions of partnering that incorporated new codes for touching, for support, and for the achievement of pleasing configurations. Up until the end of the eighteenth century the *pas de deux* had placed great emphasis on male and female dancers performing alongside one another or traveling separately designated pathways in mirrored opposition. These dancers shared a common vocabulary of steps performed with distinctive styles stipulated for male and female dancers. By the time of the Romantic ballets partnering included sections of sustained, slowly evolving shapes where male and female dancers constructed intricate designs, always with the male dancer supporting, guiding, and manipulating the female dancer as she balanced delicately and suspensefully in fully extended shapes. And the divergent vocabularies for male and female dancers symbolized a difference between the sexes far greater than the distinct styles of eighteenth-century performers.[11]

These duets paired a noble if confused male lead with one of two female character types: the supernatural creature or the exotic foreigner. Sylphs, naiads, and wilis offered an enigmatic ephemerality, dream-like, vaporous, incomparably light. Gypsies, Creoles, and other Orientalist characters constituted the sylph's pagan counterpart. Rapturously sensual, unabashedly suggestive, these heroines after innumerable obstacles eventually consummated their romantic attachments, whereas the sylph's unequivocal Otherness usually led to tragic conclusions. In either case, the male lead indulged his longing attachment to her, seeking her out, adoring her, and partnering her with solicitous mastery.

These two female character types helped to solve the ballet's greatest dilemma, growing in intensity since the later decades of the eighteenth century, to integrate the equally pressing needs for a coherent plot and for the display of virtuoso dancing. The ballet plots typically orchestrated one kind of solution by always including festivals, weddings, or celebrations, occasions where dancing would expectably take place, as part of the action. But the female leading character played an even more crucial role in the balancing of drama and spectacle. As some form of exotic, whether foreign or supernatural, her character could easily be construed as one predisposed to dancing. Or even better, dancing might figure as the character's very mode of being in the world. Rather than a walking, talking, gesturing person, she knew best how to float, gambol, suspend, and disappear. As a dancing being, she could easily embody both the necessary passion-filled responses and the repertoire of classical steps. Her pressing desire to dance thus facilitated an easy transition from story to spectacle and back again.

The tragic ballets like *La Sylphide* and *Giselle*, depicting the impossible love between man and sylph (*La Sylphide*) or between prince and peasant (*Giselle*), used the separate vocabularies and stereotypic character types to greatest advantage. Their heroines symbolized not only love lost, but also dreams unrealized and unrealizable. The sylphide, one of a band living in the forest, represented the ideal blending of abstraction and sensuality, a ravishing sensibility, no longer found in the mundane actions of the real world. Giselle offered the beguiling spontaneity of an innocence untainted by the sterile and tedious codes of aristocratic (or urban) civilization. Upon her tragic death she transformed into a wili, yet another variety of enchanted being, defined as a girl "who loved to dance too much," and who on her wedding's eve, at the height of unconsummated sexual arousal, died.[12] The wilis appeared to mortals in the forest at night and lured unsuspecting men into a dance that could only end in their death from exhaustion. Like the sylphides, the wilis enticed men with their voluptuous ways and then vanished.

The spectacle created by low-level gas lighting and elaborate flying machinery for these tulle-skirted supernaturals offered both optical indefiniteness and opulence. Viewers witnessed mirage-like forms dissolving, vanishing, escaping the mortal with such softness. The sprites' world exuded a ravishing melancholy that transcended diversion and referenced truly lost hopes. The sylphide's death after her mortal lover had removed her wings carried a moral and aesthetic significance comparable to the great literature of the Romantic period. Giselle's poignant and miraculously successful efforts to protect her beloved prince from the rapacious wilis resonated with a kind of hope and courage that transcended her specific moment.

Yet the success and durability of these ballets derived not only from their powerful scenarios and sumptuous spectacle, but also from the plentiful opportunities for virtuoso display. Celebrations for the impending wedding in *La Sylphide* showed off the skills of a large *corps de ballet* and several soloists. The witches' dance that opened Act II proffered the high leaps and jumps as well as the contorted acrobatics that audiences adored. Giselle's village commemorated the harvest with a danced celebration, and the wilis in Act II danced Giselle's initiation, the death of the gamekeeper Hilarion, and their pursuit of the prince. These scenes staged group precision at complicated steps and traveling patterns along with dazzling individual expertise. The disposition of dancers in space and the sequencing of dances within these scenes always orchestrated a hierarchical display of skills, contrasting *corps de ballet* with soloists in ways that revealed as they confirmed the very training process that built a great dancer.

The drive to develop new levels of competence at dancing can be traced to the consolidation of the ballet lexicon with its specification of positions, steps, and variations at the beginning of the eighteenth century. Dancers had endeared themselves to audiences for generations by developing some new proof of their dexterity and grace. What distinguished the early nineteenth-century quest for virtuosity was a new conception of bodily responsiveness evident in the training procedures for dancers and also in the high expectations for skill at social dancing and the approach to physical discipline taken in the nascent physical education movement. By the early nineteenth century, dancers no longer studied individually a regimen designed specifically for their physical type and inclination, but instead attended large group classes where they learned standardized sequences of exercises with designated shapes to which all bodies should conform.[13] The pedagogical goal of these classes, informed by the science of anatomy, was to develop the body's strength and flexibility so as to enable more turns, higher leaps and leg extensions, and longer balances. The social dance repertoire reflected a similar concern with expanding physical achievement – more complicated rhythmic patterns, beats of the foot, jumps, and shifts of weight. At the various *bals* and *fêtes* where social dancing occurred, this quest for virtuosity signaled a body that functioned less as a medium for communication than as a showcase for accomplishments.[14] The very fact of the emergence of a new discipline of physical education corroborated this conception of the body-showcase by identifying a set of exercises for the sole purpose of developing bodily strength and equilibrium.[15] In the eighteenth century many activities including dance had claimed a healthy body as an added benefit for those who pursued them. Now, the body had a thing-ness that required maintenance in and of itself. A hundred years earlier dancing had constituted a meta-discipline that prepared the body to execute gracefully all actions whether those of sports, warfare, or the daily behaviors of proper social comportment.[16] Now, the practice of theatrical dance, like the regimens of physical education or social dancing, implemented a body that was isolated by and contained within the specific program of exercises it pursued.

If the physical demands of virtuosity leached from the body any connection to a signifying sociability, they did not de-sexualize it. Rather, the objectification of the body accomplished in these physical regimens rendered it a more neutral and compartmentalized receptacle for an abundance of sexual connotations. Yet, in the same way that codes of partnering put the female body forward for the viewer's delectation, so too, her body bore the vast majority of all sexualizing inferences. Newspaper critics described and compared female dancers' body parts in excruciating and leering detail. An immense literature of gossipy pamphlets sprang up that recounted as a kind of biographical profile the amorous liaisons and sexual escapades of female dancers.[17] The disdainful yet salacious tone, the suspicion of prurience in these publications, distinguishes them from the more modest literature summing up the glamour and power of eighteenth-century ballerinas. Even the definition of the "wili" as the girl who loved to dance too much implied a transparent conflation of dancing with sexual intercourse that extended to the ballet generally. Thus the ballet, even as it danced out an ethereal world of idealized enchantment, also proffered lovely ladies, scantily clad, engaged in a blatant metaphor for sensual and sexual actions.

Capitalist marketing strategies initiated in the early nineteenth century supported and enhanced the objectified dancing body and the commodified female dancer.[18] They pitted one ballerina against another in intensive, objectifying advertising campaigns and opened up backstage areas where wealthy patrons might enjoy the company of dancers before, during, and after the performance. Rather than evaluate a performance within the context of a given genre, or even character type, viewers were encouraged to focus on female stars with merciless comparative scrutiny. The progressive segmentation of the body occurring in physical education, anatomy and the new science of phrenology further supported the fascination with isolated parts of the female dancing body. Poorly paid dancers and insubstantial government support left the institution of dance vulnerable to exploitation, both sexual and specular.[19]

If the female body quietly endured the evaluation of viewers, it nonetheless repelled their gaze through its demonstration of ephemerality itself. As it danced through the exotic trappings of these productions, it conveyed a sumptuous ethereality that rendered viewers mute. Unable to grasp the beauty that vanished as it moved, viewers succumbed to gossip about the dancers, to criticism of their physique, or to rhapsodic evocations of dance's inexpressible loveliness. No translation into words of choreographic action or its danced execution seemed possible. Although eighteenth- and early nineteenth-century choreographers had written the scenarios of their ballets for the program and for publication, choreographers skilled at the conventions of this vaporous ethereality could no longer be expected to write, much less to contrive, the plots for ballets. A scenarist was now called upon to formulate the storyline which the choreographer then evoked through danced action. Nor could any form of notation preserve this action. Like the unattainable love it typically portrayed, choreographic form left its only trace in the bodies that had performed it.

The ballet's evanescence, its reputation as decorative and pleasurable entertainment, aligned it with a host of feminine attributes. Dancing in general accentuated the moderated and flowing use of the body uniquely suited to women, and it provided the nurturing guidance necessary during that romantic and most feminine moment in one's life, late adolescent courtship. The concern with physical presentation, with mannerly and decorous behavior grew out of a uniquely feminine sphere of influence. Theatrical dance, now dominated by female dancers and by female characters, offered a delightful treat more than an edifying experience. Artistic endeavors likewise became feminized within a public sphere dedicated to political and economic governance. Of all the arts, dance, with its concern for bodily display, its evanescent form, and its resistance to the verbal, distinguished itself as overwhelmingly feminine in nature.

The harder-edged bodies, the abstract geometries, the athleticism found in today's productions do not substantively alter the surround of cultural and aesthetic issues, inherited from the nineteenth century, that continues to define ballet today. If not globally, then at least in the United States and Europe, the countries that have exported ballet, the divide between classical steps and representational gestures, the quest for virtuoso display, the division of labor along gender lines, the reputation of dance as non-verbal diversion – all these features remain central to ballet's identity. Despite the security of the choreographic validity of exquisite physical forms, the menacing question of what the ballet is about still looms large. To the extent that the choreographer aspires to represent any facet of human feeling, interaction, or drama, some vocabulary, whether pantomimic or modernist must be deployed. And its gestures must somehow reconcile with the basic ballet vocabulary and with the mandate to present virtuoso dancing. Ballet training, more painful and demanding than ever, produces the audacious and rapturous brilliance that consistently motivates audiences to interrupt the performance with their applause. Even in the most avant-garde companies, distinct vocabularies for male and female dancers endure. Where the ballet vocabulary has blended with modern, jazz, and postmodern movement traditions so as to blur stylistic and lexical distinctiveness, the pointe shoe with its attendant demands on the female dancer survives to assure viewers of the genre. Despite a recently acquired respectability for the male dancer, ballet continues to be conceptualized as a feminine art, especially when compared with music, painting, or poetry. It is dominated by women, even though men hold key artistic and managerial positions. It lacks the permanence of an accessible notation system, and seems sublimely incapable of translation into words.

What no longer endures of the nineteenth-century tradition, (or is it merely glossed over?) is the blatant sexual inflection of the ballet, its extroverted signaling of gender identity and sexual desire. Today's audiences seem not to view the exposed crotch of the ballerina in *arabesque promenade* as genitals. They do not view the moment where her thighs slide over her partner's face as she descends from a high lift as oral sex. Nor do they see her gentle fall onto her partner's prone body as copulation. The formality of balletic bodily shape and line dominates all coding of body parts and conventions of touching. Nineteenth-century audiences likewise accepted the aestheticized coding of body parts that the ballet had developed, even if many men sat in the front row in order to peek up the dancers' bloomers.[20] Still the nineteenth-century productions broadcast the synthetic possibility of spectacle as simultaneously physical, sexual, glamorous, romantic, and aesthetic. To sort through to what has been lost or somehow transformed in contemporary ballet requires a return to Romantic period performances with specific attention to their vectoring of the viewer's desire.

Renowned critic Jules Janin provided this assessment of ballet's structuring of desire in 1844:

> The grand danseur appears to us so sad and so heavy! He is so unhappy and so self-satisfied! He responds to nothing, he represents nothing, he is nothing. Speak to us of a pretty dancing girl who displays the grace of her features and the elegance of her figure, who reveals so fleetingly all the treasures of her beauty. Thank God, I understand that perfectly, I know what this lovely creature wishes us, and I would willingly follow her wherever she wishes in the sweet land of love. But a man, a frightful man, as ugly as you and I, a wretched fellow who leaps about without knowing why, a creature specially made to carry a musket and a sword and to wear a uniform. That this fellow should dance as a woman does – impossible! That this bewhiskered individual who is a pillar of the community, an elector, a municipal councillor, a man whose business it is to make and above all unmake laws, should come before us in a tunic of sky-blue satin, his head covered with a hat with a waving plume amorously caressing his cheek, a frightful danseuse of the male sex, come to pirouette in the best place while the pretty ballet girls stand respectfully at a distance – this was surely impossible and intolerable, and we have done well to remove such great artists from our pleasures. Today, thanks to this revolution which we have effected, woman is queen of ballet. She breathes and dances there at her ease. She is no longer forced to cut off half her silk petticoat to dress her partner with it. Today the dancing man is no longer tolerated except as a useful accessory.[21]

Janin succinctly observed the alignment of masculine identity with a public domain and of feminine identity with a private domain and the inevitable destinies of male and female performers within such an alignment. Male dancers, so chunky and thick on the one hand, so dangerously effeminate on the other, should be banished from the stage. These "frightful danseuse(s) of the male sex" only contaminated, through their doubly failed performance of gender, the viewer's rightful access to the "pretty dancing girl." Her mission and message, utterly obvious according to Janin, was to lead the viewer through the "sweet land of love." Her body, through the act of dancing, would reveal treasures of beauty and sensuality unavailable in any other context.[22]

Although fashion in the early nineteenth century had created of all women a kind of spectacle, theatrical dance constituted one of the few cultural events that framed women, and specifically women's bodies for view. As public personages, the details of their daily lives infused their identities on-stage with prurient intrigue.[23] Their participation in a market economy — buying the claque's applause and publicity from critics like Janin, selling sexual privileges in order to pay for dance classes — was familiar public knowledge. Among the aging aristocrats and business tycoons who could afford to "contribute to their careers," the dancers were referred to as fillies who could be mounted, re-mounted, or exchanged for a new mount.[24] Still, they maintained a kind of dignity that even Janin's demeaning tone could not deny them, one that derived from their expertise at dancing and their dedication to a life in the arts.

As a variety of public woman, female dancers nonetheless bore the burden of spectaculariz-ing expectations for their performance, and they were subject to strategies of containment that controlled their effect on public life. Their bodies, morselized by training and by the viewing gaze, were described as "Nordic," or "gangly," or "with the legs of a gazelle."[25] These terms belied not only the compartmentalization of the body but also the conflation of body parts with characterological attributes. Dancers no longer aspired to represent realistic characters on-stage. Instead, their bodies' parts stood in for various states of being — love, longing, wickedness, pathos, nurturance, dementedness, etc. And these states lined up along axes defined by ethereality and fleshliness, abstinence and rapaciousness, piety and succor. Their physique's natural inclination to evoke these states mattered more than their skill at acting. Thus even as they captured the public's eye with their willingness to put the body on display, their skills were minimized in favor of their natural physical endowments.

In the plots for ballets, female characters uniformly served as the desired personage, and they also registered the bulk of the pathos — in scenes of lamentation, madness, or delight. Male characters' longing overwhelmed in magnitude and intensity any reciprocal gestures the female characters might proffer, yet they also stood by with incapacitated stoicism as the objects of their desire became seized by the torment or ecstasy that the plot produced. Female bodies, absorbent of the feelings and conflicts circulating through all the story's characters, trembled with sexual and emotional fervor. Their solos, the rewarding climax of any scene, were the ones all other bodies watched. Using their exceptional prowess at dancing, these women could express what no other bodies could. Dancing occurred at the site of these bodies as both an indescribable event and an expression of the indescribable.

If these female lead characters gave their male counterparts the dispassion necessary, as Janin observed, to govern, they also sustained male sexual potency. The separation of the dance vocabulary into gendered parts placed female soloists as the central and final object of the specular gaze, yet allowed the male character to remain in control of this charismatic object. The choice and development of female characters likewise worked to preserve male sexual superiority. The wilis, for example, through their challenge to men's sexual endurance, augmented and bolstered male sexual capacity. The few who "died" at their hands in no way undermined the enhanced reputation for sexual prowess that the wilis' existence secured for all men. Other Orientalist and pagan female characters functioned in a similar if less dramatic way. Their renowned sensuality and sexual forwardness reflected directly and positively onto the male character whose inclination it was to pursue and master them.

Scenarists invented a remarkable number of female character types who could assure a potent yet stoic male identity, and these types functioned similarly, in their use of gender-specific vocabulary, in both tragic and comic plots. Although they filled the stage with their voluptuous variations, these female leads never achieved a strong or profound sense of identity. In the tragedies, the point at which they would begin to develop characterological depth most often coincided with the story's demand for the explosive registering of feeling. In that display of pathos, the body was frequently undone.[26] Once their function – as the mark of that which was not male – was jeopardized by the impending need to know them more intimately, the plot wiped them out. All that remained were the endlessly duplicated minor ballerinas, the *corps de ballet*, who, because of their massive number and routinized action, posed no threat of a palpable personhood.[27] In the comedies, heroine and hero would eventually unite, yet the plot and the casting of characters gave little depth to either. Neither lead encountered any substantive conflict through which personality could be revealed. And the fast-paced encounters, extrications, and flirtations that composed the action could only be seen as plays of appearance, especially since a large number of the male parts were played by women.

The popularity of the female travesty dancer grew in tandem with the individuation of masculine and feminine vocabularies of dance movement in the early nineteenth century.[28] A common role in boulevard and variety-show productions from the turn of the century, the travesty role made its way into the Opera in the 1820s.[29] Although the seriousness of tragedy continued to demand a male lead character, the frivolity of comedies and divertissements increasingly called for female dancers in the male roles. Reviews complimented the travesty dancer on her skillful partnering and her graceful ability to display the female lead's talents. They praised her shapely legs, well revealed by the men's *pantalons* she wore. Her presence, perfectly acceptable, even desirable because the two bodies worked so well together, signaled no intimation of homoerotic possibility, no sense of illicit, much less scandalous, behavior. It rested upon, even as it advertised more widely than ever before, a tradition of travesty that since the early 1800s had seen no possibility of or "any affecting consequence" in the love of one woman by another.[30]

The travesty dancer through her blatant burlesque helped to subdue the charismatic power of the female lead. She also seemed to solve, through its elimination, the problem of the effeminate male. Especially in the comedies where true suffering and unbearable consequences never appeared on stage, the male dancer's leaps and turns, even more, his decorous gestures and gaudy costume gave his gendered identity an uncomfortable ambiguousness. The tragedies' plots also tainted him with the same wimpishness. In *La Sylphide* circumstances rather than an act of will caused him to abandon his fiancée and follow the sylphide into the woods. In *Giselle* he stood by aghast and watched as his peasant-love, now cognizant of his treachery, danced herself, by fits and starts, to death. Thus the feminized context of the ballet with its exploration of bodily, sentimental, and opulent aesthetics left little room for a man to move.

It left a great deal, however, for him and for the male viewer who identified with him, to look upon. First, there was the spectacle of the female *corps de ballet*, all those similarly dressed bodies moving in unison like merchandise lined up on a shelf. He could savor the knees of one, the neck of another, engulfed in a glorified female sensuality that required no commitment and no obligation. Then, there were the ballerinas, the ones most desired, most sought after, whose individual physiques and talents inspired different varieties of erotic reverie. Through identification with the male lead, he could likewise adore her, partner her, and possess her. Or if the male lead was played by a woman, her body added yet another kind of feminine form, one that summoned up the voyeuristic erotics of two women dancing an amorous duet together. The whole organization of balletic spectacle presumed the primacy of the male heterosexual viewer whose eyes would be satisfied by a display of voluptuous feminine forms.

But how did the synthesis of choreography and plot guide his desire? As specified in the scenarios and also in the dancing itself, the dominant message in all the ballets amplified upon the desirability of heterosexual coupling. Male and female characters always united or else failed, tragically, to unite. Where the leading couple was successful, the narrative drive towards their union reverberated, in its images of progress and expansiveness, with the promise to realize a new society. At the same time, it affirmed in the procreative unit the secure foundation of the nation. Father passed daughter along to her new husband, ensuring simultaneously the perpetuation of the lineage and male control over it. The female character, even when she asserted a preference for spouse to which her father eventually capitulated, served to mark the exchange between men. The male viewer, identifying with the male lead, confirmed his own sensitivity to and mastery over woman and story. And he participated tacitly in the exchange of woman among men by witnessing the heroine's transfer from father to husband.

Where the leading couple failed, the impedance could be traced to the impossibility of achieving union across class or blood lines. Here male characters accumulated a misguided and tormented persona, stoic, pathetic, but also autonomous. The number of introspective moments performed on-stage built up a character in deep conflict. He alone suffered the agony of the antagonism between social proprieties and deepest desires. He alone danced out that agony with the ballerina – the perfect representation of the impossibility of resolving that conflict. This autoerotic display engulfed all other characters' identities. Even the ballerina was recast as a dream-like conjuration of his torment-filled fantasies. Did the sylphide really exist, or was she simply a symbol of the unrealizable aspirations that divided his soul? This power to summon into being all the facets of his desire and the conditions of their impossible fulfillment imbued the male character with a kind of self-sufficiency that again proved his superiority. Through identification with this hero, the male viewer could nurture his own fantasies using feminine forms to stand in for all impediments and solutions to his happiness.

And what if a woman played the role of the male lead? The popularity of the female travesty dancer in enacting these heterosexual scenarios and her reception as recorded in the press, point towards additional, mutually reinforcing trajectories of desire for the male viewer. The anxiety provoked by the effeminate male dancer resulted not only from a sensuality and decorativeness entirely inappropriate for the male position in society, but also because it referenced a homoerotic aesthetic. The heterosexual valuing of sexuality and sexual preference that dominated both public and private domains, forced an interiorization of homosexual desire and a closeting of same-sex social and sexual practices.[31] Since male interest in grace, lightness, and physical appearance was prohibited as unmanly, any male enactment of these values could easily be construed as homoerotic expression. By insinuating the female body into the male character, the homoerotic connotations of the performance were preserved without any compromise to male superiority. Her travesty garb was material evidence of the conventions of closeting through which male homosexual desire was sublimated. This type of closeting worked to facilitate male bonding, whether in a homosexual or heterosexual context.

The "man" who was not himself invited the erotic attachment of both male sexual orientations. The homosexual male viewer could fantasize the two women as standing in for men, while the heterosexual male viewer could risk the fantasy with no consequences to his reputation. The entire stage thus became a closet for the exercise of male desire.

But if the travesty dancer showed a "man" who was not himself, she equally showed a woman whose pretense posed no threat of uncontrollable sexual appetite or uncontainable passion. Where the female ballerina embodied an explosive charge, the travesty dancer's appearance invoked only perverse delight. Her crossing-over diffused the power of the ballerina and also provided the perfect wrapping for the ballerina as eroticized commodity. She purveyed the ballerina/commodity to the spectator, functioning neither as a member of the patriarchy nor as a menacing "wili." Her transgressive and revealing garb exacerbated the desire to possess the ballerina at the same time that it authorized the sale. Thus the ballerina and her inverted double, the travesty dancer, gestured towards four complementary features of the patriarchal order: as desired mate within the heterosexual union, she fulfilled the procreative half of the social contract; as spectacularly charismatic fantasy, she proved the self-sufficient superiority of the male character; as the entity of exchange within a homosexual or heterosexual male economy, she ensured male potency and rationalized their entitlement to governance; and as the fetishized promise of sexual acquisition, she ordained male capitalist competition within a society of consumption.

All of these readings foreclosed the possibility of a feminine expression of desire whether heterosexual or homosexual. The strict division of labor that placed woman in a purely reproductive function required of her appearance in public the complete eradication of her desire's expression. The heterosexual viewer could only identify with the female leads as objects of a masculine desire. The woman interested in same-sex erotic attachment would necessarily labor so intensively to read against the dominant choreography of desire that she might well have left the theater in search of working-class productions whose eclectic offerings included vicious satires of "high" art successes and also a great range of hyperbolic enactments of gender and sexuality. On the Opera stage, however, the only resistance to the foreclosure of feminine desire took place through the act of vanishing, or disappearing in the act of performing the feminine function. Yet this strategy of vanishing looked exactly like the vanishing that established her charismatic identity. The male viewer thereby controlled both homosexual and heterosexual viewing privileges at the expense of two kinds of "men" who were not themselves – one who dressed like them and another who was entirely concocted by them.

Gone, for the most part, are the complicated stories and the dozens of distinct characters, and certainly the travesty dancer no longer figures as a genre of leading character in contemporary ballets. Instead, when male and female leads extend an arm towards one another and begin their *pas de deux*, this expansive sweep gestures the full statement of their desire to be together. This is how, for example, the audience knows that Balanchine's Apollo has chosen Terpsichore over the other two muses, that he cherishes her expertise at fitting movement to the architectural structure of the music over prowess in drama or poetry.[32] But aren't all three muses versions of the charismatic ballerina whose powers of inspiration secure even as they challenge male authority? Doesn't Apollo sit to the side and evaluatively admire their dancing thereby guiding the audience's gaze towards them? Doesn't he drive them as prancing horses pulling his chariot up into the sky to meet his destiny as god? Don't their legs fan out behind him as protective aura, decorative armor, radiant testimony to his glory?

The legs. The ballerinas' legs. Sheathed in unblemished nylon from high hip bone to pointe shoe, most often a distinct color and texture from both skin and costume, they seem at times almost detached from the rest of the body. Their astonishing straightness, length, and the flexibility of hip and thigh muscles that permits their extreme separation from one another contrast with the supple, softly flowing arms and arching torso. Then the pointe shoe, a recapitulation of the leg's length and line, forms a slightly bulbous tip at the end of the ankle's thinness. So much of the choreographic focus goes to the articulation of these legs and feet, how the direction they take will establish a certain tension between mobility and precariousness. The tiniest, fastest steps across the floor on pointe (the *bourrée*), the balance on pointe with one leg extended high to the side then sweeping to the back, the turns in place or traveling – all these moves show her standing on so little. She becomes so insubstantial yet so resilient. Straight legs float in space; bent legs open out into straight legs; legs turn soft in order to accomplish some ornamental foot gesture, then re-lineify to point out the lines across the stage space that extend beyond them, to pronounce the precise angle that separates them from one another. In this moment of re-erection, they reveal the creation of the abstract line running from pelvis to toe that draws the musculature to it. The power of these legs springs from their fleshly realization of an abstract ideal.

Nineteenth-century reviews of the female dancers, iconographic representations, costuming – all established the erotic pre-eminence of the ballerina's legs. Breasts or bellies, physical features associated with motherhood, garnered no attention. The legs, unveiled for the first time, indicated a kind of sexual access to the dancing body even as they deflected awareness of the ballerina's "non-natural" status as a non-childbearing character. These late twentieth-century legs, however, do not glow in the same way. Emblazoned in theatrical space rather than coyly shimmering under a translucent skirt, their allure augments as they mutate from stiffness to pliability, from precision to effortlessness. They celebrate vital physical vigor and, at the same time, the triumphant quest for rational form.

The legs belie the phallic identity of the ballerina. They signal her situatedness just in between penis and fetish:[33]

> *She* looks like but isn't a penis. Her legs, her whole body become pumped up and hard yet always remain supple. Both the preparation, the dipping motion that precedes the etched shape, and the graceful fade from an extended pose show deflation, but always on its way to re-enflation. She never twists or contracts. Her sudden changes of direction and shifts of weight, always erect, resemble the penis's happy mind of its own, its inexplicable interest in negligible incidents. Yet, clearly, she is not a penis; she is a woman whose leg movements symbolize those of a penis.
>
> *She* attracts like but isn't a fetish. Her charisma comes from no single or identifiable source. She synthesizes strangely dissonant elements – legs with whole body, beauty with athleticism, physicality, and rationality. Although some may hoard her used pointe shoes or focus fixedly on the proportionate lengths of her arms and legs, she resists the alienated

severing of part from whole necessary to create a fetish. Her whole body and performance persona, despite the extremes to which they have been cultivated, remain intact.

She enacts desire and the inevitable loss of the object of desire. She is there and then elsewhere, in his arms, then running to the other side of the stage, in a given shape then transforming to another. A perpetual mutating of form, she attracts, invites, beckons and then disappears. To lose her is to lose that which is desired above all else, the imaginary, that pre-verbal, womb-ish world of sound, light, and movement. Her every move promises recuperation of that world and, in the very same gesture, shows its vanishing.

She gives figure to signification. In her, the chaos of body transmutes into rational form. The years of bodily disciplining have refigured fleshly curves and masses as lines and circles. Geometric perfection displays itself at both core and surface. Bodily shapes present one stunning design after another, notable for their silhouette and also for the interiorized configuration of lines running parallel to the skeleton around which the musculature is wrapped. Via this geometry her movements turn mess into symbol.

Supporting, underlying, founding this phallic identity is the ballet's perpetual upward thrust. The choreographic and stylistic demands of ballet take the weight of the body and make it disappear into thin air. Everything lifts up, moves towards height rather than depth; everything gestures out and up, never in, never down. This obsessive aeriality reinforces the erection of the penis-like balle-rina. It helps transform movement into the void of space, thereby facilitating dancing's vanishing and confirming its rational principles. By gesturing upwards into the realm of abstraction itself, the dancing proves its fraternal relation to music and mathematics.[34] Its grammar, evident in its geometry of forms, manufactures Pythagorean equations.[35]

The Romantic ballet, its choreographic conventions and its narratives, prepared the ballerina for just this phallic destiny. The same principles of desire and loss, the same charismatic glow now evident in the movement sequences themselves, originally manifest in the danced plot. Whether as sylphide or gypsy, the ballerina embodied an unattainable desire. Dance style allotted her elusive ethereality or ungovernable vitality. The plot often contrived her character so as to enable the dis-placement of the phallic attachment onto race or class. The ballets danced out the impossibility of love through a representation of the impossibility of non-permissible love, love that transgressed class and racial or inter-species boundaries. As a figment of the imagination, as in the sylphide, or as an independent and volatile gypsy, she augmented male sexual potency just before she vanished. Or if she passed from one male partner to the next, she lubricated the exchange of their sexual pow-er. When those partners were played by female dancers, female bodies whose lack of a penis could arouse no fears of castration, then the ballerina sexualized commodity exchange. Her body, fetish-ized both on- and off-stage, offered itself up to the viewer from the same abstract distance as that from which the burgeoning capitalist market offered its goods.[36] In the absence of a castrating father or castrated mother, the ballerina floated as freely from obligation as all purchases procur-able within a monetary medium. She danced out the erotics of acquisition under a system that measured all objects with a common symbolic denominator. In all these mutually reinforcing roles, the ballerina conferred phallic power upon male viewers by enacting their scenarios and appearing as their fantasy projection.

*

Between the Romantic ballet and her late twentieth-century descendant, two events of enormous choreographic significance intervened that have influenced the ballerina's phallic inheritance. First, at the beginning of the twentieth century, women as soloists who choreographed and performed their own dances began to occupy the stage, appropriating the phallus for themselves. Unpartnered and refusing to realize any choreographic vision other than their own, they detonated the classical stage and its sexual politics. Earthbound, preoccupied with flow from core to peripheral body and back, rather than from body out into space, they claimed "natural" physical processes rather than rational aesthetic tradition as inspiration for their movement choices. Yes, they were gazed upon, but they did not die at the end of their dances. Instead, arms plunging upwards and legs shooting down into the ground, they stood proudly, thereby collapsing the phallus into themselves, becoming the phallus themselves. Their charisma resulted in part from their ability to capitalize on and, at the same time, disrupt the sexual economy of viewing to which their audiences were accustomed. Their ascendance to the stage was partnered by a second major choreographic change – the premier of the gay male dancer.

The ballet tradition's uneasy relationship to these choreographic initiatives has yet to be assessed, and it deserves a kind of consideration that space here does not permit. However, one ballet, Fokine's *Petroushka*, suggests itself as a model for the kind of prescient story of ballet's initial response to the modern dance aesthetic. Opening on the hubbub of a mid-nineteenth-century Russian fair, *Petroushka* introduces an ancient wizard-like puppeteer whose mysterious allure charms the populous into attending his small theater. The curtains are drawn back to reveal three puppets: the exotic, brutish Moor; the mechanical, virtuoso Columbine; and the contorted, sincere Petroushka. In this brief display Petroushka's love for Columbine enrages the Moor and they burst the boundaries of the theater only to be restrained by the discontented puppeteer. Petroushka, banished to his private cell, acts out the mournful tale of his unrequited love and his frustrated incarceration at the hands of the puppeteer. Then in his own cell the Moor, in the midst of worshipful devotion to a coconut, is visited by Columbine, who kicks and pirouettes around him in an effort to attract his attention. Having finally succeeded by sitting on his lap, she is annoyed to see Petroushka enter. His further entreaties towards Columbine enrage the Moor, and their frantic chase spills out into the street, where, much to the crowd's dismay, the Moor kills Petroushka. The wizard, exhausted and irritated, shoves his way through the concerned onlookers to demonstrate that Petroushka is only a puppet, a bag of straw which he yanks from the ground with terrifying authority. Dragging the puppet back to his theater, he closes for the night. But as he begins to exit the stage he suddenly sees the apparition of Petroushka, gesturing menacingly from the rooftop above the theater. Overwhelmed with fear, he runs out as Petroushka persists in a melancholy yet taunting laugh.

This ballet presented an almost transparent critique of czarist Russia with Petroushka, standing for the pathetic commoners, struggling under the czar-puppeteer whose portrait hung in his tiny room. It could equally be construed as one of the first renderings of modernist subjectivity: man, no longer noble or good, and woman, no longer a goddess or a whore, acted out the destinies that Fate had provided. Alienated from their means of production, they performed their small dramas whose impact only resonated in the hollow laugh of a ghostly afterlife. I want to propose a third interpretation, one which sees in the puppeteer the choreographer Fokine who recognized that he was working at the faultline of an enormous aesthetic rupture. Captivated by the dancing of Isadora Duncan only a few years earlier, he cannily appraised what the ballet tradition had to offer: the exotic and lavish trappings of other-worldly places that activated desire (the Moor), and the virtuoso yet mechanized vocabulary of spectacular dancing (Columbine). Petroushka represented the new expressivist agenda as proposed by Duncan with its radical overhauling of the very conditions under which vocabulary, subject matters, and viewing experience might be constructed. Fokine, inheritor of the ballet tradition that had choreographed the law of the father, could only respond by running from the ominous threat of aesthetic rebellion.

Yet Petroushka, played by Nijinsky, introverted and pathetic, lacking all erectness, and dominated by a controlling male partner, represented the inverse of the female choreographer who had assimilated the phallus. Clearly identified as homosexual in an age that had recently recognized homosexuality as a category,[37] his performance in *Petroushka* and other ballets constructed an entirely new character type – the male performer as queered phallus. Deviant yet magnificent, always cast in the role of the exotic, Nijinsky specialized in a serpentine, even contorted bodily shaping combined with the highest leaps ever made.[38] It was he who died or vanished at the end of Fokine's ballets, and he who came back like a queer male "wili" to haunt the stage at the end of *Petroushka*. Nevertheless, Nijinsky went on to choreograph three ballets that self-consciously staged the same patriarchal dynamics on which the ballets of a century before had been founded: the autoerotic supremacy of the male position in *L'Après midi d'un faune*; the female as sacrificial object of exchange among men in *Le Sacre du printemps*; and the sexualized encounter as commodity in *Jeux*.

Thus *Petroushka* forecast the ballerina, always the vehicle for a male choreographic vision, as estranged from the feminist response of modern dance, and it also predicted the gay male choreographer/performer easily insinuated into the stable patriarchy of the ballet and the volatile sorority of modern dance. *Petroushka* also portended a division of labor between ballet and modern dance in which ballet no longer provoked empathic connections to its danced characters so much as to the superbly moving beauty of its form. Modern dance, by contrast, explored the authenticity of human feeling whether embodied in identifiable characters or in movement qualities.[39] As in the character of Petroushka, the growing gay male presence in both traditions remained entirely closeted thereby submerging any distinctive homosexual aesthetic deep within musculature of the tradition. The leggy, anorexic, hyper-extended ballerina issued from this matrix of aesthetic concerns.

But what if *Petroushka*'s poor puppeteer in his panicked exit from ballet's dilemmas were now, almost a century later, to run headlong into the ballerina-as-phallus? Would she machine-gun him down with her pointe shoes, or, better yet, trade them in for combat boots? Would she "out" all the gay male choreographers, viewers, and critics – those "frightful *danseuses* of the male sex" – who have consistently ignored her plight? What kind of a deal could she make? How might she mobilize to secure a choreographic place for her female body and a narrative space for her feminine desire? Could she somehow contrive to both terrify and enchant his fleeing figure so as to short-circuit the traffic in women? Could she take inspiration from the gender-failure of the nineteenth-century male dancer and the courage of the female dancer to create a new identity, dangerously ambiguous or constantly changing that would elude the viewer's grasping gaze? Could she collaborate with the choreographer/puppeteer on a movement lexicon that would enable her to dance on the graves of Lacan as well as Freud and thereby teach them a new move or two? These are the questions, I believe, that those seven-year-old girls must ask as they draw their hair back into a bun, pull on their pink tights, and head downtown in Hong Kong, Havana, New York, Buenos Aires, Sydney ... for their weekly class.

NOTES

1   *This is the argument that has been made in the classic dance history books such as Lincoln Kirstein's* The Book of the Dance: A Short History of Dancing *or Walter Sorell's* The Dance Through the Ages.

2   *For a comprehensive analysis of conventions of partnering in the ballet conducted in the context of a comparative study of ballet with modern dance and contact improvisation, see Cynthia Novack's* Sharing the Dance: Contact Improvisation and American Culture.

3   *Novack and Ann Daly are among the first to launch an inquiry into gendered roles in dance. See also Daly's "The Balanchine Woman: Of Hummingbirds and Channel Swimmers."*

4   *The whole history of ballet's migration from Europe begs to be written. I want to allude to the colonialist implications of this migration here, yet it lies outside the bounds of this essay to undertake a full history or even to probe the relevance of postcolonial theory to the global dissemination of ballet.*

5   *The initial apprehension of this potential identity for the ballerina came from my attempt to understand the full impact of nineteenth-century innovations in ballet technique and vocabulary. As the argument in the text indicates, the separation of the ballet lexicon into distinctive vocabularies for male and female dancers occurred seemingly in tandem with a marked increase in the popularity of the travesty dancer. These three performance roles suggested a set of oppositions and contra-distinctions that could be mapped onto the Greimasian quadrangle. According to Fredric Jameson whose work on Greimas can be found in* The Ideologies of Theory: Essays 1971–86, *the fourth location on the quadrangle reveals the hidden ideological content of the entire system of relations. The quadrangle as I have been able to develop it reads as follows:*

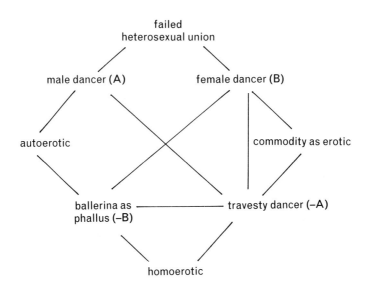

6   *Another kind of answer might result from an inquiry into ballet's structuring of expression, as compared, for example, with that of opera. In* The Queen's Throat: Opera, Homosexuality, and the Mystery of Desire, *Wayne Koestenbaum identifies opera's special expressive power as a product of its communication via the ear:*

> *The listener's inner body is illuminated, opened up: a singer doesn't expose her own throat, she exposes the listener's interior. Her voice enters me, makes me a "me," an interior, by virtue of the fact that I have been entered. The singer, through osmosis, passes through the self's porous membrane, and discredits the fiction that bodies are separate, boundaried packages. The singer destroys the division between her body and our own, for her sound enters our system. I am sitting in the Met at Leontyne Price's recital in 1985 and Price's vibrations are inside my body, dressing it up with the accoutrements of interiority. Am I listening to Leontyne Price or am I incorporating her, swallowing her, memorizing her? She becomes part of my brain. And I begin to believe – sheer illusion! – that she spins out my self, not hers, as Walt Whitman, Ancient-of-Days opera queen, implied when he apostrophized a singer in "Out of the Cradle Endlessly Rocking": "O you singer solitary, singing by yourself, projecting me, | O solitary me listening, never more shall I cease perpetuating you ..."*
>
> *I follow a singer towards her climax, I will it to happen, and feel myself "made" when she attains her note.*
>
> (Koestenbaum 1993, 43)

Koestenbaum argues that this ability to create interiority is partly responsible for the attraction of gay and lesbian audiences to the opera. Elizabeth Wood and Terry Castle (among others) affirm and expand on Koestenbaum's assertion with their proposals that the quality of the voice, its sonority, flexibility, and its resonant "low notes" as a source of attraction for lesbian listeners. See Wood's essay "Saphonics" and Castle's "In Praise of Brigitte Fassbaender (A Musical Emanation)." Gays and lesbians have attached themselves to the voice's production of song, to the operatic spectacle, and to the diva for distinct yet sometimes overlapping reasons. They read into and against the grain of the performance so as to find systems of values that resonate with the complex status of their sexual and social identities in contemporary society. But where the body serves not as the site for the manufacture of expressive signals and instead as the very substance expressed, the opportunities of empathic connection to the performer proliferate differently. No one minds the corpulent, awkward bodies that produce those luminous sounds in opera; the sounds themselves are what excite. In ballet, however, the bodies are what matter, and identification with the dancing body, especially the ballet body, is far less likely to establish the kind of interiority for the viewer that the voice can.

7   Here I am referencing Gayle Rubin's famous article "The Traffic in Women." Her essay was one of the first in what has become a sustained critique within feminist theory on the role of the woman as the most fundamental category of goods exchanged within a culture.

8   Koestenbaum eloquently describes the gay male experience of identifying with the diva during her performance at the opera. I suspect that the ballet performance functions similarly in that the gay viewer ignores the obvious heterosexual thrust of the narrative, and differently, in that neither male nor female dancer serves as the exclusive focus of his attention. Rather, it is the generalized climate of physical and sensual grace which the ballet offers that makes it so popular among gay men. Significantly, whereas the opera also boasts a strong lesbian following, the ballet holds little if any interest for the lesbian viewer. One of the goals of this essay is to theorize this difference.

9   Here I am alluding to Donna Haraway's exploration of the opportunities for political resistance offered by the Cyborg in "Manifesto for Cyborgs: Science, Technology, and Socialist Feminism in the 1980's," and by the Monster of "The Promises of Monsters."

10   For an excellent overview of the Romantic ballet in its cultural surround, see Eric Aschengren's "The Beautiful Danger: Facets of the Romantic Ballet."

11   Here I am referring to the shift from a one-sex/two-gender model to a two-sex/two-gender model outlined by Thomas Laqueur in Making Sex: Body and Gender from the Greeks to Freud and eloquently summarized in this description of male and female essential differences:

Les prédispositions particulières de l'homme et de la femme sont telles, que le premier, ayant la force en partage, semble né pour commander et être obéi. Par là il doit être sujet à des passions plus violentes que la femme, qui, faible, douce et soumise, ne semble criée que pour aimer et consoler, obéir et plaire. Par *conséquent l'attitude de l'homme doit être noble, fière et impérieuse; sa pose pleine de fermenté, la rectitude du tronc invariable, et la position de la tête fixe; tandis que la position de la femme doit être timide, remplie de mollesse et d'agrément: tout chez elle est souplesse et ondulations gracieuses; sa tête, mollement penchée, a toute la candeur de la pose enfantine.*

Dans les fonctions ordinaires de la vie, l'homme est plus froid; il est d'une sensibilité plus profonde que la femme au milieu des grandes influences; s'il emploie le geste, c'est toujours avec une superiorité d'expression et d'entraînement, surtout pour la manifestation des sentiments énergiques. La femme, dont les idées sont plus nombreuses et plus nuancées, les mouvements plus souples et plus faibles, emploie des gestes variés et sans énergie.

Dans la démarche et l'expression, l'homme, dont la taille est moins balancée et l'attitude plus ferme, se meut avec plus de force et d'aplomb que la femme; sa démarche prend un caractère de virilité et de résolution; son regard est ferme et méditatif; sa diction, énergique, positive et régulière; sa voix, sonore, impérieuse et sans éclat. Chez la femme la démarche est légère et élégante; son regard plein de douceur, de sensualité et de finesse. Dotée d'une sensibilité dont les modifications sont infinies, elle parle souvent avec excès, presque toujours d'une manière agréable; son élocution est gracieuse et brillante; sa voix, douce, flûtée et claire: sa respiration, active et variée, prend un caractère particulier en conséquence des déplacements qu'elle fait éprouver aux seins.

(B*** and Ball 1846, 41–2)

12   *This description is taken from the published scenario for the ballet* Giselle, ou les wilis, *by Vernoy de Saint-Georges, Théophile Gautier, and Jean Coraly.*

13   *Carlo Blasis describes the new pedagogy in his* Traité elementaire, theorique et pratique de l'art de la danse.

14   *An account of the changing priorities for social dance practice is provided by Jean-Michel Guilcher in his* La Contredanse et les renouvellements de la danse française. *A more detailed analysis of social dance practices is given in Sarah Cordova's "Poetics of Dance: Narrative Designs from Staël to Maupassant."*

15   *In* Le Corps redressé: histoire d'un pouvoir pedagogique *Georges Vigarello provides a powerful and convincing history of the changes in postural pedagogy and bodily comportment from the seventeenth century to the present.*

16   *Louis XIV's original charter for the Academy of Dance specifies dance's contribution to the arts of war and theatrical entertainment. A host of dancing manuals from the early and middle eighteenth century reiterate dance's value as a foundation for proper conduct, attractive appearance, good health, and success in all endeavors.*

17   *Publications appearing in the 1840s that disseminated gossip about primarily female artists include the following: Touchard-LaFosse,* Chroniques secrètes et galantes de l'opéra, 1665–1845, *Anon*. Le Foyer de l'opéra, *Anon*. Le Monde d'amour, *and Anon*. Les Filles d'opéra et les vertus de table d'hôte.

18   *The most notorious instance of this is Louis Véron who took over the Paris Opera as a private venture from 1830–33. His* Mémoires d'un bourgeois de Paris *details the various strategies he implemented for making the Opera a profitable enterprise.*

19   *The most comprehensive analysis of the daily circumstances of dancers in this period is provided by Louise Robin-Challan in "Danse et danseuses l'envers du décor, 1830–1850."*

20   *They also participated in more fetishizing adventures. As recounted by Margot Fonteyn for the video series "The Magic of Dance," Marie Taglioni's fans cooked and ate her pointe shoes following her last performance in St. Petersburg.*

21   *This is Ivor Guest's translation from his book* The Romantic Ballet in Paris, *21.*

22   *In her essay, "The Legs of the Countess," interpreting photos taken of the Countesse de Castiglione, Abigail Solomon-Godeau raises many of the issues discussed here and provides important evidence that corroborates the mid-nineteenth-century status of women in the arts.*

23   *A sudden surge within French publications of gossipy biographies that focused on dancers' liaisons occurs in the 1830s and 1840s.*

24   *In his* Petits mémoires de l'opéra, *Charles de Boigne claims that Véron was a genius at publicity, repeatedly announcing that a production was close to its final performance (p. 8). He calls the mother or sister an essential piece of the ballerina's equipment, "un meuble de rigueur comme l'arrosoir" (p. 19). He also observes that:*

> *A l'Opéra l'avancement ne se donne pas à l'ancienneté, mais au choix. On ne gagne pas ses grades un à un; d'un bond on saisit, on enlève le sceptre. On arrive de Londres, de Naples ou de Vienne avec un nom tout fait. Quelquefois avec un talent trop fait.*
>
> *(de Boigne 1857, 23)*

> *And he compares the ballerina to a horse, remarking derogatorily that horses look good after battle but the dancer:*

> *Après son pas, elle n'est même une pauvre après la lettre! Epuisé, haletante, presque morte, elle se soutient à peine; elle souffle comme une machine à vapeur; son visage, peint à la colle, a déteint et ressemble à un arc-en-ciel; son corsage est mouillé, souillé par la sueur; sa bouche grimace, ses yeux sont hagards; quel spectacle!*
>
> *(ibid., 33)*

Dancers, unlike horses, never get a vacation:

> *Huit jours de repos les condamnent à un mois d'entrechats forcés. La classe de danse a remplacé l'inquisition, avec cette différence qu'à la classe, pour se faire administrer la question, les patientes payent cinquante francs par mois et par tête. Le maître de danse est sans pitié pour ses victimes: il les presse, les tourmente, les harcèle, les gronde. Jamais un moment de repos! Jamais un mot d'encouragement: Il commande et elles obéissent. Tournons nous! s'écrie-t-il; et toutes de rester, tant qu'elles peuvent, talon contre talon; les genoux tendus et les pieds sur la même ligne. Cassons nous! Ajoute-t-il; et vous voyez tous ces pieds et toutes ces mains exécuter la manœuvre avec un ensemble parfait. Il s'agit, tout en tenant la barre de la main droite, de poser le pied gauche sur la même barre, et de changer, au commandement, de pied et de main; et au milieu de ces tortures, il faut sourire.*

> (ibid., 35)

25   See Gautier's Gautier on Dance *for exemplary instances of the morselized female body.* Guest's The Romantic Ballet in Paris *also includes many quotations from the newspapers that described dancers' performances.*

26   *See Catherine Clément's* Opera, or the Undoing of Women *for a deeply moving analysis of the varieties of "undoing" for nineteenth-century opera heroines. Their fates parallel those of the ballet's leading female characters.*

27   *In her article "Film Body: An Implantation of Perversions," Linda Williams finds built into the very structure of the cinematic apparatus a fetishizing function for the female body "whose first effect is to deny the very existence of women." Specifically with regard to the work of Muybridge, whose photographic investigations of motion help form the cinema's origin, she claims that the threat posed by the female nude determined two strategies of containment for the female body in the photographs. Either the female subject was ensnared in a scene suggestive of a narrative, or she was reduplicated so many times as to erode any power she might have. These two strategies map easily onto the Romantic ballet's frequently tragic fates for leading female dancers and to its reduplication of the female body to form the* corps de ballet.

28   *Lynn Garafola's pioneering essay "The Travesty Dancer in Nineteenth Century Ballet" provided a much-needed feminist intervention into the subject of the travesty dancer. Further historical research is required in order to understand the exact nature of their popularity and the relationship between travesty appearances at working-class theaters and at venues like the Opera.*

29   *One of the most famous travesty performers of the early nineteenth century was Virginie Déjazet (1797–1875) who initiated a range of travesty roles at the Théâtre des Variétés. For thirty years she played roles as "gamin de Paris, coquette, débardeur,* *duc, marquis, acteur, jeune homme timide, tambour et même officier d'artillerie." She even played Napoléon with a huge army. See Grand-Carteret,* XIXe Siècle: classes, mœurs, usages, costumes, inventions. *At the Opera Louis Milon's ballet* Les Pages du Duc de Vendôme *(1820) featured women including the highly popular Emilie Biggotini as one of the four pages. A more standard use of travesty, however, began in the 1840s and 1850s.*

30 *This is a reference to a review from 1806 of the ballet* Les deux Créoles *whose production at the Théâtre de Porte St Martin featured a female dancer in the role of the male lead. The reviewer's response to the performance was as follows; ". . . and the love of one woman for another is scarcely affecting."* Journal de l'Empire, *4 July 1806. The situation was apparently quite different in England and in the medium of drama where female travesty performers became a threat by the early nineteenth century. See Kristina Straub's essay "The Guilty Pleasures of Female Theatrical Cross-Dressing and the Autobiography of Charlotte Charke" in* Body Guards, *142–66.*

31 *Foucault's* The History of Sexuality *initiated an inquiry into the various discursive practices that work to define categories of sexual experience and sexual preference. David Halperin and others have suggested that homosexuality as a category emerges out of societal insistence on the public-normal as heterosexual and the private-abnormal as homosexual that occurred in the late eighteenth and early nineteenth centuries. See Halperin's* One Hundred Years of Homosexuality: And Other Essays on Greek Love.

32 *The fitting of movement to the architectural structure embodied in the music is one of Balanchine's most often claimed choreographic goals.*

33 *In this four-part definition of the ballerina-as-phallus, I am following the general Lacanian thesis that sees in the phallus the law that divides symbolic from imaginary. The phallus's function in this capacity as it affects the experience of subjectivity and desire is worked out in Lacan's essay "The Subversion of the Subject and the Dialectic of Desire in the Freudian Unconscious." I am also relying on Teresa de Lauretis's critique of the phallus in* Alice Doesn't; *Charles Bernheimer's re-assertion of the similarities between the phallus and the penis in "Penile Reference in Phallic Theory"; and Michael Taussig's explication of the relationship of the fetish to the totem in "Maleficium: State Fetishism".*

34 *In* The Art of Making Dances, *Doris Humphrey describes the desirable relation between dance and music as one that brings the feminine dance together with her "perfect mate but not master" (p. 132). I am proposing a different relation between ballet and her "sister" arts based on a homosocial male aesthetic economy.*

35 *For additional feminist perspectives on Pythagorean aesthetics, see Sue-Ellen Case's "Meditations on the Patriarchal Pythagorean Pratfall and the Lesbian Siamese Two-Step" and Susan McClary's "Music, the Pythagoreans, and the Body".*

36   *The analysis I am undertaking here parallels and takes inspiration from Jean-Joseph Goux's "The Phallus: Masculine Identity and the 'Exchange of Women'". Goux's is a complex and elegant thesis, two aspects of which are important to the argument presented here. First, Goux works to historicize the very conception of the phallus by considering its role in "primitive" societies and in their myths and rituals, then in nineteenth-century and early twentieth-century capitalist societies, and now in a postcapitalist, postmodernist landscape. He argues that the phallus itself, our access to it, and its relation to modes of cultural production have changed distinctively in each of these periods. Second, he connects the identity of the phallus to the identity of capital, claiming for each an analogous degree of abstract functioning in relation to their respective economies of desire and material production.*

37   *One of Halperin's arguments in* One Hundred Years of Homosexuality *is that the separation of public and private forces a notion of homosexuality as an inverted sexuality. The resonance between Halperin's theorization of late nineteenth-century homosexuality and Nijinsky's performances is striking.*

38   *Michael Moon expands on Nijinsky's gayness in his article "Flaming Closets."*

39   *Frederick Ashton is the most notable choreographer who attempted to reach across this divide.*

History/theory – criticism/practice

MARK FRANKO

"TORTURE AT THE TYPEWRITER"

Three modern dancers circa 1946 – One Who Seeks, She of the Ground, and He Who Summons – perform amidst a field of Isamu Noguchi's phallic stelae at New York City's Plymouth Theatre. *"You go back and torture yourself at the typewriter. If you can get the first paragraph out, it isn't too bad, but to sit there and that first paragraph won't come is agonizing. You're full of impressions, but you're not giving out."*[1] Three "discourses" – one discursively critical, the second intensely performative, the third intervening in their historical relationship to unsettle the duality performance/discourse – move alongside one another in the symbolic twilight/dawn of dance studies: John Martin's journalism and aesthetics, Martha Graham's 1946 dance work *Dark Meadow*, and this essay scrutinizing their dialogue. At this particular juncture of the criticism/practice split in modernism, roles are reversed: Graham becomes the "mind" and Martin the "body," Graham the "male" and Martin the "female," Graham the "cogito" and Martin "space" or *res extensa*.[2] **One Who Seeks sinks backward against the floor before the most centrally located and tallest stele; Erick Hawkins, dressed in a half skirt, peers out from behind the monument; May O'Donnell bears witness stiffly, pointing at Graham's supine figure; Martin watches from the darkened auditorium, his body straining to empathize with these figures, to grasp their...? The curtain falls.** *"I was in a state of despair, and as I passed along the back aisle, my colleagues were waiting for me ... 'John, what are you going to say? What was this about, John?' I gave my usual wisecrack, 'I don't know, I haven't read the* New York Times *yet'"*[3] *(Figure 2.1)*. On the horizon of this inquiry into practice/criticism is a reformulation of that other duality history/theory in the context of aesthetic modernism.

The first section of this essay, "Torture at the Typewriter," intertwines Martin's theory of dance history and his critical reception of Graham with a running description of *Dark Meadow*. Collaging Martin's discursive rehearsals of modernism with Graham's performed modernity is designed to reveal that modern dance has not benefited from an adequate critical account of its aesthetics and politics. The second section, "Panicked in the Theater," juxtaposes Martin's oral account of his bewildering first exposure to *Dark Meadow* in 1946 (the year of my birth) with my interpretation of the reconstructed work seen in 1968 and 1993. I understand Martin's quandary over how to write about *Dark Meadow* as a direct result of his earlier inability to theorize Graham's modernism. The third section, "The Writing Cure," correlates the findings of the first two with Martin's reviews of *Dark Meadow* in order to reflect on the relationship between history and theory in dance modernism.

Created at the dawn of the cold war, *Dark Meadow* was located on the threshold of two worlds as well as on an invisible dividing line between Graham's earlier Americana cycle (1934–44) and her later Greek myth choreographies (1946–58).[4]

Evidencing a choreographic nostalgia afloat between her past and future, *Dark Meadow* was unique despite structural similarities with Graham's other large-scale works of the 1940s such as *Letter to the World* (1940) and *Appalachian Spring* (1944). *Dark Meadow* was unique in its esoterism, recalling earlier formalist works such as *Primitive Mysteries* (1931). **Playing One Who Seeks, Graham stands on the lower platform edge of an ovalescent object that rises gently behind her, angled at the wings.** In 1946 Graham reasserted high modernist qualities that had been less evident in her work since popular front aesthetics of the mid- and late 1930s had engulfed American choreographers in a concerted expression of nationalism.[5]

Martin found *Dark Meadow* particularly perplexing – indeed, as we shall see, traumatic – in part because it threw him back upon an earlier avant-gardism that he had not come to terms with despite his books on dance history and aesthetics based on the observation of modern dance.[6] **Hands raised above her head, One Who Seeks surveys the audience. She seems engaged in seeing without seeing.** This essay's three sections reconsider the events on the stage, in the audience, and in the newspaper composing room when Martin first saw *Dark Meadow*. **Five female choristers circle one another at the center of the stage. They perform jumping, thumping leg, and swaying hip movements.** I evaluate that evening's traumatic encounter as the return of an unresolved critical dilemma Graham posed Martin at the veritable inception of American modern dance. **One Who Seeks appears to knock on the ground with her feet. She repeats the same gesture in the air with her arms.**

Perhaps *Dark Meadow* perplexed Martin because it lacked the dramatic momentum frequently present in 1940s modern dance. *"She was never one to create dances without some dramatic basis."*[7] **One Who Seeks spins around, her body contracted over her legs.** Its illusory time frame in whose approximately forty minutes nothing concretely transpires endows *Dark Meadow* with an anti-climactic and unportentous aura. It seems to inhabit a dramatic vacuum. Although actions necessarily develop through time, this only serves to enhance their ambiguities. **One Who Seeks paces the back of the stage, arms lifted, one leg after the other trailing behind her in the air. As she arrives to the front of the stage her movements grow more forceful and begin to resemble those of the chorus which, in turn, adopts some of her vocabulary.**

Nevertheless, the relationship of the two main protagonists – One Who Seeks and He Who Summons (originally danced by Graham and Erick Hawkins) – does imply some discernible dramatic structure. One Who Seeks is summoned to a romantic entanglement with He Who Summons, presided over by She of the Ground.[8] Suggestions of narrative, however, do not themselves constitute narrative with respect to this work's high modernist hermeticism.[9] Graham's aesthetic modernism is an ambiguating practice.

Modernism challenged critical discourse to account for ambiguity without imposing reductive thinking on its necessity. Just as it emerged on the American concert stage of the late 1920s with Graham and others, New Criticism was developing formalist critical premises to account for modernist literary practices.[10] *"People laughed at them; the press and everybody else didn't know what it was all about. They thought it was another crazy art fad."*[11] Yet despite Martin's continued influence on the way we think about historical modern dance, he failed to produce a critical account of dance modernism. More important, his failure created an artificial split between history and theory which is only now beginning to be recuperated by dance studies. **Back to the audience, One Who Seeks faces the central stele. Then she withdraws to her oval platform as He Who Summons steps out from behind the monument as if conjured forth by her. She of the Ground also enters from the wings by cutting between One Who Seeks and He Who Summons.** In the 1930s, Martin may have come close to but he ultimately fell short of a foundational opportunity to articulate a formalist dance criticism. By the 1940s his position had hardened.

My interest in Martin's encounter with *Dark Meadow* is neither to contextualize the situation of modern dance nor of Martin himself in the 1940s. Rather, I ask what went wrong from the start between Graham and Martin. *"You're off your feet; you have nowhere to stand. You have to go with a reasonably open mind, which is probably the hardest thing anybody has to do."*[12] Like the return of a trauma, *Dark Meadow* exposed a fundamental misapprehension in Martin's critical response to Graham that by 1946 had already accumulated more than a decade of history. More crucially, his response to *Dark Meadow* calls his earlier critical assumptions into question. Let us begin at the beginning.

"When I began on the Times, *the modern dance was just starting."*[13] Martin launched a new relationship of dance practice to criticism in 1927, a journalistic reviewing that was also to furnish the basis for the history and aesthetics of modern dance. **He Who Summons performs a solo of skittering hops (many backwards), jumps accompanied with clapping of hands, and low hovering spins similar to those already executed by One Who Seeks.** This is not to say that Martin confused history and aesthetics with reviewing *"based on snap judgments."*[14] Rather, he distilled his reviews after the fact into books. Thanks to his extensive personal history of spectatorship, his aesthetic judgments and theories of dance history could claim an empirical basis. But reciprocally, Martin's aesthetics maintained the immediacy and fragility of a dance review. **His arms are frequently extended straight ahead of him, which lends his presence an aggressiveness, a nuance of menace.** *"You were just thrown into an unknown area. You wondered what in the world was going to happen; what you were going to say."*[15] **Throughout his solo, One Who Seeks sits on her oval disk. She does not observe him.** *"There is no literature, to speak of, in English on the subject* [of modern dance]," Martin noted, *"and the only source of enlightenment has been the actual performances of the dancers themselves."*[16] **He Who Summons comes to a halt before the central stele. She of the Ground danced through his solo's final moments, accruing greater energy to his jumping and running.** *"Suddenly, from some unexpected source and for some inexplicable cause, something happens on the stage and you say 'Ah, that's it; this is where I start; here I have a contact at last.'"*[17] **One Who Seeks leaves her disk and circles the stage repeatedly in low wide spinning turns.** The critical technique of writing from the "ah!" underlines the "intuitionistic imperative" of phenomenology underpinning Martin's

approach.[18] Martin's journalism and his aesthetics, although formally separate, share a common project: to uncover the founding critical presupposition of the "ah!" **She of the Ground comes to rest before the oval object.** This is important because when Martin moves beyond his reception of the dance to his presuppositions of writing, he moves definitively out of performance and into language. This departure from the specificity of experience constitutes a phenomenological bad faith since the need to "come to grips linguistically with the phenomenon as it gives itself to experience" is abruptly abandoned for the solution to a "problem."[19] **One Who Seeks exits.** There is none of the "re-languaging" in Martin's writing that Maxine Sheets-Johnstone has proposed as "part of phenomenological accounts."[20] **He Who Summons cups his hands to his lips as if calling out while dancing energetically with She of the Ground. They stop together before the central stele.** This, too, is significant because Martin's critical project is fundamentally phenomenological in its outlook. Of course, Martin was in no technical sense a philosopher, but his claims of impressionistic criticism are interwoven with the phenomenological/modernist viewpoint. "To have sensations in the presence of a work of art," wrote Joel Spingarn in 1931, "and to express them, that is the function of criticism for the 'impressionistic critic.'"[21]

Prior to the 1980s, dance studies was dominated by the phenomenological attitude summed up for our purposes by Hegel: "I am directly conscious, I intuit and nothing more, I am pure intuition; *I am – seeing, looking* ... I take my stand on one immediate relation."[22] Similar pleas for intuitive immediacy as a form of receptive spectatorship suited to historical modern dance have distinguished its performance as immediate (unmediated) experience. The fit between modern dance and phenomenology is almost too perfect since "[phenomenology's] source of sense in general is always determined as the act of *living*, as the act of a living being, as *Lebendigkeit* (vibrancy)."[23] Much modern dance wished to impact upon its audience quite literally as a vibrant phenomenon: its sense was only derivable from within a mystique of experience as immediate.

While the germ of Martin's observations is already present in his reviews, he did not consider the review itself to be a theoretical genre. *"Looking back, I see that it was of great interest to me to develop the ability to be the first dance critic in the field. ... Nobody knew then, or knows now what the exact qualifications are."*[24] Instead, his books transmute the critic's experience in the theater into a sweeping conceptualization of dance history and aesthetics whose unfolding horizon was the new modern dance. **Enter the full chorus of They Who Dance Together in couples, two by two.** What conceptual framework, against which the advent of modern dance might be realized in its full historical significance, do Martin's books provide? **They Who Dance Together insert a black cloth stretched over a thin wooden frame forming a cross into the top of a phallic object to the right of the central stele.**

Martin developed an historical context for his aesthetics in *Introduction to the Dance* (1939). He focuses his account of dance history through an anthropological functionalism, dividing dance into three vaguely historicized but also conceptual modes: the *recreational*, the *spectacular*, and the *expressional*. Each mode having emerged at a particular historical moment, as Martin explains, nevertheless continues to function as an aesthetic/anthropological option in the present. **He Who Summons places himself behind the middle of three phallic objects occupying the right side of the stage. His face appears behind the cross that has been inserted into the prop. One Who Seeks places herself before it and pulls the black material down from its armature, revealing some of Hawkins's upper body.**

Each of Martin's modes – the recreational, the spectacular, and the expressional – offers the viewer a set of culturally defined options and insights. **Pulling the black material over her head, One Who Seeks walks over the train it forms extending behind her in a long diagonal strip.** Recreational dance, roughly speaking, corresponds to the ritual practices of dance in traditional cultures; spectacular dance corresponds to the Western theatrical practices of dance most readily associated with classical ballet; expressional dance corresponds to the modern dance burgeoning in America and Germany when Martin wrote. **One Who Seeks lies on top of the black fabric, rolls off it, runs around the stage's periphery and stops facing the phallic object behind which He Who Summons stands. She reclines on the cloth and crawls along it toward her oval property.** These three modes, as already mentioned, are not exclusively limited to the definition of dance historical moments. They presuppose cultural attitudes towards dance that remain encoded in its particular existing forms. (*Dark Meadow*'s roles subtly allude to Martin's modes: She of the Ground to recreational dance, He Who Summons to spectacular dance, and One Who Seeks to expressional dance.)

Martin's most productive distinction is between recreational and expressional dance because these represent two poles of a spectrum: the historical origin and the radical present. As such, they implicate one another dialectically. This situation is particularly characteristic of aesthetic modernism: that is, expressional dance is modernist because of its investment in a primitivism. Martin explains that modern (expressional) dance emerges from recreational dance, and although it surpasses recreational intent, it also incorporates some of its characteristics in modern society. **One Who Seeks lies on her back, lifts the edge of the cloth over her head, sits up, and rocks forward over her folded legs.** Martin makes the following additional claim in order to justify the wisdom of his categories: recreational dance is *not* spectacular; rather, *"it is practiced wholly for the benefit of the dancer himself and gives no consideration to possible spectators"* because it is *"inseparable from the social and religious aspects of living."*[25] **Wrapped in the cloth, One Who Seeks writhes and rolls sideways; she walks with the cloth over her head, moving it forward beneath her feet as she advances.** By contrast, spectacular dance exemplifies what is meant by "classical" dance since it *"adapts materials already so created with an eye to either their formal qualities, their surfaces, their sensational appeal, or their aesthetic values."*[26] **One Who Seeks kneels, turns, and ends in a cross-legged position on the floor with the cloth over her head like a mourner.**

Having established these somewhat arbitrary distinctions – for clearly spectacular dance also has anthropological investments and, by the same token, "recreational" dance is also cultural performance, and thus has spectacular components – expressional dance becomes problematically poised between these two. **She of the Ground**

skitters, her knees fully bent as if in a seated position, to the front of the oval object and lifts it upright, revealing its smooth white underside. The crucial difference is that recreational dance is not *"art"* for Martin, but spectacular dance *is*, albeit of a bad kind that manipulates aesthetic materials while rejecting *"subjective impulses."*[27] **The oval object becomes different. Now it stands higher off the ground, no longer a platform but a sort of vertical couch.** Martin thinks classic art is the superficial manifestation of Western culture. For this reason, modern dance radically opposes it. Yet, modern dance must still lay claim to the status of art, and not just of (physical) culture. It must wrest this status from spectacular dance. **One Who Seeks lies on the black cloth. He Who Summons lifts the cross off the phallus and holds it aloft.** Expressional dance *"attempts to prevent the loss of subjective impulses of the recreational dance, and to make them the basis for direct communication with the spectator."*[28] This is why one can argue that expressional dance is new (modern), indeed revolutionary.

Here we arrive at the crux of Martin's conception of dance history – and the polemical situation of modern dance within it – and we confront this conception's liabilities as well. Similar to recreational dance, modern (expressional) dance redeems social and religious values without regard to objective form (hence its primitivism). Nonetheless, expressional dance is not actually recreational because of its spectacular qualities of display. Yet unlike spectacular dance, it displays itself directly, as it were, from a mobile subjectivity (hence its modernism). It has no prior model or basis in tradition. **She of the Ground takes the cross from He Who Summons and strums it like a lyre as she exits.** Modern (expressional) dance affords an experience of the sublime, *"newly imagined fields," "the conceptual,"* without relinquishing the psycho-logical immediacy allying it with ritual and play as compensatory cultural activity.[29] Modern dance, in other terms, spans a chasm between ritual and "art." **One Who Seeks rocks forward again with the cloth pulled tightly over her head.**

Given this tense collusion of expression and spectacle, Martin is at further pains to differentiate the direct (unmediated) communication of modern dance from the *mediated* communication of spectacular dance. Indeed, his entire concept of expressional dance hinges on the distinction between mediacy and immediacy. **Three male choristers jump onto the stage and lift the cloth from One Who Seeks.** The "direct communication" of modern dance is unspectacular to the degree that it is rooted in *"vicarious participation in the dancer's movement and its emotional associations"* for the viewer.[30] This affiliates spectacle with intellectualism and stresses the private quality of modern dance spectatorship. **Male choristers jump with the cloth and it billows in the air.** The deep kinetic empathy modern dance arouses banishes any surface visual allure. **The men drape the cloth over a phallic object.** Martin's theory of metakinesis, which I shall discuss shortly, turns on a theory of spectatorship as vicarious kineticism. **Four female choristers enter.** That is essentially the argument of *Introduction to the Dance* which does not further elaborate Martin's theory of history as much as amass details supporting the argument's descriptive basis. **One Who Seeks reclines on her disk in its new, more vertically oriented position.**

Let us now probe further into the paradoxical situation of Martin's conception of

modern, expressional dance. **The chorus exits.** Martin imposes another important caveat regarding expressional dance that further distances it from recreational dance and allies it, however uneasily, with spectacular display. Although expressional dance should omit the visual extroversions of classical movement, it should nevertheless also avoid dangerous lapses into obscurity. **He Who Summons runs to One Who Seeks and leans over her. Their first duet begins** *(Figure 2.2)*. Martin exhorts expressional dance to a startling compromise:

> *There must be certain adaptations in the objective direction, as a matter of course. In the first place, the use of these [subjective] impulses must be taken out of the field of transient and uncontrollable inspiration, out of the virtual possession and hysteria which often dominate them in primitive society, and brought within the bounds of voluntary manipulation. In the second place, they must be rendered subject to the response capacity of the spectator instead of being solely for the emission of the dancer's own inner overcharges.*[31]

In other words, the "ah!" should be choreographed into a modern dance. Let us focus at greater length on this movement of *"subjective impulses"* in the *"objective direction"* for the purposes of transparent, but no longer immediate, communication. **He Who Summons lifts One Who Seeks off her oval property onto his knees** *(Figure 2.3)*. This is the most disastrous moment of Martin's theory for it is here that he dispossesses Graham's modernism of its subjective properties. **Balancing her on his knees, He Who Summons spins One Who Seeks violently in circles. Freeing herself, she rolls on the floor; he follows and crawls over her.** The desired objectivity is culled, as one might surmise, from recreational dance: *"Such behavior as this [recreational behavior], indeed, is the germ of the whole matter; when we bristle with rage, or start with fright, or resort to gesticulation when at a loss for an adequately expressive word, we are practicing the beginnings of dance."*[32] Thus, Martin reduces second-generation modern dance to a latter-day Delsartism or primitive expressivism, even as his phenomenology or metakinesis is always already proceeding towards discursive "explanation" designed to clarify the ambiguities of performance.[33] **He Who Summons follows One Who Seeks on his knees, holding her by the waist as she lunges ahead of him. One backs away from He on her knees; He pursues One, lifting his knees in the air.** Martin's awareness of this problem is expressed in his hesitations about the scope of mimesis:

> *The mimetic faculty is employed not to reproduce actuality as an end in itself, but only to provide a means of meeting the spectator where he is in the world of actuality. Once this is done, representationalism is abandoned for those abstractions and distortions that will lead away from the actual into the conceptual.*[34]

◓ Fig 2.2 One Who Seeks clings to her oval object. Martha Graham and Erick Hawkins in *Dark Meadow* (1946). *Photo:* Arnold Eagle.

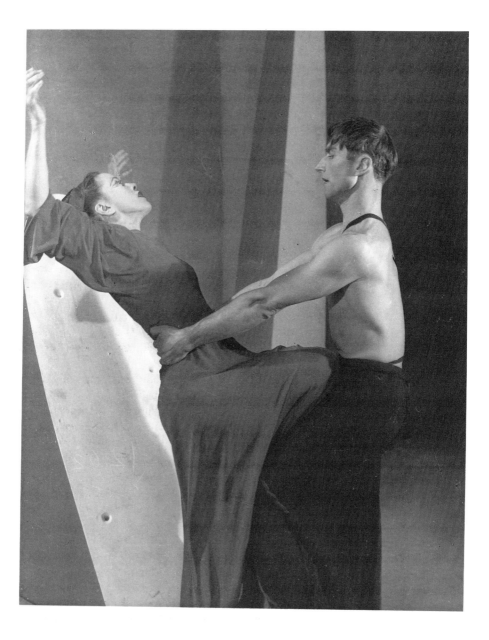

Note here that subjective impulse is referred to as abstraction. Abstraction, which Martin also understands as the distortion of recognizable forms into unrecognizable ones, can only be legitimately practiced, he argues, if we know what the original forms were, that is, if we recognize the elements of distortion. **He Who Summons returns One Who Seeks to her property and retreats back to his central stele.** This constitutes a pedagogical demand that modernism encode its ambiguities unambiguously, and thus is itself an egregious distortion of the goals of abstraction. **She of the Ground runs diagonally with vigorous gestures at the ground.**

Now I want to argue that this conceptual quandary should be directly related to Martin's misapprehension of Graham's earliest work. Consider that Graham herself never wrote about mimesis except to shun it. **"Dance is an absolute,"** she wrote. **"It is not knowledge about something, but is knowledge itself."**[35] **She of the Ground removes the black cloth from the phallic object downstage and exits throwing the cloth in the air repeatedly. She seems to exult in this action.** Martin did qualify absolute dance as one in which dance's *"essential substance and the dimension in which it exists is unveiled."*[36] But he never reflected on how critical language could acquit itself of the challenge absolute dance posed without at the same time radically betraying it with importations of mimesis at the origin of distortion/abstraction. This shortcoming is, of course, endemic to the phenomenological enterprise as such. As Jean-François Lyotard has noted: "the phenomenological enterprise is fundamentally contradictory as designation in language of a prelogical signified in being."[37] **One Who Seeks retreats behind her oval property: only her head shows.**

Historically and theoretically, Martin's legacy has obscured Graham's early belief in absolute dance as autonomy from mimesis. This early belief returns forcefully in *Dark Meadow* after a long period of retreat within mimetically oriented works of the 1940s. **He Who Summons stands behind the central stele: only half of his body is visible. They Who Dance Together reenter.** Announcing that dance was its own cognitive activity – "knowledge itself" – Graham severed practice from the symbolization of behavior as visible human intent, and conventional representations of emotions.[38] **He Who Summons dances down center stage clapping his hands and hurling his chest in and out which forces his body to arch and cave in violently.** Graham's definition of absolute dance was modernist in that it posited a somatized self "presentifying" itself to others as the form of its own content, purged of subjectivism.[39] **He Who Summons falls to the floor and stands again repeatedly.** But, although Graham's own discourse summoned interpretative quests to engage it, her very definition of dance as **"knowledge itself"** warned that natural language could not uncover the knowledge dance itself performed. **One Who Seeks tips the oval property over her back and back toward the ground with herself crouched beneath it.** Could natural language perform this knowledge, criticism would "say" dance in that art form's unique self-containment as a formal substance and in

Fig 2.3 He Who Summons removes One Who Seeks from her oval object. Martha Graham and Erick Hawkins in *Dark Meadow* (1946). *Photo:* Arnold Eagle.

its absolute consubtantiality with the embodied world within which it presents itself. **She attempts to encrypt herself.** In both cases, dance practice might find itself radically uncovered and assailed by criticism. **He Who Summons turns the oval property back to its upright position. Three male choristers enter and insert feathered darts into the surface of the oval form.** To appeal, as Martin does, to mimesis as a basis for dance's *"absolute"* is certainly to take Graham in a misconstrued direction. As if attempting to circumvent his critical dilemma, Martin's metakinesis was a project of absolutist dance criticism designed to overcome the incommensurability of the discursive and the performative through a phenomenology of perception: *"There is a kinesthetic response in the body of the spectator which to some extent reproduces in him the experience of the dancer."*[40] **She of the Ground enters wearing a long, flowing black cape.**

Martin's theory of spectatorship recurs ultimately to an empathy through which the spectator (predominantly male) *"feels"* the rationale for innovative form produced by the (predominantly female) dancer's body: *"Movement, then, is the link between the dancer's intention and your perception of it."*[41] **She of the Ground covers the downstage phallus with her cape and slowly kneels so as to make the phallic object appear to rise as she uncovers it.** But in this very *"muscular sympathy"* modern dance became assimilated to *"the irrational medium of bodily movement"* and thus segregated from the cognitive dimensions of writing.[42] This solution only serves to further distance performance from its verbal translation. *"If she became angry with somebody while in a cab, she would just open the door while the cab was moving and step out. She would jump out of windows and do other things. She was just a wild creature."*[43] Although Martin had written that the artist *"is concerned with personal, amoral, functional results exclusively,"* he counted the *"inwardness"* of Graham's artistic temperament as a liability.[44] Thus, he presented his critical enterprise as a gendered phenomenon in which the critic (predominantly male) partakes of an *"extra-intellectual experience"* by *"feeling for"* an artist (predominantly female), and then expresses the ineffable in language.[45] *"It's significant that when she began to find herself, after having resisted form and discipline so long, her technique and movement was and still is directed inward."*[46] But he also wrote: *"The intellect is manifestly the wrong receiving instrument for that which by its very nature excludes rational statement, for it must thereby also exclude rational perception and reception."*[47] **One Who Seeks performs a solo characterized by pressing both arms into the floor as well as approaching and withdrawing from her oval property.** *"Martha spoke marvelously and when I went home my wife said, 'What did Martha have to say?' I said, 'Oh, she was marvelous. She said . . .' 'Oh,' she said, 'what did she have to say?' I said, 'She said, she said . . .' I hadn't the remotest idea what she'd said, but I had come away with a clarification and a real experience."*[48] For Martin, Graham's qualities as a dancer inhabited her way of using language which was entirely performative, that is, opaque to the so-called rational mind. A particularly nasty brand of paternalism but also a virulent anti-intellectual bias can both be traced back to Martin's writing.[49]

Martin recognized Graham's "absolute" only to the degree that he glimpsed the formal autonomy of modern dance from mimesis. But he could go no farther than to say that modern dance *"realized the aesthetic value of form in and of itself as an adjunct to this expression [of inner compulsion]."*[50] **She of the Ground enters carrying a chalice before**

her. One Who Seeks reaches into the chalice and removes a red cloth. One Who Seeks wipes her hands in the cloth. The content of modern dance, however, is "absolute" for Martin because compelled by a unique self; form, on the other hand, is only autonomous by virtue of the way it marks an impersonal sublime.[51] Thus the need for a metakinetic receptive process, because movement only conveys *"grasped but intangible emotional and mental experiences," "inexpressible through the media of reason and intellect."*[52] Modern dance is both hopelessly subjective (irrecuperable by language) and ecstatically sublime (recognizable in language). But he must read his *own* body in order to translate the inexpressible into intellectual media. Martin calls form a *"substance,"* that is, not a sign but a referent, a *"self-contained"* movement *"related directly to life."*[53] It must be experienced first hand, and physically interiorized. **They Who Dance Together meld their bodies together. Everyone says it is an archaic ritual, probably a fertility ritual** *(Figure 2.4).* These two propositions – the sublime and autonomous form – if they could be synthesized, take up Graham's claim that modern dance **"is knowledge itself."** Dance does not pass through the sign but is itself content actualized in movement. *"Martha could come in and read the telephone book, and it would be a great experience because she is a great performer. She could perform a list of alphabetical names and you had a wonderful time, but couldn't review it."*[54] Thus, when Martin's theory does approach Graham's, it is at the expense of an outspoken sexism, or of his own sex change. Martin's problem is that the formal absolute he allows into the critical realm is vitiated by another of his critical requirements: form must remain an *"adjunct"* to conventional expression theory that begins at *"inner compulsion."* Martin proposes a Romanticism within modernism: *"The modern dance has actually arisen in fulfillment of the ideals of the romantic movement . . . making its chief aim the expression of an inner compulsion."*[55] **She of the Ground enters with a thin metallic mobile of seven points ending in small circular disks creating a semi-circular spread. She inserts this mobile into the phallic object furthest downstage.** Martin's thought hovers between formalism and emotivism, tending in the final analysis to enlist Graham in a project of emotivist literalism.[56] So, for example, he writes: *"The body is the mirror of thought. When we are startled the body moves in a quick, short, intense manner, etc."*[57] In Martin's thinking, undifferentiated zones of feeling are merely initially hidden correspondences that can be seen to emerge in conventionally established body languages or sign systems. **One Who Seeks and He Who Summons enter from opposite sides of the stage and face one another. For the first time, they move together slowly and harmoniously. The chorus enters and dances for the first time diversely and differently.** In 1946, the year of *Dark Meadow*'s premiere, Martin wrote: *"He* [the dancer] *utilizes the principle that every emotional state tends to express itself in movement, and that the movements thus created spontaneously, though they are not representational, reflect accurately in each case the character of the emotional state."*[58] A very rudimentary semiology undergirds the lived experience of dance, making Martin the purveyor of a vulgar phenomenology. In 1937, art critic Meyer Shapiro identified abstraction as a situation in which "personality, feeling, and formal sensibility are absolutized."[59] By contrast, Martin's literal reading of "feeling" as emotional state undercuts his grasp of modern dance's poetic of the absolute. Although not fully representational, Martin's absolute

dance is no longer immediate in its communication, but derived from an already established formalization of mood upon which a subjectivity comes to erect itself. Martin's aesthetics limps between two unreconciled views like a phenomenology paradoxically aspiring to a non-sensory status, or a semiology that cannot abjure belief in the primacy of an embodied world without signs.

In this curious divide between a formalism and an emotivism Martin deluded himself as to the role of his intuition. In one of his earliest reviews of Graham, he symptomatically reproached her sense of abstraction for being failed drama: *"Her mask is less plastic than her body and is singularly limiting to her emotional expression.... Though her dramatic intention is clear and true, her means of projecting it are slight.... When her primary concern is decorative she achieves the happiest results."*[60] In this particular review, Martin wishes to dissuade Graham from drama and to recommend she pursue lyricism. This is to say that Martin's position on the sublime is as unstable as his position on aesthetic autonomy. He thinks metakinesis accomplishes a reading of dance in the material terms of dancing, yet his *"meta"* only allows (in the photographic sense of an image) kinetic equivalents for that which already exists in language. This slippage is masked by his vision of criticism as "a consumer service": the language of criticism needs to be understood by a wide range of readers not having seen the performance. Thus, the demand for clarity is nothing other than the commercial trade-off in which sublimely unrepeatable form is reported on as a commodity whose consumption will perform what Martin promises. Dance will reproduce itself as commodified experience for other spectators. The theoretical need for mimesis thus stems not merely from a truncated solution to an interpretive problem, but is actually commanded by the economics of newspaper journalism. In this sense, too, criticism represents an inevitable compromise for practice.

Form, in the final analysis, is what moves performance into a discursive, not a performative, universe, and intuition is merely that faculty able to locate form *"Ah!"* in its surrogation for content: movement as the unequivocal expression of an emotional state which itself reveals the semiological root of the distortion. *"The whole story of Martha's arrival at maturity as an artist was her conquest of herself."*[61] Despite Martin's allowance for *"the aesthetic value of form in and for itself,"* his account minimizes ambiguities and thus forecloses Graham's modernism. **She of the Ground leads One Who Seeks around the stage until they reach the central stele. He Who Summons reaches out from behind it. One Who Seeks sinks down backwards before it** *(Figure 2.5)*.

The questions about Martin's critical and aesthetic reflections can be summed up as follows: how can a modernist aesthetic characterized by the disjunction of form and content be conceptualized as *"adjunct"* to emotional impulse which itself couples form with content in an unproblematic manner? The issue is somewhat obscured by the fact that Graham's work during the 1930s and into the 1940s transmuted from a

◐ Fig 2.4 **They Who Dance Together** (*Dark Meadow* (1946)). The central stele is pictured as well as the phallic object furthest downstage in which She of the Ground has inserted a mobile. *Photo:* Arnold Eagle.

modernist to a more mimetic choreographic mode, perhaps under pressure from Martin, but also for political reasons discussed elsewhere.[62] The choreographic response to this paradox, however, can be pinpointed in *Dark Meadow* and in Martin's loss of language while encountering it. **Another flowered mobile descends from the central stele. One Who Seeks stands alone. The curtain falls.**

"PANICKED IN THE THEATER"

"I had quite an ordeal with one of Martha Graham's premieres."[63] He Who Summons first appears from behind a tall phallic construction center stage. His directed gaze and energetic attack exert an almost sinister purpose and some pretension to authority over One Who Seeks. *"Martha Graham did a premiere of a work called* Dark Meadow, *with a score by Carlos Chavez, and it was a perfectly bewildering piece and that point never came where I said 'Ah, now I see.'"*[64] One Who Seeks gravitates towards an oval shape on the left side of the stage. Her object suggests a promontory from which she surveys the stage at the work's opening, and later becomes a couch or tomb from which He Who Summons removes One Who Seeks, as well as a target into which three choristers insert feathered darts, and a table over which One Who Seeks and He Who Summons momentarily commune. *"There was nothing; the 'umms' and the 'ahhs' were all you could review of this piece,* Dark Meadow.... *I had to rush back and write, heaven knows what."*[65]

She of the Ground is a linking rather than autonomous figure, dancing in patterns reminiscent of One Who Seeks's, yet also gravitating to the phallic object closest to the audience. She of the Ground's spatial orientation is not to any particular locus of the stage or to an object on it but to the ground itself as a covering layer which supports figures and objects of the choreography. She of the Ground is a foil for One Who Seeks's detachment from biological determination, life cycles, etc. That is, One Who Seeks is not "of the ground" in that her relation to biological determination is "chthonic," prior to or beyond ego-logical closure.[66]

They Who Dance Together present a more conventional representation of romantic and sexual imbrication. As a chorus, They connect the doings of the three soloists.[67] The groupings of They Who Dance Together, occupying the center of the stage, are amorous and "of the earth," solemnly lyrical although not lascivious. Although the two soloists could be formally apprehended as "exemplary choristers," the model couple whose image is anonymously multiplied by the chorus, the relationship of soloists to chorus is actually asymmetrical. Never interacting with They Who Dance Together, the two soloists are distinguished, even as One Who Seeks stands apart from the earthiness of She of the Ground, as they who do *not* dance, they who engage only with circumspection in the lyric state. They Who Dance Together propose a model of

◁ Fig 2.5 The final moments of *Dark Meadow* (1946). May O'Donnell as She of the Ground stands over Martha Graham as One Who Seeks. Erick Hawkins as He Who Summons appears from behind his phallic monument. The sprig of leaves descends at the right of the photo. *Photo:* Arnold Eagle.

experience that the soloists only engage in with circumspection.

The performance of this work undergirds no person's self-defined psychological coherency either on the stage or in the audience. *Dark Meadow*'s world is both non-objective and extra-subjective. It therefore thwarts and frustrates the critical operation Martin theorized as metakinesis. *"'John, what are you going to say? What was this about, John?' I gave my usual wisecrack, 'I don't know, I haven't read the* New York Times *yet.' But they really had me because I didn't know what to say – I had not found any point of contact."*[68] *Dark Meadow* goes further than perhaps any other modern dance work in staging the choreographer's subjectivity while purging it of her subjectivism. Could metakinesis function only on condition of the dancer's *impersonality*, whereby without a mimetic bridge of determined transliteration, the dancer's performance is introjected by the spectator precisely because there are no "I–you" boundaries demanding the spectator identify behavior. It is precisely because the dancer presents herself as depersonalized – a human object of subjectivity – that unmediated communication might be thought to occur.

Carl Gustav Jung, whom Graham was reading intensively at that time, recounts a dream which led to his "conviction that there are archaic psychic components that have entered the individual psyche without any direct line of tradition": the dream of a meadow that is also a dark grave.[69] Jung's dark meadow dream spurred his personal realization that the unconscious had a "social" or collective nature.[70] The dream's imagery distinguished between earthly and psychic depth in that the dreamer discovers a crypt beneath the meadow's layer of earth.[71] Graham's project of addressing an audience at the collectively unconscious level suggests that spectators construe performance as archetype, defined by Jung as "unconscious content that is altered by becoming conscious and by being perceived."[72] *Dark Meadow*'s architecture of oneiric and sexualized forms suggests an archetypal space in which bodies and objects become co-constituents. *"I struggled through the review. I wrote, as frankly as I could, that this was the most bewildering piece Martha had ever done, and you had to make your own judgments of what it was about. It was moving, but, in effect I said that I really didn't know what it was about, as honestly as I could."*[73] In Jung's terms, archetypes are a lowest common denominator of shared symbol, "forms without content," and thus fundamentally social because their source of meaning is universally shared.[74] Graham's Jungianism concealed a strategy for laying 1930s' accusations of obscurity to rest by socializing the cryptic. *Dark Meadow* was her perverse way of democratizing modernist ambiguity for a "broader," indeed a "universal," audience. Yet, for an archetype to be archetypal – that is, universal and effective – it must comprise a potentially esoteric level of abstraction, since its formal generality obscures the specificity of its content. Graham here reproduces Martin's conundrum, and confronts us with the paradoxical logic of metakinesis as crypt. *Dark Meadow* is cryptic in the etymological sense of that term. "The crypt," explains Jacques Derrida, "constructs another more inward forum [within the public forum of open exchange] ... sealed, and thus internal to itself, a secret interior within the public square, but, by the same token, outside it, external to the interior. The inner forum is (a) safe, an outcast outside inside the inside."[75] If one were to eliminate its vulgar emotionalism, could not metakinesis designate a mode of archetypal transmission in which the sublime is precisely depersonalized subjectivism, "form without content," yet intuitively grasped as content laden? The collective unconscious addressed by *Dark Meadow* is as much indebted to Merleau-Ponty as to Jung: it operates as a transcendental ego. That is, it has transcended individuality and erased differences between spectator-subjects. The collective unconscious is a way of bracketing "traditional prejudices" more radically than Martin is able to admit.

Because *Dark Meadow* seems to respond choreographically to Martin's theory of meta-kinesis and this is best illustrated with reference to its roles. Taken together, they form a Jungian allegory of objective and subjective, discursive and performative, outside and inside. The Jungian division of human behavior into Intuiting, Thinking, Sensing, and Feeling can be correlated with *Dark Meadow*'s physical inscriptions of effort, via Rudolf Laban, in this way:[76]

GRAHAM		LABAN		JUNG
He	→	*Space*	→	*Thinking*
She	→	*Weight*	→	*Sensing*
One	→	*Time*	→	*Intuiting*
They	→	*Flow*	→	*Feeling*[77]

Each role's "signature" gesture is the physical correlate of a behavioral function in Jungian theory.[78] For example, Thinking can be manifested choreographically by stressing spatial awareness. The spatial focus and purposefulness of He Who Summons indicates the rational faculty. She of the Ground indexes Sensing: the weight factor of She is predominant in the downward thrust of her runs. Similarly, Intuition is manifested in the sustained attitudes on one leg of One Who Seeks when circling about the stage at the beginning of the work. One Who Seeks's movement differs from the others' chiefly in her upwardly outward focus. "Intuition," writes Jung, "is more like a sense-perception, which is also an irrational event in so far as it depends essentially upon objective stimuli, which owe their existence to physical and not to mental causes."[79] The intuition of One Who Seeks is located differentially between the thinking of He Who Summons and the sensing of She of the Ground, although intuition privileges sensing. *"Then I edited my copy and was taking it from the composing room to the copy desk when in the middle of the composing room, the moment I had been waiting for in the theater hit me. 'At last I see what this is about. I see where to stand.'"*[80] Finally, the attitude of the chorus to Flow is heightened by their intricate couple work featuring both restriction and lyricism: they embody Feeling. One Who Seeks, He Who Summons, and She of the Ground stand apart from the chorus and comment on Flow as a model. In fact, the three soloists critique flow by disassembling it into time, space, and weight, respectively.[81]

If feeling is conventionally the most performative of the discursive categories, space is ostensibly the most discursive of the performative ones. These poles are gendered in *Dark Meadow* much as in Martin's writing. Yet, at the same time, they are displaced in the landscape, so to speak, in the architecture of sexualized objects: an environment for the dancer-subjects but not an essentialized identity. And by the same token, the movement signatures corresponding to these functions are only relative: each of them is also found in the other to some degree. The articulation of relatively weighted discursive and performative registers such as thinking, sensing, intuiting, and feeling by physical accentuations of space, weight, time, and flow respectively displaces narratives of dramatic representation. The choreography maps instead floating borders between discourse, performance, and sexual identity. Moreover, One Who Seeks is not only the pivotal border figure but also a figure of the metakinetic critic at a puzzling juncture between emotion and form, body and sign, *soma* and *sema*, feeling and thinking. In other terms, with respect to Martin as an audience, Graham as One Who Seeks actively reappropriates intuition, confiscates it from the transliterations of Martin's "ah!" Criticism, in the role of Martin in the audience, could no longer be sure of what it saw because it saw itself mirrored in One Who Seeks. Naturally, Martin was perplexed as he looked his own critical operation in the mouth. He was full of impressions but not giving out, as he said, describing critical torment at the typewriter. *"I turned in the copy because it was the deadline. I couldn't do anything about it, but I went back and wrote a completely different review for the Sunday column. That was one of the most terrible moments of my thirty-five years on the* Times.*"*[82]

"THE WRITING CURE"

What did Martin actually say about *Dark Meadow* in print? *"What she has done is a miracle of sheer invention, but invention not on an intellectual plane, but on the subjective level of pure intuition."*[83] *Dark Meadow* appears to have turned the tables on Martin, inducing him to seek the dance's own discursive translation of itself. For what other reason could he ask that the work be invented on an intellectual plane? The dance reflected his own perplexity, staged his critical quest to know what it was, and resisted his flawed critical strategies. *Dark Meadow* exposed metakinesis as "exchangism," that is, as an emotionalism whose forms are ready-made language.

For these reasons, Martin described *Dark Meadow* as a fertility ritual in which, presumably, anything with an air of mystery and affirmation goes. *"The work emerges as an extremely archaic ritual. According to the program note it is 'a reenactment of the mysteries which attend the adventure of seeking.' If that seems vague it is no more so than the general purport of the action."*[84] Interestingly, Graham reacted negatively to the idea of ritual. One year after the premiere, she wrote a new program note: **"This dance is not a drama of any event nor is it an attempt to portray ritual."**[85] *"If you look back over her [Graham's] programs and over the notes, she writes with her head completely in the clouds. Her unintelligible program notes are vague, but they mean something to her, and she puts them in the program."*[86]

Although Graham most likely drew on Jessie Weston's *From Ritual to Romance* for the sexual motifs of chalice and lance and the idea of quest, and although there is vegetation imagery in *Dark Meadow*, fertility as such is an earthly rather than a chthonic theme. Furthermore, summoning is at odds with seeking in that the purposefulness of male culture and the intuition of female culture do not mesh. Whereas He Who Summons is integrated with his architectural extension/abode and seems driven by purpose, One Who Seeks maintains an adaptive rapport with her ovalescent property because its connotations change unexpectedly and also because One Who Seeks is tentative as a seeker in her relation to space. That about the object which adheres to the body (the "male"), and that about the body which adapts to the object (the "female"), frames the fluctuating performance of gender in *Dark Meadow*. Unlike fertility ritual then, *Dark Meadow* actually deconstructs fertility because One Who Seeks, although summoned, does not dance. One Who Seeks does not entirely pattern herself on They Who Dance Together. At the end of the work, she remains alone.

Martin's insight in the composing room was to abandon the intuitive quest. In his Sunday column he wrote: *"To approach it in the conventional attitude of a work on a dramatic theme is to miss it altogether; whatever its program notes may imply to the contrary, it is as abstract as any symphony. Looked at from this angle, the meadow appears far less dark."*[87] *"All I require is to have had an experience.... The experience is felt in the irrational part of your being rather than the more often used rational parts."*[88] If Martin's first reaction was to see a failure of form in an excess of subjectivism, his second reaction was to see a surfeit of form in a practice of abstraction. Had he explored how these two extremes are in fact one and the same, Martin might have begun to articulate, albeit somewhat belatedly, modernism in dance.

Martin's previous failure to account for the disjunction of form and content and their superior union beyond representation produced a trauma cured on Sunday by writing the word *"abstraction."* *Dark Meadow* shadowed the mystery of interpretation while bracketing the inevitability of reproduction; it reembodied intuition dispassionately, a-sexually, chthonically, and thus disabled Martin's *"response mechanisms,"* *"clogging [them] up with extraneous theories."*[89] Martin himself would probably never agree: *"Since theories are largely matters of words,"* he wrote, *"words are perhaps the best possible means for exploding them."*[90] *"Thus a verbal attempt to clarify the spectator's approach to the dance becomes largely a clearing away of the underbrush of erroneous theory."*[91] This would appear to be his final word.

Throughout this essay, I have wanted not to call Martin's aesthetics "theory." That term might better be reserved for the contributions to this volume. I wish to distinguish the sense of theory from Martin's brand of aesthetic criticism in that theory moves between and across discursive and performative poles without artificially reducing their tensions.

Beyond the conflict between criticism and practice narrated here, there is also a broader historical–theoretical question. It is the following: Theories of modern dance can no longer be developed by arguing metakinesis, aesthetic Jungianism, or their like. The collusion of history and theory, rather, occurs where bodies, modernisms, and politics emerge in practice as dancing. **A sprig of leaves emerges from the funerary monument. A curtain falls on history as on the spectacle of criticism's traumatic silence before the counter-spectacle of dance as its own theoretical practice. The meadow glimmers darkly. We saunter thoughtfully up the aisle and exit onto wet pavement.**

NOTES

1   Reflections of John Joseph Martin, *unpublished typescript, Oral History Program, UCLA, 1967, p. 79. I thank the Department of Special Collections, University Research Library, UCLA, for permission to quote from the typescript of this oral history interview, referred to henceforth in notes as* Reflections. *I also thank Linda J. Tomko for calling my attention to the existence of Martin's oral history, and Arnold Eagle for permission to reproduce his photographs from the original* Dark Meadow *production*.

2   *Martin reviewed dance performances for the* New York Times *from 1927 until 1962. He took a special interest in American modern dance whose development paralleled that of his own career as dance critic. Graham's first independent concert was in 1926. Martin's major statements of aesthetic theory can be found in* The Modern Dance *(1933),* America Dancing *(1936), and* Introduction to the Dance *(1939)*.

3   *Martin,* Reflections, *84.*

4   Dark Meadow *had its premiere on 23 January 1946 with Erick Hawkins, May O'Donnell and Graham herself in the leading roles. The work remained in active repertory until 1953 not to be revived again until 1968. This essay is based on my viewing of the 1968 revival danced by Mary Hinkson, Matt Turney, and Bertram Ross, but more significantly by the single New York performance given* Dark Meadow *on 19 October 1989 at which time Christine Dakin, Donlin Foreman, and Thea Nerissa Barnes performed the principal roles.*

5   *See "Graham in the Proletarian Moment," in Mark Franko,* Dancing Modernism/Performing Politics *(Bloomington: Indiana University Press, 1995).*

6   *This is not to say that* Dark Meadow *could be visually confused with Graham's earlier work. It contains choreographic innovations only possible in 1946, and which project ahead into the 1950s, as well as recognizable elements of postwar modernism such as myth and Jungianism. What I do wish to suggest is that its willful esoterism was more in the spirit of Graham's choreographic beginnings than of the directions her work later assumed.*

7   *Martin*, Reflections, *105.*

8   *This narrative has been noted by Marcia B. Siegel: "Dark* Meadow *is about this woman's confrontation with love." See her synopsis and analysis of the work in* The Shapes of Change. Images of American Dance *(Boston: Houghton Mifflin Company, 1979), 190–8.*

9   *Do narrative elements constitute concessions to "representation," a term Martin applied to a literal-minded mimeticism he thought indispensable to modern dance? I argue that they do not.*

10   *See John R. Willingham, "The New Criticism: Then and Now," in* Contemporary Literary Theory, *ed. G. Douglas Atkins and Laura Morrow (Amherst: University of Massachusetts Press, 1989), 24–41. Visual artists, on the other hand, quickly abandoned abstraction when faced with social crisis in the early 1930s. See Andrew Carnduff Ritchie,* Abstract Painting and Sculpture in America *(New York: The Museum of Modern Art, 1951). "During the years of economic depression and threats of war in the '30s the abstract wave in America, if such it can be called, was relatively weak and unimportant compared with the tremendous swell of American scene and Social Realist painting" (p. 64).*

11   *Martin*, Reflections, *61.*

12   *Martin*, Reflections, *78.*

13   *Martin*, Reflections, *61.*

14   *Martin*, Reflections, *80.*

15   *Martin*, Reflections, *78–9.*

16   *John Martin,* The Modern Dance *(New York: Dance Horizons, 1972), 1. He goes on to note: "All theory which is more than hypothetical must be by deduction from the practice of the best artists" (ibid.).*

17   *Martin*, Reflections, *78–9.*

18   *The phrase is Jacques Derrida's in his* Speech and Phenomena and Other Essays on Husserl's Theory of Signs, *trans. David B. Allison (Evanston: Northwestern University Press, 1973), 97.*

19   *Maxine Sheets-Johnstone, "Phenomenology as a Way of Illuminating Dance," in* Illuminating Dance: Philosophical Explorations, *ed. Maxine Sheets-Johnstone (Cranbury, NJ: Associated University Presses, 1984), 135.*

20   *Johnstone, 136.*

21   *Joel Elias Spingarn,* Creative Criticism, and Other Essays *(Port Washington, NY: Kennikot Press, 1964), 5.*

22   *G. W. F. Hegel*, Phenomenology of Mind, *trans. J. B. Baillie (New York: Macmillan, 1961), 155.*

23   *Derrida*, Speech and Phenomena, *10.*

24   *Martin*, Reflections, *77.*

25   *John Martin*, Introduction to the Dance *(New York: Dance Horizons, 1965), 133–4.*

26   *Martin*, Introduction, *137.*

27   *Martin*, Introduction, *141.*

28   *Martin*, Introduction, *141.*

29   *Martin*, Introduction, *142.*

30   *Martin*, Introduction, *141.*

31   *Martin*, Introduction, *141.*

32   *Martin*, Introduction, *133–4.*

33   *On American Delsartism, see the essay in this volume by Nancy Ruyter.*

34   *Martin*, Introduction, *142.*

35   *Martha Graham, "Dancer's Focus," in Barbara Morgan*, Martha Graham. Sixteen Dances in Photographs *(Dobbs Ferry, NY: Morgan & Morgan, 1941; reprinted 1980), 11.*

36   *Martin, "The 'Absolute Dance,'" in* The Modern Dance, *90–2.*

37   *Jean-François Lyotard*, Phenomenology, *trans. Brian Beakley (Albany: State University of New York Press, 1991), 68–9.*

38   *This argument is developed in Franko, "Emotivist Movement and Histories of Modernism: The Case of Martha Graham," in* Discourse 13/1 *(Fall/Winter 1990–1), 111–28, and in an expanded version of that essay in* Dancing Modernism/Performing Politics.

39   *This disjunction was also theorized as an excessively proximate unity, which leads to the same difficulty as modernist disjunction of form and content for any theory of representation. The term "presentification"* (Darstellung) *is borrowed from the psychoanalytic terminology for hysteria in which hysterical symptoms are "actualized" by the body without becoming the organic expression of psychic material. See Monique David-Ménard*, Hysteria from Freud to Lacan. Body and Language in Psychoanalysis, *trans. Catherine Porter (Ithaca: Cornell University Press, 1989), 55 and 110–11.*

40   *Martin*, The Modern Dance, *48.*

41   *Martin*, The Modern Dance, *12.*

42   *Martin*, The Modern Dance, *12 and 10.*

43   *Martin*, Reflections, *104.*

44   *Martin*, Introduction, *130.*

45   *Martin*, The Modern Dance, *65.*

46   *Martin*, Reflections, *104.*

47   *Martin*, The Modern Dance, *37.*

48   *Martin*, Reflections, *83.*

49   *Left-wing dance critic Edna Ocko pinpointed these tendencies in Martin's metakinesis as early as 1937:*

> *[Martin's] recipe for the enjoyment of modern dancing: "When entering the theater it is well first of all to leave as much of the intellect as possible in the check room with the hat. . . . When the performance begins, abandon all effort to figure out what it means. . . . Merely relax and let the muscles do the thinking. These rules, if applied, would actually deny the validity of some of the most significant contributions made in the modern dance today. How can one disregard the visual and pictorial aspects of the dance? Blind oneself to the dancer's selection of costume? Ignore the effects of lighting and color? . . . If we checked our intellects with our hats, our plight at a modern dance recital would be sorry indeed!"*
>
> *(Ocko 1937, 34)*

50   *Martin*, The Modern Dance, *6.*

51   *"The basis of each composition in this medium [expressionistic dancing] lies in a vision of something in human experience which touches the sublime." Martin*, The Modern Dance, *59.*

52   *Martin*, The Modern Dance, *10 and 63.*

53   *Martin*, The Modern Dance, *36–7.*

54   *Martin*, Reflections, *83.*

55   *Martin*, The Modern Dance, *6.*

56   *This can be demonstrated in critical language which does not fundamentally differ in this respect from the reviews to the books. Martin's critical evaluations of Graham ensnare her in a sustained double bind between formalism and mimesis. From his first review of her work in 1927 until his last oral comments on* Clytemnestra, *the "have it both ways" tenor of his commentary leaves one wondering whether Graham also straddled this divide or not. I believe that, at least initially, she did not.*

57   *Martin*, The Modern Dance, *8.*

58   *See John Martin, "Dance as a Means of Communication," in* What is Dance?, *ed. Roger Copeland and Marshall Cohen (Oxford: Oxford University Press, 1983), 22.*

59   *Meyer Shapiro, "Nature of Abstract Art," in* Marxist Quarterly 1 *(January–March 1987), 88.*

60   *John Martin, "Final Dance Recital by Martha Graham,"* New York Times, *20 April 1931, 15.*

61   *Martin,* Reflections, *104–5.*

62   *The most telling indication of this shift is Graham's statement of the body's instrumentality in the service of a self: "The acquiring of technique in dance has been for one purpose – so to train the body as to make possible any demand made upon it by that inner self which has the vision of what needs to be said." Martha Graham, "A Modern Dancer's Primer for Action," in* Dance as a Theatre Art, *ed. Selma-Jeanne Cohen (1941) (New York: Dodd, Mead, 1974), 139.*

63   *Martin,* Reflections, *83.*

64   *Martin,* Reflections, *83.*

65   *Martin,* Reflections, *83.*

66   *James Hillman has drawn such a distinction between underground and underworld, between* ge *(earth) and* chthon *(Hades or death). See his* The Dream and the Underworld *(New York: Harper & Row, 1979), 35.*

67   *In the original version there are four women choristers but only three couples; later versions show four couples. Early program notes divide the dance into four sections: "Remembrance of the ancestral footsteps," "Terror of love," "Ceaselessness of love," and "Recurring ecstacy of the flowering branch." It is nevertheless difficult to distinguish sections. By the 1970s these subtitles were no longer used.*

68   *Martin,* Reflections, *83.*

69   *Carl Gustav Jung,* Memories, Dreams, Reflections, *ed. Aniela Jaffé (New York: Vintage Books, 1963), 23. This material was presumably not available to Graham when she titled her work in 1946. Yet Graham was then in analysis with Frances Wickes, a Jungian analyst who may have had access to this material.*

70   *The collective unconscious was "not individual, but universal. . . . It is, in other words, identical in all men and thus constitutes a common psychic substrate of a suprapersonal nature which is present in every one of us." Carl Gustav Jung,* The Archetypes and the Collective Unconscious, *trans. R. F. C. Hull (Princeton: Princeton University Press, 1980), 3–4.*

71   Dark Meadow *is intended to provoke reflection on primary processes without visualizing or dramatizing the unconscious as such. Graham would take that approach in the following year with* Errand into the Maze *(1947). For a discussion of*

Jung's influence on Dark Meadow, *see Suzanne Shelton, "Jungian Roots of Martha Graham's Dance Imagery," in* Dance History Scholars Proceedings *(Riverside, CA: Dance History Scholars, 1983). The background of this article is extremely helpful, but my interpretation differs from Shelton's by not sharing the perspective according to which "Graham didn't understand the dance herself and wasn't sure where it came from." Ibid., 129–30.*

72 *Jung,* Archetypes, *5.*

73 *Martin,* Reflections, *83.*

74 *Jung,* Archetypes, *48.*

75 *Jacques Derrida, "Fors," trans. Barbara Johnson, in* The Georgia Review *31, no. 1 (Spring 1977), 68.*

76 *See Carl Gustav Jung,* Man and his Symbols *(New York: Anchor Books, 1964), 60–1.*

77 *Vera Maletic explains the interrelation of these concepts in Laban's theory in her* Body–Space–Expression. The Development of Rudolf Laban's Movement and Dance Concepts *(New York: Mouton de Gruyter, 1987), 157.*

78 *"Each individuated character in a Graham dance is likely to have a recognizable style, established through both movement qualities and signature gestures." Evan Alderson, "Metaphor in Dance: The Example of Graham," in* Dance History Scholars Proceedings *(Riverside, CA: Dance History Scholars, 1983), 115.*

79 *Jung,* Man and his Symbols, *61.*

80 *Martin,* Reflections, *83.*

81 *In saying this, I disassemble time, space, and weight from flow which, in Laban's effort shape theory, actually enables their appearance. The entire dissociation of flow from other factors seems nevertheless suggested in Graham's early work. In* Primitive Mysteries, *for example, the choreographer performed motionless with the exception of exits and entrances.*

82 *Martin,* Reflections, *85.*

83 *John Martin, "A World Premiere Danced by Graham,"* New York Times, *Thursday, 24 January 1946, 31.*

84 *Martin, "A World Premiere," 31*

85 *See David Sears, "Graham Masterworks in Revival," in* Ballet Review *25 (Summer 1982), 31.*

86 *Martin,* Reflections, *109.*

87 *John Martin, "The Dance: 'Dark Meadow,'"* New York Times *(27 January 1946), section 2, p. 2.*

88   *Martin*, Reflections, *88–9.*

89   *Martin*, Introduction, *14.*

90   *Martin*, Introduction, *14.*

91   *Martin*, Introduction, *14.*

The re-turn of the *flâneuse*

LENA HAMMERGREN

What I have spoken of as being done in a house can also be done in public buildings, or on a long journey, or in going through a city, or with pictures. Or we can imagine such places for ourselves. We require therefore places, either real or imaginary, and images or simulacra which must be invented.

(*Quintilian on* loci *as tools, in* Institutio oratoria)

"I don't understand you," said Alice. "It's dreadfully confusing."
"That's the effect of living backwards," the Queen said kindly. "It always makes one a little giddy at first."
"Living backwards!" Alice repeated in great astonishment. "I never heard of such a thing!"
"But there's one great advantage in it, that one's memory works both ways."

Lewis Carroll (Through the Looking-Glass)

SITTING IN THE LIBRARY

Let me imagine a *locus* for myself; a place that is both real and phantasmic. It is a lush recreational area, flanked by grass-covered hills and a canal widening into a small bay. It is a void in which I will imprint a no longer existing city of glass and steel. I will move through this memory terrain whilst writing, drawing from the memorized places the images I have placed on them.[1]

The two introductory citations are worlds apart, but they meet on this page and in their concerns about the art of memory. Their juxtaposition (one that must always be unorthodox) might never be fully clear in what follows. Yet, they both provide stimulation for conceiving the half of the text that is not printed. This half requires of the reader the use of an artificial, that is trained, bodily memory, an aid in turning the durability of printed words and the photographs into fleeting images and sensations. This bodily intertextuality necessarily complements our experience of reading, viewing, and of writing.

So, I am writing from a trained memory and from a position gained through the appropriation of the moving figure of the *flâneur*. The text brings together a fictional stroll with bodily memories of activities such as, for example, walking, sitting down, floating, looking out through windows, kicking, crouching, contracting, releasing, and various ways of "making do." These tools/memory-aids will be used in search of Swedish body politics of the 1930s.

A jump from France ...

My *flâneur* strategy is primarily inspired by the writings of Walter Benjamin, and James Clifford's article "On Ethnographic Surrealism."[2] The moving figure and the mobile perspective of the *flâneur* seem suitable for the historian who has a particular interest in moving and dancing bodies. But, it is a composite figure who is fictionally and historically constituted and I will remark upon a few aspects that are crucial to my appropriation of the strolling persona.

In literature, the figure of the *flâneur* essentially accounts for the experience of men, since they had the freedom to drift alone in the cities, whereas women were confined to private spaces.[3] Women could not leisurely inhabit the public spheres on their own, without putting their social rank and reputation at risk. It has been pointed out that prostitution was the only female version of *flânerie*.[4] These street-walking women did not, of course, pursue their sauntering in a leisurely manner since the male gaze directed every move. It is therefore important, I argue, to reconstrue the central aspects of the *flâneur*, unless one is merely content with reversing the gender roles instead of trying to change them. So, in assuming the (formerly non-existent) role of a *flâneuse*, in order to make the historiographical gesture of redistributing value-charged categories, this *flâneuse* will reject sight as the single magic key that will unlock society's hidden secrets.

Visual penetration has always been the crucial element in the activities of the *flâneur*, be it characterized as "the casual eye of the stroller," "the purposeful gaze of the detective," the "detached gaze of the foreign visitor," or the "look inward into the mind and memory of the perceiving subject."[5] Now, these looks, glances, gazes, peeps, stares, and observations all seem to support the notion that seeing is equated with acquiring and mastering knowledge, but I intend to extend and alter the metaphors of vision and to progress from observing in the mind to observing and responding in the flesh.[6]

There are two discernible strands within the *flâneuse* strategy: surrealist practices and the pedestrian activity. From Benjamin I have got the image of the *flânerie*, that is, to stroll through the streets of history, along the paths constructed by my intended research topic.[7] I am trying to "enter" a particular space to adjust the historian's body (my own) in that past space, and yield to recollections springing from a bodily memory that is mine, and yet, belonged to strangers. (Following Alice's, or rather the Queen's example, this points to a third manner in which the memory can be used.) How is this possible? Well, let me say that it is not really I who plunge into the past. It is not the actual writer, it is, in Foucault's words, "the 'author' as a function of discourse."[8] In my reading of Foucault, his analysis also foregrounds the author's position within a text. Hence, what we conceive of as the author and the author's intervention in discourse "are projections . . . of our way of handling texts: in the comparisons we make, the traits we extract as pertinent, the continuities we assign, or the exclusions we practice."[9]

However, the actual writer does, in a sense, plunge into the past. A past becoming the present. I am referring to how "source material" can operate kinesthetically on the writer. How does my body react while entering that particular space?[10] What bodily sensations do I get? How does it feel to touch an object, to adjust to a normative bodily code, to sit in a chair, to look out over a landscape, to move in a particular dress, to compare "this" body to "that" body? As "participants" we might be able to detect and react to the symbolic power manifest in bodily signs, in gestures, postures, demeanors, and gaits, but also in buildings of glass, flowerbeds, yogurt, and cocktails (hence, the figure of a stroll in a flea market seems appropriate, see note 7). In this sense, the kinesthetic discourse is a strategy which we perform with ourselves as tools, with the possibility of embracing all kinds of "source material." As a result we would privilege the bodily experience of space, furniture, trees, doorknobs, words, clothes, etc., over their visual appearance. We would sense them before we visualize them, or at least use sight merely as a mediating sense. In privileging this bodily experience we call up memory associations, that is, we activate an artificial bodily memory.[11]

Ivar Lo-Johansson, a Swedish working-class writer, is close to suggesting the effects of such a bodily experience: "A doorknob, a perspective window, a piece of furniture made with sobriety would all, in a short time, affect the family living in the house, producing open-minded and transparent thoughts and feelings."[12] Ivar Lo, no doubt, privileges the sense of sight, but doorknobs and furniture are things which one repeatedly touches and which mold one's body in the everyday practice of living in and using a house.

The *flânerie* is, as Benjamin argues, a specifically revealing activity. When he strolled through the crowds in the big cities, it was in studied contrast to their hurried, purposeful activities, and it was in this disjunction "that things reveal themselves in their secret meaning."[13] It was "only the *flâneur* who idly strolls by [who] receives the message."[14] My approach is different. I do not intend to reveal any hidden meanings, and I do not conceive the historian as someone with absolute powers. The staging of a promenade in a past, or, better yet, imagined space, reveals the historian in her strategic (and studied) act of composing a history. It becomes a play about historiographical boundaries which I try to bend in my own imagination. The image of staging the promenade is helpful, since the drama analogy "helps us develop images of ourselves as persons engaged in serious play – spontaneously responding and recreating our environment, not by building eternal structures, but by constructing temporary ones to solve immediate local difficulties."[15]

The other strand of the *flâneuse* strategy is to defamiliarize. Usually we try to render the unfamiliar comprehensible, but I am investigating the possibility to act in, as James Clifford describes it, "a reverse sense, by making the familiar strange,"[16] and therefore engage myself in surrealist practices, separating things that belong together, uniting disparate events, and reversing dominating orders. Now, I am writing about the 1930s, and it would be difficult to argue that there is something particularly surreal in dealing with the minutiae of this temporal unity. But, in staging my position (i.e., as author) within it as a participant observer, I hope to achieve some aspects of the surreal. Simply put, I try "to use, manipulate, and divert"[17] the space of history as a properly "scientific" discourse together with its particular laws. It must be stressed, that I use the term surrealism in a slightly different sense than Clifford. I concentrate on the part of the aesthetic "that values fragments, curious collections, unexpected juxtapositions."[18] This loosely applied notion of the surreal has to do with my efforts to practice a "surrealist ethnography" rather than its converse.[19]

There is an additional point to my choice of the surrealist strategy. Clifford remarks that the "postwar context was structured by a basically ironic experience of culture," and that surrealism itself "began with a reality deeply in question."[20] I find this notion of reality as no longer a given and familiar environment crucial, both in that it influenced conceptions of the body, and as a guide in finding corresponding structural devices for writing about this experience. I am intrigued by the possibility of seeking techniques of representation from this same source.

... to Sweden

One of the reasons why I have chosen the 1930s is that the twentieth-century socialization project, "the Swedish model," is still in its formative stage at this time. Although a favored object for studies of social change, this progressive project has seldom been analyzed with regard to the way in which physical preparedness was understood to be integral to the reform.[21] In order to further situate my historiographical gestures in specific contexts, I want to center this text around the 1930 Stockholm Exposition of functionalist trends. Once, this event was perceived as something of a turning point, but today there seems to be broad consensus as to its lack of significance, especially with regard to how visitors conceptualized their lives in a functionalist era.[22] I have already mentioned above that I am interested in the redistribution of value-charged categories. In writing about the 1930 exposition I will repeat the undoing of its mythical status as a turning point in the history of architecture, but, at the same time, reactivate its significance as a staging ground for socially and culturally constituted bodies. Hereby, the familiar history of Swedish architecture would be defamiliarized, as well as the dance history, when moving and dancing bodies will appear in what is for them a hitherto non-significant context. By reactivating the exposition, and writing about how "bodies" use – and what they make of – its images and space, I will introduce the body in a context and in a time where it has been kept inactive. And it has remained quiescent in spite of the terrain being rather well-trodden.

> I was strolling along the main street of the 1930 Stockholm Exposition. It was summer and very hot. The sun of the new decade shone on my head. They had built a completely new city of steel, glass, and concrete on the plain that earlier on had been a void. Houses, restaurants, and spectator stands looked like birds, lifting off with stiff wings. Everywhere people talked about the new architecture that would give birth to a new feeling about life. . . . I was walking around looking for the new human being.[23]

One of my co-*flâneurs* through the exposition will be Ivar Lo-Johansson. When he wrote the paragraph above he did not, in retrospect, think he found what he was looking for. Alas, he was usually looking for her in the wrong place; in one of his favorite bars where the male avant-garde artists of the time used to sit and brood, waiting for the "new women" to enter into their lives. He openly stated that he "visited Pax exclusively in order to meet women. I found them remarkable and beautiful, I admired them. I was hunting for Poetry and Woman."[24] In retrospect Ivar Lo was disgusted by his friends' humiliating attitudes towards women, but "I could not refrain from thinking that this was ultimately the consequence of my own relation to women. They were playthings that I used when I had some time off."[25] He never frequented any of the many gymnasia where people of various ages and social classes practiced the new life style. Gymnastics was the most rapidly growing popular movement, an activity which its practitioners viewed in light of the desire to change day-to-day life in the present and the future; to experience a gigantic revolution.

> We are living in the middle of the revolution of the body, we hardly notice it, but it is more

powerful than all political changes. It grows out of the same reasons, the world must be transformed, the lives of people must acquire other forms . . . in order to endure life one must have physical powers . . . a machine to live with.[26]

It must be stressed that this experience (even if it sounds familiar), has little to do with our contemporary notion of the body with its credo of "baptism by sweat," which promises us paradise if we perform the act of worship in a fitness club. The text from which the quotation above is taken, speaks of a strategy where the desire to conquer the body became part of everyday practice. To strengthen the body (and the mind) was a thoroughly genuine change, intended to daringly stretch the body in an arc towards a progressive future, rather than to achieve self-mastery: "What hardships could the body endure? For how long could one remain in the water? How far could one cycle during a day? . . . The answers were still not given."[27]

During the first half of the twentieth century, the importance of the new *Körperkultur* is noticeable throughout Europe. In analyses of body culture, the most common framing device seems to be nature – perceived as a cultural paradigm. Gymnastics (preferably outdoors), vegetarianism, scouting, cross-country skiing, hiking, camping, sports – they all comprise activities that take shape and come into play as expeditions into the external and internal nature.

Here, I need to make a very short excursus into European theatrical dancing. From a dance historian's point of view the 1920s through the 1940s was a period of frenzied activity. The forms encompassed were many and varied, for example, natural movement, exotic music-hall dancing, *Theatertanz*, modern dance, *Ausdruckstanz*, futuristic machine ballets, and classical ballet. It is difficult to distil from this wide array "nature" or "the natural" as the single common framing device, and I will argue that we find at least two. (This will appear more important when the physical culture is situated within the framework of the 1930 exposition of functionalism.) If one can be conceptualized in terms of natural/organic/harmonious qualities, then the other is its opposite: artificial/mechanized/fragmented qualities.[28] So, rather than accepting nature as the framing device for this particular history, I will use "natural" and "artificial" as two (seemingly) oppositional categories which informed the shaping of Swedish bodies during the 1930s.

STILL IN THE LIBRARY,

but entering the terrain

The entrance, through a tall iron-bar gate, is festive, with rows of flagpoles lining both the promenade, which runs alongside the waterfront through the exhibition area, and the *corso* (the main street) that leads past the exhibition halls. Behind me is safety. If I look over my shoulder, I can see the Nordic Museum with its national romantic features. From there, it is not far to the beautiful boulevard *Strandvägen* with its nineteenth-century upper-class homes, and along the quay the small steamers and pleasure boats, all of which feels reassuringly normal. This sense of comfort and familiarity changes radically at the entrance. The impressive construction, with its long and slender supporting columns, has the appearance of an ancient Greek temple. But it is guarded by some very contemporary ushers in bellboy costumes. Upon entering, one takes on a play-acting persona and soon becomes aware of the exciting theatricality that fills the air. The theatrical no longer remains a place apart from the ordinary ordering of society, instead it becomes a major controlling metaphor of structure. Here is the new future, speaking its lines from a stage onto which we are all summoned to act our parts (and invited to partake of a "theatrical" writing). At least one visitor rejects this air of theatricality, which is partly connected to the imposing presence of advertisement. "For a spectacle it is, and a very modern one. A spectacle, which in the spirit of the time sets greater store by pleasure than edification."[29] Whether we like it or not, the entrance into the theatrical space remakes our bodies – it activates the body as an important generator of knowledge.

Continuing my walk along the waterfront, I arrive at the vast festival area, *Festplatsen*, accommodating 50,000 people. This is the nave of the exhibition. On my right this place is bounded by water with diving platforms and swimming lanes. On my left is a parabolic-roofed bandstand. Straight ahead lies the main restaurant – a striking three-storey building of glass and iron.

Eating

> It must be difficult for a sullen and bitter bachelor auditor to find a table in this functionalist inn, where he, unseen and with no possibility of looking out, can devote himself to dark dreams, because . . . [here] one is met by and intoxicated with the view over water and lovely groves, castles and church towers.[30]

I am struck by the kinesthetics of this gloomy auditor blinded by dazzling light, and of the old life shattered into pieces. The remnants of the past – the "inn," with its connotations of a cocooned coziness and a snugly wrapped body curled up in the corner – are transformed by the future: the "functionalist," with its liberating interplay of iron, glass, landscape, and transgressing bodies. Sense the auditor's cramped posture – a bodily seizure deriving from the experience of loss of control. Sense your tensed muscles and your contracted rib cage! Or, soak your body in the sensations of open space, and of energy flowing through your limbs! In this space, eating is no longer an act of enclosed privacy. It is no longer a feeding of invisible bodies, it is a shared experience of nurturing bodies, of displaying them, and of supporting them in their suspended leaps towards the future. A future, for which the body must be aptly prepared.

The very appropriate name of this restaurant is *Paradiset* (The Paradise) which appears in big neon letters at the top of the building. It is, however, not the only locale constructed for the pleasure of and "visionary" discourse of eating and drinking. Eating politics are highlighted through advertisements in the daily program brochures, which offer sandwiches, coffee, pastries, and cocktails: a *Groggy Paul*, an *Asplundare*, and a *Zeppelinare*,[31] to be savored in, for example, *Porla-grottan* (The Porla Cave) or *Gröna Udden* (The Green Cape). The building that catches the eye is a milk bar. It is eye-catching not by virtue of its architectural features which are less striking than those of the other buildings, but rather because of the politics of eating suggested by its goods. Here, they serve different kinds of milk products, among them the hitherto unfamiliar Bulgarian yogurt. The price of a simple meal is completely in line with the "visionary" aspects of eating. A yogurt and a piece of wholesome rye crispbread with cheese cost only a few cents more than a fattening Danish pastry. Here stands the very image of the new body culture, materialized in an architectural space in close and cooling proximity to the water. Strengthening this image is a rooftop sundeck with seating and parasols for customers wishing to celebrate this particular merging of bodily health, food, and nature.

Turning back

But let me return to *Festplatsen*. It has a gently sloping design, not unlike a flattened-out section of an ancient Greek amphitheater. It is as though it has been levelled (made more democratic?) and turned into a site for expanding modern bodies. Although there are spectator seats provided, the major part of the space is planned for moving rather than just sitting passively. It is a place for gatherings; a void transformed into a primal modern scene, pregnant with the curved, angular, and irregular patterns of sauntering people.

Resting and reflecting

The terrain's spatial order reflects the ideas which support the planning of new housing complexes and individual homes, examples of which are also exhibited at the exposition. The Swedish functionalists consider the home as the site for privacy, sleep, and studies. Their ideal is collective housing, with shared spaces for cooking, eating, childcare, socializing, and exercising. However, most of the housing projects do not include this type, since it is considered a little premature for Swedish circumstances. The implicit message is that social life should be spent outside of the home, preferably in the big open spaces that are planned to divide each block of apartments from the next. People's quest for outdoor activities is imposed on every structural feature of the home, as well as on the very spacious exposition area itself. Kitchens are smaller and more laboratory-like; the living rooms are no longer seen as the primary site of families' social-entertainment activities – and they are also made somewhat smaller; the home should be efficiently planned, a plan ordered under the sign of hygiene, sunshine, air, and light.[32]

The sharp distinction between private and public spheres is blurred – in a rather interesting way. Private space is transformed into an additional narrative of the public body culture. The formerly clear distinction between male and female spheres is also disturbed in turning the "female" kitchen into a "male" laboratory. In all likelihood, the ideology of domesticity for women is largely retained, but the new architectural order points to an inadequacy of that ideology in practice. The efficiency implied by the kitchen-as-laboratory suggests time for other activities – other, that is, than providing service to the family – to be performed privately as well as publicly.

Smelling the flowers

The quest to get close to nature is evident in the choice of location. The exposition is situated in the midst of parkland, in one of Stockholm's recreational areas – the place for bodily explorations into nature. Hence, while one is obstinately presented with glass, iron, chrome, pointed corners, flat or peaked roofs, geometrically sharp lines, unadorned exteriors, one also marvels at the lush verdure, the many rowing boats for hire on the glittering water, and the flowerbeds interspersed between the buildings. Ivar Lo-Johansson is perplexed and rejects this particular policy of re-ordering:

> Familiar flowers grew in flowerbeds close to the shiny constructions of steel . . . [the flowers] had to be watered with peasant-water [he deliberately uses this non-existing word] so they would not die. . . . I looked out over the exhibition area, where the birds of steel were trying to take off. The usual flowers grew in the flowerbeds. Nowhere, could I find the new human being.[33]

As one's body bends down to smell the scent of flowers, its soft curve and flexible shape is trapped by, and contradicted by, those giant beings forever frozen in austere concrete and steel. No wonder then, that Ivar Lo seems to be moved at one and the same time by a will to change and by a terror of disorientation. As Marshall Berman remarks: "To be modern is to live a life of paradox and contradiction . . . to be fully modern is to be anti-modern . . . it has been impossible to grasp and embrace the modern world's potentialities without loathing and fighting against some of its most palpable realities."[34] (The surrealists would conceive of it as a desire for one's own disorientation.)

Staggering

Suddenly, Ivar Lo is hit by a revelation and for one brief moment he grasps the meaning of the unexpected: "In one of the more modern apartments in the exposition – an apartment so functional and shiny that it flashes – there is a rocking-chair."[35] He staggers, he is shocked. Why have they placed such an old and odd object in this modern city? Why this piece of anachronistic furnishing? The answer is simple: It is "a symbolic rocking-chair that still remains in the Swede's otherwise so modernly refurnished fantasy."[36] But Ivar Lo cannot hold on to this insight, since it appears to him to be an obstacle preventing progress. He fails to realize that in order to fully sense modernity, our bodies might occasionally need to be held in the comfort of a rhythmically rocking motion, which mirrors our lives moving forwards, then back again, and forwards. . . .

Ivar Lo is trying to orient himself in a world where the familiar is attacked by the unexpected – where nature is juxtaposed with artificiality. The organization of the whole exhibition area is founded on this jarring proximity of artifice and nature, a discourse which also informs the body politics and hence codes the dancing. Although there is a remarkable variety of performing bodies, their various forms of performance all manifest the same juxtaposition of the natural and the artificial as the 1930 exposition itself.

Chafing

Movement and dancing are the central activities – and the axis around which everything turns is the main restaurant's glass rotunda. In the evening, as the daylight wanes, this functionalistic paradise is transformed into a stage-cum-window-display. Through its transparent walls one can watch people dancing and eating (activities for which they have paid either an entrance fee or the price of a rather expensive dinner), and it is the site we all must pass on our way through the exposition. The well-lit rotunda "is like a rock in a river, against which the stream of people chafe on their way towards the sea – the amusement park."[37] This is an intriguing description – the chafing bodies whose strength could shatter the glass monument. And where is this powerfully pulsating and vital crowd of people headed? Excited by the displayed dancing (several journalists describe watching these dancing couples as the most popular evening entertainment), they are moving along the water, and then uphill towards the amusement park where they can engage in a less expensive body culture, one that is performed in outdoor dancing venues.

Waltzing

Social dancing is, together with reading and writing, considered an integral part of contemporary general knowledge. There are of course those who reject this high esteem placed in the appreciation of dancing. Once, in a restaurant, Ivar Lo explains that he cannot dance, and he is met by a very surprised reflection: "Are there people who can't dance?" "That's strange."[38] Ivar Lo disagrees, because he interprets the social dancing mainly as being part of a capitalistic and bourgeois life style.[39] Others believe, however, that people "dance in order to rest the soul while the legs follow the rhythm. The soul rests and the body is exercised. Dancing is adapted to its purpose in our times."[40] While dancing, people learn to rest, to forget their work and to restore their energy. This is also said to explain why the dances have been rather simplified. They have been made functionalistic. Broadly speaking, there are three types (aside from folk dancing): foxtrot, tango, and waltz. They are all performed in a similar manner: anti-clockwise in a circle around the room, and with simple "promenade" steps and small turns. The manner of everyday dancing is hereby adjusted to the credo of the new physical culture and the functionalist ideal of sobriety.

Exercising

Social dancing is not the only form of "mass movement" to be enjoyed. There are also large-scale gymnastic shows with thousands of amateur participants, who support their own as well as their spectators' notions of embodying a revolution. These performances stress a state of kinesthetic empathy with the collective body of others' bodies. Once, in early June, 7,000 female gymnasts enthralled their audience simply by gently turning their heads and slowly lifting their arms.[41] Undulating waves of blue-clad bodies washed over the vast field adjacent to the exposition area. Indeed a sight never to be forgotten. On other occasions, a platform for amateur as well as elite gymnastic performances is raised in the very center of *Festplatsen*, as if to remind us of the trained body's significance in shaping a new future. Physical training should not, however, become too elitist, resulting in virtuosity for its own sake – this is a credo often expressed by the journalists who review these gymnastic festivities. In the midst of austere functionalism, the familiar quality of bodies engaged in physical culture makes ambiguous the difference between natural and artificial.

This is a blurring (or bridging) of distinctions that is even more evident in the case of theatrical art forms. An incident at the Swedish Royal Opera illustrates this blurring of distinctions between natural and artificial. In a letter to be circulated among the singers in particular, the director John Forsell accuses the artists of lacking body culture.[42] They neglect to keep their bodies fit, which he finds appalling considering both the general awareness of the importance of healthy bodies and the contemporary aesthetics of the art of opera which, however artificial by tradition, gives equal stress to the visual and the aural elements.

Holding, prosaically

The 1930s is an era when revue dancing blossoms and, apart from the politics of a robotic discipline and the predominance of ornamentally arranged bodies that the dancing displays, there is something functionalistic about the movements. The functional mobility of the joints and limbs, the linearity of legs kicking in the air, the prosaic hold of partners' shoulders and waists, and the collective body replacing the individual, fit in well with the policy of sobriety. The vitiating effects of revue dancing seem to be challenged – or one is at least made conscious of a negotiating process. Chorus girls portray waves, geometrical designs, robots, dreams, "showgirls," people of the past, the present, and the future. The natural and the artificial are not only juxtaposed side by side, they are also woven together in one and the same dance. Framed within the familiar synchronized, repetitive, mechanical movement patterns, we find movements taken from the gymnastic vocabulary. The kinesthetics of these movements and postures make us aware of a playful and agile body, with "natural" movements "spiraling outward from a soulful center,"[43] and this is particularly apparent with regard to the female body.

Floating, or drowning

In the filmed revue Brokiga Blad (Motley Pages/Papers),[44] produced in 1930, there is one dance in particular where the bodies slide and mediate between nature and artifact, between sensations of organic flow, strength, expansion, and manipulated fragmentation. In this scene a man, dressed in a summer suit and a straw hat, sits on a bench and gazes through his binoculars at women in swimsuits. Suddenly, he is encircled by some of these women who admonish him jokingly for his activities. They all walk to the beach, where the singing and dancing starts. The lyrics, sung by the man, tell a story of "thrills and chills" involving encounters with various young women – and with his wife. In addition, there are allusions to contemporary events, including the appearance of John Forsell's body culture manifesto. The chorus girls line up behind the singer in conventional rows holding hands, but from then on the geometrically formed groupings give us a partly different message. The dancers stretch their arms, slap hands and thighs, do swimming gestures and knee lifts, "row boats" with their partners' legs, and perform hand and leg gestures that reveal their disapproval of the singer. Towards the end, everyone – including the male orchestra – marches into the water, where the singer is encircled by the dancers (all in swimsuits and bathing caps) and ducked – suit, hat, and all. He is plainly ill-prepared for the element or, metaphorically, the future life.

No longer do the showgirls move simply in order to please, as brilliant designs or dazzling spectacles. Now they are also involved in a project of refiguring womanhood, of reorganizing the female future body. At this time, the female body is dispersed into a plurality of possible positions and functions, where it is neither wholly "natural" and familiar nor "unnatural" and unfamiliar. The sensation of inhabiting and enjoying a versatile body, freed from the constraints of corsets and long skirts, matches the sensation of reading about the new possibilities for women in the functionalist manifesto *acceptera*. A woman can, obviously without risking redemption, "lack interest or talent for household work"; she can perhaps "be engaged in some intellectual work", and she might have "a well-paid gainful employment."[45] As unmarried or divorced women with children, we will also soon find our social positions publicly acknowledged through photographs of interior designs catering especially to our needs.

Stepping, with swinging hips

It is, however, necessary to stress the nature of potentiality concerning this reorganization of the future female body. The spirited air between the sexes is often manifested in the companionate marriage so popular in Swedish movies from the 1930s and 1940s, and it saturates the beach dance in *Brokiga Blad*. It is, however, only one of several narratives. Ivar Lo writes about how ideas of the new woman and a new morality fill the minds of the young authors. He describes a conversation in which a man claims that he can tell what mood a woman is in simply by listening to her footsteps.[46] He does not even have to turn around and look at her. Is she happy or not? If she is in a good mood, she walks with an open pelvis and swinging hips.[47] So, in opposition to the emplotment of liberation in *Brokiga Blad*, the heightened awareness of bodily signs – enhanced by and enveloped in the emerging body culture – becomes a device through which a "true" femininity is literally diagnosed, captured, and maintained. The women dancing on the beach transverse the rules set up by revue dancing, but are at the same time kept within the dominant order of performing as chorus girls behind a lead singer. A looser, more varied manner of moving replaces a more controlled way. But the new forms of movement are used in order to support strategies for localizing and fixating identities of particular kinds. At this point in time, neither narrative wins. Rather, they exemplify the negotiating process (a kind of dialogic space) that is on its way.

Crouching

In the context of the 1930 exposition, theatrical dancing is presented in the form of revues but also *festspel* (that is, commissioned festival performances). On the evening of 8 July, the *festspel Det Stora Bygget* (The Big Construction) is premiered. A platform has been raised on

Festplatsen and the set design depicts a building with various business firms and a "psychic cabinet" which advertises its services. In its separate compartments for ladies and gentlemen it measures intelligence, tests efficiency, and studies complexes and hysteria. A powerful voice from a loudspeaker, placed high on a tower-like construction carrying advertising, invites the performance to begin.[48] A firework rocket is launched and performers, representing both human characters and non-human symbolic figures, pour onto the stage in a muddle of movement, colors, and strange sound effects to the underlying accompaniment of Gershwin's "An American in Paris." A gigantic wheel in black and yellow is wheeled on-stage and a story about the modern machine culture is about to begin. It is not a happy story, imbued with a spirit of optimism in the future progress. As the narrative unfolds, it appears that everyone is oppressed and frightened by the big construction where there is no room for ordinary people to live. Some characters are even turned into wheels and robots, but after a fragmentary, jazz-influenced robotic dance they protest and demand to be made humans again.

A photograph from the performance shows the mood of the "wheel dance." People of different ages crouch and kneel in front of a podium, with hands clasped in begging postures, while padded, Michelin-like figures lie on the podium and kick up in the air. Only the genie of the wheel and cardboard cut-out humans in standardized shapes stand in upright postures. My kinesthetic sensation is as frozen as the photographic image itself, as if human bodies will forever be trapped in immobility, docile, incapable of anything but following the rules of the system. Towards the end, the genie of the future appears, but all she can do is to give comfort by invoking the dreams (enacted by a group of women, dancing in long, flowing multicolored dresses) and hopes of a time when the wheels will weave everybody's freedom instead of their captivity.

Colliding

This play (by one critic labelled unfunctionalist),[49] is perceived as a rather harsh criticism of the modern technique and advertisement culture that the exposition otherwise celebrates. It might appear a strange choice by the organizers who earlier had refused a play because it involved folk dancing and folklore which was found too patriotic and nationalistic.[50] From an ideological perspective the mechanized culture seems to be repudiated by the author as well as by the audience. It is, however, worth noting that "the machine to live with," that is, the body in its machine-like *gestalt*, is perceived differently. Many are impressed by the choreography of the robotic dance with its capacity for expressing the drama of bodies involved in gestures of torque and tension. There is also a general fascination at the manner in which each role is doubled, with a "mute" performer on stage and his or her voice spoken by another person through the loudspeakers – modern man as a marionette!

Again, one is reminded of Marshall Berman's approach to modernity. This particular event is a site of flux and turbulence. It confronts two different "machines" and is staged in a pastoral setting of concrete and iron. Here, the terror of the austere machine culture threatens the body at the same time as the agile bodily machine – with every limb and joint well lubricated – is celebrated. With the body being the very epitome of that flux, it is impossible to "step into the same modernity twice,"[51] because one's body (and attitude) is paradoxically both fully modern and anti-modern. The continuous collision between these two narratives cannot transform into reconciliation. The dialectical character gives also, in my opinion, a more satisfying image of the mechanized culture than the one given by various "technothrillers" on the theme of modernity, where the mechanical always invades human nature and thereby dehumanizes and contaminates our bodies.

In accordance with the body policy, the organizers decide not to extend the run of the successful *festspel*, since it is already planned to be followed by swimming contests.[52] Obviously, these contests comprise an equally important display for the body in performance as does the performing body on stage.

Sauntering, again

Gymnastic shows, athletic competitions, social and theatrical dancing, and, not least, the performances of the strolling bodies, are crucial to the imagined new future. It seems relatively unimportant that many of the exposition's visitors do not like the artifacts they see. Rather than simply expressing discomfort, they arrive in droves (a total of 4 million visitors is mentioned by one newspaper, and this in a country with less than 8 million inhabitants), and they begin to act out their ambiguities and resistance by the everyday tactics of appropriating the place. They start walking (together with this *flâneuse*), and the

> poem of walking manipulates spatial organizations, no matter how panoptic they may be: it is neither foreign to them (it can take place only within them) nor in conformity with them (it does not receive its identity from them). It creates shadows and ambiguities within them. It inserts its multitudinous references and citations into them (social models, cultural mores, personal factors). Within them it is itself the effect of successive encounters and occasions that constantly alter it and make it the other's blazon: in other words, it is like a peddler, carrying something surprising, transverse or attractive compared with the usual choice.[53]

While strolling, a process of manipulation and renaming starts. The proud emblem of the exposition, a pair of eagle wings, is nicknamed the razor; a bridge leading across the channel is named *Suckarnas Bro* (the Bridge of Sighs, after the Venetian bridge over which prisoners were conveyed to the place of execution); a flower show is talked about as the sunken garden; the exhibited buildings are called little boxes, steamboats or birds of steel; the slender columns at the entrance are described as long macaroni; and the less expensive restaurant at the amusement park is named *Funkis* (in Swedish, short for functionalism) in ironic opposition to the politics of expensive dinners at the main restaurant, the Paradise (functionalism is hell . . .). The movie *Brokiga Blad* continues this trend, loosely weaving its satirical storyline around four farmers who win a trip to Stockholm and a visit to the exposition, where they are fittingly modernized and initiated into the many mysteries of functionalism.

Returning to the desk

In this flux of performing bodies, it is possible to discern certain fixed points of reference, although they change shape with each interpretative turn. There are different, simultaneously existing, editions of the body. Neither edition can be comprised as fully "natural" nor "artificial," instead, they exist as sets of contradictions where each term mutually constitutes the other. We find among them the visionary (who exercises and devours yogurt), the mechanized (the intriguing mute marionette), the resisting (the stroller who re-casts the surroundings), the revolutionary (who wears away monuments by chafing her body against them), and the emancipated body (the female dancer who floats in the water while the man sinks). But they share one characteristic trait. Instead of merely mirroring their surroundings, they are all communicative bodies engaged in a process of creating and recognizing themselves "through the sharing of narratives which are fully embodied."[54]

In the context of the 1930 Stockholm exposition, it is apparent how these bodies are "formed among institutions and discourses", which "enable more than they constrain."[55] Because it is through the everyday practices of all these bodies that many (perhaps even most) of the functionalist ideas are materialized – and altered. The practitioners of this expositional space encounter various forms of control and resistance. But they find ways of "making do," and of disobeying and using "the constraining order of the place."[56] It is through the body rather than through the functionalist artifacts and monuments that the new ideas will be acted out and remembered, once the exposition is closed down.

By merely using the gaze, the *flâneuse* would not be as thrilled as she is now by, for example, sullen bachelors, rocking-chairs, the word chafing, doorknobs, fragrant flowers, or rye bread. It is, she argues, through her kinesthetic responses that their bodily and ideological implications are discovered. It is in the (emphatic) memory of the bodies that "performed" the 1930 exposition, that she finds a different story about culture – about social and theatrical dance, functionalism, and their embodiments.

NOTES

1   *See Frances A. Yates, who with this image invokes the ancient orator giving his speech with the help of memorized sense impressions, Yates (1966, 3).*

2   *Clifford (1981, 539–64).*

3   *Wolff (1985, 37–46).*

4   *Buck-Morss (1986, 99–140).*

5   *Rignall (1992, 10, 24, 158f.).*

6   *Ibid., 23. Rignall writes "from observing in the mind to observing in the flesh." I apply*

a different meaning to "observing in the flesh" than Rignall does, as he interprets the progress of Walter Scott's fictitious hero Edward Waverly, who moves from an imaginative perception in his library to observations more or less in the midst of the Jacobite soldiers. I will remain in my "library" all the time, and respond, rather than observe, in the flesh.

7　Another "figure" that inspired the composition of this particular history, originated in discovering Foucault's epiphany that came "out of the laughter that shattered ... all the familiar landmarks of my thought" while reading Borges' ancient Chinese encyclopedia classifying animals. See Foucault (1973, xv). By pulling together as species of "animal", those owned by the emperor, the stuffed ones, those who look like flies from a distance, etc., something familiar is made strange. Reading this extraordinary classification made me feel like strolling through a flea market, where curiosities are displayed in close proximity to ordinary household utensils, and, who knows, perhaps a solitary antique – a sensation not unlike working as an historian with different kinds of source material.

8　Foucault (1992, 124).

9　Ibid., 127.

10　I have found a similar approach to "entering" in Colomina (1992, 73–128). "The photograph suggested that it is intended that these spaces be comprehended by occupation, by using this furniture, by 'entering' the photograph, by inhabiting it" (p. 75). She continues "The perception of space is not what space is but one of its representations; in this sense built space has no more authority than drawings, photographs, or descriptions" (footnote 3, p. 75). My text relies on a similar approach to different kinds of source material. Note, however, that Colomina stresses the sense of sight rather than the kinesthetic touch.

11　On the difference between a natural and an artificial memory see Yates (1966, 5f.). I am expanding the understanding of a trained memory, to include not only manners of memorizing in the mind but also in the body.

12　Lo-Johansson (1976, 5). All translations from Swedish texts are my own.

13　Benjamin (1969a, 12) in Arendt's introduction.

14　Ibid.

15　Buker (1991, 236). Buker continues by further stressing the element of play in order to understand the politics of postmodernism: "it emphasizes the ways in which we are trying out new ideas. . . . There is an innocence – even ignorance – involved in our experiments, and there is a way in which we are not in control of them. . . . Perhaps our work is like play in that it is not predetermined; it is often the surprises that enables us to move ahead or take a delightful turn" (p. 238).

15　Clifford (1981, 542).

17   De Certeau (1984, 30).

18   Clifford (1981, 540).

19   Clifford makes some proposals concerning this practice towards the end of his article
      (1981, 563–4). He suggests for example, to leave the cuts and sutures of the research
      process visible. I consider "the promenade" an elaboration of these procedures,
      invoked in order to reshuffle (as Clifford puts it) the reality.

20   Ibid., 542.

21   Jonas Frykman has used this perspective in Frykman (1992, 30–42). He focuses on
      how Swedish bodies participated, through the physical culture, in forming a new
      national identity, and I am indebted to his work here.

22   Even though Frykman focuses on the physical culture, he rejects the 1930 exposition
      as ideologically important with regard to the emerging bodily identities. The
      exposition is mentioned only in terms of its artifacts and as an event that invoked
      nothing but horror and discomfort, see Frykman (1992, 39).

23   Lo-Johansson (1976, 5).

24   Ibid., 50.

25   Ibid., 54.

26   A text originally published in the social democratic magazine Morgonbris (Morning
      Breeze) in 1934, cited in Nilsson (1991, 89).

27   Frykman (1992, 33).

28   Cf. Hillel Schwartz, who summarizes the new kinesthetic of the twentieth century
      with words as "rhythm, wholeness, fullness, fluidity and a durable connection
      between the bodiliness of the inner core and the outer expression of the physical
      self," in Schwartz (1992, 104). This rather romantic description fits in well, I argue,
      with the contemporary consensus regarding a discourse on "the natural" within
      dancing.

29   Tor Hedberg, cited in Råberg (1964, 61).

30   A description from the newspaper Socialdemokraten, 16 May 1930, 11.

31   These names refer to the exposition, for example to its main architect Gunnar
      Asplund.

32   Asplund (1980, 39).

33   Lo-Johansson (1976, 6f.).

34   Berman (1982, 13f.). An intriguing, and unusual approach in Berman's analysis is his
      description of the experience of modernity as being simultaneously "for" and "against."

In his argumentation, modernity is not dominated by fixity, it is a matter of flux and of change, which "will make modern life especially elusive and hard to grasp" (p. 143).

35   Written by Lo-Johansson in the newspaper Stockholms-Tidningen, 1 June 1930, B3.

36   Ibid.

37   Ibid., B1. An article by the signature Robin Hood.

38   Lo-Johansson (1976, 132).

39   Ibid.

40   The newspaper Stockholms-Tidningen, 1 July 1930, B4.

41   The newspaper Stockholms-Tidningen, 10 June 1930, 15.

42   The letter was published in the newspaper Svenska Dagbladet, 20 August 1930, 3.

43   Schwartz (1992, 108).

44   The film was premiered in 1931 and was directed by Edwin Adolphson for SF-productions.

45   Asplund (1980, 74).

46   Lo-Johansson (1976, 55).

47   Ibid., 52.

48   The following description is mainly taken from an account of the dress rehearsal, in the newspaper Svenska Dagbladet, 7 July 1930, 10.

49   Ibid., 9.

50   Ibid.

51   Berman (1982, 143).

52   See an interview with Rolf de Maré (the creator of Les Ballets Suédois, who acts as artistic consultant for the exposition), in the newspaper Stockholms-Tidningen, 14 July 1930, 9.

53   De Certeau (1984, 101).

54   Frank (1991, 89). Frank distinguishes between the disciplined, the mirroring, the dominating, and the communicative body (pp. 36–102). In search for the communicative body he mentions Bakhtin's Rabelaisian bodies, the aesthetic practices of dance and performance, and the caring practices of medicine (p. 79).

55   Ibid., 80. For a fuller explanation of discourses, institutions, and corporeality as constituting bodies, see Frank (1991, 48–50).

56   De Certeau (1984, chapter 3).

Antique longings: Genevieve Stebbins and American Delsartean performance

NANCY LEE CHALFA RUYTER

PROLOGUE

The intention in this paper is to explore an aspect of American Delsartean performance practice in relation to its historical context. As with any such project, writing in 1993 about an experiential and presentational phenomenon of the late nineteenth century presents its own set of challenges.[1] I am purportedly attempting to learn something about a vanished practice from a distant past – and hopefully illustrate its process through time. (Isn't that the business of history?) But the minds and bodies of those who developed it and *practiced* it have disappeared; only a residue remains in their words and photographs. This past, therefore, no longer exists except in what our minds and bodies do with those traces.

Some historical dance phenomena have persisted through time by acquiring new lives in successive generations of living bodies (which implies also minds, emotions, psyches). For example, traditional dance forms from throughout the world; nineteenth-century ballets; and twentieth-century "modern" dance works have been handed down through "oral tradition." (Should we coin a new term "bodily tradition"?) Other dance phenomena, after a short or long historical break, have been reconstructed from notations, descriptions and iconographic material, and performed anew. While in either case we will never know these dances as they were to their original times and peoples, we have the *illusion* of knowing, of experiencing them – either as performers or viewers. The dances exist again – albeit with alteration – for *us*, and we imagine (hope, believe, *feel*) that they do connect us with a past, a tradition, a heritage – or an "other." In any case, according to individual taste, we find such dances attractive to do and see, just as we enjoy experiencing modern renditions of historical music and drama. All such material provides us with physical, mental, and emotional experiences we would otherwise not have. In dancing a baroque minuet, an old-style flamenco *alegrias* or one of Isadora's dance moments, we experience sensorially, imaginatively, our own version of what it might have been like to be that person of another time or place, to move as she or he moved, to live in that ambience, to drink in that experience. We add to our repertoire of personas.

Some performance phenomena of the past are available to our consciousness only through words and pictures. If we are to embody any semblance of Delsartean practice we must rely heavily on such sources because there has been no transmission through oral tradition and few attempts at reconstruction of the performance pieces. While Delsartean theory, training exercises and movement vocabulary have fed into twentieth-century modern dance practice, and thus gained a new (albeit largely anonymous) life, the performance forms became outdated long ago. And while there is sufficient source material for reconstruction of some of the repertoire, genres such as Delsartean statue posing, drills, and pantomime have generated little interest thus far: such works seem quaint, trite, old-fashioned – valuable for insights into an historical era, but not generally of interest to today's performing artists and audiences.[2]

The most crucial aspects of Delsartean performance – the bodies, the movement, the temporal and spatial qualities, the impact – have all disappeared. We must therefore search (dance?) around the edges of what was the reality (which we can never know) for traces that may help us imagine its nature. On one hand, we can apply traditional historical methodology to the practice's verbal and pictorial remains. In the case of American Delsartism these include written sources, such as treatises and articles published by Delsarteans, and iconographic material – drawings and diagrams, but most importantly, photographs, of the performers themselves and of the images (usually classical statues) upon which they modeled some performance. On the other hand, as a complement to the historical methodology, we can also embark on speculation from the experience and perspective of our 1993 bodies and minds – a kind of improvisation that takes off from the historical material. Can we trick Delsartean performance practices into taking on some life for us – and if so, will that shed any light on either the past or the present? Will that help us reconstruct the dance, at least in our imaginations?

INTRODUCTION

In the 1880s and 1890s, a complex of activity here referred to under the rubric "American Delsartism" became fashionable in the United States. It comprised theory from a French teacher of acting and aesthetics, François Delsarte;[3] practical exercises and formulas for expression based on Delsarte's work and that of his student Steele Mackaye;[4] physical training exercises; and various performance genres embodying "Delsartean" principles. Transplanted to the United States, Delsarte's "applied aesthetics" touched the lives of a considerable number of late nineteenth-century American women and introduced theory and practice that would lead to twentieth-century dance innovations in the United States and Europe.

The context for the American adaptation of the Delsarte system was elocution (training for public speaking and recitation), a field of study and endeavor which had been developing on a national scale since the 1820s. By the late nineteenth century, the elocutionary establishment included educational institutions, performance venues, publications, and a national network of professional associations. From the mid-century, some elocution instructors – particularly among the women – increasingly emphasized gesture and bodily motion, and the term "expression" came into vogue for work that was thus more inclusive. Expression included instruction in physical culture (what is now called physical education), pantomime, acting, and interpersonal communication as well as training for the speaker's "platform." The narrower study of elocution had originally been an important part of education for men – especially for clergymen, lawyers, public readers, and lecturers. As educational opportunities for women expanded, training in all aspects of expression came to be considered useful and appropriate for children, young ladies, and society matrons.

Expression was taught by various methods in the United States, but the best known and ultimately the broadest in application was the American Delsarte system.[5] In the late nineteenth century, one could find the adjective "Delsartean" applied to teachers, schools, performances, publications – and even corsets. By the 1890s, Delsartism had spread across the

United States to involve at least hundreds of teacher/performers and thousands of students. While some proponents emphasized the aesthetic principles to argue for clothing reform and artistry in everyday life, Delsartism contributed most influentially to the cause of physical culture and expression for middle-class women, constituting a context within which they could pay attention to their bodies, undergo training in physical and expressive techniques and present themselves to selected audiences in public performance.

To the traditional elocutionary fare of recited stories, poems, and dramatic selections (the favored male performance material), American Delsarteans added posing, drills, pantomimes, and (to a lesser extent) dances and dance dramas. While words might play a part in any of these new (to elocution) genres, what distinguished them was that bodily expression was not only included, but emphasized – in the communication of narratives, character delineations, and thematic ideas. Such "non-verbal" expression, however, was the equivalent of what could be (and also often was) expressed in words. The specifics of any particular piece were derived from a detailed series of expressive prescriptions based on Delsarte's theory and practice.[6] Preparation for such performance included purely physical exercises as well as training in the Delsartean canon.

In addition to their intentional content, the works also carried non-literal and unwitting meanings – about the body itself, particularly the female body in its nineteenth-century American physical, social, and cultural definition. Many of these predominantly non-verbal forms had already existed on the professional stage in Europe and the United States – performed by both men and women. They took on another life, however, in American Delsartean amateur and educational practice. The performances were given mainly by white, middle-class, urban "ladies" and their students who ranged in age from children to adults. Thus it was nearly always the female body that was *representing*, although both female and male bodies might be *represented*. These girls and women departed from everyday custom by entering a performance space, wearing special costumes, and displaying their bodies in a choreographed set of actions or poses. Both teachers and students engaged in what was for them a new, and perhaps daring, repertoire of physical and expressive activities which did not, however, transgress the traditional bounds of gentility and propriety.

The most influential American Delsartean teacher, performer, theorist, and writer was Genevieve Stebbins, and this study focuses on some of the performance material that she and others taught and presented in "ladies' matinées," school recitals and other performance contexts. Stebbins was an exemplary figure in American Delsartism. She was the first to feature non-verbal expression in Delsartean public performance and instrumental in establishing the general characteristics of the various forms. She has written prolifically about both the theory and practice of such performance. Other Delsarteans, to a lesser extent, also wrote about the genres, created original works and published production guides, but it is Stebbins's work that constituted the foundation for much that followed.

EXCURSION I:
A TOUR OF AMERICAN DELSARTEAN PERFORMANCE FORMS

Dead center: living pictures

"Living pictures," a favorite Delsartean performance activity, has a long history. One or another type of such representational posing can be traced back as far as antiquity, and the practice was prevalent in Europe on the stage and in private entertainments from at least the eighteenth century. In nineteenth-century and early twentieth-century America, it was featured in popular theater productions across the country.[7] Initially, in the Delsartean context, it consisted of statue-posing based on classical Greek and Roman models. Later, this perform-ance category also included items variously identified as "attitudes," *poses plastiques, tableaux vivants,* and *tableaux mouvants.* Delsartean attitudes were the depiction of various actions (such as pleading, rejecting, affirming) or emotional states (such as joy, fear, rage) according to American Delsartean precepts. *Poses plastiques* might designate statue poses, attitudes or full *tableaux* – the latter usually implying group rather than individual poses. These narrative *tableaux* could represent statuary, friezes, paintings, historical scenes, or original ideas and often included elaborate costumes, settings, and stage lighting, sometimes within a huge picture frame. Designating the *tableaux "mouvants"* (moving) rather than *"vivants"* (living), signified that the poses were connected by transitions in motion. Rather than a series of static moments (separated by the closing of a curtain, or a blackout), in *tableaux mouvants,* the performers were always in view and the composition as a whole involved process through time with the transitions providing continuity.[8] Music might accompany any type of posing presentation.

Close neighbors: drills and pantomimes

Delsartean drills and pantomime typically also featured posing and used musical accompani-ment. Drills usually involved a number of performers, while pantomimes were often solo. Some drills were nothing but a series of non-narrative *tableaux* on a unifying theme and connected by simple transitional movements. Others interspersed the poses with rhythmic marching or simple step patterns – often in elaborate formations – or arm and body movements – usually executed while in one place. A drill often incorporated a set of props such as hoops, fans, parasols, flags, wands, or dumbbells, and the theme might be no more than the props themselves and configurations with them. Also popular for drills were patriotic, international, and nursery subjects.[9] In contrast to drills, with their generally non-narrative content, pantomimes usually featured the interpretation of a poem, song, or story rendered through movement and poses. Popular texts included hymns (such as "Nearer My God to Thee"), bible stories, exotica (such as pieces set in the Middle East or Asia), and poems on a number of patriotic, sentimental, or humorous themes.

Fig 4.1 Clara Power Edgerly's students in "The Dance of the Muses" from her *Tableaux Mouvants and Poses Plastiques*, No. 1 (New York: Edgar S. Werner, 1894).

Far out in left field: dance

Dance – identified as such – also figured in Delsartean performance. It furnished the subject of a few *tableaux,* in which case the performers posed as if in the stopped moment of a (usually classical Greek) dance (Figure 4.1). Actual dances were presented by Stebbins from as early as 1890 and by a very few other Delsarteans. Stebbins was unique, however, in taking the dance in a new direction – in creating original dance compositions that either stood alone or carried forward the narrative of a dramatic work.

GENEVIEVE STEBBINS

Introduction

In early 1880, the probable time of her first Delsarte presentations, Genevieve Stebbins was still working as an actress on the New York stage (a career that ran from *c.* 1876 to 1885).[10] After her study of the Delsarte system with Steele Mackaye (*c.* 1877–9), her interest began to shift away from professional performance, and from 1885 on, she devoted her life to the theory and practice of physical culture and expression. Within the American Delsartean context, she achieved distinction as a theorist, educator, author, and performing artist. Stebbins moved ever closer to dance throughout her career. While she never totally abandoned

recitations and dramatic readings, her own Delsartean performances (dating to at least 1903) featured several non-verbal genres (Figure 4.2). In addition to statue posing, Stebbins performed dances and what she called pantomimes (her own original dance dramas). She also created at least nine drills for students.

Stebbins presented her material in a number of settings in New York and beyond – to predominantly female audiences. She initiated Delsarte matinée performances with her long-time colleague, Mary S. Thompson, who specialized in recitations and bird calls. Presented annually from 1887 to 1893, at the Madison Square Theater in New York City, these programs reportedly drew large and enthusiastic audiences of attractive, cultured, and socially prominent women – some of whom might then decide to study with either of the artists. These were "ladies' matinées" with few men in attendance. In 1893, Stebbins founded the New York School of Expression which she directed until her retirement in 1907. There, she presented annual commencement recitals featuring the predominantly female graduates of the school. Audience members, of course, included some male relatives and friends of the graduating class. Stebbins also performed at various educational institutions and other organizations – particularly at girls' schools or women's colleges such as Wellesley. The pattern is clear – in American Delsartean performance, women directed all aspects of production, selecting content, determining style, and designing the whole as a commodity mainly for female audiences.

Posing

In Stebbins's recitals, statue posing was a staple. One wonders what prompted this professional actress to take up such a genre which, while ubiquitous both on the professional stage and in amateur settings, enjoyed little respect as a serious art form. While there is mention that, as a child in San Francisco, she had imitated statues for family gatherings, there is no indication that posing played any part in either her subsequent training as an actress, her instruction from Mackaye, or her professional performance. But take it up she did, and by the 1890s her theoretical basis, rationale, and methodology for it were fully developed and being presented in lectures and publications as well as through her own performance.

Stebbins shared with her contemporaries a belief both in the existence of absolute and eternal principles of "true art" and in classical Greek art as the most perfect embodiment of those principles. In her view, Greek sculpture had attained a universality that could never be surpassed. Since it furnished ideal models to be emulated, she used pictures of such sculpture to illustrate expression and to teach by example. "The Beautiful and the True in human nature," she wrote, "has been expressed in its highest degree by the immortal artists of Greece. They discovered, in all its perfection, the intimate relation of the laws of expression to art."[11] Stebbins's conviction that the laws of expression developed (discovered?) by Delsarte were the same as those known in the ancient world nurtured her respect for his system and encouraged her use of it.[12] What could be better for education in the arts or for edification of an audience

◀ Fig 4.2 Genevieve Stebbins in 1892. Reproduced courtesy of the Library of Congress.

than to combine the two sources: to use Delsartean principles as a practical method for the study and reconstruction of classical models of eternal truth?

Stebbins distinguished her own statue posing from other contemporary posing on the basis of two characteristics: a focus on the expression of general rather than particular qualities and the use of designed, motional transitions between poses. While she did not denigrate the depiction of individual characters, thoughts, or emotions as a legitimate aspect of expression, her goal was the expression of "universal truth." In what she termed "artistic statue-posing," she wished to convey "the idea of absolute calm and repose of an immortal soul, possessing infinite capacity for expression, but at the same time giving no definite expression except that of capacity and power in reserve."[13] Such expression, she believed, was profound and possessed an almost mystical agency. Because of what she perceived as "purity of soul and nobility of spirit" in the Greek statues, Stebbins argued that her artistic statue posing had a "spiritual value in education, since it gives rise to noble ideas."[14] The activity of statue posing was thus generalized far beyond a limited performance genre: it was conceived as an instrument by which people – and in practice these were women – could reap spiritual as well as physical benefits.

Stebbins set forth her principles and recommendations for this genre in "Hints for Artistic Statue Posing" (in the 1902 edition of *Delsarte System of Expression*). There she states: "the only training of value in artistic statue posing is the esthetic gymnastics based on the system of Delsarte," and stresses as particularly important the Delsartean principles of "harmonic poise" and the "laws" of sequence (or succession) and opposition.[15] In Delsartean theory, poise (or equilibrium) is that state in which the legs, torso and head are in counterbalance with one another. Training in harmonic poise involved exercises that worked from a centered sitting or standing body to shifts of weight (of various extension) with the torso and head adjusting to create balance. For example, in standing, if the weight shifts to the right leg, the torso will counterbalance by shifting left, and the head, in its turn, by shifting to the right. For the Delsarteans, such physical poise in the Greek statues or in their own nineteenth-century embodiments of it corresponded to an ideal of "moral poise."[16] In their practice they thus manifested Delsarte's "Law of Correspondence" – between tangible and intangible, outer and inner, movement and meaning.

Stebbins considered opposition a fundamental necessity in statue posing. In his landmark study of the Delsarte system, Ted Shawn has noted that, in the Delsartean canon, "oppositions are expressive of force, strength, physical or emotional power," while parallelism denotes weakness.[17] Stebbins maintained that what she called "the divine lines of opposition" were integral to every Greek statue, no matter what character or subject was being portrayed; i.e., none displayed weakness.[18] At its most tranquil, opposition was present in the harmonic poise of a simple stance – in the relationship of the legs, torso, and head. In more dramatic poses, such as those portraying battle, pain, or anger, opposition occurred in greater extension and with greater force. In short, it was a characteristic necessary to every rendition; and the student of statue posing was therefore trained in oppositional modes of movement.

In its simplest form, the law of sequence dealt with the order of expression: "Expression of face precedes gesture, and gesture precedes speech." As elaborated in American Delsartean theory and particularly in relation to non-verbal practice, the concern with sequence evolved into an interest in successional movement, "the progression of the articulation of the limbs," in Stebbins's words. She compares sequence in motion to melody in music, and for transitions between statue poses she prescribed sequential movement so the change would occur like a wave, or "natural evolution" from one pose to the other.[19] We might say she was creating a visual melody. American Delsartean training featured successional movements in both straight and spiral spatial designs.

Genevieve Stebbins presented statue poses not as separated scenes, but in series of images in which the transitions figured at least as prominently as the poses themselves. Whether or not she invented this format, it was her hallmark. Stebbins's instructions to the budding statue poser give the most complete picture of the qualities she sought and presumably considered important in her own and her students' performance. After a general suggestion to use real statues or photographs (rather than drawings) for models, and to "study the poise and attitudes of these statues," she embarks on a lengthy discussion that focuses on the transitions – the movement into a pose and between poses – rather than on the poses themselves:

> Stand in front of a large mirror and attempt to make yourself a living duplicate of the picture. . . . (a) There must be simultaneous movement of all parts of body, from head to toe; (b) the motion must be magnetic, i.e., slow, rhythmic, and as unaffected as the subtle evolution of a serpent; (c) every movement must be made in conformity with the principles of evolution, i.e., the movements must unfold from within to without as naturally as the growth and expansion of a flower; (d) there must be no sudden seeking for opposition, no spasmodic attempt for sequence. . . . Every gradation of motion, from normal position to perfect image, must be one beautiful flow of physical transformation.
> . . . wherever a series of statues is gone through, one form must gradually melt into the other by the following rules: (a) Regarding each statue as an attitude expressing an impression, the rules of transition of attitude and gesture should be carefully observed, such as the arm moving in an opposite direction to the pointing of the hand; (b) harmonious balancing of arm to arm; (c) preparatory movement in opposite direction to intended attitude; (d) and, finally, rhythm of movement in harmony with character of statue or emotion depicted.[20]

One can assume from these directives that the transitions would have a sustained quality, perhaps something like that of slow-motion action on film. The emphasis is on a continuous design in space rather than any dynamics of time or energy. The poses interrupted the continuity of the transition, stopped action for a few seconds and would elicit applause. Then, almost imperceptibly, the next transition would begin.

Stebbins gives no guidance on how to emulate the statues themselves. She writes nothing about distinctions in physical quality that might be required by differences in the statues' gender, character, emotion, or action. There is no indication of costume differentiation in relation to the gender, the state of dress or undress, or the action of her models. All the evidence indicates that she (as other contemporary Delsartean statue posers) wore the generalized long and sleeveless Greek gown for all posing. And she gives no specifics on any technical matters such as timing of poses and transitions, breathing, use of props, relationship with music, use of space, or possible variation in dynamic flow.

EXCURSION II:
A TOUR OF STEBBINS'S ANTIQUE MODELS

The photographs of thirty-two classical statues illustrate the final enlarged edition of Stebbins's *Delsarte System of Expression*. These were to be used for the teaching and study of posing, and they are examples of the many subjects Stebbins herself chose to depict on stage. Despite the fact that Delsartean statue posing was an overwhelmingly female activity, the illustrations are mixed in gender: fifteen males and seventeen females. Included are gods and goddesses: four Apollos, two Venuses, two Dianas, and a host of others including Juno, Hercules, Mercury, and Minerva. There is no Dionysus. Certain historical figures are also represented – Augustus Caesar and Sophocles among them – and some mythical characters. Of the female statues, thirteen wear draped dresses that reach from shoulder to ground and reveal little or much of the body's fleshly contours (some drapes are quite transparent, and one goes so far as to bare a breast). Three statues are clad in short tunics (two baring a breast); and one is nude. Even more flesh is exposed among the male statues. Ten are either completely nude or covered only by a figleaf or drape. Augustus Caesar is shown in warrior garb with arms and lower legs bare and Sophocles in male drapery that covers most of his body. Of the four Apollos, one (Apollo Belvedere) is among the nudes with figleaf and drape. The others (Apollo Musagete and two versions of Apollo Citharaedus) depict the god in his role of musician. In each case, he wears a gown similar to women's dress that reaches from shoulders to ground; his arms are bare and he carries a cithara (ancient Greek stringed instrument). The dress resembles female garb, but in fact has no feminine connotations; it was the costume worn by professional musicians in performance.[21]

Most of the figures are in tranquil poses – with the weight predominantly resting on one leg (the foundation of "harmonic poise") and one or both arms in some kind of gesture. A few (such as one of the Apollos with cithara) have their weight almost centered with one or both arms down at their sides. The bodies are well balanced and supported, and these statues do give a feeling of calm and repose. Among the ten that represent action, three play musical instruments, one (Diana) shoots a bow, three (males) engage in violent combat, one wards off danger, another runs and the last is throwing a discus. Of these, however, only eight suggest real movement through time and space – a moment in an action that began before the pose and is moving through it on to further action. With a free-flowing quality, two Apollos with cithara are lively as they stride forward playing the instrument; Atalanta (mythical Greek huntress) runs with weight barely and seemingly briefly on the ball of one foot; and the goddess Diana plucks her non-existent bow. A constricted flow through space and time (and the opposite of repose) is embodied in four statues: the three fighters (Boxer, the Fighting Persian, and Group with a Gaul) and the frightened daughter of Niobe.

Stebbins's choice of models raises theoretical questions about her attitudes towards gender, violence, and nudity and her intent in choosing these particular types of statues to emulate. The

Werner's Magazine.

ESTABLISHED 1879.

A JOURNAL OF EXPRESSION—VOCAL AND PHYSICAL.

MONTHLY, $2.00 A YEAR.
SINGLE NUMBERS, 25 CTS.

EDGAR S. WERNER, Owner and Editor,

NO. 108 EAST 16th STREET, NEW YORK.

Copyrighted, 1894, by EDGAR S. WERNER. Entered at Post Office as second-class mail matter.

VOL. XVI.   NEW YORK, DECEMBER, 1894.   No. 12.

For Werner's Magazine.

STATUE-POSING.

"THE GAULS' LAST STRAITS."

BY CLARA POWER EDGERLY.

THE incidents connected with our group take us back about two hundred years before the Christian era, when the civilized world comprised little beyond the jurisdiction of Greece and Rome. At this time Rome had conquered Macedon and crushed Greece ; province by province of the downtrodden nation gradually became absorbed in the upbuilding of the great Roman Empire. Among the lesser kingdoms that belonged to Alexander's monarchy, in Western Asia, was that of Pergamus. This tiny province in the western part of Persia, bordering on the Ægean Sea, is of great interest to us as students, for from this place came an impetus that has been felt all through the ages. The third ruler of this fair country was Attalus I. Besides being a valiant warrior, he was a patron of art and of literature, and endeavored to make the capitol of his kingdom a rival of Alexandria. Pergamus was adorned with beautiful buildings, the remains of which can be seen to-day. Attalus made his reign memorable by his victory over the Gauls, who were at that time swarming over all Northern Phrygia. To commemorate this victory, Attalus erected the statues from which these studies in posing are copied.

The idea portrayed in the right hand group is that the Gaul, seeing nothing but death for himself and dishonor for his wife, resolves to cheat his enemies, who are rapidly closing upon him. The wife, at the thought of so terrible and sudden a death, falls fainting to the ground, from which her husband hastily lifts her, glancing in terror at the

THE GAULS' LAST STRAITS.

approaching foe. He grasps the fatal knife, and thus end their last moments on earth, moments at best frightful almost beyond conception. To die in so violent a way, and by the hand that had always shielded her, was indeed awful to contemplate. Nature happily came to her relief, and sweet unconsciousness took possession of her, so that she knew not when the dreadful blow was struck. And the husband— what of him ? He allows no tender thought of their love or their home ties to enter his soul ; he needs all his stoicism to brace him for the deed. He dare not look at her, so pale and helpless ; and, lest his resolution weaken, he glances once more at the advancing foe, ere he plunges his knife into her breast. The pose suggests the moment just before the deed.

In the group to the left, the wife has already been slain and the husband is in the act of burying the knife in his own body. His face shows no such struggle as that needed to kill his wife, and a look of strength and serenity overspreads his features as the dagger is about to find its way to his heart. The old Grecian idea that a warrior must return with his shield or on it is worthily copied here, for the Gaul thought anything preferable to captivity and its attendant misery.

On account of the encouragement which Attalus gave to learning, he was received and welcomed at Athens, and here, as well as at Pergamus, had this victory commemorated by these same groups. As the groups represent two different moments in the man's life, it takes two different figures to portray them. To avoid parallelism I have thought it best to have the recumbent figures in opposition. The position of the woman is not hard to assume if the left knee of the standing figure is bent, giving a support for the torso and arm. The arms must be grasped tightly enough to suggest the terrible mental and physical struggle through which the man is passing. In the second pose, the expression of horror gives way to a gaze of fixed determination, as he raises his head to make ready for the final blow.

passive statues are very alike in energy and even position. The performer wore the same gown for the whole series of poses. Did the interest and variety come mainly from the moving transitions and perhaps a suspended quality of the poses – rather than from any inherent interest in the poses themselves? Were the poses a rationale for quasi-dance performance, justified because of its lofty association with classical art?

EXCURSION III:
A VISIT TO ANOTHER VERSION OF THE ANTIQUE

In contrast to statue posing as a solo art, which Stebbins featured in her own performance, she and other Delsarteans presented students in group poses or *tableaux*. One of the most prominent proponents of this form was Clara Power Edgerly (1864–97),[22] who claimed that it was she who had introduced the innovation of movement transitions between poses and that she had been presenting her students in such *tableaux mouvants* since 1886. She writes that she drew on historical and mythological scenes for subject matter as well as on "well-known statues."[23]

In contrast to the lack of narrative in most of Stebbins's subjects – and their timeless quality – Edgerly's poses represent moments in particular stories. And along with other Delsarteans, she did not avoid themes that included male characters. Her performers were, of course, all women, and they, like Stebbins, wore the same general type of Greekish feminine gown whether representing females or males. The only special direction for a male role was that the girl should be tall. No apparent attempt was made to represent a male persona and the male character was typically shown in a quiet and passive rather than aggressive or active mode (for example, Paris mourning with Helen or Bacchus being crowned by Bacchantes). In one notable exception, however, Edgerly created a pose with four female students that simultaneously showed two stages of a violent scene. In "The Gaul's Last Straits" (depicting a hero faced with enemy capture and enslavement), one scene represents the Gaul in anguish knifing his wife to death, while the other depicts him in transcendence (confident that his killing is noble) holding the dead wife and now knifing himself (Figure 4.3). The violence of the subject was rare; the romanticized tragedy was not.[24]

EXCURSION IV:
A TOUR OF STEBBINS'S DRILLS

In the 1890s Stebbins developed a number of drills on various themes for educational purposes and for performance by herself and her students. Four of these were published in 1894 as an appendix to her *Society Gymnastics*. These and others appeared in *The Genevieve Stebbins System of Physical Training.*[25] Most of the drills are described for one person, but she cautions

◐ Fig 4.3 "The Gauls' Last Straits" by Clara Power Edgerly in "Statue Posing," *Werner's Magazine* 16/12 (December 1894): 401.

that it "would be a dangerous experiment for the average individual without study" to perform the drills in public – that "they require a well-developed physique, natural grace, and perfect aesthetic training to reveal that beauty of motion which has given them public favor." She adds, however, that group performance of the drills in strict unison hides individual flaws and is particularly effective for performance at commencement exercises.[26]

Of Stebbins's nine published drills, four consist of poses with transitions between; four feature decorative, expressive or abstract movement; and one is a dance. Two of those that emphasize posing are based on classical statues and depict battleground scenes. "The Roman Drill – The Amazon" is a series of athletic and dramatic poses copied from Amazon statues in the Vatican.[27] These include holding a spear, running, drawing a bow, heaving a rock, suffering a wound, charging, retreating, dealing with a broken bow and making a vow. The theme of "The Athenian Drill – The Victory" is "domination and power,"[28] which is realized through poses of an Amazon holding a spear, Diana drawing a bow, a fighting gladiator, a quoit player, a dying warrior in attack, and a warrior in defense. The image of the Winged Victory is either used as a refrain after each of the other poses "if needed to finish the musical phrase" or as the climactic final pose. The drill begins with marching onto the performing area and ends with marching off. Stebbins specifies Greek costume, but with no indication of gender or style; it may be assumed that these drills were performed in the typical feminine gown. Stebbins suggests a slow march for the music and indicates a counting structure without explaining it.

Another of Stebbins's drills based on posing is her "Energizing Dramatic Drill," a series of Delsartean attitudes alternating with movement transitions.[29] While the title is non-commital, the poses feature clenched fists and battle scenes with expressions of fright and flight, anger and attack, repulsion and horror, retreat and despair.

"Eastern Temple Drill" has a completely different quality.[30] Its theme is religious aspiration and it incorporates movements and symbols Stebbins associated with "the ceremonials found variously among the Mohammedans, the Druses, the Marabouts and the Dervishes." The poses include the "prayer form" (palms together with fingers pointing upward), the "Flame Attitude" (erect body with hands in prayer-form above head), the "cross form" (the body erect with arms stretched to the side), and the "Prostrate Attitude" (cross form with one leg behind and torso and head leaning back). In her introduction to this drill, Stebbins stresses its spiritual values; at its end, on a practical note, its exercise value "for the development of chest, back, etc."

In addition to the Roman and Athenian drills, Stebbins includes a third based on classical imagery, "The Greek Drill – The Nymphs,"[31] but while deriving from sculptural source material, this drill is unusual in privileging movement over posing. Stebbins characterizes the drill as "a study of the beautiful motion often carved to represent the various actions and sportive grace of those ideal creations of Greek fancy, supposed to people wood, water, air, and fire." The composition incorporates hip, torso, and body swaying; arm lifts and circles; a swimming motion; changes of weight; pivoting; body bends; arm and body spirals; and kneeling.

EXCURSION V:
A VERBAL TASTING OF GENEVIEVE STEBBINS'S PERFORMANCE

From 1939, Ruth St Denis's memory of 1892:

> *The curtain rose on a dark greenish background ... and there stood an exquisite woman in a costume made of soft ivory-white material that fell in gracious lines to her feet, her figure beautifully proportioned, her blonde head proud and shapely. The strong light pouring upon her made her gleam like a pearl against the dark setting.*
>
> *She moved in a series of plastiques which were based upon her understanding of the laws of motion discovered by Delsarte. Her poses were derived from Greek statuary and encompassed everything from the tragedy of Niobe to the joyousness of Terpsichore. Later she did a dance called the* Dance of Day. *At the opening of the scene, she was lying on the floor asleep, and then, awakened by the morning sun, she rose with a lovely childlike movement to her knees and bathed herself in its rays. A light rhythmic step signified the morning and the noontide; and then began the slower movements of the afternoon, presently mingled with sadness as the late rays brought her slowly to her knees and again into her reclining posture of sleep.[32]*

From 1893, reports of reviewers: In Genevieve Stebbins's statue posing,

> *[t]here is no spasmodic transformation of the body ... [the poses] flow gracefully onward from the simple to the complex. They are a natural evolution of beauty produced by the changing curve of the spiral line from head to toe, commencing with a simple attitude, and continuing with a slow, rhythmic motion of every portion of the body, until it stands before you as the most perfect representation of art.[33]*

For her series of twelve poses from classical statues, Stebbins

> *walked serenely in from a side entrance clad from throat to toe in a white Greek robe; her arms were bare and there were no signs of white powder or other makeup. She stood in front of the stage, and while the piano was played by somebody out of sight slowly assumed the form of Venus Genitrix. A moment later she swayed gently about and became the Satyr playing the Lute. The lovely audience applauded rapturously, whereat Mrs. Stebbins undulated gracefully into the statue of Melpomene.[34]*

> *To illustrate the "history of dramatic expression," Stebbins gave first the pose and movements of the Egyptian priestesses who swung the censers slowly and rhythmically in their temple worship. She then gave the Greek idea of dancing and artistic management of the body derived from [illustrations on Greek friezes, pottery and statues]. Her Greek dance was enchanting almost to voluptuousness. Then followed the sprightly Spanish and gypsy dances of a later day in which there was as much movement of the arms and body as*

of the lower limbs. Mrs. Stebbins closed . . . with the stately bows and slow paces of the minuet.[35]

Such testimonies tell us that Genevieve Stebbins was beautiful, moved gracefully and skillfully, and even possessed some measure of range in movement vocabulary and dynamic flow. How much more we should like to know!

MUSINGS

Feminist theater historian Tracy C. Davis has noted that on the professional stage, "representations of sexuality and gender are and have been male constructions (representations *of*, but not *by*, women)."[36] In contrast, on the American Delsartean stage, Genevieve Stebbins and other American women were deciding the thematic material, characters, and narratives that they depicted as well as the style of presentation — and they were presenting this material for overwhelmingly female audiences. They were constructing their own identities in the Delsartean performance context, but how did these identities relate to gender and sexuality? And what was their connection to everyday life, relationships with family members, roles in society, political, and religious beliefs?

From writings, photographs, and performance descriptions one can outline the general (as opposed to stage) image presented to the world by American Delsarteans — it did not differ from that of other female elocutionists. It was an image — and reality — of middle-class women, well-educated and well-read, socially correct, fashionable and with artistic sensibility, cultural refinement, moral fiber, spiritual depth — and independent capabilities in the public arena. These women were professionals carrying forward their careers. Whatever personal lives they had were kept private and little mention is ever made of husbands, parents, or children, except in the few cases that a family member was a professional colleague, or in occasional news items of joint travel, a marriage, or someone's illness or death. There is also never a hint of any kind of financial difficulty among elocutionists in general and Delsarteans in particular.

As a major aspect of their identity, American Delsartean practitioners presented themselves as fervent strivers for cultural/mystical transcendence — and they, as others in their class, idealized ancient Greek civilization as the perfect cultural model. The idolization of that "golden age" was an identifying marker of one committed to "the Beautiful and the True," "nobility of spirit," and "high art." Other distant cultures also attracted them — such as the ancient Middle East. In their portrayal of figures from the Old Testament and Egyptian mythology the Delsarteans again identified themselves and their art with heroic and sublime images. Their focus on such religious and mythic figures from a romanticized past brings to mind Neil Harris's analysis of what it took to legitimize the American plastic arts in the nineteenth century — a sense of religious mission, a striving towards purity and high spiritual values. The American Delsarteans seemed to employ similar strategies to justify their bodily expressions.

What prompted Stebbins and other Delsarteans to depict the images of male as well as female deities and historical figures — especially when there seemed to be no attempt at all to portray realistically the male gender through choice of costume or distinct physical qualities? Did the antiquity of the statues and characters render them gender-neutral and sexless to these women? Or, no matter how superficially, was it somehow exciting and empowering to depict male characters? Was it perhaps a harmless and tame way of trying on the persona of the powerful male without rocking the social boat? Was there any awareness or concern that the bodily presence in these statues was seemingly lost as they were translated into "living pictures" by girls in long gowns? Did the performers and viewers find nothing incongruous in this? In the antique cultures that so attracted these nineteenth-century "high-brows," women were not the only and certainly not the most powerful players. If the Delsarteans wished to play with the image of power, they needed to draw on the male images and those of the warrior women – the Amazons. And male or female warriors seemed to be a favorite subject – but portrayed in feminine gowns.

In contrast to the varying states of undress displayed by the statues, Stebbins and other Delsartean performers were chastely covered from shoulder to ankle in voluminous drapes that obscured the body. Only the arms were bare. So while portraying images, many of which revealed the body in a sensuous way, the Delsarteans maintained in their costumes the propriety expected of their class. Or did they? Was it daring for a lady to appear in a Greek gown with an uncorseted or lightly corseted body and bare arms? How did that costume make her feel? What did she experience when gazing at the image of a nude or partially nude female – or a nude male? Was it totally divorced from sexual desire in her consciousness? Was the statues' physicality totally beyond the pale of her own physicality and bodily awareness? Or was the contemplation of antique art an outlet for curiosity and fantasized desire? Did she relate the nude bodies of the statues in any way to the clothed bodies of herself, her female friends, and the men in their lives?

There are numerous photographs illustrating posings, drills, and pantomimes, often accompanied by scenarios or texts, and detailed directions on how to stage the pieces (such materials were published by Werner). Unfortunately, the photos give us very little idea of the physical tone of the performers or the movement quality of the pieces. What can be seen, besides the shapeless mass of the gown, is only the arms, the head and the neck. How ironic! The ladies are promoting bodily expression, but their bodies seem to be denied existence. The heavy and lifeless look of these illustrations may be somewhat due, however, to contemporary camera technology that required the performers to be crowded into a small space and to hold the pose for several minutes (Figure 4.4). But these images raise questions about the nature of the training itself. What, if any, conditioning exercises were included? There are exercises for flexibility and modest strength building in Stebbins's and others' Delsartean texts, but no hint as to the format of a lesson, how often the students trained or practiced, or the practical process or the training over time. How did the Delsarteans achieve the "well-developed physique," "natural grace," and "beauty of motion" that Stebbins advocated for effective movement expression?

If one could conduct an ethnographic study of the Delsartean phenomenon – enter that world as a participant–observer – it would be possible to determine more about its nature, what the activities felt like, how they were done and the social ambience. What intrigues me the most about the Delsarteans is that which is most illusive – the nature of their bodies and their bodily

Fig 4.4 "Amazon Drill" by Mrs Jamie Thompson Laird in *Werner's Magazine* 22/5 (January 1899): facing 307.

consciousness. To what extent did they achieve a depth of physicality, an integration of mind, body, emotions? With all their attention to the body, to physical culture, to physical expression, how rooted in the physical were they? How fully did they sense their own bodies? How effectively did they speak to their viewers with their bodies? Was there a sensual or sexual component in their body awareness? Did they feel flow and extension? Were they aware of manipulating time, space, energy? And did that give them pleasure? Did they feel integrated in their movement? Did their moving and posing elicit emotional states, exhilaration, any kind of "high?"

What were these Delsarteans up to anyway? Anything we can relate to the body as we know it today?

To be continued . . .

NOTES

1   *I am grateful to the members of the Choreographing History research group for jostling and expanding my mind into new directions. My musings in this prologue (as well as my "Musings" at the end) are somewhat due to that trauma.*

2   *Up to July 1994, I know of only two attempts at reconstructing Delsartean performance forms. Judy Blum reconstructed a drill of 1902 for twelve "young ladies" and has described that experience in "Reconstructions,"* Women and Performance *5/2, 1992. At the 1994 annual conference of the Society of Dance History Scholars in Provo, Utah, I gave a workshop in Stebbins statue-posing. After working on the principles of harmonic poise, sequence, and opposition, the participants posed in imitation of four contrasting statues and individually developed transitions between them. The result was quite interesting – even beautiful.*

3   *François Delsarte (1811–71) developed his aesthetic principles specifically in relation to the training of singers and actors, but saw them (and promoted them) as applicable to the plastic arts as well.*

4   *Delsarte's theory and practice were brought to the United States in 1871 by his only known American student, the all-round theater practitioner, Steele Mackaye (1842–94). Mackaye introduced a combination of his own and Delsarte's work to theater and oratorical training in the United States. From there it spread into the burgeoning physical culture movement that was particularly geared for women and children and into the amateur performance practices that are the subject of this study. By the late 1880s and through the 1890s American Delsartism was a fashion that had spread throughout the nation. For a survey of American Delsartism, see Ruyter (1979, chapter 2).*

5   *Data on American Delsartism and its practitioners has been gleaned primarily from news items, advertisements, and articles in a magazine published by Edgar S. Werner under three titles:* The Voice *(1879–88),* Werner's Voice Magazine *(1889–94), and* Werner's Magazine *(1895–1902).*

6   *See, for example, Stebbins,* Delsarte System of Expression.

7   *McCullough (1981), especially pp. 1, 6; Holmström (1967).*

8   *There are many prescriptions for staging poses, attitudes and tableaux. Typical are: Margaret Virginia Jenkins, "A Study in Attitude,"* Werner's Voice Magazine *12 (December 1890), 297–300; and Clara Tileston Power Edgerly, "Tableaux Mouvants and Poses Plastiques as Arranged and Presented at the Boston School of Oratory,"* Werner's Voice Magazine *13 (December 1891), 315–18. In addition to publishing them in his magazine, Edgar S. Werner also marketed such material in separate booklets.*

9   *For example, "Parasol Drill," "International Flag Drill," "Cymbal Drill," "Japanese Fantastics," "Nursery Rhymes Drill" and the like, published and sold throughout the 1890s. Descriptions may be found in* Werner's Voice Magazine.

10 *Biographical information on Stebbins has been gleaned from* Werner's Directory *(1887, 289); Greenlee and Greenlee (1904, 1099–100); Shelton (1978, 35); and articles in Werner's magazine and other publications.*

11   *Stebbins*, Delsarte System of Expression, *419.*

12   *Ibid., 370–1.*

13   *Ibid., 444.*

14   *Ibid., 453, 456.*

15   *Ibid., 457.*

16   *Ibid., 92–4.*

17   *Shawn (1974, 33–4).*

18   *Stebbins*, Delsarte System of Expression, *458.*

19   *Ibid., 260, 457–9.*

20   *Ibid., 459–60.*

21   *I am grateful to Professor Margaret Miles of the University of California, Irvine, Art History Department for informing me about the musicians' costume.*

22   *Edgerly (née Clara Tileston Powers) graduated from the Boston School of Oratory and then taught Delsarte there from 1885–92. In 1892, she and her husband, Julian C. Edgerly opened the Boston College of Oratory, a Delsartean training school, where she served as principal and as teacher until 1895. Biographical information from "Mrs. Clara Power Edgerly,"* Werner's Magazine *19/1 (1897), 80; and from news items in Werner's magazines.*

23   *Clara Tileston Power Edgerly, "Tableaux Mouvants and Poses Plastiques,"* Werner's Voice Magazine *13 (December 1891), 315.*

24   *Several of Edgerly's descriptions of statue-poses can be found in* Werner's Voice Magazine; *some examples: "Statue Posing: The Sacrifice of Iphigenia," 14 (October 1892), 297; "Statue-Posing: Bacchus and the Bacchantes," 14 (December 1892), 366–7; "Statue-Posing: The Gaul's Last Straits," 16 (December 1894), 401.*

25   *Stebbins*, Society Gymnastics and Voice Culture; The Genevieve Stebbins System of Physical Training.

26   *Stebbins*, Genevieve Stebbins System, *82.*

27   *Ibid., 110–14.*

28   *Ibid., 119–23.*

29   *Ibid., 97–102.*

30   *Ibid., 84–90.*

31   *Ibid., 124–9.*

32   *St. Denis (1939, 16–17).*

33   *N. A. "Genevieve Stebbins,"* Werner's Magazine 15 *(December 1893), 444.*

34   *Ibid., 445 (quoting from a New York* Sun *review).*

35   *Ibid., 445.*

36   *Davis (1989, 60).*

Dance and the history of hysteria

PEGGY PHELAN

In the inaugural text of classical psychoanalysis, Josef Breuer's and Sigmund Freud's 1895 *Studies on Hysteria*, a remarkable amount of attention is given to bodies, and to body parts, that will not or cannot move. The first of the five case histories collected in *Studies*, Breuer's account of his treatment of Anna O., and the last, Freud's account of his treatment of Elisabeth von R., contain especially fascinating and often overlooked notions of the relationship between the body and truth, the body and time, and the body and language. Here, I would like to recast the usual critical approach to *Studies on Hysteria* that accents the invention of the *talking* cure, and review another hope for a physical cure that these early case histories also express. This cure had as its foundation a deep faith in the "truth" of bodily performances.

The psychoanalytic session, at least as it was conceived in these early case histories, involved the acting out, the performative elaboration, of the symptom. While the case histories chart several different notions of performance – ventriloquism, imitation, "possession" – I will concentrate here on the ideas of dance and movement that inform *Studies*. Following the lead of Freud and Breuer, I will be concerned with paralytic feet and eloquent thighs, and with the transfers enacted in psychic and physical movements and "obstructions."

Dragging feet, feet with sharp cramps, feet that swell and limp, feet that are suddenly too heavy to move, feet that support legs frozen in contractions, give *Studies on Hysteria* a strange rhythm and rocky gait. It is upon these aching feet that psychoanalysis proposes a new reproductive system for the female body (all five of the case histories are of women). In Breuer's analysis of Anna O., "when the first of her chronic symptoms disappeared," the contracture of her right leg, the psychoanalytic method was born: "These findings – that in the case of this patient the hysterical phenomena disappeared as soon as the event which had given rise to them was reproduced in her hypnosis – made it possible to arrive at a therapeutic technical procedure which left nothing to be desired in its logical consistency and systematic application."[1] Returning suppleness and motion to Anna O.'s right leg enables both Anna and psychoanalysis itself to "take a great step forward" (*Studies*, 35). In the disappearance of the contraction in the right leg, the technique "which left nothing to be desired" was born.[2]

The birth of psychoanalysis requires the re-enactment of the event that triggered the contraction of her right leg; in that re-enactment psychic and physical movement are restored. The psychoanalytic reproduction of the symptomatic body requires two people. In these early histories, the patient and the doctor connect both physically and psychically. Freud eventually theorized the psychical contact in the transference and counter-transference. In *Studies*, however, the physical contact between the doctor and the patient is seen as a fundamental part of the cure. As Breuer observes about Anna O., "But she would never begin to talk until she had satisfied herself of my identity by carefully feeling my hands" (*Studies*, 30). Classical psychoanalysis abandoned the physical cure in favor of the clinical technique of the talking cure. A technique that depended too heavily upon touch was a huge risk for an epistemological revolution whose visionary leader was determined to be, above all, scientific. *Studies*, almost unwittingly, realizes two different approaches to the cure – and the psychoanalytic movement followed the one that left the body untouched.

Like blind men first learning Braille, the fingers of Freud and Breuer press and prod the somatic signs displayed on the hysterical bodies of the patients before them.[3] The doctors apply mental and/or physical pressure to the indecipherable bodily signifier, the symptom, until it "joins in the conversation." Different body parts of the patient join in an ongoing conversation whose subject is no longer strictly speaking "her" body but is rather "their body," the body being made and manipulated in their discursive and physical interaction. In his history of Elisabeth von R., Freud describes this technique which "left nothing to be desired":

> [H]er painful legs[4] began to "join in the conversation" during our analyses. . . . If . . . by a question or by pressure upon her head I called up a memory, a sensation of pain would make its first appearance, and this was usually so sharp that the patient would give a start and put her hand to the spot. The pain that was thus aroused would persist so long as she was under the influence of the memory; it would reach its climax when she was in the act of telling me the essential and decisive part of what she had to communicate, and with the last word it would disappear. I came in time to use such pains as a compass to guide me; if she stopped talking but admitted that she still had a pain, I knew she had not told me everything, and insisted on her continuing her story till the pain had been talked away. Not until then did I arouse a fresh memory.[5]
>
> (Studies, 148)

The "arousal" of a fresh memory reproduces a fresh body, one newly made in the somatic and verbal performance they enact. Putting his hand on her head causes pressure to build; her hand flies to a different body part which is then verbally massaged under the sign of the symptom. Elisabeth's leg's contribution to the conversation is transformed by Freud into a truth-meter, a somatic lie-detector.[6] Freud doubts Elisabeth von R.'s verbal starts and stops, her verbal narrative's beginnings and endings, but for him her thigh does not lie.[7]

In *Studies*, Freud and Breuer want to find the history of the symptom. Their search for history has led many scholars to use a kind of shorthand in thinking of the relation between history and hysteria: hysteria has been described as a disease which is the consequence of a jumbled narrative, an incoherent autobiography, a failure of historical accounts.[8] But it would be more accurate to say that hysteria represents the first disease in which psychoanalysis imagines a history of the symptom and where the patient discovers that her body's history must be spoken. The imposition of narrative order, an imposition re-performed and rehearsed in the doctor's composition of the account, provides psychic order for the body.[9] What is profoundly startling to realize, however, is that the body does not contain such an order independent of its imposition. Psychoanalysis suggests that the body's "truth" does not organize itself narratively or chronologically. The body does not experience the world the same way consciousness does: the gap between these two ways of "processing" experiences punctuates the formation of the unconscious. The function of the analysis then is to repair this join, to find a way to suture the body into time's order. The equally logical task of suturing consciousness into bodily "truth" remains outside the official domains of mainstream science and thrives in new-age philosophy and alternative medicine.

It is in this theory of the body's time that dance and psychoanalysis meet. If the body is not, *a priori*, in time, then dance can be said to be the elaboration of possible temporalities for the body that are interpreted in movement; and psychoanalysis can be said to be the elaboration of possible narrative interpretations of the body's symptom. Dance frames the body performing movement in time and space. While it is true that bodies usually manage to move in time and space, dancing *consciously* performs the body's discovery of its temporal and spatial dimensions.

Psychoanalysis is the performance in which the doctor and the patient create an interpretation of a symptom that gives the body temporal coherence. But just as the proliferation of dance styles across history and across cultures implicitly suggests the enormous range of temporal possibilities within movement performances, so too do the interpretative possibilities one confronts and rebuffs in relation to one's own body suggest the force of the desire to compose an order on the body. (It also demonstrates the role of historical, political, and cultural "fashion" involved in psychoanalytic symptoms – from hysteria as the symptom of choice at the turn of the century, to depression as the symptom of choice today – and their cures – from psychoanalysis to Prozac.) Part of the burden of establishing temporal order for the body, for both dancing and psychoanalysis, often falls to narrative. In many traditions and diverse cultures, dance takes narrative forms. For one of the things that narrative generates is temporal order. But even without narrative, dance organizes its movement across a temporal schema. And in this sense, dance, like psychoanalysis, helps join the body to time.

The first somatic symptoms Anna O. and Elisabeth von R. develop are sympathetic reproductions of their fathers' pain. These symptoms are the result of a kind of still kinesthetic empathy: each woman becomes partially paralyzed. The somatic symptoms are motivated by the daughters' desire to show love for their fathers by lending them their own bodies. If they can transfer the pain in their fathers' bodies into their own, they believe they can help their fathers live. When the somatic symptom (paralysis) fails to keep the father alive, new more dangerous hysterical symptoms emerge.

Anna O.'s paralysis is a mimetic response to her father's stillness. As he lies in bed struggling to breathe and as she anticipates his final loss of breath in the stillness of death, she herself becomes spectacularly still.[10] The paralysis is an attempt to sacrifice the movement of her own youthful, active body in order to provide the encroaching stillness another body on which to alight. If the stage is large enough, perhaps, the stillness will not have to cover the father's body so completely he will collapse, expire.

Anna O.'s cough, her breath's stutter step, begins the night she hears the dance music playing. "She began coughing for the first time when once, as she was sitting at her father's bedside, she heard the sound of dance music coming from a neighboring house, felt a sudden wish to be there, and was overcome with self-reproaches. Thereafter, throughout the whole length of her illness she reacted to any markedly rhythmical music with a *tussis nervosa* [nervous cough]" (*Studies*, 40). She hears the music playing while she sits near her father's bed. He is dying. She is watching. She is watching and not dying. Outside the dance music is playing. Her foot starts tapping involuntarily. She stills it. *Sharp intake of breath, a slight, hastily silenced cough. All she wants to do, all she wants to do, is dance. The rhythm of the music is infecting her body. Her blood picks up a little speed; she's remembering the two-step. And her romance with her father is that she cannot live without him. She is his. His girl. The apple of his eye. She is her father's daughter. She is going to nurse him back to life. She will tell him nursery rhymes, fairy tales. ("He joked with her in English, Na, how are you, Miss Bertha?"[11] Na, how are you, Papa? Papa don't die. Papa Pappenheim. . . .) The music playing inside and outside her body. In the still of the night. . . . Time is the bed and Then and Now are breathing in and out and you are one of the ones there waking, waking with a stretch joining Then and Now. Mourning the loss of him and of her body's dance. . . . Laid out there, stiff in the sheet of time, he sleeps. And she stifles her cough. Finding her mourning breath.*

In concluding his analysis, Breuer returns to Anna O.'s desire to dance and notes, "The patient could not understand how it was that dance music made her cough; such a construction is too meaningless to have been deliberate. (It seemed very likely to me, incidentally, that each of her twinges of conscience brought on one of her regular spasms of the glottis and that the motor impulses which she felt – for she was very fond of dancing – transformed the spasm into a *tussis nervosa*)" (*Studies*, 43–4).[12] By coughing instead of dancing, Anna O. changes the music's beat within her body. Her timing, one could say, is off.

But more to the point perhaps is Breuer's respect for the "meaningless" connection between dance music and coughing. It is the very triviality of dance music that produces both the desire to dance (to escape the serious meanings of her father's illness) and its denial (dancing cannot be justified because of the heaviness of his illness). Her body registers the denial of her desire by the dis-ease signaled by the cough. In the face of her father's impending death, marked by his audible struggle to breathe (he suffered from a sub-pleural abscess), a daughter with a conscience trained to "twinge" cannot permit herself to dance *and also cannot stop her desire to dance*. Her cough signals her body's renouncing of her conscious renunciation of dancing; this renunciation of renunciation is the conflict that gives life to the symptom. "Overcome with self-reproaches," her body is caught, lost in the space between sitting and dancing, between moving and watching, between exhaling and inhaling, between living and dying; gulping air in and pushing it out at the same time, she coughs, again and again.

The cough registers her somatic and temporal unmooring. It stands in for a larger uncertainty about how to move after (the law of) the father has fallen. Her psyche is "stuck in time" and to get her moving, Breuer and Anna return to the events of the past:

> *A year had now passed since she had been separated from her father and had taken to her bed, and from this time on her condition became clearer and was systematized in a very peculiar manner. . . . [N]ow she lived like the rest of us, in the winter of 1881–2, whereas [under daily hypnosis . . .] she lived in the winter of 1880–1. . . . She was carried back to the previous year with such intensity that in the new house she hallucinated her old room, so when she wanted to go to the door she knocked up against the stove which stood in the same relation to the window as did the door in the old room. . . . But this transfer into the past did not take place in a general or indefinite manner; she lived through the previous winter day by day. I should have only been able to suspect that this was happening, had it not been that every evening during the hypnosis she talked through whatever it was that*

had excited her on the same day in 1881, and had it not been that a private diary kept by her mother in 1881 confirmed beyond a doubt the occurrence of the underlying events.[13] *This re-living of the past year continued till the illness came to its final close in June, 1882.*

(Studies, *33*, Breuer's emphasis)

By reliving the previous year in such excruciating detail Anna O. makes plain that we refuse such repetition as a way of securing "psychic health." This is a psychic adaptation – there is nothing endemic to time itself that makes it impossible for the body to relive it.[14] And there is nothing in the body itself that makes such reliving impossible. The body, in short, does not share consciousness's faith in narrative order. The uneven join between the body and consciousness is packed with the expansive ooze of the unconscious.

This psychic adaptation to the convention of linear, progressive time is one of the founding principles of the social contract, a contract that in turn establishes the classificatory system by which doctors adjudicate mental health. The body is always a disciplined entity; one part of its disciplinary training is temporal–linguistic; another part is temporal–physical. Psychoanalysis pursued developing the temporal–linguistic route to the cure in part by attempting to create the talking cure as a performative speech act whose utterances transformed the body. (Just as the linguistic performative joins the statement to the action, "I promise," the talking cure sought to join the body itself to historical order.) From a system of disarticulated limbs, contractures, and paresthetic seizures, psychoanalysis sought to reproduce a free-moving, coherent, vital body.

The psychic stage on which Anna O. and Breuer danced was a stage attended by other corpses. Breaking open her "private theater" for Breuer required opening other tombs. Six years before she was born, Anna O.'s older sister, Flora, had died. When she was eight, her sister Henriette died. Thus Anna O. was literally her father's "one and only" surviving daughter; she inhabited a private theater in part because her sisters had left it. Anna O.'s real name, Bertha, was the name of Breuer's mother and of his eldest daughter. (The name of her father was Seigmund!) Breuer's mother had died when he was three; at the time of her death she was about the same age as Anna O. when they began their conversations.[15] These deaths are the historical frames through which the death of her father is experienced, interpreted, and transcribed.

In their somatic and verbal conversations, Breuer and Anna O. learn something about the relationship between language and the body. Anna O.'s conversations with Breuer are not so much a performance in which her body finds words, but rather they are performances in which her body finds time, and more particularly, finds its past. Passing into language, the somatic symptom passes into the past. To put it in a slightly different key: if we think of psychoanalysis as a mode of psychic choreography, we can see the symptom as the body's psychic movement. Psychoanalysis and choreography are two different modes of performing the body's movement. Each seeks to give the body a system of time.

The reproduction and realignment of the symptom suggest a different way to map the body's relation to time and to death. Her father's death terrifies Anna O. because she is at once remembering it and anticipating it. Her eye symptoms – periodic blindness and what she calls "clouds" – like the renunciation of her conscious renunciation to dance signaled by the cough, both confirm and disavow her image of death. Taking care of her father is traumatic for Anna O. in part because it reminds her that she has *already survived death*. This is the radical genius of her symptom. What the analysis with Breuer allows her to do is to transfer her image of death within a narrative structure that assigns images to referents, people to places, events to time.

Trauma is not an event that must be relived or re-enacted in order to be "surmounted." Rather, trauma is an event of unliving. The unlived event becomes traumatic precisely because it is empty; the trauma reveals an absence, the intangible center of breath itself. As an event of unliving, the trauma is a performance in and above the real:

> *On one occasion our whole progress was obstructed for some time because a recollection refused to emerge. It was a question of a particularly terrifying hallucination. While she was nursing her father she had seen him with a death's head. She and the people with her remembered that once, while she still appeared to be in good health, she had paid a visit to one of her relatives. She had opened the door and all at once fallen down unconscious. In order to get over the obstruction to our progress she visited the same place again and, on entering the room, again fell to the ground unconscious. During her subsequent evening hypnosis the obstacle was surmounted. As she came into the room, she had seen her pale face reflected in a mirror hanging opposite the door; but it was not herself she saw but her father with a death's head.*

> (Studies, 37)

The repetition of the event, the second visit to the relatives, reproduces the symptom: she again sees the face, and like Saul upon seeing the face of God, falls.[16] (And Breuer remarks the symptom's reproduction by repeating "again" on each side of the movement phrase: "again and, on entering the room, again.") When she falls she stops moving physically and her psychic progress becomes "obstructed." When she re-enacts the scene and again loses consciousness, she falls into her body. She *is* the body who falls. To re-join the body to consciousness nothing less than the image of death must be *re-moved*. This is the transfer that the analysis enacts.

Transfer. Transit. Transference. At the heart of psychoanalysis is an ideology of movement, of the curative potential of moving. Joining the psychic with the physical and the physical with the psychic is the task of analysis. The body's movements are the roaming rooms in which psychic "truths" are lodged. Anna O. is able to "surmount" the psychic stall that had made it impossible for her to move forward. The trauma that stops her body's movement also "obstructs" her psychic progress. While narrating her experience for Breuer, a *transfer/ence* takes place. ("But this transfer into the past did not take place in a general or indefinite manner . . ." *Studies*, 33.) The act of narrating allows her to interpret the trauma for the first time – and the interpretation itself signals the cure.

Skulls are generic: they do not usually come with a name attached. "[S]he had seen her face reflected in a mirror opposite the door; but it was not herself that she saw but her father with a death's head." The analytic cure enacts the transfer, the psychic movement necessary for the integration of the image of death as part of her history. She assigns the image of death to the other and in so doing escapes the memory of her own. The cure occurs in this moment of transference: in ascribing the image of death to her father, she also positions herself as the survivor, as the one who, despite falling faint, will again move, again live. From a killing glance in the mirror that makes her fall to the floor, to the safe rehearsal of the hallucination with Breuer, she is able to make her death history, by giving it to her father who is already "safely" dead. The phrase "but it was not herself she saw" is the interpretation of the trauma; the analysis generates the curative interpretation.

It is important to notice that the interpretation also betrays another level of the unconscious relations among Anna O.'s symptoms. The interpretation suggests that the image of her father's skull is superimposed on her image of her own face. Her body reproduces an image of his (hollow) body that the mirror reflects. Such a substitution might be said to involve a kind of psychic blurring, a confusion, about the boundaries between her body and his. This blurring occurs across verbal languages as well: she translates languages unconsciously and often makes sentences out of several different languages at once. Insofar as language reproduces the body (at least in the talking cure), Anna O.'s case suggests that bleeding between languages might also portend bleeding across bodies. This is an idea to which we will return.[17]

Anna O.'s hallucination of the death's head stands behind the second, remarkably similar, hallucination that Breuer believes is the "root of her illness." This second hallucination is re-enacted on the last day of Anna O.'s analysis. While nursing her father, "[s]he fell into a waking dream and saw a black snake coming towards the sick man. . . . She tried to keep the snake off, but it was as though she was paralyzed. Her right arm, over the back of the chair, had gone to sleep and had become anaesthetic and paretic; and when she looked at it the fingers turned into little snakes with death's heads (the nails)" (*Studies*, 38). Having already experienced the image of the death head in the mirror, Anna O. may well have believed that the image was *in* her body, oozing out of her eyes and her fingernails. She was determined not to let the death's heads alight on his body. Just as she registers her denial of her desire to dance by coughing, so too does she deny the memory of death by becoming symptomatically blind and paralyzed. The re-enactment of the trauma in the analysis allows her to let the image of death escape her body. "[B]ut it was not herself that she saw but her father with a death's head." One can see her reproduction of the traumatic image of the death's head as the beginning of its reversal which would figure her recovery as a re-birth.

In re-enacting the traumatic event, she transforms her private theater into a social space, and creates it as a space for an other, for Breuer. The final hallucination which is itself a repetition of the previous one is also re-enacted and, as in Aristotelian poetics, catharsis is achieved. "On the last day – by the help of re-arranging the room so as to resemble her father's sickroom – she reproduced the terrifying hallucination which constituted *the root of her illness*" (*Studies*, 40, my emphasis). This transference signals the passage in which the memory of death becomes a memory of *his* death: this time, the death's heads are located at the edge of her body, on her fingernails. Taking Breuer's hands into her own, "But she would never begin to talk until she had satisfied herself of my identity by carefully feeling my hands" (*Studies*, 30), she transfers her image of death to him. Together, they conclude that it is her father's death, rather than her own, that she has seen. Faced with the choice of attributing the skull to her own body or to his, she chooses his. In this sense, his death is almost reassuring. For it is the certainty of his death that gives her the psychic freedom to return to the trauma of the death's heads oozing out of her body. "The one thing that nevertheless seemed to remain conscious most of the time was *the fact that her father died.*" (*Studies,* 33) The firm fact of his death allows her to put her symptom in the past and her own body is liberated from the psychic death spaces to which she had assigned it during her "absences." Traversing her private theater is actually a movement, a passage, a physical and psychic *transference* from her body to his. In this sense the "feminine" symptom, the open question of her trauma, is resolved (in part) by masculinizing it.

No longer her secret repressed vision, Anna O. dissolves the danger of the trauma as she gives the image of death away. Nothing happens and this inaction liberates her. No one is slain by her vision of death. This nothingness covers the hole in the vision of the death's head; once placed in the past her body no longer reproduces the vision and her symptomatic blindness is, in Breuer's phrase, "removed."[18] Finding an event in the past, the death of her father, from which to divide the present from the past, also allows Anna O. to find a map for her body's movement.[19] Surmounting her fainting fall, she takes "a great step forward;" the contracture in her right leg disappears and she moves again, psychically, back into 1882, and physically, out of the sickroom (his and hers).

Hysteria, at least in the original and defining case of Anna O., involves the use of the patient's body as a stage for the body of the other. (This is why hysteria has so often been associated with women – and historically with their wombs.) In Anna O.'s case, at the beginning of her entry into hysteria, she attempted to lend her body to her father. But he had somehow already inhabited her; and her introjection (Freud's later term) of him produced two different results.[20] First, it meant she was unable to separate her body far enough from his to lend it to him as he fought death. Thus she may have felt herself to be responsible for his death. Seeing the image of the death's head in the mirror she cannot decide to whom it belongs. In falling faint, abandoning her own consciousness, she falls into her own singular body. (Her father does not faint with her, nor does the skull.) In the moment in which she falls faint, she loses her orientation in time. In transferring the image of the death's head to her father in the analysis, she also accepts that her father is dead and that she is living. (Unable to assign the image to herself or to him, she is unsure of where she is in relation to the fact of his death.)

Insisting that her memories of events of unliving were communicable (across the supple syntax of English, German, French, Italian, and Yiddish) and therefore survivable, Breuer helped Anna O. discover a "fresh" and newly animate body. As this body translated its history into stories for Breuer, Breuer translated their mutually embodied history into stories for Freud.

In such translations, different bodies are reproduced. I shall discuss only one. A crucial aspect of the cure involved the re-enactment of the trauma. The cumulative weight of these performances may have encouraged Anna O. to mark her body itself as reproductive. Her body had been newly made by their well-rehearsed conversations. And it was a profoundly new body, one outside the usual order of human reproduction.

This is the frame through which the tricky matter of Anna O.'s hysterical pregnancy must be seen. In an account full of errors,[21] Jones, whom Jean LaPlanche calls "the historian of Freud's thought,"[22] claims:

It would seem that Breuer had developed what we should nowadays call a strong counter-transference to his interesting patient. At all events he was so engrossed that his wife became bored at listening to no other topic, and before long, jealous. She did not display this openly, but became unhappy and morose. It was long before Breuer, with his thoughts elsewhere, divined the meaning of her state of mind. It provoked a violent reaction in him perhaps compounded of love and guilt, and he decided to bring the treatment to an end. He announced this to Anna O., who was by now much better, and bade her goodbye. But that evening he was fetched back, to find her in a greatly excited state, apparently as ill as ever. The patient . . . was now in the throes of an hysterical childbirth (pseudocyesis) the logical termination of a phantom pregnancy that had been invisibly developing in response to Breuer's ministrations. Though profoundly shocked, he managed to calm her down by hypnotizing her, and then fled the house in a cold sweat. The next day he and his wife left for Venice to spend a second honeymoon, which resulted in the conception of a daughter.[23]

Jones's contention that Breuer broke off the analysis because of his wife's jealousy is not borne out by the published case history, Breuer's notes about the treatment, or the correspondence he maintained with Bertha's mother.[24] Anna O. herself decided the day she would end her analysis (7 June 1882) and had accelerated her "chimney sweeping" in order to complete her cure (*Studies*, 40). Nor is Jones's implicit suggestion that Breuer displaced his "phantom" paternity by "really" impregnating his wife in Venice credible. Mathilde had delivered their youngest daughter, Dora (!) on 11 March 1882, three months before Anna O.'s treatment ended.

Nonetheless the story, however phantasmal, is worth pausing over. There is a certain satisfaction in this resolution of the history, a satisfaction that is hard to ignore. For if the performance of a phantom pregnancy has a certain allure, it comes from the expression of Anna O.'s own agency. Independently of the doctor, she will mark the effect of their collaborative re-enactments by performing her new self as an auto-reproductive body. Moreover, the pregnancy signifies the excess, the supplement that cannot be contained or interpreted by the talking cure, no matter how exhaustive, no matter how loving. This excess is femininity itself – that part of her that remains outside the discursive frame of the always already masculine case history. This excess is the place of the trauma at the heart of Freud's theory of sexual difference. As Freud developed psychoanalysis, he constructed as well a theory of anxiety about sexual difference punctuated by penis envy, the castration complex and so on – a set of psychic responses to the fear of absence. But as Anna O. experienced the analysis, she performed a theory of sexual difference which rendered her body at once reproductive and living, and "non-reproductive" and unliving. In short, her performance of a phantom pregnancy is *both* curative and traumatic.

The somatic reproduction of the trauma of absence is, and can only be, a phantom. (The trauma is traumatic because it unveils the force of the phantom – because it reveals "the nothing that is not there / and the nothing that is."[25]) Anna O.'s reproduction of her father's hollow skull in the analysis is matched by the hollow swelling of her hysterical womb after the analysis. Anna O.'s pregnancy is the reproduction of an event of unliving, a performance in and above the Real.

It is necessary to point out that the entire report of Anna O.'s phantom pregnancy comes from Freud and his historian – and not from Breuer or Anna O.[26] In his own version of *The History of Psychoanalysis*, Freud admits that Breuer "never said this [that Anna had fallen in love with Breuer] to me in so many words, but he told me enough at different times to justify this reconstruction of what happened."[27] Freud, of course, had his own reasons for wanting to believe this happened: it was the most convincing proof of his theory of the "universal nature" of the transference.[28] Since so much of Freud's history has passed for "the truth" of the history of psychoanalysis, and because the story of Anna O.'s pregnancy is continually repeated in the criticism and narrative discourse around this history, and finally because psychoanalysis itself insists that the phantasmatic event (including the phantasm of the phantom pregnancy) and the real event can be equally traumatic, I offer this reading of Anna O.'s phantom pregnancy.

Significantly, Anna O.'s phantom pregnancy returns her to *her* body, in much the way her fainting spell returned her to her body as she saw the image of the skull's head in the mirror. The phantom pregnancy marks her body as gendered, that is to say, as a body other than her father's or her doctor's. *Time is the bed and Then and Now are breathing in and out and you are one of the ones there waking and swelling, trying to find your mother tongue.* Named "Bertha" and experiencing a superimposition of languages as one of her most dramatic symptoms, the bodily speech act of her name "Bertha" contains "a birth" in English, the language of her initial conversations with Breuer. At the end of her conversation with him, perhaps she wanted to signify the (re)generation of that language in and on her body.

Ten years after her treatment with Breuer, Bertha Pappenheim emerged as a "new woman." She was one of the founders of the Jewish Feminist Movement in Germany; she was a writer; a politician; she devoted herself to caring for unmarried women with children (mothering those she had not conceived – perhaps then another return of the repressed). She lent her body and her life to the making of history, particularly to the making of Jewish feminist history.[29]

Anna O.'s case history, with or without her phantom pregnancy, re-presents the birth of psychoanalysis. Like all origins, it is also a termination point. It marks the end of historical narratives which assume that pasts are past. "For after the uncomfortable birth of psychoanalysis, time was no longer what it had been, 'before' and 'after' entering into new and hitherto unexamined relations of complicity and interference. . . . Psychoanalysis is . . . time and counter-time at once" (Bowlby 1993, 76). These intricate relations of complicity and interference are the performances which structure the history-of-the-present. These interfering complicities mark the beat of our bodies' dance through the swelling and expiring choreography of time. It is therefore appropriate that the last lines of the concluding case study of *Studies* should end on the dance floor:

> *In the spring of 1894 I heard that she [Elisabeth von R.] was going to a private ball for*
> *which I was able to get an invitation, and I did not allow the opportunity to escape me of*
> *seeing my former patient whirl past in a lively dance. Since then, by her own inclination,*
> *she has married someone unknown to me.[30]*
>
> (Studies, 114)

Having seen Elisabeth von R.'s legs joining in the conversation of another lively dance, Freud joins her dancing to marrying. Always partnered by "unknown" bodies (including our own) we attempt to make time[31] into a bed still enough to lie on. In the still of that night, we believe we will be held – until then we hold our own bodies stiff. The legacy of psychoanalysis allows us to see that bodies can be endlessly remade, re-choreographed, outside the traditional architectonics of human reproduction. Psychic health is in part contingent upon the body finding its rhythm in words and time. Choreography and psychoanalysis would do well to join in a conversation about the body's time.

POST-CURE, POST-SCRIPT

The "logical termination" of the first feminine body reconstructed by the talking cure experiences a phantom pregnancy – or at least the phantom of a phantom pregnancy is reproduced at the origin of the talking cure. Femininity is that part of bodies that logic can only treat as a question: the feminine body, the psychoanalytic body, can only take an interrogatory form. Is she or isn't she? Is she or isn't she making it up? Hysterical pregnancy stages the drama of the question of "the body" – the traumatized body, the seductive body, the pregnant body – on the body of the woman. Employing the technique which left nothing to be desired, psychoanalysis sought to interpret what women desire.

As a phantom, hysterical pregnancy is the somatic figure which raises the question of the woman's desire in relation to masculine logic and culture. What does she want? with him? with herself? for herself? The fact that semen is not necessary for the hysterical pregnancy to take its shape implies that the "past" which paternity is so anxious about (an anxiety that fuels the historical drive of the talking cure) is also irrelevant to the performance of the symptom of femininity. Part of what is captivating about the hysterical pregnancy is that the baby never appears; the pregnancy is overwhelmingly powerful because it makes visible the possibility of a body clinging to a permanent present. (One is pregnant while one is hysterical. Nine months has nothing to do with it.)

It is here that the phantom pregnancy rejoins the question of dance. Pure symptom, Anna O.'s phantom pregnancy points to the limit of the talking cure. Insisting that her performative symptom always exceeds narration and the will to mastery enacted by "masculine" discourse, Anna O.'s phantom pregnancy *is* her body's long deferred, long desired, and long renounced, dance. At the end of the cure, she partners herself and touches, perhaps for the first time, her feminine body. And it swells. Her hollow hollers. (And he "fled the house in a cold sweat" (Jones 1954, 247).)

Anna O.'s dance figures her body in the pure present. This is the only tense in which dance itself can exist. Arlene Croce, writing about the problem of reconstructing Balanchine's ballets, especially his *Agon*, notes: "Like all ballets, it has no past; it happens in the moment."[32] But if the ballet is to have a future, like Anna O., it must face the question of history and the attendant challenge of its reproduction/reconstruction. As Balanchine's ballet enters the pedagogical institution, conscious interpretation of technique is turned into science. The pivot of this interpretation revolves around the question of the femininity of *the* Balanchine ballerina. The success or failure of Balanchine's ballet will be determined and measured by the movement phrases performed by the feminine body. She will be required to have a technique that "leaves nothing to be desired" and she will be measured according to her skill at reproducing his vision of her moving. And the performance of this transfer/ence is the true *agon* of dance history and the history of hysteria.

What I am attempting to suggest here is that the irreducible kernel of femininity, as a symptom forever in need of interpretation, also returns us to the challenge of reproduction and reconstruction. For if the psychoanalytic symptom is feminine in the manner I have been describing, once it is "re-moved," how is femininity re-enacted? The conjunction of Anna O. and Balanchine's ballerina suggests that femininity is re-enacted through the reproductive body – through a staging of the body as reproductive in the case of Anna O., and through a staging of the body as a "reconstruction" in Balanchine's ballet. That such acts are phantoms only underlines the power of transit, the belief in transformation, to which both time and the body continually cling.

Patriarchal culture's violent renunciation of the existence of femininity has helped to create a feminine body capable of renouncing that renunciation. The feminine body is, profoundly, an auto-reproductive body, one who continues to reproduce symptoms and movement phrases which dance across the slippery stage of the paternal order.

This essay then, written in a deliberately feminine style by a daughter of dead fathers (Freud, Breuer, Balanchine, my own), seeks to reproduce the dance of femininity within the psychoanalytic body. Recognizing that the classical psychoanalytic body is now also a textual body, I want to turn one more time to Freud's sense of his own dancing. Writing in London in 1938 after being forced to leave Vienna, Freud returns to a piece of writing he could not quite renounce. *Moses and Monotheism*, a deeply speculative and extraordinarily bold investigation into the Mosaic tradition which insists on monotheism, is a text that Freud cannot quite believe, and yet cannot quite leave off. Reproducing his own situation as a non-believing Jew who is nonetheless identified and endangered as a Jew in anti-Semitic Vienna, Freud returns to the story of Moses and seeks to replot his origins, his travels, his history. In the second prefatory note to the third section of his analysis, a note written as he begins his exile in London, Freud writes: "To my critical faculties this treatise, proceeding from a study of the man Moses, seems like a dancer balancing on one toe."[33] Questioning the body of the work he was nonetheless determined to write and to reproduce, Freud balances, like Balanchine's ballerina, between history and hope. In the precariousness of that balance one can glimpse a body capable of escaping our "critical faculties's" beliefs about time, bodies, traumas, histories, women.

NOTES

1   *From Breuer's case history of Anna O. in Freud and Breuer's* Studies on Hysteria, *35.
     Hereafter cited in the text as* Studies.

2   *Insofar as psychoanalysis can be said to be a theory of desire, Breuer's description of
     its technique as that which "left nothing to be desired" is overdetermined.*

3   *For more on the instances and justifications for massaging patients see* Studies,
     *51–6. In Peter Swales's fascinating essay, "Freud, His Teacher and the Birth of
     Psychoanalysis," he reports that "an entry from many years later in the diary of
     Sandor Ferenczi would indicate that Freud must have described to his pupil [Ferenczi]
     how, during his early years in practice, he had even lain on the floor, sometimes for
     hours at a time accompanying a patient [Frau Cacilie M. of* Studies*] through
     hysterical crises" (1986, 50).*

4   *More precisely, her right thigh (see* Studies, *168).*

5   *This passage, and the sexual connotations of its language, "arouse," "climax," and so
     on, is thoughtfully analyzed by Joline Blais (forthcoming).*

6   *My own "critical" words rejoin their conversation – but I can press on only the textual
     body the doctors have created, and of course, my own.*

7   *This formulation of the body as "joining in" also appears in Freud's case history of the
     wolf-man, where "his bowel began, like a hysterically affected organ, to 'join in the
     conversation'" ("From the History of an Infantile Neurosis"). There is much to
     discover in the distinction between a loquacious bowel in a male body and an
     eloquent thigh in a woman's.*

8   *This reading of hysteria is ubiquitous: see White (1989) for a representative example.*

9   *Sometimes it may provide an "excess" of order. Breuer's narrative case history ends
     with Anna O.'s cure, but as Albrecht Hirschmuller has demonstrated, Breuer knew
     that Anna was not "well" when the analysis concluded. (She was, however, "well"
     when Breuer wrote his case study.) See Hirschmuller (1989). The point I want to
     emphasize here is that Breuer's "act" in writing the case study is a willful
     re-imagination of their past that repeats Anna O.'s re-imagination of her own. And my
     narrative construction here repeats the act of re-imagining the past they re-imagined
     together. In joining their conversation I experience, again, the physical and psychic
     imperatives to discipline the textual body, and learn again, how much an "act" of
     imposition it is – for me, for Breuer, and for Anna O.*

10   *In the "Preliminary Communication" of* Studies, *Freud and Breuer report Anna O.'s
     paralysis: "A girl, watching beside a sick-bed in a torment of anxiety, fell into a
     twilight state and had a terrifying hallucination, while her right arm, which was
     hanging over the back of her chair, went to sleep; from this there developed a paresis*

of the same arm accompanied by contracture and anaesthesia. She tried to pray but
could find no words; at length she succeeded in repeating a children's prayer in
English" (pp. 4–5). In Breuer's case history, the "prayer" is a nursery rhyme. The case
history, like psychoanalysis more generally, partakes of the nursery rhyme, the fairy
tale, and the prayer. In Anna O.'s case the allegorical implications are especially hard
to ignore: a young unmarried woman cares for her father; she exhausts herself and
falls ill; he dies; when he does, she becomes even sicker. The mother calls in the good
doctor who loves her like a father and cures her. And they all live happily ever after. In
embryo, then, here are the same seeds which develop into narratives of Revolution
(the ailing father and the death of the State); of Romance (the reintegration of the
household); of scientific progress (from chaos to clarity) and of Redemption (from
suffering to salvation via faith in the cure).

11   From Breuer's original notes (the notes he used to compose his case history); in
     Hirschmuller (1989, 279). Anna O.'s talking cure is doubly marked as translation from
     one sign system (the body) to another (speech) by virtue of the fact that she
     unconsciously translates everything into English (see Studies, 26). The echo of her
     father's call ("Na, how are you, Miss Bertha?") is most likely reproduced as Breuer
     hypnotizes her and asks her, in English, how she is. She eventually "joins in the
     conversation" by (re)producing nursery stories. This interpretation lends credence to
     Freud's (early) view of the transference – here, from the father to the doctor.

12   It seemed very likely to me, incidentally, that each of these repetitious citations were
     an attempt to partner – for I too am very fond of dancing – to partner Anna O.'s stutter
     step with prose.

13   For Anna O.'s mother, one of her daughter's most alarming symptoms was the loss of
     her ability to speak her "mother tongue" (German); it is therefore fitting that it is her
     mother's words, her private diary, that maps Breuer's reading of the temporal "truth"
     of Anna O.'s symptoms.

14   The repetition of course marks the time as "different" – that is to say, as a "second"
     time. In physics, classical thermodynamics proved that the same events can occur
     forwards or backwards in time. Much of Freud's theory of the drives is predicated on
     classical thermodynamics. For a discussion of contemporary physics' notion of a
     "second time" see Phelan (1993, 126–9).

15   For an exhaustive reply to Jones see Hirschmuller (1989, 129–30).

16   For a fine reading of "fall," "fallen," and "falling" in Freud's case histories of women
     see Fuss (1993).

17   For now though let me just note that in the bleeding from Breuer's German to the
     English of the Standard Edition this question of translation is re-enacted.

18   When blindness, the absence of sight, vanishes, the eye/I decides it is safe to return. Note that the symptom which negates must itself be negated before it can disappear. Thus the double narrative transcribed by Breuer also corresponds to the double narrative (the two negations) which enable the symptom's "removal."

19   Michel de Certeau (1988) argues that the "making of history" always requires the production of a division between the past and the present. Insofar as psychoanalysis is the search for the history of the symptom, the "historical cure" reproduces the interpretation of this division. See especially pp. 1–15.

20   Lacan's famous dictum, "woman is the symptom of man" is reversed by Anna O. Her father is her symptom. One wonders, of course, what transpired between the two of them. (I know very well this is not recoverable, but just the same, when I read this I wonder): "One evening she told me a true story of long ago, how at night times she would creep in to eavesdrop on her father (at that time, night nurses could no longer put up with her), how she slept in her stockings for this reason, then on one occasion she was caught by her brother, and so on. As soon as she was finished she began to cry out softly, demanding why she was in bed with her stockings on" (from Breuer's case notes, in Hirschmuller, 1989, 288). And what was she eavesdropping on? What conversation was she seeking to join, there with her "creep"ing, dancing feet covered in stockings? And what is in that "and so on" after her brother "catches" her? In the published case history, Breuer notes that one cause of Anna O.'s symptomatic deafness had its origin in the trauma of being "shaken angrily by her young brother when he caught her one night listening at the sickroom door" (Studies, 36). And why does this critical hallucination feel so familiar?

21   For a discussion of the many errors in Jones's account see Bowlby (1993, 72–81) and Hirschmuller (1989, 126–32).

22   Laplanche (1976, 67).

23   Jones (1954, 246–7).

24   The correspondence and case notes are reproduced in Hirschmuller (1989).

25   Wallace Stevens, "The Snow Man" (1972).

26   I am not trying to suggest that the transference and counter-transference played no part in Anna O.'s case history. I am trying to question, however, Freud's version of it. Breuer, writing in 1907, did say that Anna O.'s case history taught him a lot, "I learned a very great deal: much that was of scientific value, but something of practical importance as well – namely that it was impossible for a 'general practitioner' to treat a case of that kind without bringing his activities and mode of life completely to an end. I vowed at that time I would not go through such an ordeal again" quoted in Paul Cranefield (1958). It certainly seems clear that Breuer's counter-transference was not worked through with Anna O., any more than her transference with him was successfully analyzed.

27 *Quoted in Bowlby (1993, 73).*

28 *For a fuller treatment of this motivation see Bowlby (1993).*

29 *See Kaplan (1979), Freeman (1972), and Hirschmuller (1989) for full accounts of Bertha Pappenheim's life and work.*

30 *Part of the reason that Anna O.'s hysterical pregnancy is so difficult to decipher is because all of the case histories end so "novelistically."*

31 *Time and its attendant copyists – narrative and history.*

32 *Croce (1993, 84).*

33 *Freud,* Moses and Monotheism, *71.*

Lifelessness in movement, or how do the dead move? Tracing displacement and disappearance for movement performance

HEIDI GILPIN

You have remained in the state of having left. And I
have made a film out of your absence.

Marguerite Duras[1]

An image haunts me: I see a wall, industrial grey with random markings and dents, as in a factory perhaps, the edges of which are obscured by diagonal shadows of blackness. On this wall there is the faint shadow of a body in mid-air, with arms and legs intact and reaching outward as in a leap, but no other identifying characteristics. The space around this shadow is enormous, there is so much wall; and the body creating the shadow is not visible, already vanished from sight. This image appears whenever I think of performance: it recalls the state of disappearance that is for me the foundation of an event, and marks the desired stasis that will prove that it ever took place, that it could ever be recorded in some displaced form. It also marks the impossibility of retracing an event for any other purpose than to create a fictional narrative derived from it. We can never know what took place, because the image etched in memory is transformed the moment we attempt to reexamine it. Performance, through its embodiment of absence, in its enactment of disappearance, can only leave traces for us to search between, among, beyond. If the act of interpreting performance could be reconciled with its impossibility, perhaps that which has vanished would reappear in altered, unrecognizable forms, as its own fearless undoing and unknowing of events.

This text marks the initial traces of a search for and examination of the workings of displacement and disappearance in performance. It does not propose to be a demonstration of the function or existence of displaced and vanished events; rather it indicates certain points on a map of survival tactics present in the performative spaces of moving bodies. The failure of performance to be fixed within the representational field is an underlying issue that motivates these pages; critics often do not register that what they are writing about is a representation. Much critical writing about movement in performance presumes the fixability and reproducibility of the performed event, and thereby romanticizes its ephemeral character. This is evidenced by criticism's frequent recourse to description as a discursive mode in order to recreate, fix, and some would argue, sentimentalize, the performance event.[2] I see little value in sentimentalizing disappearance. Rather, I would like to celebrate disappearance as a powerful source of compositional and hermeneutical information. It is precisely the unstable and unfixable nature of bodies in performance which demands attention at this point in the development of bodily discourses – indeed, we must begin not only to let the body go, but also to revel in its absence, and in the traces engendered by its passage from presence to absence.

Both displacement and disappearance are resonant issues that inform strategies for the composition and interpretation of contemporary performance, and in particular contemporary

European movement performance.[3] To pursue these concerns, I will examine a selection of critical resources which elaborate displacement and disappearance and their resonances; this will involve a discussion of repetition as an act of philosophical and practical significance. I will then offer a brief consideration of the work of the Polish visual artist and theater director Tadeusz Kantor, not to discuss the importance or reception of his work (which has already been done so well), but rather to expose how his work problematizes displacement and disappearance, and in so doing proposes movement performance as a mechanism for survival.

DISPLACING MOVEMENT

Jacques Lacan begins one of his seminars on the Unconscious and Repetition by recalling an interrupted seminar a year earlier in which he developed the theme of anxiety. To nostalgia he dedicates the following poem by Louis Aragon, from *Fou d'Elsa*, entitled "Contre-chant":

> *In vain your image comes to meet me*
> *And does not enter me where I am who only shows it*
> *Turning towards me you can find*
> *On the wall of my gaze only your dreamt-of shadow.*
>
> *I am that wretch comparable with mirrors*
> *That can reflect but cannot see*
> *Like them my eye is empty and like them inhabited*
> *By your absence which makes them blind.*[4]

Aragon's poem, and Lacan's positioning of it within the domains of nostalgia, anxiety, repetition, and the unconscious, speak to the particularities of performance, and offer us material significant for the *reading* of performance, toward a reading of moving bodies.

What this poem calls forth is an acknowledgment of the disappearance of the body which performance insistently makes manifest: the impossibility of ever *really* seeing – actually perceiving – movement. What does it mean to perceive movement? What we only ever have, it seems, is an image, and most often not even that: just a "dreamt-of shadow" (*une ombre rêvée*) of an image. So in vain do images come to meet us, from various spaces: a stage, a "performance space," an electronic screen of some kind; sometimes incorporating living bodies in their actual states of present-ness, of presents, sometimes displaying shadows of bodies once alive, but no longer agents of their own movement, auras of energy once transmitted and now "captured" in another medium that cannot begin to mimic the originary moments of movement. All these images can do is reflect, in their blind state, our own absence – according to the last four lines of Aragon's poem. It is our absence, if we follow the poet, which makes these reflecting mirrors of performance blind. But what does it mean to be inhabited, like mirrors, with the absence of an image, or the image of absence? And would we have to be wretched in such a state, as Aragon suggests? Is seeing the sense without which all others flail and fail to transmit *affect* – the affects of a performance, for example?

Norman Bryson discusses the idea that visual experience is never fully organized by a centralized ego: there is always an excess in vision over and beyond what the subject can master in sight. Bryson argues:

> Trompe l'œil *painting unfolds in exactly this area of insufficient control, where instead of the objects' obeying the subject's sovereign gaze, they slip out beyond it and usurp the visual field: they "look back" on the observer, as though there were no right by which human observation takes command of its surrounding world and imposes its own order upon it from a position of visual centre. The veiled threat of* trompe l'œil *is always the annihilation of the individual viewing subject as universal centre.*[5]

If we take these thoughts on vision and autonomy into the realm of performance, *trompe l'œil* painting resembles the power and subjectification of performance, the performers exerting a surveillant control over the observer that threatens the observer's security of position, interpretive power, and perceptive ability. If in fact "the annihilation of the individual viewing subject as universal centre" is the danger which in Aragon's poem threatens blindness and absence, then the task of interpretation is one that requires the courage to address ambivalence, contradiction, and the distorted and fragmented proliferation (without the subject's control) of possibilities. I would like to argue for the power of such notions as potentially enabling and empowering strategies for the development of modes of interpretation where moving bodies – many kinds of movement performed by many different bodies – are concerned.

Moving bodies fascinate not only because they (or a particular moment of their present-ness) have vanished the moment we acknowledge having apprehended them – or the shadow-image of them – but also because they force us to displace our previous notions of what movement is, even when we observe a repeated performance of the "same" phrase of movement, for example, and discover that it is never really the same.[6] As Freud suggests in *Moses and Monotheism*, the word *Entstellung*, or distortion, signifies not only disfigurement, but also *dislocation*: "We might well lend the word 'Entstellung' (distortion) the double meaning to which it has a claim but of which today it makes no use. It should mean not only 'to change the appearance of something' but also 'to put something in another place, to displace.'"[7] The act of perceiving movement enacts its own displacement. In the act of movement, of "putting something in another place," there is the displacement of a body. In the act of interpreting movement, then, there is the displacement of a displacement. Insofar as Freud has observed that *Entstellung* also incorporates disfigurement (when he writes that it is "to change the appearance of something"), he refers to the most common definition of *Entstellung*: "to deform, disfigure, deface, mutilate, distort (a meaning, etc.), garble (an account), misrepresent."[8] This definition has a proliferating number of relevant interpretations for performance, as well as for the act of interpreting performance. If to move involves displacement (distortion, deformation, disfigurement), then to interpret such movement inevitably involves the same kinds of mis*representations. That these distortions have been seen as a failure of the observer/critic to "capture" the performance "accurately" – as if there could be an "accurate" reenactment of a performance (which is often non- or extra-linguistic) in linguistic form – is perhaps one of the reasons that performance criticism reveals itself as falling short of "the real thing."[9] It seems to me that such distortions could, alternately, propose unexplored modes of developing a performative discourse on the subject of performance.

It is the act of interpretation that requires attention in this light. Jacques Derrida distinguishes between two interpretations of interpretation:

> *The one seeks to decipher, dreams of deciphering a truth or an origin which escapes play and the order of the sign, and which lives the necessity of interpretation as an exile. The other, which is no longer turned toward the origin, affirms play and tries to pass beyond man and humanism, the name of man being the name of that being who, throughout the history of metaphysics . . . has dreamed of full presence, the reassuring foundation, the origin and the end of play.[10]*

These two forms of interpretation are irreconcilable; they stand in opposition to each other. Derrida suggests that we must live them both simultaneously in order to learn from the particularities of their oppositions.[11] In his work on dreams, Freud demonstrated that the act of interpretation constitutes a process of deformation which establishes its only claim to legitimacy. Samuel Weber writes about the act of interpretation precisely *as* such an act of disfigurement:

> *As a movement of* Entstellung, *then, interpretation must be conceived not as the more or less faithful reproduction or re-presentation of an antecedent, self-identical object, meaning, or "presence," but as a process of repetition and dislocation, the limits of which must always remain more or less problematic and unstable.[12]*

Such a performance of interpretation assumes the positive and enabling functions of instability, of the ambivalence of repetition with dislocation, that must be considered in response to the question: How do we read the body in performance? If it is movement we are concerned with, that is, the notion of movement in performance and performance in movement, then perhaps we should reconsider Antonin Artaud's statement, in one of his last writings, that ". . . Dance / and consequently the theater / have not yet begun to exist."[13] If dance, if theater, if movement performance have not yet begun to exist, if they are still to be born, and if, as Derrida argues, "whatever can be said of the body can be said of the theater,"[14] there seems to be an unstable agreement here between the displacement and simultaneous disappearance of the body in performance, and the questioning of the "real" nature of theater (read performance) altogether. The act of disappearance is the most enabling, fascinating, difficult, and unavoidable performance we can enact or witness. Disappearance, like displacement, proliferates its own presence within absence,[15] its own birth within death.[16] The act of disappearance can be witnessed only in the moment of its passing, at the threshold between presence and absence, between birth and death. On the wall of Aragon's gaze, and in the blindness of his eye, absence inhabits, "the theater is born in its own disappearance . . . ,"[17] and the possibilities of interpreting performance begin.

FREUD, KIERKEGAARD, AND REPETITION, OR HOW TO MANIFEST DISAPPEARANCE

By implication or desire, performance is constantly oriented towards the impossible desire to stop disappearance. If disappearance is a condition of performance, repetition is a crucial strategy that calls attention to the very fact of disappearance, that manifests the absent presences of that which has disappeared.[18] Walter Benjamin alerted us to the functions of repetition within an increasingly industrial society where aesthetic and other products are reproduced through myriad processes of mechanization.[19] Freud explored the psychic processes of repetition linked to trauma: a child's *fort-da* game of disappearance and return (mimicking the disappearance and return of the child's mother) exposed for Freud how an individual, through the repetition of a traumatic experience, could take on an "*active* part" in relation to that traumatic event.[20] This repetition, which allows one to take on an active role in relation to the trauma experienced by *enacting* the very event that caused the pain, is an act, a re-presentation, a performance. Performance, in this sense, is a survival mechanism, for Freud a form of healing, a cure. By its relation to performance in this context, repetition is a crucial part of this mechanism that enables survival, that allows for the tolerance and endurance of trauma. My attention to repetition as a significant device of contemporary European movement performance is, then, motivated by a desire to witness survival mechanisms at work, to observe which traumas are repeatedly being enacted on stage, and to explore the nature of these traumas and their performances.

Within late twentieth-century culture, everything is reaccessible. We can continually repeat, continually go to have the same thing, we can play packman forty times, listen to the same CD over and over, watch forever the same video, we can see the same movie again and again: our access to repeated experiences gives us the illusion that we can control the future and perhaps, the past. This is an illusion we deeply crave. Freud argued that the repetition compulsion exhibited a desire for control:

> The manifestations of a compulsion to repeat . . . , when they act in opposition to the pleasure principle, give the appearance of some "daemonic" force at work. In the case of children's play we seemed to see that children repeat unpleasurable experiences for the additional reason that they can master a powerful impression far more thoroughly by being active than they could by merely experiencing it passively. Each fresh repetition seems to strengthen the mastery they are in search of. Nor can children have their pleasurable experiences repeated often enough, and they are inexorable in their insistence that the repetition shall be an identical one.[21]

Movement performance looks at the longing to control experience and reinscribes over and over the failure to achieve it. Whether this is pleasurable or not for the spectators of such reinscriptions remains a question. If we follow Freud's reasoning, if a spectator perceives an event repeated on stage as unpleasurable, according to Freud, such an event is most probably traumatic for that person, and she or he would seek to gain control over this event by enduring its repeated enactments. For the choreographer, the use of repetition upon certain phrases of movement, upon certain events, indicates that such movements or events might be either unpleasurable or pleasurable. In either case repetition in performance indicates a desire to master, or at least comment upon, the event being repeated.

Curiously, Freud focuses a few lines later only upon the pleasure associated with repetition, when he states that repetition itself is about pleasure: "None of this contradicts the pleasure principle; repetition, the re-experiencing of something identical, is clearly in itself a source of pleasure."[22] Freud also admits that repetition foregrounds the desire for new forms of expression, for new interpretations of experience: "... it may very well be that, in addition to the conservative instincts which impel towards repetition, there may be others which push forward towards progress and the production of new forms."[23] Although Freud does not explore this particular point any further in *Beyond the Pleasure Principle* (perhaps because such production of new forms would elicit *unpleasurable* aspects of repetition?), the idea that the compulsion to repeat has as its source a desire for the new is clearly applicable to the function of repetition in the work of Tadeusz Kantor, where the force of multiple repetitions of the same phrase of movement challenges the spectator to discover new reactions and to create new interpretations of that phrase.

In "Further Recommendations in the Technique of Psychoanalysis: Recollection, Repetition, and Working Through (1914)," Freud argues that the repetition compulsion is a substitute for the ability to access memory: "We must be prepared to find, therefore, that *the patient abandons himself to the compulsion to repeat*, which is now replacing the impulse to remember...."[24] He asserts that resistance and repetition are intimately connected:

> *Moreover, the part played by resistance is easily recognized.* The greater the resistance the more extensively will expressing in action (repetition) be substituted for recollecting.... *Resistances determine the succession of the various repetitions.*[25]

That resistance and repetition exist in a causal relationship presents questions one might pose of the movement performance directors who employ repetition as a significant structural element in their choreographies. What scenes, situations, or issues do they find necessary to repeat? What do these repetitions reveal about what they consider traumatic? What do the specific elements chosen for repetition reveal about what might be resisted, or what does not want to be recollected? According to Freud, the compulsion to repeat is the patient's way of remembering.[26] If such performances of repetition are merely substitutions for or resistances to recollections, to readings or acknowledgments of memory, as one could interpret contemporary movement performance to be, what role does memory play in movement composition? And what gets left out, if anything? Is repetition enacted upon a complete (traumatic or other) moment? Or are parts of this moment elided, removed, amputated?

Søren Kierkegaard's philosophical/fictional *Repetition: A Venture in Experimenting Psychology*, written in 1843, is especially relevant in the context of performance, and in relation to these questions of trauma, resistance, recollection, and movement. In this wonderfully complicated text, Kierkegaard's psychologist narrator Constantin Constantius sets out in search of "pure" repetition, but discovers that such a thing is impossible: "The only repetition was the impossibility of repetition."[27] One could interpret Kierkegaard's text as a prediction, which he puts forth in the opening passage cited below, that the great subject for modern philosophy would be repetition. Although the philosophy of this century seems to have failed to fulfill Kierkegaard's promise, I would argue that contemporary movement performance *does* take up the challenge Kierkegaard put forth in *Repetition*. In the late twentieth century, the project of philosophy, which Kierkegaard attempted to secure within a field of representation via repetition, situates itself in movement performance. One could further suggest that the failure of philosophy to secure its own field, as Kierkegaard would have had it, mirrors the failure of movement performance to secure its own representational field.

In this light, it is particularly interesting to note that Kierkegaard made this challenge to philosophy based on the discourse of theater, performance, and dance, and that in fact what he may have been trying to do with this text was link theater, performance, movement, and philosophy. *Repetition* begins with a philosophical parenthesis, in which Constantin reflects upon the nature of repetition and recollection via movement. I will quote the opening lines of the text at length because they exemplify the arguments and issues I have suggested above. What is extraordinary about this opening passage is its incessant reference to movement and stasis, and in its initial lines, to a non text-based movement performance:

> *When the Eleatics denied motion, Diogenes, as everyone knows, came forward as an opponent. He literally did come forward, because he did not say a word but merely paced back and forth a few times, thereby assuming that he had sufficiently refuted them. When I was occupied for some time, at least on occasion, with the question of repetition – whether or not it is possible, what importance it has, whether something gains or loses in being repeated – I suddenly had the thought: You can, after all, take a trip to Berlin; you have been there once before, and now you can prove to yourself whether a repetition is possible and what importance it has. At home I had been practically immobilized by this question. Say what you will, this question will play a very important role in modern philosophy, for **repetition** is a crucial expression for what "recollection" was to the Greeks. Just as they taught that all knowing is a recollecting, modern philosophy will teach that all life is a repetition. . . . Repetition and recollection are the same movement, except in opposite directions, for what is recollected has been, is repeated backward, whereas genuine repetition is recollected forward. Repetition, therefore, if it is possible, makes a person happy, whereas recollection makes him unhappy – assuming, of course, that he gives himself time to live and does not promptly at birth find an excuse to sneak out of life again, for example, that he has forgotten something.*[28]

This passage performs what it asserts: its argumentation mimics the imagined actions of Constantin. The first line presents a theoretical denial of motion countered by the "actual" movement of Diogenes. Without verbal language, Diogenes refutes the assertion of stasis with his own motion. Likewise, Constantin, who was rendered motionless and incapable of movement by the question of repetition at home, is able to further the question with movement, or at this point at least, with the *idea* of movement: with a plan of travel to Berlin. Constantin similarly exhibits how recollection and repetition are the same movement, first by recollecting Diogenes' movement in the past, and then by repeating such a movement (to deny stasis with motion, to deny the resistance to the importance of the question of repetition with an active engagement with this question) through his own future movement to Berlin. That Diogenes paces *back and forth a few times*, embodying a performance of repetition, is a detail Constantin seems to ignore verbally but to articulate physically with his idea (put into action in the course of the narrative) of a second trip to Berlin. For he will go to Berlin with every intention of repeating each detail about his first trip there: he will stay in the same hotel, go to the same café, eat in the same restaurant (all of which gave him pleasure during the first trip) and most importantly in terms of his own desire, go to *the same theater to watch a dancing girl.*

That Constantin should link repetition with happiness, recollection with unhappiness, is provocatively reenacted in Freud's assertion above of repetition as a source of pleasure. Freud's subtle resistance to the possibility that repetition could be a movement forward (in Constantin's terms), a movement toward new knowledge, along with his assertion that repetition is enacted upon both pleasurable and unpleasurable events, suggests that the question of repetition may contain an impossible paradox, if we are to associate Constantin's idea of happiness with Freud's notion of pleasure. In keeping with his argument that repetition produces happiness, Constantin is predictably devastated by the impossibility of repetition:

> The little dancer who last time had enchanted me with her gracefulness, who so to speak, was on the verge of a leap, had already made the leap. . . . When this had repeated itself several days, I became so furious, so weary of the repetition [of the failure of repetition], that I decided to return home. My discovery was not significant, and yet it was curious, for I had discovered that there simply is no repetition and had verified it by having it repeated in every possible way.[29]

Constantin's representation of the search for repetition is performed via the much desired performance of the dancing girl at the Königstädter Theater.[30] This performance is described not in terms of how the particular movements she performed the first time were different from the second time, but rather in terms of a leap which was suggested, alluded to, prepared for during the first performance, and completed during the second. Is it perhaps because an imagined leap is always greater than an actual leap, because the possibilities of imagination were fulfilled through actual movement, that Constantin is so disappointed in this dancer?

Later in the text, Constantin argues that repetition transcends (i.e., it would not get stuck in a completed actual movement, such as the dancing girl's leap), this time in relation to philosophy: "Modern philosophy makes no movement, as a rule it makes only a commotion, and if it makes any movement at all, it is always within immanence, whereas repetition is and remains a transcendence."[31] Again we find the assertion that modern philosophy should but does not meet the requirements of adequately attending to repetition (transcendence) via movement. What Kierkegaard's *Repetition* puts forth, then, is the possibility of reconnecting the projects of philosophy and performance, specifically, of philosophy and *movement performance.*

One could also say that *Repetition* tells the story of a young man (called "the young man" by Constantin, who acts as his confidant) who falls in love, undergoes a crisis, and abandons his beloved for the *idea* of love. As Robert Pogue Harrison suggests, Constantin "finds in this melancholy youth an opportunity to study the patterns of a higher spirituality: 'The idea was in *movement* in the young man's love, and for that reason I was interested in him.'"[32] Through Constantin's eyes, we observe the young man transcend his beloved and transform her into an object of recollection. As Harrison argues: "Recollection figures here as a category of poetic consciousness: it consists in poetic recuperation of the loss of immediate presence."[33]

Thus we return to the relation between repetition and recollection discussed above, now further complicated by the concept of loss – more specifically, the concept of loss of presence – which is at the core of live performance generally. Loss of presence is particularly apparent in a theater of movement performance, where most often only the presence (and not the verbal language, for example) of bodies on stage is apparent one moment, vanished the next. This loss must be recuperated through the act of recollecting, which according to Freud, is a substitute for repetition. Either we repeat the performance of absence, of abandonment, or we recollect the disappearance of this performance. The use of repetition in contemporary European movement performance productions could be read, then, as an attempt to recollect what cannot be recollected; as an acknowledgment of the impossibility of recollection; or more specifically, as a critical acknowledgment of the impossibility of *understanding*, of capturing somehow, that which cannot be recollected.

Constantin's assertions about the impossibility of repetition coupled with the potential impossibility of recollection focuses our attention on the kinds of stasis trapped within movement, or the sorts of absences that are exposed within performances of presence. What constitutes such impossibilities? What elements are removed in order to manifest presence on a stage; what moments of stasis must be eliminated in order to display movement?

What does it mean to disappear?[34] Not surprisingly, all definitions of this verb expose a term of performance and movement. We also find a term of absence, immobility, invisibility, and death: "to pass from view; to cease to be: pass out of existence or notice."[35] The *OED* offers: "1a. To cease to appear or be visible; to vanish from sight. b. Of a line or thing extended in space, which ends by gradually ceasing to be distinguishable, or 'dies away' by blending with something else; to be traceable no farther. 2. To cease to be present, to depart; to pass from existence, pass away, be lost."[36] Disappearance engenders this definition: "The action of disappearing; passing away from sight or observation; vanishing." The first example the *OED* offers of the usage of the term disappearance dates from 1712, and surprisingly calls forth the issues of memory and recollection discussed above: "Not likely to be remembered a Moment after their Disappearance." The act of disappearing, then, involves both movement and the cessation of movement: to pass from sight, and to cease to be present. It also registers a lack of representationality: the disappeared can no longer be represented because they can "be traceable no farther," they have vanished from sight, which also suggests, as does the definition above, that they have vanished from existence, from presence. According to dictionary definitions, dying is indistinguishable from disappearing. Death, like disappearance, is a passing from presence to absence, a movement from figuration to disfiguration – physically and in memory. The possibility that presence, once it is no longer traceable, is also no longer part of our memory of it, is deeply disturbing. How is it possible to forget what was once present? How can such a forgetting be tolerated responsibly? How do we enact this memory, even if it is through a performance of absence? How can absence be performed?

That the disappearing person, object, or idea is (as was suggested in 1712) "not likely to be remembered" immediately after their disappearance, is a topic Cathy Caruth addresses via latency and the act of forgetting, again in relation to traumatic events. What is truly striking, Caruth writes,

> is not so much the period of forgetting that occurs after the accident, but rather the fact that the victim of the crash was never fully conscious during the accident itself: the person gets away, Freud says, "apparently unharmed." The experience of trauma, the fact of latency, would thus seem to consist, not in the forgetting of a reality that can hence never be fully known; but in an inherent latency within the experience itself. The historical power of the trauma is not just that the experience is repeated after its forgetting, but that it is only in and through its inherent forgetting that it is first experienced at all. . . . If return is displaced by trauma, then, this is significant in so far as its leaving – the space of unconsciousness – is paradoxically what precisely preserves the event *in its literality.* For history to be a history of trauma means that it is referential precisely to the extent that it is not fully perceived as it occurs; or to put it somewhat differently, that a history can be grasped only in the very inaccessibility of its occurrence.[37]

Thus disappearance paradoxically manifests precisely what we presume it makes absent. It enables not only appearance, but perception, apprehension, experience, and memory. If, as Caruth suggests, forgetting an event allows us to experience it for the first time; if the departure of movement preserves movement; and if history can only be *grasped* (and it is interesting that Caruth uses a term of physical movement in this context) in its ungraspability, then the fundamental fact of performance is that it is enabled by its vanishing, that it exists through its disappearance, that it is made possible by its very impossibility.

TADEUSZ KANTOR: MANIFESTING DISAPPEARANCE, MECHANIZING DEATH

> No foreign sky protected me,
> no stranger's wing shielded my face.
> I stand as witness to the common lot,
> survivor of that time, that place.
>
> Anna Akhmatova[38]

Heinrich von Kleist's 1810 essay "On the Marionette Theater"[39] challenges us with the idea that a mechanical body could possibly be more graceful than a living human body; that a false leg, or prosthesis of any kind, could be more graceful than a natural organ. This essay dreams of a "divine" puppet which would transcend the laws of grace and gravity and outdance human dancers. What fascinates us in puppet theater is the animation of lifeless objects, the putting into motion of dead bodies. Whether these bodies are composed of amputated limbs, or whether they are physically unified objects severed from a life force, the role of marionettes in late twentieth-century theater significantly posits issues of living, dying, disintegration, and disappearance that are literally played out in much recent European performance work. Puppets, or mannequins, as impossible living bodies, are called upon to represent the movement of life more effectively than actual breathing bodies.

The Polish theater director, visual artist, and writer Tadeusz Kantor (1915–90) created an œuvre full of such impossible living bodies, that manifested Kleist's dream. Focused on the search for and performance of disappearance, Kantor created an extraordinary range of visual and textual material, in addition to happenings and theater productions with his internationally renowned company Cricot 2. Kantor was a prolific writer, producing poetry and numerous manifestos and essays that both describe his theater work and challenge spectators to rethink the role of theater as a machine of reality rather than fantasy. He argued for the theater to manifest reality – not a representation of reality, but its own reality –: "The theatre has to avoid creating the illusion of the reality contained in the drama; the reality of the drama must *become reality* on the stage."[40] In text and performance, Kantor created what he called Autonomous, Informel, Zero, and Impossible Theatres, as well as the Theatre of Death and an extraordinary contraption of wood and metal called the Love and Death Machine.[41] These works present a deeply moving exploration of lifelessness and vitality, and of the physical, intellectual, and psychic experience of the movements of living and dying in the twentieth century. Kantor's vision – of theater as painting, of "poor" objects, of mannequins, of the wax figure as dead actor, and of presence via absence – resonates with, among other concepts, repetition, displacement, and disappearance, and suggests divergent ways in which the futures and histories of bodies can be conceived and performed. His work displays bodies as testimonials to the mechanizations of life and death, and the fragmentary traces of both.

Tadeusz Kantor's writings and theater productions demonstrate the possibilities of disappearance as a mechanism for movement composition in performance. Although dis-appearance functions differently as a concept and as a physical act for each director who engages it, Kantor's manipulation – and representation – of the movement from presence to absence and vice versa in his productions, exemplifies a perspective common to many contemporary movement performance directors: a consciousness that death and absence are the foundations of performance. Although Kantor is typically described as a director of theater, much of his theatrical vocabulary is anchored in movement: gesture, mime, repetitive movements of figures and mechanical objects, music, and voice are the bases for his form of performance. In his productions of the 1970s and 1980s, very little text is used except in the way that gesture and movement are used: as one of many elements that construct a stage picture. In one of his most well-known productions, *The Dead Class*, words are spoken (in Polish), but they are often nonsense phrases, unfinished sentences, interrupted phrases: they compose an array of repetitive linguistic material that requires no translation because the gestures and movements that accompany it make the scene absolutely evident without words. In theaters where translation is usually printed in a program when a performance takes place in a language foreign to its audiences, Kantor's *Dead Class* is accompanied by a program, but no translations. In this piece, the focus of all meaning production is on the stage picture and the movement that takes place within it.

The Dead Class was first performed in 1975 in Cracow, Poland, and has subsequently been performed in theaters throughout the world.[42] The setting is a very simple old-fashioned school room, with long pew-like benches facing front. The actors who play the students are old; their faces are painted the palest flesh color, giving them a very aged – or corpse-like – appearance. The Cricot 2 company actors who perform this work are mostly non-professional; they are "people whose own lives and dreams are interwoven through the piece."[43] The teacher of this class could be said to be Kantor himself, for he is on stage throughout, watching, gesturing, conducting the pace, length, and direction of this series of dream-like sequences. Kantor describes the characters of *The Dead Class* as neither individualized nor clear-cut and unambiguous; they are compilations of fragments severed from any context:

> As if pasted or stitched together from ill-matched parts: remnants of their childhood, the vicissitudes of their (not always creditable) lives, their dreams and passions, they fall apart and become transformed with every minute, and through this continuous motion and theatre running riot, they progress inexorably to their final form which is irrevocably transfixed and is to encompass the Entire Memory of the Dead Class. Final preparations are hastily made for the Grand Game with Emptiness.[44]

Since all this is happening in a theater, however, Kantor writes that the actors, faithfully sticking to the rules of theatrical ritual, take on some roles from a play, although they seem to attach very little importance to them.[45] The "students" seem to be performing answers to heard and unheard questions: they babble responses, murmur loudly among themselves when a question seems difficult to answer, repeat questions manically, terrified that any answer they propose may be incorrect. Their faces project tremendous fear of authority, and of being caught doing something wrong, as they wait for one of their fellow students to answer the question of the moment. The actors' movements appear mechanical, almost automated, carried out by a "momentum of general habit,"[46] and there is the sense that they desperately perform someone else's lines or movements arbitrarily, just to perform something, anything at all. Gaps are everywhere in motion: sentences stop midway, without even an expression of embarrassment at having forgotten the rest; and gestures go uncompleted. The futility of the scene is overwhelming. Kantor writes that the "*pupils*, old men and women, some with one foot in the grave, *some who are already absent* . . . they put their hands up in class in the universally known gesture and remain like that . . . as if they were asking for something, something final. . . ."[47] Kantor's acknowledgment of present absence – that some characters who are already absent, who have already disappeared, continue to perform motions of presence, like raising their hand in this classroom – is a provocative demonstration of the significance of absence and disappearance in performance.

Eventually the students leave the school room, only to enter it again in an extraordinary march of repetition that circles around and around the school benches: bodies carry other bodies, or mannequins, wax figures, and dolls. Some actors and/or mannequins are attached to mechanical objects, others to the backs of the "living" figures. In this "theatre of death," as Kantor calls it, it becomes difficult to discern whether any bodies on stage are living: some are moving, others are static or lifeless, but even the moving figures seem to be from a dream of the dead. The mechanical quality of their movements makes every figure seem to be under the control of someone or something else. Mechanical objects appear on stage: a figure called "The Woman with A Mechanical Cradle" is chased around the benches and forcibly put on a strange-looking contraption listed in the program as "The Family Machine." It is a manually operated mechanism: a bench with two side boards, which, when the woman lies on the bench directly facing the audience, repetitively and mechanically make her legs open and close. Later a "Mechanical Cradle" appears, looking like a small coffin, with two wooden balls inside, which produce an abrupt and merciless clatter as a mechanism jerks the cradle back and forth. The woman sings a lullaby, linking birth and death in a desperate lament.

These opening moments of *The Dead Class* offer a sense of the power of death and mechanical life in Kantor's theater: whether object or person, these figures take on representations of lifelessness and horrific futility through the very mechanical nature of their movements. Kantor created a mechanical object he called the Death Machine, which enacts, in its own movements, the futility of the actors' movements on stage. He describes this machine in "The Zero Theatre *or* The Theatre of Nullification" (1963) under the disturbing category title "Elimination by force":

> The Death Machine
> (a shapeless construct made out of decrepit chairs)
> shoves the actors aside, throws them "out,"
> exterminates
> by its sudden, robot-like movements.
> There remains a ridiculously small space for
> acting and living. Actors resist
> being pushed aside,
> try to keep their balance and cling to the surface
> as does a drowning man; wage a hopeless struggle
> but fall off.[48]

The anti-narrative nature of Kantor's productions underscore an attention to the imperfect, the fragmented, the traumatic, the fallen. He transforms the performance space into a testimonial space. Much like oral testimonies of trauma survivors, whose narrative material or account of a past experience fragments as the victim or witness approaches the core of the trauma, Kantor's productions are collage-like compositions of fragmented scenes, disconnected moments of diverse historical, personal, visual, and spatial experiences.[49] As Carolyn Forché writes:

> The narrative of trauma is itself traumatized, and bears witness to extremity by its inability to articulate directly or completely. Hence the reduction of a century to a series of staccato images in Adonis's "Mirror for the Twentieth Century": "A coffin bearing the face of a boy / A book / Written on the belly of a crow / A wild beast hidden in a flower / A rock / Breathing with the lungs of a lunatic: / This is it / This is the Twentieth Century."[50]

Where figures in Kantor's productions enact the relation between performance and death, Roland Barthes discusses theater's relation to death in the context of photography. Barthes exposes the possibilities of present absence, of the performance of death, in figuration:

> We know the original relation of the theater and the cult of the Dead: the first actors separated themselves from the community by playing the role of the Dead: to make oneself up was to designate oneself as a body simultaneously living and dead: the whitened bust of the totemic theater, the man with the painted face in the Chinese theater, the rice-paste makeup of the Indian KathaKali, the Japanese Noh mask. . . . Now it is this same relation which I find in the Photograph: however "lifelike" we strive to make it (and this frenzy to be lifelike can only be our mythic denial of an apprehension of death), Photography is a kind of primitive theater, a kind of **Tableau Vivant**, a figuration of the motionless and made-up face beneath which we see the dead.[51]

Curiously, the terms with which Barthes describes photography display the qualities of stasis, and of simultaneous presence and absence, with which we can describe not only Kantor's theater work, but also the work of many contemporary movement performance directors and choreographers. Kantor's theater performs the role of death in its enactment of life, which is often as motionless as the photographic images Barthes considers.

Mannequins, or wax humanoid figures, are a common presence throughout Kantor's texts, theater, and visual art. Kantor exposes the impossibility of life and death by representing each with its opposite, much as Cathy Caruth discusses absence or inaccessibility as the force that makes presence or apprehension possible: living actors mimic dead bodies, corpse-like mannequins represent life. Often the life-size mannequins on Kantor's stage seem so much more alive than the pale-faced actors that we must wonder which truly portrays life, and which death. Kantor begins his 1975 essay/manifesto "The Theatre of Death" with a discussion of the marionette as the true source of theater:

> 1. Craig's Postulate: to bring back the marionette. Eliminate the live actor. Man – a creature of nature – is a foreign intrusion into the abstract structure of a work of art.
>   *According to Gordon Craig, somewhere along the banks of the Ganges two women forced their way into the shrine of the Divine Marionette, which was jealously hiding the secrets of the true THEATRE. They envied the ROLE of this Perfect Being in illuminating human intellect with the sacred feeling of the existence of God, its GLORY; they spied on its Movements and Gestures, its sumptuous attire and, by cheap parody, began to satisfy the vulgar taste of the mob. At the moment when they finally ordered a similar monument built for themselves – the modern theatre, as we know it only too well and as it has lasted to this day, was born. A clamorous Public Service Institute. With it appeared the ACTOR. In defense of his theory Craig cites the opinion of Eleanora Duse: "to save the theatre, it must be destroyed, it is necessary for all actors and actresses to die of plague . . . for it is they who render art impossible. . . ."*[52]

Later in this text Kantor disagrees with Kleist, who, "for the same reasons as Craig, demanded the substitution of the actor by the marionette...."[53] Kantor argues that mannequins are clearly stamped with the sign of death: "The mannequin as manifestation of 'REALITY OF THE LOWEST ORDER.' The mannequin as dealings of TRANSGRESSION. The mannequin as EMPTY object. The DUMMY. A message of DEATH. A model for the actor."[54] Subsequently, he writes that the mannequin in his theater must become a model "through which pass a strong sense of DEATH and the conditions of the DEAD."[55] Kantor suggests that mannequins have a transgressive force, for they have always existed on the peripheries of "sanctioned Culture;" and have always been treated condescendingly as curiosities. For this reason, he argues, mannequins fascinate us:

> The vague and inexplicable feeling that through this entity so similar to a living human being but deprived of consciousness and purpose there is transmitted to us a terrifying message of Death and Nothingness – precisely this feeling becomes the cause of – simultaneously – that transgression, repudiation, attraction ... and fascination.[56]

The connections between Kantor's impressions of the mannequin and the issue of disappearance that I would like to mark here concern the question of what it means to perform living, what it means to enact dying, and how it is possible to apprehend the performance of either. Kantor argues that the movement of future theater should not be to replace the live actor with the mannequin, as Kleist and Craig wanted:

> This would be too simple and naive. I am trying to delineate the motives and intent of this unusual creature [the mannequin] which has suddenly appeared in my thoughts and ideas. Its appearance complies with my ever-deepening conviction that it is possible to express life in art only through the absence of life, through an appeal to DEATH, through APPEARANCES, through EMPTINESS and the lack of a MESSAGE.[57]

Again we find a confirmation, now in Kantor's words, that presence can only be conveyed by absence (even the repetition of absence), that a lack of message is precisely what signifies, and that the performance of emptiness makes a perception of existence possible. Kantor confirms the role of the non-living figure in his theater as its life force. The mannequin, lacking signifying markers, is capable of taking on many meaning-bearing codes: for Kantor, it is a formless being that can be made to signify anything. Remarkably, Kantor's own performances on stage functioned, perhaps, as a metaphor for the mannequin.

In a tradition particular to Kantor's Cricot 2 company alone, Kantor appeared and remained on stage during each performance of every production, gesturing directives to the actors, indicating when a sequence of sound or movement should begin, how long it should last, what kinds of cadences or crescendos it should have, and generally conducting the performance much like a musical conductor. Kantor would approach an actor and move him from one spot on stage to another, or adjust a costume, mannequin, or movement taking place. His interferences were central to the continuity of the performance itself. After Kantor's death in 1990, the company continued to tour certain productions for about a year, but at this point has ceased to perform. The actors said (in conversations in New York in 1991) that performing these works made no sense to them without Kantor on stage.

Kantor was very conscious of his role as conducting director; his production titles often referred directly to his own experience or desire, as in his last two productions: *I Shall Never Return*, created in 1988, and *Today is My Birthday*, performed in its unfinished state after Kantor's death in 1990. This last production was particularly difficult to perform without Kantor present, because in rehearsals for the performance, he was positioned seated at a table downstage center with full view of all the movements of the spectacle taking place before him. He was even listed in the program as an actor, whose role was ''The Proprietor of the Poor Room of the Imagination.''[58] His static position on stage throughout this production (in rehearsal) made it all the more difficult for the actors to perform it without him after his death. Since the program indicated Kantor's position during rehearsals to the audience, spectators were also made hyper-conscious of Kantor's present absence during the performance. In this way, Kantor managed, with his own death, to enact the principles that motivated his theater from its beginnings: that death must be witnessed, that absence must be performed, and that life can only be perceived through its disappearance.

Tadeusz Kantor's productions are testimonials; they re-present displaced artifacts of disturbing moments of individual and collective history. In his attempts to confront terrifying realities, Kantor's work honors the disappearances of life, experience, memory, and vision that color the history of this century, and offers traces of these disappearances in moving forms.

The very last text in the program for *Today is My Birthday* appears in memoriam, on an all black page, facing another all black page with a small photograph of Kantor. I would like to end with this text not only as a memorial marker of Kantor's present absence, but also because this passage marks the paradoxical nature and significance of the performance of absence for contemporary theater with a suggestion that the theater is not where we assume it to be – that the theater is elsewhere. The text is a quotation by Kantor that comments on his own presence on stage. Read in the context of his death, however, this text translates the meaning of the stage and the threshold between the performers and the spectators, between the living and the dead, into another dimension where the stage is as much life as it is death, and where the act of disappearance is forever central to life and to theater, yet impossible to capture in words or visions:

> . . . *I am back on stage again.*
> *Probably I'll never explain*
> *till the end this habit of mine*
> *neither to you nor to myself.*
> *As a matter of fact not on stage,*
> *but on the threshold. . . .*[59]

NOTES

1 *Marguerite Duras*, The Atlantic Man, *as cited in* Two by Duras, *trans. Alberto Manguel (Toronto: Coach House Press, 1993), 48. Original French edition:* L'Homme atlantique *(Paris: Les Editions de Minuit, 1982).*

2 *Certainly the material of bodily movement in performance is of a malleable nature; historically it has created much controversy over how to write about it, in part due to the ambiguity, as with speech, that such malleability affords. As a result, critical writing about dance performance, as I argue, tends to shy away from interpretation in favor of description. Dance critics' accounts, according to Randy Martin, maintain "a close rapport between the memory of an event and its documentation in order to do justice to the very specificity of dancing" (Martin, "Overreading Dance: Addressing the Narrative of Context through Bill T. Jones' Promised Land," Irvine, 10 May 1993, manuscript, f.8). Dance critics have commented that the ambiguity of dance, like Freud's acknowledgment of the ambiguity of words, creates an inescapable difficulty. In* The Interpretation of Dreams, *Freud writes that "words may be regarded as predestined to ambiguity" (as cited in* The Standard Edition of the Complete Psychological Works of Sigmund Freud, *translated from the German under the General Editorship of James Strachey, in collaboration with Anna Freud, assisted by Alix Strachey and Alan Tyson (London: The Hogarth Press, 1960, reprinted 1971), vol. 5, 340); in* "Gradiva" *(1907) he remarks that the ambiguity is made possible "by the malleable nature of the material of speech" (Standard Edition, vol. 9, 85). Edwin Denby asserts that "the handicap to method in dance criticism has always been that its subject matter – dancing that can fascinate as an art does – is so elusive" (Denby,* Dance Writings, *New York: Alfred A. Knopf, 1986, 537, emphasis mine). I would argue that this elusiveness is precisely the strength for writing about movement, not its weakness.*

3 *Movement performance is a term I have coined to accommodate the myriad genres of performance involving moving bodies currently being enacted on stages and screens in the late twentieth century. For a more detailed discussion of this term, see the introduction to my* Failure, Repetition, Amputation, and Disappearance: Issues of Composition in Contemporary European Movement Performance, *Ph.D. dissertation, Department of Comparative Literature, Harvard University, May 1993.*

4 *Original French:*

> *Vainement ton image arrive à ma rencontre*
> *Et ne m'entre où je suis qui seulement la montre*
> *Toi te tournant vers moi tu ne saurais trouver*
> *Au mur de mon regard que ton ombre rêvée*
>
> *Je suis ce malheureux comparable aux miroirs*
> *Qui peuvent réfléchir mais ne peuvent pas voir*

Comme eux mon œil est vide et comme eux habité

De l'absence de toi qui fait sa cécité

Translation as cited in Jacques Lacan, The Four Fundamental Concepts of
Psycho-Analysis, *ed. Jacques-Alain Miller, trans. Alan Sheridan (New York: Norton,
1981), 17, from Section I: The Unconscious and Repetition: "The Freudian
Unconscious and Ours." Original French edition:* Le Seminaire de Jacques Lacan,
Livre XI: Les quatre concepts fondamentaux de la psychanalyse *(Paris: Editions du
Seuil, 1973). Louis Aragon, Le Fou d'Elsa (Paris: Editions Gallimard, 1963), 73. In*
Failure, Repetition *cited above, in the context of a discussion of amputation and
elimination, I refer to the startling fact that in Aragon's text, this poem was spoken by
a character (An-Nadjî) to celebrate a circumcision.*

5   *Norman Bryson*, Looking at the Overlooked: Four Essays on Still Life Painting
   (Cambridge, MA: Harvard University Press, 1990), 143–4.

6   *Søren Kierkegaard, as I will discuss below, argues for the impossibility of "pure"
   repetition after an extended attempt to seek it out: "The only repetition was the
   impossibility of repetition." Kierkegaard, "Repetition: A Venture in Experimenting
   Psychology," in* Fear and Trembling/Repetition. *Kierkegaard's Writings, VI, ed. and
   trans. Howard and Edna Hong (Princeton: Princeton University Press, 1983), 170.*

7   *Sigmund Freud*, Standard Edition *23 (London: The Hogarth Press, 1978), 43.*

8   The New Cassell's German/English Dictionary *(New York: Funk & Wagnalls, 1962).*

9   *The assumption that criticism should* translate *performance into another medium is
   perhaps its first failure. "'Memory's images, once they are fixed in words, are erased,'
   Polo said. 'Perhaps I am afraid of losing Venice all at once, if I speak of it. Or perhaps,
   speaking of other cities, I have already lost it, little by little.'" Italo Calvino*, Invisible
   Cities, *trans. William Weaver (New York and London: Harcourt Brace Jovanovich,
   1974), 87. I would argue rather for the transformation of criticism into its own
   performance, into a creation of an other event inspired by a performative event but by
   no means attempting to reenact it. I am grateful for conversations with Peggy Phelan
   on the subject of "performative writing," an idea she enacts and addresses in*
   Unmarked: The Politics of Performance *(New York and London: Routledge, 1993).*

10 *Jacques Derrida, "Structure, Sign, and Play in the Discourse of the Human
   Sciences," in* Writing and Difference, *trans. Alan Bass (Chicago: University of
   Chicago Press, 1978), 278–93, p. 292. Original French edition:* L'écriture et la
   différence *(Paris: Seuil, 1967), 427.*

11 *Samuel Weber explores this point further in* Institution and Interpretation
   (Minneapolis: University of Minnesota Press, 1987), 3–4.

12 *Samuel Weber*, Institution and Interpretation, *80. For an illuminating discussion of*

interpretation and Entstellung, *see* Weber, *"The Blindness of the Seeing Eye: Psychoanalysis, Hermeneutics, Entstellung," in* Institution and Interpretation, *73–84.*

13 *Antonin Artaud, "Le théâtre de la cruauté," in 84, nos. 5–6 (1948), 11–135, p. 127.*

14 *Jacques Derrida, "The Theater of Cruelty and the Closure of Representation," in* Writing and Difference, *232–50, p. 232.*

15 *One could make the argument that the void, the erasure, the absence and invisibility that movement performance offers is not only a metaphor for the unknown, but as such (via Freud and Lacan), also a metaphor for woman. Calvino's cities all bear women's names, and play with the idea that to discover, penetrate, reveal, translate a city may nevertheless not be to capture it, although there may be an endless quest of desire to do so. "All the rest of the city is invisible. Phyllis is a space in which routes are drawn between points suspended in the void: the shortest way to reach that certain merchant's tent, avoiding that certain creditor's window. Your footsteps follow not what is outside the eyes, but what is within, buried, erased." Italo Calvino,* Invisible Cities, *91. See also Alice Jardine,* Gynesis: Configurations of Woman and Modernity *(Ithaca: Cornell University Press, 1985). Susan Rubin Suleiman's reading of Lacan with Marguerite Duras's* Le Ravissement de Lol V. Stein *in relation to knowing, writing, and the performance of feminine discourse (which is "not always where one expects to find it," p. 118) as an object of hope, offers compelling material with which to propose such an argument. See Suleiman, "Duras/Lacan: Not Knowing as Entanglement," in* Subversive Intent: Gender, Politics and the Avant-Garde *(Cambridge, MA, and London: Harvard University Press, 1990), 110–18 and passim.*

16 *The body without organs is an example of the generative power of the acknowledgment of absence. Gilles Deleuze and Félix Guattari address this concept in* A Thousand Plateaus: Capitalism and Schizophrenia, *trans. and foreword by Brian Massumi (Minneapolis: University of Minnesota Press, 1987), 149ff. Original French edition:* Mille plateaux, *vol. 2 of* Capitalisme et schizophrénie *(Paris: Les Editions de Minuit, 1980). About this body, they write: ". . . it is an inevitable exercise or experimentation, already accomplished the moment you undertake it, unaccomplished as long as you don't. This is not reassuring, because you can botch it. Or it can be terrifying, and lead you to your death. It is nondesire as well as desire. It is not at all a notion or a concept but a practice, a set of practices. You never reach the Body without Organs, you can't reach it, you are forever attaining it, it is a limit" (149–50, emphasis mine).*

17 *Jacques Derrida, "The Theater of Cruelty and the Closure of Representation," in* Writing and Difference, *233.*

18 *Repetition has been the focus of a great deal of philosophical, psychoanalytic, and literary study, not to mention its importance to the fields of music, physics, film,* *architecture, history, the visual arts, and quantum mechanics. Repetition contains notions of movement and performance within its very definition.* Webster's Dictionary *(9th edition, Springfield, MA: Merriam-Webster, 1986) offers the following: "the act or an instance of repeating or being repeated; MENTION, RECITAL." It is curious that this definition begins with "the act," immediately indicating a performance, a movement of some kind, and that the definition includes not only terms of performance generally, but also a term of linguistic performance specifically. "Mention" acknowledges a particular kind of movement. Its definition begins as did that of repetition: "the act or an instance of citing or calling attention to someone or something...." Within the concept of repetition, then, is a linguistic performance, an emphatic act, as well as a performance of movement.*

19   *Walter Benjamin, "The Work of Art in the Age of Mechnical Reproduction," in* Illuminations, *ed. with an introduction by Hannah Arendt, trans. Harry Zohn (New York: Schocken Books, 1969), 217–51. Herbert Blau has written extensively and brilliantly about issues of disappearance, repetition, recollection, transformation, and death in performance. See, among many of his other texts, "Look What Thy Memory Cannot Contain," and "The Thought of Performance: Value, Vanishing, Dream, and Brain Damage," in* Blooded Thought: Occasions of Theatre *(New York: Performing Art Journal, 1982), 72–94 and 25–48; and especially "Universals of Performance; or Amortizing Play," and "Shadowing Representation" in* The Eye of Prey: Subversions of the Postmodern *(Bloomington and Indianapolis: Indiana University Press, 1987), 161–88 and 189–206.*

20   *Sigmund Freud,* Beyond the Pleasure Principle, *trans. and ed. by James Strachey, introduction and notes by Gregory Zilboorg (New York and London: W. W. Norton & Co., 1961), 10.*

21   *Freud,* Beyond the Pleasure Principle, *29, first emphasis mine.*

22   *Freud,* Beyond the Pleasure Principle, *30.*

23   *Freud,* Beyond the Pleasure Principle, *31.*

24   *Sigmund Freud, "Further Recommendations in the Technique of Psychoanalysis: Recollection, Repetition and Working Through (1914)," first published in* Zeitschrift, *Bd. II, 1914; reprinted in* Sammlung, Vierte Folge, *cited here in the translation by Joan Riviere in* Therapy and Technique, *ed. and with an introduction by Philip Rieff (New York: Collier Books, Macmillan, 1963, 157–66), 161, emphasis mine. I address the connection between memory and repetition with regard to Pina Bausch's work in "Amputation, Dismembered Identities, and the Rhythms of Elimination," in* Other Germanies: Questioning Identity in Women's Literature and Art, *ed. Karen Jankowsky, Carla Love, and Thomas Jung (Albany: State University of New York Press, Postmodern Culture Series, forthcoming).*

25   *Freud, "Recollection, Repetition and Working Through," 161, emphasis mine.*

26 Freud, "Recollection, Repetition, and Working Through," 161. On the topic of repetition and representation (insofar as memory incorporates representations), see Judith Butler, Gender Trouble: Feminism and the Subversion of Identity (New York and London: Routledge, 1990), esp. 29; 31–3; 115–16; 139–50; and James A. Snead, "Repetition as a Figure of Black Culture," in Out There: Marginalization and Contemporary Cultures, ed. Russell Ferguson, Martha Gever, Trinh T. Minh-ha, and Cornel West, with foreword by Marcia Tucker (New York: The New Museum of Contemporary Art, and Cambridge, MA and London: MIT Press, 1990), 213–30.

27 Kierkegaard, "Repetition: A Venture in Experimenting Psychology," in Fear and Trembling/Repetition. Kierkegaard's Writings, VI, 170.

28 Kierkegaard, Repetition, 131, emphasis mine.

29 Kierkegaard, Repetition, 170–1.

30 Kierkegaard, Repetition, 170.

31 Kierkegaard, Repetition, 186.

32 Robert Pogue Harrison, "Heresy and the Question of Repetition. Reading Kierkegaard's Repetition," in Textual Analysis. Some Readers Reading, ed. Mary Ann Caws (New York: The Modern Language Association of America, 1986), 282.

33 Harrison, "Heresy and the Question of Repetition," 282.

34 The conclusion of this section which focuses on disappearance, appeared in abbreviated form in my "Aberrations of Gravity," ANY (Architecture New York) 5: Lightness (March/April 1994), 51.

35 Webster's Dictionary.

36 The Oxford English Dictionary (Oxford: Oxford University Press, 1971; reprinted 1985). Emphasis mine.

37 Cathy Caruth, "Unclaimed Experience: Trauma and the Possibility of History," Yale French Studies 79, Literature and the Ethical Question, ed. Claire Nouvet, 1991, 187, emphasis mine.

38 Anna Akhmatova, "Requiem, 1935–1940," trans. Stanley Kunitz and Max Hayward, in Against Forgetting: Twentieth Century Poetry of Witness, ed. Carolyn Forché (New York and London: W. W. Norton, 1993), 101.

39 Heinrich von Kleist, "Über das Marionettentheater," originally published in Berliner Abendblätter, 12–14 December 1810.

40 Tadeusz Kantor, on the "Independent Theatre," in Daniel C. Gerould, "Tadeusz Kantor: A Visual Artist Works Magic on the Polish Stage," Performing Arts Journal 12, vol. IV, no. 3 (1980), 27–38, p. 29, Kantor's emphasis.

41   *For an excellent introduction to Kantor's work, see* The Drama Review, *vol. 30, no. 3
(Fall 1986), Special Issue on Tadeusz Kantor, which includes "The Writings of Tadeusz
Kantor 1956–1985" with numerous manifestos (on the Autonomous and Informel
Theatres and the Theatre of Death) and other texts; Jan Klossowicz, "Tadeusz
Kantor's Journey;" Michal Kobialka, "Let the Artists Die?: An Interview with Tadeusz
Kantor;" a comprehensive bibliography compiled by Michal Kobialka; and
photographs of performances. On the Machine of Love and Death, see Krzysztof
Miklaszewski, "Tadeusz Kantor: Exegi monumentum . . . or 'The Love and Death
Machine,' " interview with Krzysztof Miklaszewski,* Le Théâtre en Pologne/The
Theatre in Poland, *11–12/351–2 (November–December 1987), 3–8. For Kantor's
manifesto "The Impossible Theatre," see "Le théâtre impossible,"* Les Lettres
Françaises, *12 July 1972. See also Michal Kobialka's collection of Kantor's writings in
English, along with an excellent critical study of Kantor's theatre:* A Journey Through
Other Spaces: Essays & Manifestos, 1944–1990, *by Tadeusz Kantor (Berkeley and Los
Angeles: University of California Press, 1993).*

42   *It was presented at the Edinburgh Festival, in London, and in Amsterdam in 1976; at
the International Festival in Nancy and at the Autumn Festival in Paris in 1977; in
Florence, Milan, and Australia in 1978; and in Mexico and the United States (at New
York's La MaMa Theater) in 1979 (and again at La MaMa in 1991). It was by far the most
frequently performed of all of Kantor's productions.*

43   *Jan Klassowicz,* "The Dead Class *Scene by Scene," trans. by Karol Jakubowicz,*
Gambit: International Theatre Review, *vol. 9, nos. 33–4 (1979), 107–35, p. 108.*

44   *Tadeusz Kantor, "Characters in* The Dead Class," *trans. by Karol Jakubowicz,*
Gambit: International Theatre Review, *vol. 9, nos. 33–4 (1979), 137–40, p. 137,
Kantor's emphasis.*

45   *Kantor, "Characters in* The Dead Class," *137.*

46   *Kantor, "Characters in* The Dead Class," *137.*

47   *Kantor, "Characters in* The Dead Class," *138, second emphasis mine.*

48   *Tadeusz Kantor, "The Zero Theatre or The Theatre of Nullification, 1963," trans. Michal
Kobialka,* The Drama Review, *vol. 30, no. 3 (Fall 1986), 133.*

49   *Shoshana Felman articulates testimony as an essential way to relate to the traumatic
events of contemporary history, many of which are represented in displaced and
fragmented form in Kantor's work: "As a relation of events, testimony seems to be
composed of bits and pieces of a memory that has been overwhelmed by occurrences
that have not settled into understanding or remembrance, acts that cannot be
constructed as knowledge nor assimilated into full cognition, events in excess of our
frames of reference." Felman, "Education and Crisis, or the Vicissitudes of Teaching,"
in Felman and Dori Laub,* Testimony: Crises of Witnessing in Literature,

Psychoanalysis, and History *(New York and London: Routledge, 1992), 5. See also an extraordinary collection of testimonial writing:* The Collective Silence: German Identity and the Legacy of Shame, *ed. Barbara Heimannsberg and Christoph J. Schmidt, trans. by Cynthia Oudejans Harris and Gordon Wheeler (San Francisco: Jossey-Bass Publishers, 1993).*

50   *Carolyn Forché, "Introduction,"* Against Forgetting, *42–3.*

51   *Roland Barthes,* Camera Lucida: Reflections on Photography, *trans. by Richard Howard (New York: Farrar, Straus & Giroux, 1981), 31, emphasis mine.*

52   *Tadeusz Kantor, "The Theatre of Death. 1975,"* The Drama Review, *vol. 30, no. 3 (Fall 1986), 137–8, trans. by Voy T. and Margaret Stelmaszynski, reprinted from* Canadian Theatre Review, *16 (Fall 1977), Kantor's emphasis.*

53   *Kantor, "The Theatre of Death," 138.*

54   *Kantor, "The Theatre of Death," 142.*

55   *Kantor, "The Theatre of Death," 144.*

56   *Kantor, "The Theatre of Death," 143.*

57   *Kantor, "The Theatre of Death," 143, Kantor's emphasis.*

58   *Tadeusz Kantor,* Today is My Birthday, *18–23 June 1991, La MaMa E.T.C. Theater, New York, program. Presented by La MaMa in association with The New York International Festival of the Arts. An introductory note to the program states: "On December 8th 1990 Tadeusz Kantor died in Cracow. He was 75 years old. The night before his death he directed the dress rehearsal of his last production 'Today is my Birthday.' The Actors of Cricot 2 stage the performance as Tadeusz Kantor left it, with the exception of his empty chair onstage." This chair remained loudly "empty," throughout the performance. A note in this program to Kantor from the actors reveals that the title of the production was very clearly a reference to Kantor's own birthday: "We, the inhabitants of the Room of Imagination of Tadeusz Kantor, we, whom you have invited for your 75th birthday, we . . . have responded to the calling of the powers which are stronger than ours and have arrived to perform functions assigned to us. It is our moral obligation and duty to do so for all that you taught us and we, faithful to you, transmit from the boards of your theatre into the world" (p. 2).*

59   Today is My Birthday, *La MaMa program, June 1991.*

Dancing in the field: notes from memory

SALLY ANN NESS

12 April 1993   UC Irvine, Humanities Research Institute[1]

You are looking at work still in motion, actually just coming into motion or entering a "performative mode."[2]

I am "drafting a new form of text."[3] This text fails to shine as a polished product. It says "no" to the document.[4] It will open up a space for new perceptions of the writing work of ethnography as it connects human beings to each other – subjects, readers, others, writers, objects, selves, etc. It [produces] a failure of completion, capable of representing ethnographic events as ongoing occurrences, happening now, currently transforming.[5]

These notes are involved in several temporally concentric ethnographic processes: they are part of the initiation of what will become a five-to-seven-year study of tourism and performance in insular Southeast Asia, a project now in its infancy with only a few months of fieldwork accomplished; they also follow up a previous eight-year effort to come to terms with an earlier experience of living in this part of the world.[6] These texts are my "written *downs*":[7] subjective, spontaneous, private, unpublishable narratives of some incidents that occurred in Indonesia and the Philippines, during a summer of fieldwork in 1992. They include failures of objectivity, states of confusion, excessive pleasures that are traditionally excluded from published accounts,[8] exposing the difference between "what one feels oneself to be and what one would claim in public."[9] They are first encounters or arrival stories, moments when the subjectivity of the ethnographer has traditionally been allowed to be incorporated into the "writing up." They focus on establishing rapport through dance, on embodied knowledge as a means of transcending other identity categories.

They are not my memories intact. They are keeping my memories from dying. "They" are also worth keeping alive and intact as *corpora*, as "bodies of text," not as a replacement for [the] monograph form of writing, but to show, as Kirsten Hastrup suggests, "there need be no 'loss' from fieldwork to writing."[10]

I don't want my [published] writing to deny, mask, sacrifice, or replace notework, but to enliven it, to represent that temporal boundary[11] when you move from being still "in the writing": to the moment when you decide to allow something to "stand as writing," the moment when you find you are now willing to "only tell what you know."[12]

That moment – that decision about when to let writing stand as credible publishable ethnographic work – is governed by the ethnographic corporation.[13] It is one of its most strictly governed movements. My task:

- A text that breaks with the logic of the ethnographic corporation, in this case by *telling* something "way too soon."

- A text that writes against the separation of the ethnography and the memoir,[14] a text written between author and fieldnote-maker, the fallible, multivocal, inconsistent, imaginative individual who existed when the notes were written down, who has since outgrown herself, but who is also an outgrowth of the earlier figure, who maintains a limited substantive continuity as an organism and as a form of memory.

All ethnographic work is inherently in motion, unfinishable, partially true, in James Clifford's terms committed *and* incomplete.[15] These excerpts are merely "written-up" – transfigured into a piece of ethnography – in a form that foregrounds vividly that vital unfinishable condition.[16]

EPISODE #1: A TOURIST'S DANCE LESSON IN UBUD,[17] BALI, INDONESIA

12 May 1992: Finding a teacher   *Ubud, Bali*

I'd gone to the tourist information center earlier. The arrows directed me into a not-yet-finished room, but on a second try I found the counter. When I asked about a lesson, the woman behind first said Wednesday afternoon to go to the Puri;[18] I said I had less time. She then said this afternoon at 3:00. I wasn't sure she understood, but could get no further with her.

At 3pm, I appeared at the Puri. Three or so guys outside sold me a ticket first;[19] then got it that I wanted to find a teacher. One said "his friend" could do it, another said there were four or five ladies coming who could do it and to wait. I went into the Puri and sat on the pavilion where the *gamelan*[20] was set up. Little girls were playing on the others; soon they started to put on sarongs. I waited about half an hour. Another tourist, in long pants and printed *barong* shirt was waiting also. He didn't speak to me. After a while the little girls started to disappear into the inner courtyard. The guy waved me to follow them if I wanted to watch the rehearsal . . .

At around 4:30 a woman came over to me. . . . The woman gave me her card and we made a 7:30 date for Thursday. She described her location. Her rate was 10,000 [rupiah] an hour – what I'd heard was the going rate. She seemed surprised I wanted only one lesson, but she was willing. Her English was as good as the tourist workers' in general. Rina was her name.

I left elated, having accomplished my mission. Clearly, no set pattern for one-time dance lessons was yet standard tourist fare. Also, there were not yet tourist-oriented specialists – Rina was clearly also a local in-house teacher – the "real thing." Laura [a Balinese dance expert and longtime Ubud resident] looked at her card later and said she was an ASTI[21] graduate, but she didn't know her personally. The dance network is large enough for some anonymity.

14 May 1992: Lesson day   *Ubud, Bali*

I was up at 6:30am for my lesson. No one at the main desk knew of Jalan Suweta[22] so they told me to go down to the main street and ask. I was surprised to find that the street was right there at the Puri and #7 was only 100 meters off. I stopped for coffee and got *nasi*[23] as well (1500 rupiah), and got to the house at 7:35am.

Rina said hello, and that she thought I'd decided not to come since I was five minutes late. So much for Balinese time.[24] She asked where my sarong was – I apologized (even though she had said nothing about bringing one).

I took off my shoes and we started. The lesson went for almost an hour including a break. She gave me eight or so exercises and then we stopped. Then we got up and started through them again. She was very complimentary and wanted me to come back. She had had several students from the West and Japan. They usually came for one or two months. I was the only one-timer so far. She used English to count and knew some body part words. Most of her corrections were non-verbal – I felt like a tree with branches that she arranged.

Experiences with the technique:

- My triceps (just the shoulder cuff area) hurt intensely from elevating the arms.

- The *celedet* ("eyes looking") was completely foreign; I couldn't even monitor my own blinking. it seemed deeply unjust, giving up the freedom of the eyes.

- The joint relations of the arm were too complex to mirror or remember; mainly I grasped the principle of rising [symbol used] in the elbows [symbol used].

- The top of my hand and lower arm hurt from the hyperextending; I realize what a project it was to keep sending energy out of the palms in these moves; mine kept buckling into flexion.

- The lower body seemed not so foreign; the plié with hyperextension at least felt like a learnable technique and my legs didn't tire as quickly as my arms had.

- The hand postures were completely beyond me; I was able only to begin to master the thumb patterning of contract and stretch [symbols used] and see that the index fingers led the wrist flips. the amount of Bound/Quick[25] needed for these actions was extraordinary.

- In the arm pattern "*ngalut*" which is like a figure 8, I couldn't follow the trace form of the hands; it seemed odd to me that I couldn't; there was something about the hand situation that made the rotation unreadable to me.

- Walking with head, weight center, hand/rising in counter balance felt good; the strength of the step, the sway of the weight felt very feminine and centered; there is something serene and joyful about this step style – and humorous.

Ben[26] was saying that he liked Wayan's[27] technique at Swastika[28] of getting the tourists to dance. Then, Ben said, it was the tourists who looked ridiculous. I must have looked ridiculous also, but Rina was more understanding than Ben. I think Wayan is onto something. The complexity of the technique was made much more accessible to me as a student. I gained enormous respect in that hour, and some concrete awareness of my own specific limitations. Every tourist should be put through a lesson.... The local economy is resistant to short-term exchange, however. It is not the tourists who have cut themselves off....

EPISODE #2: A TOURIST DANCE LESSON IN DAVAO CITY,[29] PHILIPPINES

20 June 1992: The lesson   *Davao City, Philippines*

[This dance lesson occurred during the "audience participation" finale of a tourist dance performance I attended at the restaurant of Davao City's most ostentatious tourist hotel. I had been told by local acquaintances about regular dance shows at the Inn and had contacted the company director, Karen, a few days prior to this performance. Karen agreed to be interviewed by me on this occasion.]

The [hotel] was a disappointment from the start.... At the desk they were uncertain if there would be a [tourist/cultural dance] show, but called back and sent me on around. I passed the Vinta Lounge, Bagobo and T'boli meeting rooms,[30] none of which looked at all distinctive, and headed for a large open-air pavilion showing a buffet and a dance stage. It was empty, surrounded by an enormous lawn scattered with tables on a large beach. Since night was falling I couldn't see much of the grounds or take pictures.

The restaurant was empty. The waiter recognized my reservation and showed me to a corner table marked "reserved," which seemed absurd under the circumstances. They put on a Sousa-like march that somebody mocked in the background and took my order for some calamansi juice, suggesting I go to the appetizer section. I tried the *kinilaw*[31] and seaweed and some German potato salad, some macaroni salad, and a chicken marinade (?) – everything just as it should be. While eating, one of the waiters I questioned (they had nothing to do) said there were only forty-five guests (185 keys in the hotel).

I ate in an hour, wanting to be done by 7pm in case Karen[32] arrived on time....

Guests began to trickle in around 6:30pm. Some English-speaking men sat near me, one making a comment directly to me about the light and my reading. I smiled, half hoping to be drawn in and half hoping Karen would show and change their image of me abruptly. Karen did show, not until 7:45, but she did show. It had been raining thru dinner so my hopes weren't that high about seeing the show and I expected to find out from the desk that they'd cancelled. But I was in luck.

She arrived quietly, wearing a silk print outfit of the standard elite style. Her hair hung simply in a slight wave just past her chin. Her face was serious, she smoked and ordered brandy (I joined her). She seemed unamused by me and unhappy though not hostile. I decided almost immediately not to try to win her over, but to just speak directly from my heart. She struck me as a sober, engaged person of character, an interesting person, an individual who'd faced some dark hours independently. I decided she could judge me for herself and we'd know sooner than later if something might work out.

I started complaining about the lack of good floor space and she connected, understanding my need and sympathizing, saying I'd have to build one if I wanted something good and that it was too bad I hadn't come when she'd had her studio downtown. She later asked me if I might be interested in giving a seminar on interpretive dance, and I knew I was in by the enthusiasm in her voice and face. . . .

She told me a little about her dance company:

- Started in 1976 (4?) and continued thru the present, even while [karen and her husband] had lived in Cebu (1982–1990: NPA[33] threats and strikes forced them to flee and start over from zero).
- One mother/daughter pair was dancing, also a mother and son.
- The performers ranged from thirteen to thirty-eight years of age.
- The dancers live all around the area, making it difficult driving them all home.
- one just finished his nursing credential (all proud).
- They get fed two times each performance and rehearsal.
- They rehearse two times a week.

The Inn pays 2500 pesos for each performance because it is a regular deal.

- The hotel is now managed by . . . a Swiss/German couple who recently replaced the longtime manager who died.
- The [managers] will be leaving in July when Intercontinental pulls out of the hotel, leaving it entirely in local hands.
- Karen believes the new management won't renew her agreement, since they have less appreciation for Philippine culture than the foreigners did (a fact she found ironic).

Other performances ran for 4000 pesos:

- City Hall for VIP occasions.
- Family occasions.
- Christmas celebrations.

(Pearl Farm Beach Resort[34] has a tentative invitation for July for 4000 pesos.)

The choreography for the performance was based on Karen's own work and research (no Bayanihan[35] borrowing). She encouraged her dancers to be "natural" in their performance, showing the audience their own enjoyment – the effect was genuine; the Effort life[36] of the smiles of these dancers was Drive level and posturally supportive. The audience was won over by it, me included. Bali seemed very far away . . .

- The performance was a series of three suites:
  Muslim tribes[37]
  Maria Clara[38]
  Rural dances[39] (*tinikling*).
- Bayanihan "suite" format identical.
- Some costumes were original Bogobo.
- Length of dances was less than three minutes each.
- Visual appeal successful – no lag in scenes.
- Accompaniment: *Kulintag*[40] and combo on guitars.

At the end, audience members were invited to learn the *tinikling*[41] and I was first. They didn't stop until I'd missed, which took a long time. I was a hit – one of the men at the next table wanted to shake my hand and [another] said, "you really mastered it." Karen said to my partner "*dancer siya*"[42] by way of explanation, which was enough to make the whole trip worthwhile. I felt I'd passed a rite of initiation and had a rapport with the company that was an excellent start for the future.

27–9 May 1993   *Riverside, California*

These notes speak in different ways about two different lived interactions, two participatory arrival experiences, two varied instances of embodying knowledge upon a first encounter. The contrasting records provide an opportunity to theorize more fully the significance of embodied knowledge in the production of ethnographic relations, as well as in relation to the writing of ethnographic literature (the construction of monographs, the "writing-up"). As Judith Okley has observed, the latter activity is more than "pure cerebration" as it has sometimes been depicted.[43] Writing-up – and these episodes are [particularly exemplary] cases in point – necessarily involves some sort of recounting of bodily memory.[44]

Obviously, everything written since the entry from Davao [is now] a recounting of my body, triggered by the notes but not fully expressed in them. In making this piece of ethnography, I express [and will forget] even more of my lived experience of the episodes. [I thus proceed with] making the "written-up" [incurring] a loss of life. [This entry takes more out of my body than any other, being nothing other than remembered expression of the now absent field sites. My body is little more at present than a writing memory.]

To further clarify the contrasts in the episodes recorded:

(1) *As regards the knowledge embodied:*
In both Bali and Davao episodes, what was given for practice were patterns of bodily conduct that had transgenerational histories of regular articulation, patterns that had been made sense of in ways regarded as common by untold numbers of dancers in each culture. Yet, despite the common fact of their being body-oriented, the knowledge imparted in these patterns was of very different sorts. In the Balinese case the patterns were designed for an individual body,

preparing to dance in a highly codified movement technique, heroic character roles from epic sacred narratives; in the Davao case, the *tinikling* step pattern was designed to coordinate the unison locomotive action of relatively unmarked bodies dancing in partnership amongst a field of moving objects. What one needed to learn to achieve performative adequacy and understanding of each of these dance forms revealed very different aspects of self-awareness and lived experience.

In the Balinese case, the knowledge imparted and embodied was of several kinds. There were recipes for counterbalancing the dance of multiple exertions at play with one another throughout the dancer in performance.[45] The recipes in performance assumed the character of systemic proprioceptive feelings of pressure. They might be verbalized as "*Whiles*," "pushing (myself) up here" *while* "pressing (myself) back there," *while* "lifting this (area of myself)," *while* "flexing that (area of myself)," *while* "bending this," *while* "spreading that," *while* "tilting this," *while* "holding that," etc. These instructive impulses stabilized within the standing being the routing of intense pressing energy investments throughout the body. The effect was a stabilization that enabled the most extreme intensification of those investments sent simultaneously into different areas of the dancer.

The density of the bodily areas energized in this dance of "whiling" altered continually, necessitating a continuous reassessment of the exertions themselves. And, so, there were also maps of checkpoints where assessing and reminding oneself of one's investments and their effects could most easily ensure steady traffic among the forces travelling throughout the regions of the dancing figure. Many joints were marked for relational checking and rechecking in such a way, elbows *vis-à-vis* shoulders, knees *vis-à-vis* hip joints, but also other kinds of areas, such as palms, the inner surfaces of the fingers, and thumbs.

In addition to the proprioceptive systemic monitoring, there were also trail routes given for dancing actions. These paths traced ways through a microcosm delimited by the physical reach limits of the body. Tracking devices, ephemeral cairns-in-memory delineated intricately twisted journeys for the upper limbs and more straightforward passages for the lower limbs. The imaginary cairns of this invisible territory were more viscerally than visually locatable, learned in danced duplications of another dancer's travels, the imitative act reproducing in one's own movement-sphere both the map and the territory of the teacher.

To dance the steps of the *tinikling* – at least the single-step pattern that I was given to learn on the hotel's stage that rainy night – I needed knowledge about more than how to conduct myself inside some reachable imaginary microcosm. There was a partner to deal with less than an arm's length away, a man confronting me face to face, holding both of my hands, a body whose steps, grasp, smile, and gaze, were to be considered at my every step. The knowledge embodied in my dance was in part a knowledge of his dancing, his buoyancy, his timing, his agility, his finely measured touch. It was a knowledge that became embodied through my hands, which "listened" avidly to his in order to move with him, reading the energy patterning manifest there and following it, absorbing it, reflecting it as movement dispersed throughout myself, up my forearms and down into my feet, seeping from the distal ends towards my center of gravity. We had only a very small area of contact. We were not even joined with our whole hands, our thumbs were not intertwining, only our palms and fingers loosely rested inside one another, making this monitoring a fragile activity, requiring a sustained, though not powerful and not critical, attention. Yet, enhanced by visual readings of the movement, the hold was more than enough of a lifeline to produce a rhythmic merger in our steps. It was evident we both knew in our dancing how to read a partner's grasp for these sorts of messages. We went on together matching each other's stride and spring and hold under more and more stressful conditions when the dance progressed to faster and faster tempos. Innumerable minute adjustments of pressure, speed, and direction, were registered, "heard" and understood performatively through the linking of our hands. The knowledge embodied was of both a very general and a very individual sort.

Unlike the Balinese dancing lesson, I was not solely in command of my balance in this *tinikling* balancing act. In addition to my human partner guiding me manually through the steps, there were poles in motion under my feet, whose rhythmic meeting and parting continually undermined my stance, threatening my uprightness, now one way, now another, perpetually dislocating me, causing me to spring from foot to foot, now putting me alongside, now in between, now in between [other foot], now along another side of the poles. I was always changing feet, but not always changing pole sides, encountering in this way rapidly changing, though mesmerizingly repetitious, circumstances designed to catch me off-balance.

The *tinikling* is a dance made for learning about temptations, entrapments, and diversions, and about understanding cumulative disorientation. There is the temptation to keep worrying about the meeting of the poles, about their parting, to track them with one's eyes, and to decide upon where to step on the basis of this tracking, using a logic of relative placement destined to fail as the dance's tempo quickens. The knowledge embodied in the dancing is in some sense a knowledge of what *not* to do, how *not* to use the hands (to try to find a supportive base for one's own weight in one's partner's grasp – the hands must learn to join delicately in part to avoid throwing one's partner off-balance), how *not* to use the eyes (to watch the moving poles beneath; one's eyes are more helpful fixed on one's partner – having/being a partner is helpful in establishing a relatively safe haven for one's gaze), how *not* to use one's legs (as seekers of unoccupied territory; the legs must learn to ignore the dance of the poles, trusting the regularity of that movement, the legs need know only their own springing rhythm and when to step in place, when to step side – a knowledge unrelated to their orientation to the poles, they need to be thought through *less* than a naive observer might think), how *not* to use one's feet (to find solid ground; the feet must accustom themselves to exploring the air, striking the ground so as to become airborne).

With respect to all of the elements involved in the dance, knowledge of the *tinikling* step consisted of strategies of other-oriented tuning, tuning in and tuning out information arriving from sources beyond my own body. The conditions of the dance necessitated planning for the monitoring of and adjusting to other animate beings' behaviors.

To say simply that one has "embodied knowledge" doesn't take a reader very far in comprehending a specific lived experience of embodiment. These episodes of dancing produced radically different kinds of movement knowledge, about the self as an individual and as a partner, about stability and mobility in relation to balance. The skills developed in each case varied, their acquisition exposed different aspects of lived experience and personality. The embodiments themselves put the relationships developing on two different footings.

(2) *As regards the learning processes of embodiment:*
A basic difference in these episodes as recorded appears in the context of embodiment – in the markedly different learning situations themselves, which would seem to have determined to a great extent not only the patterns of instruction and the relationships that evolved out of them, but also the production of the notes as well. In Bali, my desire for instruction was overt and premeditated, and the dance event recorded was constructed at my request with a teacher who labeled herself as a professional conducting herself in a "lesson" situation. It took well over an hour. The notes reflect a rank novice's attempt to glean as much information as possible from the learning experience, mapping out an entry into a foreign technique, articulating the limits of my initial attempts to make bodily sense of the largely inaccessible forms.[46] In Davao, in contrast, I had had no intention of learning anything myself on the occasion recorded. I was persuaded to participate by a performer who himself had next to no stake in the teaching *persona* he briefly adopted for the sole purpose of getting me into the company's closing act. The "lesson" in the latter case was an impromptu, momentary, extremely task-specific occurrence, geared as much towards "embodiment" as the former episode had been towards "knowledge." The notes made, and particularly those unmade in words but kept in memory,[47] reflect less a novice's first encounter than a more deeply felt relation of familiarity to the process of embodiment that went on in the brief *tinikling* partnership, to its status as a subjectively unforgettable act of embodiment primarily because it entailed prior experience to such an extent that the knowledge acquired felt as if it had already been learned, before it had ever been encountered.

Yet, different as the two learning events may have been in these contextual respects, they nonetheless produced relationships that were remarkably similar in one aspect, an aspect that itself served to unfound, although only for brief instants, the contextual differences. I am referring here to the effects of the dancers' embodiment of "instructivity," their seemingly total engagement in that knowledge-imparting mode, and the temporary relationship of identity that this instructivity produced. In both cases, in Bali and in Davao, teaching/learning the dance required a number of acts of forgetting, momentary, but in their moments, all-encompassing.

These momentary relations may have been magnified by the fact that in both episodes linguistic instruction played a very limited role in the learning process, with only a few aspects of the dance translated into speech terms and exchanged along linguistic lines. Rina used language mainly for counting, to keep the exercises moving along at an even tempo and to mark the routes of the arm and hand gestures at given temporal intervals. She would say "one, *two, three, four,*" as she performed some action and would look at me on the stressed numbers so as to cue me to look at her and where she was as she paused in her dancing to say these numbers. Or, she would count as she guided me through a movement phrase, stopping my limbs on a certain count so I could feel the relationships before progressing. It was by means of these rearranging actions that I began to sense the recipes and checkpoints noted above. Unlike my partner in the *tinikling*, there was no fragility in Rina's handwork. Her adjustments were firmly determined, sculpted with a couturier's precision around the bony landmarks she was manipulating. The power I felt contained within her hands was greater than that which lay within my arms, or within my entire ribcage. It was an easy matter to yield to her replacements and find a wealth of explanatory information embodied in them. The verbal counts became like proper names for moments in the dancing that were primarily tactually defined, so that a certain pose would "be" *the* "one" of an eight-count progression. This crude accounting function was the main purpose served by language in the lesson, except for the announcement of body parts in English that served as the titles of the exercises themselves. The rest of the time, I imitated, observed contrasting demonstrations, and took tactile corrections.

Rina's relation with me was produced mainly in terms of what she could feel and see about my imitativeness, and my adjustability once informed of a modification. Her knowledge of me was largely focused on observing how consistently I re-incorporated corrections after her instruction, how capable I was of taking one of her suggestions "to heart" and making a habit of it in my practicing for the remainder of the lesson. The pace of our exchange of knowledge was not lost on her. She told me in a definitive tone near the close of the lesson that I needed "one month" of practice and would then be dancing on a par with advanced performers. By the break in the lesson, she had me demonstrating spine stretches from "modern dance technique," and she was following along, commenting in movement (demonstrating the contrasts) on the absence of hyperextension in the lower spine, which was itself essential in the Balinese style of dance.[48] The time allotted for the lesson cut short this exchange, but the exercises traded back and forth, however cursorily, began to develop a shared activity sphere for Rina and me, a basis for relating to one another marked mainly by body parts and their articulations, unidentified, *at least performatively*, as anything save anatomically specific.

My *tinikling* partner in Davao, likewise, used next to no language in our "lesson." He first positioned me between the not yet moving poles, and then demonstrated the three weight-shifting moves of the step pattern (one side, two in place, always alternating feet). If this procedure was accompanied by some sort of spoken elaboration, it was lost on me in my fixation on the stepping demonstration that was occurring in relation to the poles. As I was being led reluctantly up to the performance space, I had reasoned to myself that, if I were to get through this surprise exhibition gracefully at all, I would have to imitate my partner's dancing carefully and stay in synchrony with him. As the poles began to move and we began to dance, I followed my partner without mishap. All I heard him say after the dance began, as we were springing in and out amongst the poles, me gradually loosening what I soon realized was an inappropriately firm grip on his hands, and spending my energy rising spinally up "off of" my legs, were the words, "higher," and "faster." He said them repeatedly, more and more breathlessly, as the pace of the poles' movements accelerated. I didn't understand the reason for these utterances at all initially, didn't even register them as being directed at me, until they had been repeated more than once, I was so completely absorbed by what I was learning about the game implicit in the *tinikling* form, intrigued to find it was ultimately more about staying light in one's weight center than about aiming accurately into the ground with one's feet, and that the lightness of the grasp seemed the final test of one's mastery. Everything seemed to be going along fine; I had slipped out of "learning mode." With a feeling of mild shock at the recognition that I was being addressed and advised by these terms, I eventually took the verbal cues to mean that I should lift my feet "higher" off the ground as I danced, which made the stepping all the more staccato in its phrasing, closer to *petit jeté* than to minimal jogging, and that I should expect to feel a "faster" tempo along with him. He must have repeated the words a dozen times each, his tone becoming more insistent each time, which puzzled me because I could feel his tempo wasn't changing. Aside from these ambiguous commands, however, all of his contributions to the exchange were made through movement. In movement, he was not ambiguous, setting himself up as a behavioral example cuing me both through his hands and by exaggerating the initiations of his steps for me to see. The clarity of this gesturing only increased as the dance progressed, so that he continuously re-enabled me to follow him as long as I was managing to hold up my end of the performance. By its end, the performance had produced an understanding between us, a very limited understanding, tested in co-action, that referred to a few isolated facts about body parts and articulations, how eyes and feet might be connected, how handshakes and jumps coordinated, how temporal stress could be mediated, how the poles could be avoided.

There may have been little ability to resort to verbal translation in each case, since both instructors spoke only limited English, and I more limited Indonesian and Filipino, but, more to the point, there was even less motivation. We dealt with "how to go on," how to keep effecting embodiment, through observation, movement, and touch. What these expert dancers shared, in my experience, despite their different investments in the instructive scenarios, was an immediate responsiveness in the act of registering my apprehension of their dance. When I was performing their material, they produced physical affirmations by *returning to the dance.*

(3) *As regards the consequences of the embodiment:*

"Doing fieldwork exposes you to the judgments of others." Jean Jackson (1990).[49]

The consequences of these episodes of embodiment have yet to fully manifest. Rina, after our lesson, simply invited me to study further, expressing regret that my stay was so short. I have practiced her exercises regularly since the lesson and wonder what progress she will note upon my return. Karen, after the show, invited me back to her home, where we spoke for a while as her company ate supper. A few days later, I was invited to be a guest at a resort she owned and operated. When I left Davao for Manila, she put me in touch with her friends there in the dance world, some of the leading figures in the country. It would be impossible to say what the precise contribution of the episode may have been in establishing the beginning of a rapport that crossed cultural boundaries in such a significant way for my research. My having made a public spectacle of myself may be viewed as merely a fortuitous start in a chain of events that provided only an initial opening for a conversation that quickly acquired a momentum of its own. It may have been the magnification produced by the spectacle context more than the successful act of embodiment in and of itself that influenced the connection and identified me simply as a "dancer" for Karen. In any case, however, the dancing produced a relationship that included a highly specific common experience.

Learning how to embody new forms of movement in cross-cultural encounters exposes in a highly specific way some of one's most personal judgments to others, and in this respect can accelerate a certain kind of body-based intimacy in the production of ethnographic relationships. Rina witnessed how I knew to tilt my pelvis, how unused I was to shifting my gaze without blinking, how difficult it was for me to keep my shoulders lifted up around my ears and to keep my knees bent to their maximum flexion. My partner in Davao learned how well acquainted I seemed to be with the kind of footwork he performed, how my breathing patterns changed when fatigued, how my hands shook and perspired under stress. Regardless of the differences in the knowledge embodied in both episodes, the work done established a personal connection whose immediacy and mutuality was less open to question than any I managed to establish in other situations. The episodes stand out in my experience in this regard. A professed interest in embodying knowledge, regardless of the success or failure of the attempt, is more likely to expose one's self in an engaging way in cross-cultural encounters than perhaps any other form of interaction.

I am afield. Note: dancing.   (Dancerly writing "down")
I am afield note-dancing.   (Writerly writing "down")
I am a field notedancing.   (Dance experience)
I am a fieldnote dancing.   (Writing "up")

14–24 August 1993   *Davao City, Philippines*[50]

Once again in Davao, I give the last word to a site of embodiment. It is a word that has taken more than one year's time and more than 30,000 miles travelled to produce. The production of ethnographic literature typically (or at least in classic examples) relies upon such transcontinental, temporally extended "choreography." These notes have overscored that corporeal patterning by registering the necessary movements and placements (sites) of the text's composition. Solo (or pseudo-soloist) moves, global pathways, landings among diverse cultural sites, acts of embodiment, recollection, and text-making, all form vital elements of an ethnographer's corporeal score, an existential dance of fancy leaps, exotic gestures, and bizarre positionings.

In Riverside, I planned to devote this final "made in Southeast Asia" section to "theory," theorizing about the making of ethnographic literature and the composing of the "written-up," about the geopolitics of the "mono" in monographic writing.[51] This privileged "final" writing, which drives the ethnographic enterprise, entails a loss of life (gained at field sites), the choreography of which can be better understood once it is recognized as precisely that, as a "corpo-reality" in which lived experience is transformed into expression written out through acts of disembodiment. Supported, influenced, galvanized and disciplined by field notes, recollected experience is dismembered as it is articulated linguistically in the construction of the work of literature.[52] It was to this ultimate phase of text production that I meant to turn, to question the classical corporeal score of ethnography and its use of recollection in conjunction with the removal of the ethnographer's body from the field site. The present composition has gone literally to great lengths in this final entry to deviate from the classical score, to release memory from all but its most vital role in writing up, to produce itself from a different existential patterning, the theoretical benefits of which I discuss below.

Being in Davao, however, I realize that this plan for theory-making was a more site-specific plan than I had realized in Riverside. Such a theoretical discussion would have been inconceivable here. The tropical climate alone would have pre-empted it, as Nietzsche might have expected.[53] I still attempt to execute the plan, but I could never have envisioned it. It is by virtue of memory alone that I make here what I should in theory make nowhere else. It is theory here that must now be simply recollected, all associated disadvantages included. It is the field site that has the benefit of being at hand. That was the plan. And the plan has been affected by the experience I am now living, inevitably, predictably affected. Davao will have a last word, of mine, of its own.

Concerning the "choreography" of ethnographic production, this writing has been composed so as to de-simplify what I have termed the classical ethnographic score. The score designates a largely mythical practice, but is still ideologically and pedagogically influential within the discipline.[54] The classical production involves the close integration of two movement patterns: (1) a reversible move of the ethnographer's body of the greatest imaginable/feasibly constructible magnitude:

> home office – field site – home office.

This trans-cultural re-positioning is synchronized with (2) the action sequence of:

> research conceptualization – participant/observation (embodiment/notework) – writing-up.

The dual movement processes create an arrangement in which acts of embodying cultural knowledge (gathering culturally novel forms of lived experience) are positioned in complementary geographic and historical distribution with reading and writing-"up" – literary activity. "Writing-up" in particular occurs at a site where only memory work (not ongoing lived experience) regarding the field site makes a bodily contribution to the most literary phase of text-making.[55] The ethnographer's memory and otherwise physical figure are thus dissociated in the classical score as these two aspects of the self are sequenced in the process of text-making. As Kirsten Hastrup has noted, fieldwork experience becomes memory before it becomes text.[56]

The bodily dissociation of the ethnographer parallels a similar site-related process of dissociation as well, as the field site becomes opposed to the home office with respect to the relative absence and presence of analytic work and writing of a literary calibre. The alterity of the field site can thus be inaccurately enhanced, the "Field" inappropriately reified as a non-literary place where embodied knowledge of other sorts is predominant. Writing-"up" at a designated "field" site can thus act also as a writing "against," against the splitting of the writer's person sequentially into simply memory and simply body, and against the "de-literacizing" of the written site.

The imposed dichotomy of home/field is an arbitrary projection, a by-product inherent in the composition of the classical score. The effect is akin to the by-product inherent in the monographic format resisted by this polygraphic notework. The "*mono*-graph" creates an effect of *authorial* (versus personal) omnipresence (or unipresence), an author whose *writerly* faculty is independent of the site it writes about, and, in fact, in some cases insistent on being dissociated from it.[57] This effect is countered in the monograph genre only via the relatively weak strategy of adopting an "ethnographic past" tense and/or providing notes on the research process in supplementary material. The monographic style denies the significance of the processual development of authorial consciousness and assigns the home office the exclusive role of authorial residence. Monographic texts thus relinquish or repress what Derrida has termed the "spacing" of the text,[58] the textual presentation (the literary representation) of the gaps and movements involved in the writing experience itself, which in ethnographic work are geographically and geopolitically marked (and thus salient). A monographic text does not expose inherent displacement(s) that affect and delimit its realm(s) of analytic presence. Unlike the present entries, which are the substance of an abbreviated monograph stripped of its rhetorical omnipresence, monographic writing pretends to be a homogeneous text, the performative writerly element acknowledging no voids, no spacing, no contradictions, no alternation of positions with regard to the making of the narrative.

Such are the distortions inherent in the classical style of ethnographic production. It designates none of its own distance to the *writing* body no longer living in the field. Note forms, in contrast, privilege heterogeneity – both of the sites of production and of the authorial self ("I am afield note-dancing").

In loosening the coordination of traveling and writing-up, I insert a dislodgement in the classical ethnographic patterning. By writing in the space of that dislodgement I am making room for questions about how relationships between the speech acts of cultural anthropology (now dominated by its ethnographic literature) and its episodes of cross-cultural meaning-making congeal, crystallize, and develop.

The alterations in this corporeal score have been designed so the field sites in this composition are not restricted to non-literary episodes of embodying knowledge and intermediate, substandard acts of inscription/denotation. What has been vital to the production of this text, rather than any standardized corporeal patterning or movement sequence, has been its insistence on a certain kind of writerly body in motion, a body that participates and is affected by other bodies,[59] that learns, remembers and forgets others, a body that de-corporates its memory on the move. Ethnographic work requires such a traveling body, always shifting its sites of lived experience, visiting diverse cultural locations, carefully aiming and timing its displacements and replacements so as to draw connections in between them.[60]

Which brings me to what is other than my memory, to what interferes with my recollection, to what insists on being written today.

[*Readers be advised: the spacing here is particularly disjunctive*]

In Davao, I go out daily walking the streets alone. Such is the behavior of an orphan who can't afford even jeepney fare, but it is an unchangeable habit nonetheless. I pass by San Pedro Street, Legaspi Street, and Bonifacio Street on my way to and from Magallenes, the street where I live. Spanish is well represented on the city plan. Even though official maps have been revised to make use of postcolonial heroes, force of spoken habit still works in the first conqueror's favor.

Since my return to Davao, I have been haunted on these streets. This is not a surprising occurrence for someone odd enough to go around alone. The local *spiritu* are sometimes called "white ladies" – very tall female supernatural figures who wear long flowing white gowns and have long flowing hair. They look like me. I have even been taken for such ghosts on occasion.

They are souls not yet at rest who require the further prayers of the living, who may invade the spaces of the living unpredictably, appearing inside cars or gardens or homes or in unlit places out in the open after dark (the *are* like me). They terrify their witnesses. They discourage solitary activity.

My ghost, however, is no white lady, no human figure at all. It appears in the form of a concept. It is the brainchild of Arjun Appadurai's overly sanitary model of global cultural flow and disjuncture,[61] of Kirsten Hastrup's concept of violent cultural intrusion[62] and of Gayatri Spivak's concept of the postcolonial wound.[63] I am haunted here in Davao by a certain notion of "aperture" or, rather, of "aperture-ing" that I observe manifesting on a cultural scale. Like a ghost, it seems invisible to others. It pursues me relentlessly, at every step and every turn. It has pursued me all the way from Irvine, California.

I go out onto the street and I see on the glass doors of businesses signs that read, "OPEN" (not the Visayan "*bukas*"). I feel depressed. I look along the street and I see the English signs: "Kerosene Sold Here," "Dormitory Facilities Available," "Hairdresser: Aesthetic and Facial Care," "New Victory Dental Supply." I fight a growing panic edged with anger. The swimming pool at the Apo View Hotel[64] has a sign: "Rules and Regulations"; all nine are listed in English. Disappointment deepens as I read easily down the list. When I look among the newspapers pinned up for sale on the wooden cabinets that line the uneven sidewalks of the city's main avenues, I read a labyrinth of headlines: "Drug pusher gunned down," "Dureza implicated in Palo murder-rape case?" "Massacre kills 3, hurts one person," "Flashflood leaves 4 dead, scores homeless, 3 bridges down." Only a few newspapers are not in English.

Each word of English stings me. I see each as an aperture, a minute tear in the local symbolic fabric. Every "Sorry," every, "Welcome," every "Entrance," every "Free Delivery," every "Please Come In," sets off a transnational alarm. Another unguarded neo-colonial opening awaiting English-speaking abuse, another symbolic mistake. Each sign hurts, becoming more cause for regret. Every English word I see appears injurious, and there are millions of them, all dangerous invitations for foreign consumption in foreigners' terms. The streets I walk bleed uncontrollably from the millions of grams of English there inscribed. The city has become like one of its own miraculous *santos*; its stigmata cover every surface. They even hang in the air, spoken signs gushing their cultural blood. Innumerable wounds are rendered daily, hourly, by the second. I am covered in blood. I do not want to make any more of these signs.

When the children on the street call out to me, "Good afternoon," "Hello," "Where are you going?" I choke on my English replies they call forth, unable to prevent this visceral response. I gag at the thought of being an unwitting aperturist. I smile, saying nothing, closing off the verbal exchange, passing out of earshot with just a facial gesture of goodwill and gratitude instead. I do not want to abandon Davao consumed by some unearned guilt. I do not want to leave the city to multinational forces of "development" and their in-house collaborators, or to all those who capitalize on limiting international interactions to such easily denigrated encounters, where the foreigners are always "ugly" foreigners with always all of the same flaws. But witnessing the bleeding hurts me also now.

Claude Lévi-Strauss once characterized anthropological fieldwork as a kind of war, as essentially war-like in its opening of virginal lines of communication between peoples and cultures, even when that communication was not practiced under the banner of colonial or missionary oppression.[65] The definition seems somewhat self-imposing when applied to Davao, where most of the residents encountered by an incoming First World professional are themselves members of transnational families, one or more in the immediate family residing abroad. Davao is already millions of *grams* away from any kind of "first contact" scenario, any essential opening of communication. The traces of such events are antique artifacts, family heirlooms – material for archaeologists and historians.

The situation of Davao pre-empts any Lévi-Straussian confrontation or opening of anything that might be construed as "virginal." How could such apertures be made at a site already so overloaded with leaking figures, a site where it is possible to choreograph an ethnographic practice situated entirely within the openings of others, where the field is less an unopened land than an open market, a honeycomb of long-established apertures. How does one wage the "anthropological war" with the wife of the Commissioner of the San Francisco Airport (also the daughter of the city's "Grand Hotel" owner)? or with the mother of a Chicago psychiatrist (also a founding member of several of the city's most active women's organizations)? or a former AFS exchange student to Pasadena (also a kidnapping victim of local Islamic separatist terrorists)? or the father of a "neo-ethnic" choreographer who holds an MFA from Ohio State University (also a resident of Davao since the era of pre-World War II Japanese-run abaca plantations)?

The scenario of ethnography as primary aperture-ing leaves unconsidered the contemporary predicament of sites where trans-cultural communicative openings are highly unoriginal, well-practiced, and generally gilded in layers of polysemic ambiguity. "English" typically works as a cloaking device, serving to confuse while it lures a foreign speaker into an apparent aperture – but that discussion is for another essay. I am still covered in cultural blood. It precludes text-making enterprises that achieve anything other than the creation of novel openings, or perhaps the enlargement of existing opened wounds – no possibility of a writing that might work to seal-off or plug existing openings, no writing of closure or limited access. It denies writing that reveals its own inevitable half-telling-ness,[66] its own "spacing."

These note entries seek to ensure the visibility of their own unfoldings and foreclosures, reflecting the further possibilities for interpretation and invention still available in subsequent site-specific compositions. The gaps in between the dates of writing make openings – voids that are not apertures but closures to the flow of information, closures of the writer's presence, announcing the limits of the view, the turnings of the gaze. They make the steps of composition clearer as well as the no-man's land between the steps. They make the ruptures in the ethnographic process literary realities.

Davao was and is my field site. I remember it, but don't *simply* remember it. Since I live in it now, it re-members me as well. It is not simply a *position* in a process of writing for some theoretical interest, assumed to be of universal relevance or origin. And, it is I who adopt positions here, theoretical and otherwise. It is I who will have to leave them when I leave this place, and discontinue the stories following from them, theoretical and otherwise, that I might, other-wise, have told.

[*Readers are invited to return to the opening Irvine entry to conclude their reading.*]

NOTES

1   *The notes in this chapter have not been written at the date of the entry. They have been added subsequently in multiple writings. The first entry, 12 April 1993, which represents an oral presentation made at the Humanities Research Institute from detailed notes, has been edited by means of both omission and recombination. Subsequent entries, with the exception of the final entry (see note 50), have been edited only by means of omission. Brackets [ ] are used in the text to indicate information added to the entry after its writing date.*

2   *"Work" on this occasion, referred to my body as well as to the fieldnotes that had been distributed to the group. The "performative mode" is defined by Peggy Phelan as "a writerly present that corresponds with the present invigorated by the performative now." See Phelan, this volume. In the performative mode, as I employ the term, the process of the writing experience remains vital to the reading of the text, including both reader and writing author in the text's foundational discursive development.*

3   *Anthropologist Dan Rose, in "Ethnography as a Form of Life" (1993, 216), argues that the standard methodological scenario asserted in anthropological training – which constrains the relations developed in the field – depicts a radically fractured ethnographic activity sequence in which the reading and "serious" (publishing-oriented) writing are (falsely) separated out from the fieldworking phase, denying the fact that fieldworkers actually do inhabit a writerly present while on site. Research projects that challenge this mythic sequence of reading, fieldworking, and ("real") writing, generate a greater awareness of cross-cultural inquiry as lived experience by what James Clifford, in* Writing Culture *(1986, 13), has termed a specification of its discourse. Research representing in relatively graphic detail its own immediate relations of production exposes the initial rendering of the symbolic aperture out of which information from the site is flowing, as well as the boundaries across which it is moving (field/home; other/West; private/public; personal/professional; individual/institutional, etc.).*

4   *Michel de Certeau, in* The Writing of History *(1988, 72–7), argues that the creation of a "document" is both a founding gesture for the discipline of history and a means of exiling whatever it is that becomes "the documented" from the sphere of practice, in order to secure its status as an object of knowledge. The production, study, and reproduction of "documents" involves an inherently hegemonic operation by which state-level power structures reify, institutionalize, and make knowable through acts of (mis)representation objects of intellectual inquiry. Saying "no" to the document in this case involves retreating from the production of a text that would reduce the people involved to mere objects of anthropological inquiry, either by making comprehensive knowledge claims about their practices or by formulating conclusive arguments about their cultural predicament. See also Phelan, this volume.*

5   *On the capacity of failure to establish aperture, see Heidi Gilpin (1993), "Failure,*

Repetition, Amputation, and Disappearance," and "Static and Uncertain Bodies." On
the processual nature of ethnography, see Judith Okley, Anthropology and
Autobiography (1993); see also Simon Ottenberg's discussion of fieldnotes as
reflections of the growth process of ethnography in Fieldnotes (1990, 139–60).

6   See Ness (1992), Body, Movement, and Culture.

7   The phrase was coined by J. Fabian to distinguish the work of site-specific note-taking
from the construction of published monographs (see Fabian as cited in Okley 1993, 3).
Notework is generally viewed as a relatively "low" form of writing, considered more
chaotic, less reliable, more transparent, less analytical, more subjective, less
thoughtfully conceived, overly rigorous, confined to descriptive detail, impulsive,
compulsive, conceptually incomplete. The contradictory characteristics attributed to
notework indicate the intimacy of its role in ethnographic research, which may cause
it to vary greatly from project to project, from site to site, and from researcher to
researcher. In this regard, notework is a particularly salient index of the heterogeneity
of ethnographic research.

8   See Clifford (1986, 13). Clifford argues that this exclusionary tactic was employed in
pre-1960s classical ethnographies in order to preclude too close a connection
between "authorial style and the reality represented." The omission of the author's
subjectivity served to establish other referents in the text as objectively
representable.

9   A difference noted by Mary Russo, remarks made in discussion session, Irvine, 5 April
1993.

10   See Kirsten Hastrup, "Writing Ethnography; State of the Art" (1992, 117). What is not
lost in the presentation of the note material per se, Hastrup argues, is its influence
on a fieldworker's "form of life," its contribution to the performance of cross-cultural
interactions while on site, what Jean-Paul Dumont in Visayan Vignettes (1992, 5),
refers to as "the living texture of social life." What is saved and made into print is the
specificity of the fieldworkers' author function that continually intervenes in the field
research. Departing from Hastrup, however, what is saved in this particular instance
of writing as well is something saved from linguistic representation altogether,
something saved from becoming a part of the writing-up. What is not lost is an array
of memories of lived experience that will remain partially embodied precisely because
they will never be completely written-up and/or down. They will not be fully expressed
as words on a page, the complete expression of which would require a disembodiment
of the lived experience, an absolute forgetting. Rather, some memory will remain as
known by heart, still inhabiting and affecting my body, still potentially dynamically
corporeal. Most, however, will be given to the text.

11   Remarks made by Mary Russo in discussion session, Irvine, 5 April 1993. Jean
Jackson in Fieldnotes (1990, 14), has also characterized fieldnotes as being
threshold-like or liminal, situating them between memory and publication, still en

route *from an internal and other-cultural state. As regards the potential masking effects of published writing Jean-Paul Dumont (1992, 2–3), has also noted the tendency of anthropologists to mask the emergent aspects of their own writing process for the sake of a "fallacious coherence" in their published work, arguing that "the apparent coherence of an ethnographic situation is always the result of a writing, not to say rhetorical, effort, achieved at the cost* of doing violence to the evidence" *(my emphasis).*

12   *James Clifford (1986, 9), quoting a Cree hunter in Montreal describing his frame of mind when deciding to testify in court concerning the fate of his hunting lands in the new James Bay hydroelectric scheme.*

13   *"Corporation," as used here refers to the institutionally sanctioned and sponsored frameworks – legal–rational cultural formations – that support and contain ethnographic inquiry in the U.S. See Dan Rose (1993), "Ethnography as a Form of Life," for an extended discussion of the ethnographic corporation.*

14   *As Eric Bruner (1993) has recently argued in the introduction of* Anthropology and Literature, *the separation of the memoir from the ethnography creates a false dichotomy that distorts the lived experience of fieldwork when it is rendered into textual form. Uniting the memoir and the ethnography in published accounts restores a lost degree of accuracy to the memory work generating cross-cultural representation. It also serves as a critique of the still powerful realist manner of ethnographic discourse that requires a sharp separation between subject and object in order to retain an authoritative narrative voice. As Okley (1993) in* Anthropology and Autobiography *has suggested, strategies that insert personal narrative or employ other autobiographical techniques in the "writing-up" phase of ethnographic work can assist persuasively in this critique insofar as they serve to insist on a critical scrutiny of the ethnographer's position with respect to its admission of marginalized individuality (its construction of an authorial "I" that will not make a claim to generalizations within a dominant discourse, but will say "in my experience"; an I that is open to a critique of being non-representative), and on the given narrative as being one of many possible renditions of the represented collective lived experience engaged in by the fieldworker. Such effects encourage anthropological readerships to acknowledge their involvement in an enterprise that works to create or maintain apertures through which information flows out of "other" cultures into the West.*

15   *See Clifford (1986, 7). See also Jean-Paul Dumont (1992, 2), who has characterized anthropological writings as evoking realities that are always localized, partial, and ephemeral.*

16   *"Writing-up" – the making of ethnographic literature – can produce various transformations. Among those mentioned in essays on the subject are: articulating a general validity beyond the moment of recorded events, cultivating an engaged clarity, allowing the reality that begins to emerge during fieldwork to take shape in*

writing, recounting specific ways in which the ethnographer learned about the culture experienced, recognizing openly writing's own overdeterminedness by forces ultimately beyond the control of either an author or an interpretive community, making the familiar strange and the exotic quotidian, recognizing writing's own marginal situation between powerful systems of meaning.

17 *Ubud, located inland about an hour's drive from the tourist beaches near Bali's capital city, Denpasar, is the principal site of Balinese art tourism, particularly for the performing arts. Tourists seeking a cultural/ethnic experience are attracted to Ubud and its surrounding* desa *(village-level communities) to attend dance and music performances, and to visit the galleries and studios of expert painters, sculptors, and carvers. Ubud has been a tourist destination for decades. It can currently accommodate a range of tourist clientele, from student travelers to international celebrities.*

18 *"Puri" means palace. The puri grounds in Ubud included a large courtyard surrounded by several pavilions where nightly dance performances were staged. During the afternoons, several days a week, schoolchildren learned Balinese dances there as well.*

19 *The ticket sold was for that evening's tourist performance of traditional Balinese dance.*

20 *A* gamelan *is a traditional Balinese gong orchestra. Classical Balinese dance is typically accompanied by* gamelan *music.*

21 *ASTI (Akademi Seni Tari Indonesia – Academy of Indonesian Dance Art), renamed STSI (Sekolah Tinggi Seni Indonesia – School of Indonesian Fine Art) in 1992, is Bali's state academy of the performing arts. The school has acquired a reputation for excellence in technical training of performing artists over the course of the last few decades under the leadership of I Made Bandem, a senior scholar of Balinese performance studies and a world-class master of Balinese dance theater. While it is still possible for students of Balinese classical dance to study with local masters at a variety of* desa *who have no connection with the academy, STSI is currently the predominant site of native dance training at the expert level in Bali. The success of the academy is having a significant impact on the dance arts of Bali, since the style of dance employed there is taught to students coming from all over the island, who learn it and bring it back to their* desa, *where it supplants the local style. Rina's ASTI certification indicated that she belonged to an accredited circle of Balinese dance experts.*

22 *Jalan Suweta or "Suweta Street" was Rina's address.*

23 *"Nasi goreng" is a typical breakfast dish of fried rice and vegetables.*

24 *My acquaintances in Bali jokingly used the phrase "Balinese time" to refer to what was assumed to be a standard practice of announcing that a given future event was* going to begin at a certain time and then expecting that the event would actually begin much later than the time indicated.

25   These terms are taken from the technical vocabulary of the Effort model of Laban Movement Analysis (see Dell (1970), A Primer for Movement Description, Laban and Lawrence (1974), Effort, and Bartenieff (1980), Body Movement; Coping with the Environment). "Bound" refers to the apparent quality of controlling the flow of movement through the body (as opposed to a visible intent to release that movement flow out and beyond the body's limits). "Quick" refers to the apparent quality of acceleration of the movement impulse, a condensation of the dynamic of duration.

26   Ben was a US scholar in Bali researching a book on performance.

27   Wayan was a renowned master of classical Balinese dance and former teacher of Ben.

28   A tourist establishment in Bali staging regular shows of Balinese dance.

29   Davao City, the principal port of Mindanao Island, is currently in the formative stages of developing a tourism industry. The province was targeted by the nation's Department of Tourism as a top priority development site shortly after the Aquino administration came to power. While the site has no history of tourism, it has been compared to Bali by tourism officials in terms of its potential as a destination, given its ethnic diversity and scenic beauty. The advent of a tourist economy is apparent in Davao in several respects: the appearance of professionally designed postcards portraying newly opened natural reserves and cultural sites, the construction of a number of pensions, hotels, and resorts, the improvement of the provincial airport (planned to become an international port of entry), and the employment by the larger resorts and civic organizations of dance companies who perform an array of traditional dances from the region on a fairly regular basis. The tourist dance economy of Davao is at a much earlier stage of development than is that of Ubud, and its dance forms are drawn from a relatively wide array of cultural communities and practices. Moreover, there is no provincial equivalent of the STSI academy of Bali. Dances are taught and practiced at private homes, family-operated studios/schools, and in physical education programs from primary grades through college.

30   "Vinta" is a sailing vessel traditionally used by Islamic peoples inhabiting the coastal areas of the southern Philippines. "Bagobo" and "T'boli" are two of the most well-known non-Islamic, non-Christian cultural communities of Mindanao, whose textile work is widely admired throughout the nation.

31   White fish marinated in coconut milk, vinegar, garlic, and onion.

32   The company choreographer and artistic director.

33   The New People's Army is the armed wing of the Communist Party of the Philippines.

34   Located on nearby Samal Island, Pearl Farm Beach Resort is the area's most luxurious resort destination. Originally an actual pearl farm and marine biology station, the

resort recently re-opened in 1992 after having been completely remodeled to accommodate first-class European tourists.

35 *The Bayanihan dance company is one of the Philippines' most famous internationally touring ensembles, presenting stylized renditions of the traditional dances of the Philippines to audiences all over the world. Karen had worked extensively with the company's artistic directors and was fully capable of creating duplicates of the Bayanihan performances.*

36 *"Effort" is used here as a technical term from the Effort model of Laban Movement Analysis (see Dell (1970); Laban and Lawrence (1974); and Bartenieff (1980), as previously cited). Defined as, "a mover's attitude toward investing their energy in movement," Effort qualities are theorized as being the visible manifestations of four general dynamic factors (Time, Space, Weight, and Flow) that comprise all movement events, but only become apparent as qualities when a movement process engages a modification of one or more of them. When three factors are simultaneously engaged in a movement process, a "Drive" level of Effort investment is observable.*

37 *"Muslim" is a shorthand classifier for choreography modelled on the dance practices of the Islamic ethnic groups of the southern Philippines. The costumes, musical accompaniment, and choreography of these dances is markedly different from those of non-Islamic Philippine groups. Dances may include the use of ornamental fans, malong textiles, and bamboo poles, over and amongst which the dancers process.*

38 *"Maria Clara" is a shorthand term referring to the relatively formal, Hispanic social dance practices of lowland communities, associated with elite Christian culture. "Maria Clara" refers to a specific woman's costume of Hispanic design.*

39 *"Rural dances" refers to choreography modelled on the relatively informal dance practices of lowland Philippine communities, associated with laborer and peasant classes. Dances include fiesta-oriented game events and social partner dances.*

40 *The kulintang is a gong ensemble found throughout the southern Philippines. It generally consists of one or several large hanging gongs, a drum, and an array of eight smaller gongs set horizontally in a single line on a wooden frame.*

41 *The tinikling is a widely practiced, well-known, social game/dance performed by rural lowland Christian Visayan communities at fiesta time and on other special occasions (see Alejandro (1972), Sayaw Silingan; Fajardo (1979), Visayan Folk Dances, and Aquino (1983), Philippine Folk Dances). The tinikling involves a dancer stepping into and out of mildly treacherous temporary spaces created and collapsed by two other players' continuously moving a pair of parallel bamboo poles towards and away from one another in a rhythmic sequence. The effect is vaguely similar to jumping double ropes. See Gregoria Baty-Smith (1990) for a detailed analysis of the dance form.*

42 *"She [or he] is a dancer."*

43   *Okley (1993, 16), cites Fardon in* Localizing Strategies *(1990, 3), in this regard.*

44   *Okley (1993, 16), argues that the immersion of the anthropologist for an extended period of time in another culture results in a life experience that involves the whole being, and which subsequently requires the whole being's participation in making sense of recorded material. In semiotic terms, the symbolic reality of the fieldwork ensures that the iconic capacity of the record – its descriptive effectiveness – however detailed, will never exhaust completely its dicent indexical aspect. Given that the notes represent symbols, there will always be more to recollect.*

45   *This aspect of Balinese classical dance technique has been theorized in terms of its epistemological salience by Gregory Bateson (1972) in his analysis of what he termed the Balinese "steady-state" cultural temperament in the essay "Form and Function of the Dance in Bali." While Bateson's theory is untenable, given its extremely reductive character, as well as being empirically insubstantiable, his attempt is nonetheless one of the few in the literature of cultural anthropology of his period to suggest that the body may be a site for the production of knowledge that is generalizable to all other domains of cultural life and action.*

46   *I am indebted to Randy Martin and his remarks in discussion, 12 April 1993, for leading me to this observation. Another basic difference reflected in the record, which influenced the writing more strongly than I was aware of at the time, concerns the degree of mastery achieved in these learning experiences. The Balinese dance lesson was largely a failure in this respect. The lesson ended with very few actions accurately or fully embodied. The notes are mainly a record of the limits of learning with respect to specific body areas. The degree of detail and description given corresponds to the specificity of the failure experienced. The notes sketch out the magnitude of the still unlearned and possibly unlearnable realms of knowledge embodied in the technique. The length of the entry is an inverse measure of the sense of mastery of the technique.*

   The same follows in the Davao episode as well, although in this case the opposite result was achieved. Against the odds, having been selected out of the audience to perform inexpertly, to prove by contrast the virtuosity of the company members, I was set up to fail by my partner when he directed me to achieve "higher" and "faster" movements. As we finished and the warmth of the applause struck me, I realized that my performance to all watching was something out of the ordinary. The feeling of being such a public success was a profound relief. Perfect strangers had reconfirmed the expertise that would serve as the basis of mutual respect in my future dealings with this company. The memorableness of the occasion warranted little recording. Indeed, I remember as I wrote the entry that I felt certain I could remember the evening in detail without the aid of fieldnotes. In this episode again, the volume of the notes is an inverse measure of the sense of mastery of the technique.

47   *What Simon Ottenberg has referred to as "headnotes" (1990, 5), remembered* *observations, unwritten knowledge incorporating a concept of ethnographic salience.*

48   *Another feature Bateson remarked upon as well in "Form and Function of the Dance in Bali" (Bateson and Holt 1970).*

49   *From Jackson's essay in* Fieldnotes *(1990, 18).*

50   *This entry, unlike the preceding ones, has been subject to some editing, done in Riverside, California, as it was entered into a word processing format. It was first written-up entirely by hand without a laptop or other computer support in Davao. Ironically, it approaches most closely the monographic style it claims to resist.*

51   *The "monograph," defined technically as a treatise that provides detailed factual information on a particular subject, is one of the basic documentary formats of ethnographic literature. Modeled historically on writing in the natural sciences, monographs are typically considered to be the first form of publication an ethnographer "writes up" after completing fieldwork, and which is most specifically written for other practicing anthropologists. Ethnographic monographs originally were essentially descriptive accounts, that reported as comprehensively as possible on every aspect of the specific culture observed. However, in contemporary cultural anthropological work, "monographic" writing (writing which concentrates on a single research interest, ethnic situation, or fieldwork site) has overtaken comparative and more generalizing forms of ethnological writing as these alternative forms have become stigmatized as neo-colonial master narratives that mask without relinquishing chauvinistically ethnocentric perspectives.*

52   *As Okley (1993, 16), has argued, and as the Riverside entry of this chapter exemplifies, fieldnotes are inherently incomplete records, often no more than a trigger for the embodied knowledge – lived experience held in memory – that once expressed constitutes the actual subject of written-up ethnography. Memory, Bourdieu has noted in* Outline of a Theory of Practice *(1977, 94), can be nothing other than bodily habitus. In this regard, writing-up can rely at least as much upon divestitures of memory/bodily dismemberings, as it does upon re-presentations and enhancements of field writings. The divesting of lived experience in the rendering of the text, the physical aspects of retrieval, recollection, and expression in memory work are what I am referring to as "corpo-realities." Their influence on the text-making process is literally formative. See also note 10.*

53   *Nietzsche in* Ecce Homo *argues, "The influence of climate on our metabolism, its retardation, its acceleration, goes so far that a mistaken choice of place and climate can not only estrange a man from his task but can actually keep it from him: he never gets to see it" (cited in Gasche, "Ecce Homo or the Written Body," 1985, 12). Keeping me from having seen the theoretical task at hand in Davao, for example, were a series of fungal skin rashes, brought on by the polluted tropical climate, that took forty days to cure, during which time I was under doctor's orders to "avoid perspiring" and to follow a daily regimen involving multiple washings, and time-consuming applications* *of medicinal lotion. The treatment interfered with every aspect of life and work, and, if ever it was abandoned, the resulting discomfort made analytical writing impossible.*

54 *See, for example, Dan Rose's account of the model of the standard logic of ethnographic inquiry (1993, 194) he learned from graduate anthropological methodological training and from reading the products of ethnographic research. Rose's progression also isolates acts of reading and writing from the experiences of fieldwork. See note 3. See also remarks about writing-up "from afar" in Dumont (1992, 4, 6).*

55 *See note 52 on the corporeality of memory.*

56 *See Hastrup (1992, 125).*

57 *Some anthropologists argue that being off-site is critical to the activity of writing-up, although the issue is a subject of debate. See Ottenberg (1990, 146–8).*

58 *See remarks in* Positions, *80–96. See also Jean-Paul Dumont's remarks on false narrative coherence in ethnographic writing-up (1992, 2–8).*

59 *In Spinoza's terms a "dynamic body (versus a kinetic body); one defined by the effects that constitute it and of which it is capable. See Deleuze, "Ethology: Spinoza and Us" (1992, 625).*

60 *The interest in moving from a here/there perspective on diverse cultural sites towards the intersubjective creation of a world of "betweenness" is one of the primary motivations for interpretive ethnographic writing. See Hastrup (1992, 118) and Tedlock's remarks in* The Spoken Word and the Work of Interpretation *(1983, 323–4).*

61 *See Arjun Appadurai (1990), "Disjuncture and Difference in the Global Cultural Economy." The model depicts a postgeographically determined global situation in which shifting "scapes" of media-generated, financial, technical, ethnic, and ideological materials form cultural disjunctures and transcultural inter-relationships as a result of their heterogeneously fluid states. I characterize the model as "overly sanitary" in the sense that it is written-up in a neutral voice, reified without affect or particular emphasis given to the human suffering incurred by the conditions it objectifies. I would not argue that Appadurai's strategy is flawed or inappropriate. I simply note that from the field position I was in, it appeared "overly" sanitary. See also Robert Martins, "'World Music' and the Global Cultural Economy" (1992, 240–1) for a critical assessment of the model.*

62 *See Hastrup (1992, 123).*

63 *See Spivak (1992, 770).*

64 *Named for the nearby Mount Apo, a spectacular volcanic peak that has become a dominant symbol for the city's tourism industry.*

65   *See Michael Jackson citing Jacques Derrida's remarks concerning* Triste Tropiques *(1989, 107).*

66   *What Jean-Paul Dumont (1992, 7) refers to as "displacing the responsibility for interpretive closure." See Michael Jackson,* Paths Toward a Clearing *(1989, 109).*

Fete Accompli: gender, "folk-dance," and Progressive-era political ideals in New York City

LINDA J. TOMKO

On clear days in May, early in this century, hundreds of schoolgirls tumbled onto the Sheep's Meadow in Central Park. Signalled by a waving flag, they rushed forward in one great tide towards maypoles that had been erected for their schools. Running, cheering, they collected themselves in the grassy meadow and commenced a vernal festivity known as a park fete. The opening dance for park fetes was almost always the *Carrousel*, a Swedish singing-game. Each group of girls performing the *Carrousel* organized themselves around a maypole in two concentric circles. The inner-circle girls linked hands, the outer-circle girls placed hands on the shoulders of the inner-circle girls standing in front of them. They slid and stamped, first left, then right; they "danced around in circles" remarked one newspaper reporter, "and bewildered the people who were watching them."[1] Following the *Carrousel* the girls shouted their individual school cheers and continued with a series of "folk-dances" from European lands, like an Italian *Tarantella*, or *Sellenger's Round*, an English country dance. Alternating with the dances were team athletic games like shuttle relay, punch ball, and ball-throwing games.[2]

A brass band cued the start of the dances, no participant left the area during an activity, and dances were performed by all participants at the same time. Presented in this way, a dance like *Reap the Flax* would appear to viewers as fifty or more groups of girls forming straight-line phalanxes and alternating these formations with single-file chains winding circular patterns; then squares of girls through which dancers wound like thread through spinning wheels; and finally single-file chains winding serpentine patterns. The maypole assigned to each school supplied the spatial point of reference for each group of girls and the underlying organization of the dancing field as a whole. In the final *May-pole Dance*, girls encircled the poles once more, then braided bright ribbons around them by dancing in circles of ever-diminishing radius. The winding complete, the girls "unshipped" the poles and carried them off the field, supporting them along their length. At a signal, all the participants ran full tilt towards the bandstand at the center of the meadow, yelling and waving banners emblazoned with their schools' name or the words "Girls' Branch," the name of the sponsoring organization. Stopping just short of the bandstand, the girls cheered Elizabeth Burchenal, the park fete organizer, and sang the *Star-Spangled Banner*. Tired and probably dusty, scores of girls then turned homeward with their schoolmates while Boy Scouts on clean-up detail took to the field, picking up litter, stray hair ribbons and banners left behind.[3]

Clad in white, light dresses; singing, playing, and dancing on the grass – what could be more natural for American girls at the turn of the century? Many things, actually. The presence of schoolgirls dancing in the metaphoric heart of New York City constituted a departure of major significance for the female sex and for dancing in the early twentiety-century United States. Park fetes, their organization by the Girls' Branch of the Public Schools Athletic League, and their claiming of public space for female dance practices provide historians with an important vehicle for reassessing one image of women dancing, for denaturalizing the easy association of females, the out-of-doors, and playful dancing in American culture.

This reassessment forms part of the larger project of history writing, a project that can be articulated as identifying change through time, theorizing its causations, and acknowledging its effects in the past and present. One change in the practice of history writing, the advent of gender as a category of analysis, has since the 1960s enriched the repertoire of strategies that historians bring to bear in that project. This essay explores park fetes for insights they offer into the reciprocal relationship between women and dancing in the Progressive era: insights into ways in which notions of femaleness were being contested, recast, or formulated anew; and ways in which dance proved instrumental in women's assertion of professional and political agency. In this the essay introduces new kinds of analytical treatment to the study of dance. It locates dance in institutional contexts at a pivotal time for organization and bureaucracy formation in the twentieth-century United States. It also links dance to women's activity in constituting new social identities as "professionals" when "separate spheres" ideology began to wane in Progressive-era America. And, the essay furthers current critical inquiry into the body as the domain of women, analyzing a key point in the twentieth-century extension of the body–woman bond to a body–woman–dance linkage.

Scrutiny of park fetes offers as well the chance to stake new ground for writing histories of *dance*. Dance history writing as an academic pursuit in the United States dates largely from the 1960s. Scholarly products of this pursuit have typically taken the form of chronologies (devoted to individual careers, dance companies, productions of a given work); choreographic analyses of particular works or movement styles (often documented with dance notation scores); and biographies of significant performers, choreographers and producers/impresarios.[4] Such studies have done crucial service in "establishing the record," in documenting careers, works, and lives in various dance genres. In a young academic field dealing with a subject of vaunted "ephemerality," such drives to capture, preserve, and document the object of inquiry are fundamental. Yet to focus solely or primarily on setting forth for dance "what happened" is to treat history, the product of history writing, as a synonym for "the past." To establish the record should not be confused with the crucial, to the historian inextricably linked, steps of discerning pattern, articulating change through time, and theorizing its causes and effects. To take these analytical steps in dance history writing is to acknowledge the project for writing history as it is practiced in the history profession itself. To take these steps also positions the dance historian to make use of recent critical theory emphases on embodiment, power, representation, and interpretive communities.[5] To do so sustains a comprehension of dance as a cultural practice – an activity and meaning system embedded in a context, constituting, responding to, changed by, implicated in the lived layerings of meaning-making. To write histories of this cultural practice connects dance to the ways we have survived.

From their inauguration in 1908, park fetes grew in size to include by 1916 more than 50,000 schoolgirls, drawn from all the boroughs in New York City. Girls learned the dances to be performed by joining after-school folk-dance clubs organized by the Girls' Branch. Twenty to forty girls in a club, one or two clubs to a school, they met on rooftop playgrounds or in gymnasiums at their schools, playing games and learning dances for six months each year. Classroom teachers provided the instruction; they in turn had studied how to teach folk-dances in classes organized by Elizabeth Burchenal. At first tapping teachers and children in nine schools, by 1916 more than 273 schools took part in the enterprise. Regular newspaper coverage, both textual and photographic, extended public awareness of the park fetes and the Girls' Branch yearly work which they culminated. How can we account for this focus on the "education of the girl child," this dedication of resources and city-wide attention to the young and the female?[6]

WHY THE CHILD?

Focus on the girl as child culminated a century-long demographic transition in the United States. Between 1800 and 1900 the average number of children born to white women declined from 7.04 to 3.56 nationwide. The reduction was most visible among the middle class and among people who lived in towns and cities.[7] This decline constituted a radical change in family size and was joined by new ideological emphasis placed on nurturant parenting, in contrast with eighteenth-century models of more distanced, patriarchal parenting. Put simply, fewer children meant proportionally greater resources available for each child within family economies. This normative focus gained an official profile with the 1913 founding of the federal government's Children's Bureau. A second demographic shift contributed to the signal consciousness of and concern accorded children by the first years of the twentieth century. Immigration flows accelerated into port cities like New York and San Francisco, with labor demands from the new mass-production industries pulling immigrants deep into Midwestern cities like Chicago. In cities like these, eight out of ten residents were immigrants or children of immigrants in 1900. Housing stocks in urban areas were seldom adequate to the increased demand; city schools struggled to accommodate swelling populations of schoolchildren. Ideals of child-centered parenting combined with keenly felt population pressures in New York City to focus educational, civic, and reform attention on children as a group.

Focus on the child as girl resonated exquisitely because the hold exerted by a "separate spheres" ideology of gender roles was being contested in certain ways and to certain degrees in the first several decades of the twentieth century. "Separate spheres" ideology emerged during the economically tumultuous nineteenth century, offering relatively clear-cut gender roles and "safe harbors" of identity. This prescriptive ideology charged women with responsibility for child-rearing, upholding morality, and maintaining the home as haven. As Barbara Welter has summarized them, the characteristics expected of women in this value system were piety, purity, morality, and domesticity. Women were expected to deploy these practices and values in the home, the private sphere, as opposed to the public sphere of commerce, politics, and the professions in which men were enjoined to make their mark. The values and activities prescribed for the two sexes were thus complementary: men were to brave the rough and tumble of competition in the burgeoning industrial economy pursued on *laissez-faire* lines; women were to balance these calculating, aggressive strengths with their countervailing qualities of nurturance, spirituality, and intuitive equipoise.[8]

WHY THE GIRL?

Whatever the certainty these gender roles provided in precarious times, the limitations they placed on women's aspirations and activities provoked protest and resistance that grew demonstrably as the nineteenth century waned. It must be recognized that performance of these prescriptive gender roles was realizable in distinctly class terms. In New York City, for example, working-class women – native-born, immigrant, women of color – daily confronted the public world of work when they labored as garment workers, flower makers, milliners, or domestic labor. Clerical work, which grew by leaps and bounds in the United States from 1880 to 1920, saw an increase of nearly one million female workers between 1910 and 1920.[9] Public and private realms of activity were not neatly separated for these people; prescription clashed with actual practice at a fundamental level. Protests against this ideology and resistance to the restrictions it imposed on women's activities proceeded from various groups and class positions during the Progressive era. Women workers participated in the founding of the Women's Trade Union League, a cross-class coalition supporting labor activism by and for women's gains. Campaigns to win female suffrage shifted strategy from state-by-state approval to the quest for a constitutional amendment. Rallies, marches through Manhattan streets and even a suffrage pageant in 1914 brought agitation for women's voting rights to public attention. Women were succeeding in gaining access to higher education, particularly through admission to female colleges like Vassar, Wellesley, Smith, and Bryn Mawr, beginning in the 1860s and 1870s. Struggles for access to professional training were still being fought at the turn of the century, with successful individuals then fighting to win actual entry to professional institutions – university posts for female academics, hospital posts for female doctors and surgeons, etc. Through a variety of women-organized reform efforts, such as settlement house work, public nursing, and charity organization societies, middle-class women claimed public sphere roles on the basis and as an extension of the nurturing roles assigned them by separate spheres ideology. Sketched briefly here, such instances of resistance to and recasting of separate spheres ideology demonstrate that the "woman question" was vividly and concretely at issue, in New York City as in the nation. Focus on the girl child partook of this concern.[10]

Several kinds of concerns and conditions thus came together and prepared the salience of Girls' Branch activities for Progressive-era New Yorkers. Park fetes are easy to read on one level as pastoral gambols, but to do so would amount to reading them out of the historical record. Park fetes can also be read as embodied assertions about issues of gender and childhood in American work and public life. Bringing together schoolgirls in the public spaces of New York City parks, park fetes mingled and focused contending and changing perceptions about the sorting or taxonomy of activities appropriate to females and the distinction or demarking of realms appropriate to female agency and self-making. They provided annual workings out of the struggle with and about female gender role prescriptions as they intersected contemporary concerns about immigration and ethnicity, urban living, even government.

Folk-dancing on these occasions provided a physical discourse through which to argue gender and claim public space. But why dancing? Why this activity and not some other? The answers to this are several and proceed, I believe, from a Progressive-era understanding, both intuitively felt and explicit, of the significance of the body in establishing identity.[11] Certainly the physical body commanded increased scrutiny and recognition in the late nineteenth century as a discourse of nature, or evolutionary development, achieved prominence. Darwinian theory, preceded in the United States by the work of Spencer, theorized the human

WHY DANCING?

body as a wholly natural entity, its development governed completely by biological processes. Supporters and opponents argued passionately, seeking to sustain or qualify this view and the political and social implications which flowed from it. Arguments on all sides, however, had to deal in some way with an emphasized primacy of the natural world over against the cultural or social.

It was on the ground of such discourse that physical training, the cultivation of the human body, gained centrality in public education and as a focus of social concern. Various systems of physical training had been implemented in public schools since the Civil War, in part a response to the physical condition of soldiers recruited in that conflict. Growing demand for physical training teachers in the 1880s and 1890s led to the founding of numerous normal, or teacher training, schools for physical education. The Sargent Normal School, run by Dudley Sargent in Boston, and the International YMCA Training College, located in Springfield, Massachusetts, were only two of the leading institutions of this kind. And an ambitious group, the American Association for the Advancement of Physical Education, constituted itself in 1885 as an organization concerned both to theorize the cultivation of the human body and to establish physical education as a professional domain.[12]

As the journals and conference reports from the period reveal, the new profession of physical education took as one of its chief responsibilities the analysis of physical training systems suitable for use in public schools. The issue was substantive, for competing systems hailed from a number of different national sources and operated on quite different principles. The physical plants available to the public schools had to be taken into consideration as well. Practical implementation of any physical training system met large obstacles in most grade schools. It was common for classroom teachers, rather than trained specialists, to give the instruction to the students in the same rooms used to teach academic subjects, and children performed the exercises in the space between desks, in the aisles, or sometimes in the school hallways. In many cases, ten minutes of each hour were given to the instruction, and the focus was correction of postural defects caused by long hours sitting at school desks. The advent of organized athletics at the end of the nineteenth century, and their rapid commodification in professional sports, posed a related problem for evaluation by physical training professionals: could, and should, team sports like football and basketball be added to curricula?

A kind of body consciousness thus suffused various efforts and groups at the turn of the century: efforts to reconcile religious beliefs and economic thought with evolutionary theory, for example; and the crusading work of physical training innovators who demonstrated a type of nationalism in weighing foreign-born systems against newly minted American systems and sports. Riddling these several kinds of concerns about the body were questions of gender. One vein of social theorizing mobilized evolutionary doctrine and human physiology to define gender roles for women. For example, in his 1873 *Sex in Education* Edward Clarke asserted that biology was destiny for women. Because the cognitive work required for higher education drew on and depleted blood from the nervous and reproductive systems, he maintained, it unfitted women for childbearing, and might make them infertile, physically weak, and mentally ill. It followed that higher education for women was to be avoided.[13]

Some twenty-five years later, psychologist and "child-study" movement founder G. Stanley Hall tried to extend evolutionary theory to psychic matters and linked cultivation of the body with development of the mind. Speculating that ontogeny recapitulated phylogeny, he declared that individuals' neuromuscular development recapitulated "race history," or the evolutionary stages of development experienced by members of their race. Within this framework, males and females recapitulated the physical and psychical differentiation of the sexes and the corresponding divergence of social functions and roles that flowed from these sex differences.

Hall's 1905 treatise *Adolescence* pursued these themes in two-volume detail, recommending revisions and changes to be made in school curricula of the day. These recommendations embraced the importance of exercise to child development. Hall wrote that "muscle culture develops brain-centers as nothing else yet demonstrably does." It followed that to train the muscles was to train the mind; "for the young, motor education is cardinal." Hall identified play as the ideal form of exercise, in which every movement was "instinct with heredity." When playing, children rehearsed "the activities of our ancestors, back we know not how far, and repeat their life work in summative and adumbrated ways." Children's play retraced the oldest elements of muscle history first, and as they matured retraced progressively more recent history. Those activities which were most instinctive, untaught, and non-imitative, he maintained, were the most spontaneous and exact expressions of children's motor needs. Hall identified dancing as "one of the best expressions of pure play" and elaborated a number of examples of its use in historical societies. He pinpointed rhythm as a key characteristic of dancing and asserted that rhythmic movement was the source, in some pre-civilized time, of all work, play, and art.[14]

Evolutionary theory, the pre-eminence accorded physical training, and mobilization of physical differences to instate gender role differences; these contemporary concerns about the body came together in important ways in Hall's child psychology and advocacy of dancing. Hall's articulation of a body—mind linkage and his theoretical intertwining of gender roles with physical and psychical capacities came to bear on Girls' Branch folk-dance practices through the mediating figure of Luther Halsey Gulick. Gulick accepted appointment in 1903 as Director of Physical Training in New York City schools. A personal and professional friend of Hall's, he also maintained collegial friendships with Thomas Denison Wood and Patty Smith Hill, innovative physical training and kindergarten pedagogy academics employed at Teachers College. Gulick himself had developed and worked in the department of physical training at the International YMCA Training School from 1887 to 1900. He edited the *American Physical Education Review*, journal of the re-named American Physical Education Association, beginning in 1901 and resigned that post to assume presidency of the organization in 1903. This nationally prominent physical training figure walked into a newly consolidated city school system and worked to harmonize the differing principles and systems used by physical training staff employed in the city's previously autonomous boroughs. Despite the changes and innovations that he made, Gulick was not satisfied that the physical training needs of students were being met. The solution he instituted expanded physical training work through planned programs of after-school athletics, and it was in girls' athletics work that dancing backed by Hallian psychology took pride of place.

Gulick first initiated after-school athletics programs for boys, founding the Public Schools Athletic League in 1903. The PSAL was organized as a voluntary organization, receiving conceptual support and the use of school facilities, but not financial backing, from the Board of Education. The PSAL met with success, and Gulick lent his support to a woman-organized proposal for the provision of girls' work. Thus in 1905 he recruited Elizabeth Burchenal from her Teachers College physical training post to assist him in developing athletics work for the Girls' Branch of the Public Schools Athletic League.

Gulick brought to the formulation of girls' work his considerable experience in developing and implementing physical training systems, plus theoretical familiarity with Hall's work. Burchenal brought experience as a teacher, in both commercial and academic settings, of a variety of physical training skills, plus a personally developed expertise in teaching folk-dance. Gulick's published materials explain the theories that underpinned Girls' Branch work. His 1910 *The Healthful Art of Dancing* reveals with clarity the extent to which Hallian psychology informed Gulick's thinking and the support he provided for Burchenal's teaching of folk-dancing.

After an initial year of experimentation with gymnastics, folk-dancing, and athletics (team games and contests of skill), the Girls' Branch Board of Directors concluded that the girls found folk-dancing to be the most interesting of the three activities; that more girls could participate in such dancing in a given space than in the other activities; and that folk-dancing afforded cooperation with other home and school activities which athletics and gymnastics did not.[15] The first of these conclusions is of more than passing importance, for in Hallian psychology, children's expression of interest was taken to confirm the "racially old" validity of an activity.[16] The second conclusion indicates an early awareness of economies of scale in an organization which would by 1916 serve over 50,000 girls. The third conclusion, I believe, reflects the recognition by Girls' Branch sponsors of the bridge that after-school folk-dancing was capable of effecting between the prescriptive realms of public and private spheres for females. That the tenor of such bridging was expected to be conservative, to weigh on the side of preserving the separate spheres status quo, seems clear. Yet accounts of Girls' Branch work and of the year-end, culminating park fetes reveal that folk-dancing provided a flexible practice for struggling with, for contesting, issues of gender, ethnicity, and social order.

How did this dancing address, trouble, argue, and worry these and other issues of power and the allocation of resources in Progressive-era society? In what ways did technical vocabularies, choreographic forms, or movement qualities embody political concerns or propose alternative arrangements?

DANCING ARGUED POWER?

One of the most palpable problems that the Girls' Branch introduced folk-dancing to redress was the failure of urban dwelling conditions and public schools to provide necessary and adequate resources, conditions, and guidance for children's bodily development and healthy play. The design of schoolroom desks and classroom protocols binding children to their seats, stationary, for five hours a day made for bad posture, imbalance in strength of abdominal flexor and spinal extensor muscles, and poor development of internal organs, Gulick maintained. Yet school physical training programs frequently had to be squeezed into the aisle space of classrooms; gymnasiums were not universal school facilities; paved rooftop playgrounds sometimes provided the significant open space available for play. Similarly, densely packed, row-house blocks in working-class neighborhoods afforded few internal play areas, and streets in these neighborhoods doubled as commercial space for vendors and clogged, dusty, thoroughfares for horses, carts, and trolleys as well as pedestrians.

When not impossible, it was seldom safe to run freely, throw distances, or collect in groups on these streets.

Gulick and the Girls' Branch were not alone in formulating an urban environmental critique: the inadequate – unequal – distribution of fundamental resources of sunlight, air, and square footage for safe play motivated several contemporary reform efforts in New York City. The Outdoor Recreation League mobilized to claim park space located squarely within densely populated neighborhoods in the city's several boroughs, and it insisted upon spaces that permitted users to walk and play on the grass, not simply skirt it in defined paths. Charles Veiller and Richard Watson Gilder mounted campaigns to protest tenement building design and construction and recommended models which promised greater access for each dwelling unit to sunlight, moving air, and sanitation facilities. Settlement houses like University Settlement and Henry Street Settlement established children's clubs and provided meeting rooms for club activities; they also built gymnasiums for recreation by users of all ages. It should be noted, of course, that these reform efforts responded to conditions of city living as the effects of industrial labor and *laissez-faire* economic competition. Rather than challenging generating causes, they aimed to ameliorate them.[17]

Gulick's writings specify several particular features of folk-dancing that made this movement vocabulary particularly suitable for redressing the imbalanced distribution of urban recreation resources and the damaging effects of school regimens. First and foremost, folk-dancing required large muscle movement. Since the effect of exercise was a function of the body "in proportion to the number of foot-pounds of energy expended," he wrote, this large-muscle use made folk-dancing an extremely efficient means to achieve health. It also produced a big impact on circulation and respiration. And folk-dancing realized these gains and proved capable of accommodating large numbers of children – clustering girls in couples, lines, circles, and other group formations – while requiring relatively small amounts of space.

With these descriptors Gulick wed an ideology of efficiency, one that resonated strongly with contemporary applications in mass-production technology as well as domestic management, to the privileging of "health" that undergirded demands for and supplies of physical training as a cultural practice. This-turn-of-the-century construction of folk-dancing confirms the late twentieth-century theoretical recognitions of the body as "the very site of material inscription of the ideological, the ground where socio-political determinations take hold and are real-ized," as Teresa de Lauretis has put it.[18] What goes understated in the claims made by Gulick for folk-dancing is the degree to which such dancing permitted Girls' Branch work to distance itself from European systems of physical training imported in the previous century. A competing system such as Swedish Ling calisthenics, for example, surely offered the kind of muscle use, circulatory, and respiratory benefits that Gulick extolled in folk-dancing. However, the Swedish system was faulted in American physical training literature for relying on drills directed by barking commands from an instructor to keep activity going. It thus introduced a rigidity and authoritarianism at odds with Hallian values of spontaneous and instinctive play. And although Gulick never made the point in print, the conduct of a folk-dance, once learned, could remain in the hands and feet of the girls dancing it, with memory of sequence and musical cues from the accompanying score supplying the "directives." The German Jahn system of physical training eluded criticisms of inflexibility, to an extent, because it combined certain amounts of free play with other structured work on specialized apparatus. The need to acquire apparatus for each and every school, however, made the system costly to implement. Testimony by Jessie Bancroft reveals the ways in which folk-dancing satisfied methodological criteria that other systems failed to meet. A Girls' Branch organizer and member of Gulick's city schools physical training staff, Bancroft recalled

> the happiness that came to the little children of the East side through the folk dancing. Up to that time their serious, sad, unsmiling faces were noted by all visitors to the schools, who could but feel a great depression from it. This unchildlike seriousness was the aftermath of pogroms and massacres and exile. But after the folk dancing came, the smiles crept over those little faces like sunshine after a cloud, and brought some, at least, of their childhood's rightful heritage of laughter and joyousness.[19]

References to "serious, sad, unsmiling faces," "unchildlike seriousness," and "childhood's rightful heritage of laughter and joyousness" confirm the Girls' Branch subscription to an ideology of play-filled, care-free childhood and a moral sense that children possessed "rights." Citing "pogroms and massacres and exile" as the source of East side children's grim miens, Bancroft indirectly acknowledges the immigration and population pressures threatening a widely held social construction of childhood. She reports that folk-dancing provides the solution, and she likens it to sunshine. Weather changes are spontaneous, like folk-dancing, she implies; the unpredictabilities of climate comport with the impetuous, unplanned qualities of instinctive play.

In the characteristics it offered as a movement vocabulary – the scale, vigor and ongoingness of its motions; the possibility it held out for spontaneous, relatively independently sustained execution and enjoyment – folk-dancing thus gave bodily presence to ideologies of health, efficiency, and even a certain American nationalism, at the same time that the Girls' Branch was wielding these practices to offset or push back the physically enervating effects of city living, high population density, and constraining public school facilities.[20] Demonstrative and remonstrative capacities of this dancing intermingled.

In deploying folk-dancing as an instrumentality for recreation and for offsetting unequally distributed urban resources, the Girls' Branch tried to recuperate/compensate for certain effects of urban living and a burgeoning industrial economy. It did so, however, without calling for fundamental change in the generating structures of those effects. In other aspects of its functioning, though, Girls' Branch park fetes asserted the need to rethink Progressive-era modes of social organization, notions of individual personhood, and the *laissez-faire* principles that underpinned them.

At their advent in Revolutionary-era America, principles of *laissez-faire* economic competition had promised that the general good would be won through the free competition of individual actors in a self-regulating market. A radical doctrine at the time, the conservative implications of *laissez-faire* economic and political organization had become clear by the end of the nineteenth century. And the implications were clear to players operating from a variety of positions. Railroad management, the first to exploit new techniques of bureaucratic organization, also had been among the first to discover the costs of unrestrained competition, turning then to oligopolistic models of deploying capital. On the opposite side of the economic relationship, labor forces during the nineteenth century quickly discovered the disabling effects of an ideology that identified workers as singular units, collective action among whom was legally limited or disallowed as infringement upon individual rights. Farmers during the 1890s supported features of the Populist platforms like community ownership of storage elevators, the subtreasury plan, and inflationary free silver measures because they offered some instruments, collectivities, and leverage to individual producers in negotiating brutally competitive international markets for agricultural products.

In social terms as well, the "free agency" promised by capitalist organization had seemed to augur freedom from traditional limitations on aspiration, opportunity, and position that had characterized earlier models of corporate, hierarchical, reciprocally responsible societies. Amidst cycles of economic booms and panics, the flourishing of separate spheres ideology, and continuing social struggles over race in the nineteenth century, however, it became clear that successful achievement of such free agency was heavily weighted towards white males, even if economic security was unpredictable for most. The costs and benefits of pure competition, the possibilities of "individual agency," and the procedures for effecting right relationships between individuals and collectivities were issues that animated political and economic debates as industrial development achieved the stage of mass-production industry and the country's population became increasingly urban.

That human bodies bore the brunt of these contesting issues was clear to labor activists, to community workers, and to schoolteachers and administrators in New York City. Gulick saw in the selection and organization of after-school athletics the opportunity to work out through bodily interactions better balanced relationships between individuals and the groups in which they functioned. Support for this view, clearly proceeding from preoccupation with race history, could be found in Hall's *Adolescence* where he remarks:

> . . . [play's] social function develops solidarity and unison of action between individuals. The dances, feasts, and games of primitive people, wherein they rehearse hunting and war and act and dance out their legends, bring individuals and tribes together.[21]

At the outset, Gulick and the founders of Girls' Branch work rejected free play because strong youths could realistically be expected to take the floor with games and stunts, displacing the weaker and less aggressive children to the edges of the room or playground, where they would engage in more passive play. Only a few children would reap the full physical benefit intended for the many; only organized play could ensure the equal distribution of benefit. The loss of freedom and individual choice that this decision entailed was more apparent than real, Gulick explained:

> We are only beginning to learn what freedom means. It is not the privilege of doing, irrespective of everybody else, what one wants to do. That would make the tramp the ideally free man. Freedom lies in the recognition and joyful acceptance of relationships. In organized play, where every child is a unit in a larger, mutually responsible, and mutually responsive whole, all reach a higher and more significant stage of individualized

freedom than is possible on the unorganized, free-for-all playground.[22]

The playground clearly stood as a microcosm of society in this formulation; the physical was clearly connected to the political. And relationships, that stuff of everyday life in which women were supposed by separate spheres theory to excel, constituted the kinetic substance of "freedom." By singling out relationships in this way, Gulick's words made a claim for female agency in the construction and dynamic functioning of social order. What is operating as well in the Girls' Branch instituting of folk-dancing is the recognition, to which theorists have come (again) in the 1980s and 1990s, that the "political" could not be limited or defined solely as "having to do with state power."[23]

The complement and distribution of dancers participating in a park fete gave kinetic and visual shape to Girls' Branch concerns about connections between individuals and the collective. The dances presented required groups of individuals or couples to perform the same steps and gestures simultaneously. Girls' Branch handbooks stipulated that group dances should not be done by fewer than ten girls, and no soloists were singled out. To be sure, leaders of lines were required at times, but they emerged from and dissolved back into the group. With the exception of the basketball throw, the games that interspersed the dances in the course of a park fete were all team games or relays. Handbook descriptions of park fetes consistently claimed that, by design, it was impossible to distinguish individual girls among the many. Efforts were thus focused to make park fetes embody and facilitate realization of individual qualities through combined effort in a group activity rather than focusing on performance as heightened presentation of particular sensibilities, personalities, or emphasized figures. This position was reinforced, summarized, finalized, in the traditional closing dance of the park fete – the *May-pole Dance* was incapable of execution without the cooperation of individual girls in a single unified process.[24]

The forms created in the course of various folk-dances realized in spatial terms the emphasis Girls' Branch work placed on integration of individuals and groups. *Reap the Flax* and *May-pole Dance*, described above, create recognizable patterns as they progress: lines, circles, and serpentines for the first; concentric circles for the latter. The English morris dance *Laudanum Bunches* deploys sets of six girls, each set arrayed in parallel lines of three dancers each, for much of its duration. A sense of the importance of recurring forms such as these can be gained by working out or re-constructing park fete dances that are recorded in Elizabeth Burchenal's publications. A typical dance description provides a piano transcription of the music and a breakdown of the choreography into several sections. The analysis of each section includes textual descriptions of step-units to be performed (slides, hops, stamps, turnings); relationships and physical contact among the girls (hands on shoulders, taking hands, for instance); and characterizations of the spirit and brio that should animate the movements. Occasional photographs intersperse the text and these frequently select moments in the dance when activity coalesces into geometrical shapes. Most of these photos appear to have been made on occasions other than park fetes, with photos from 1909 and the next several years taken on rooftop play areas or ground-level playgrounds.[25]

Choreographic emphasis on geometric form was intersected by, at times mediated by, the effort qualities of the girls' dancing. This intersection must be discerned from a second type of photograph. Newspaper coverage of park fetes regularly featured photographs, typically taken either at close range or from distant vantage points. It is the longshot photos that seize the *May-pole Dance* in its crystalline moments, girl-bodies etching closely dotted circles, circles bulging into ovals with the curvature of the camera lens. The fixing of moments that close-up shots offer, however, brings the reader/looker up short. Here clarity departs and flurry abounds. Bodies framed at full length, or sometimes waist-up only, reveal their smiles, their swaying torsos, stretching limb-reach, throat-bared heads. These photos reinscribe the tumult of the field, the horizontal multiplications of efforts, the absence of overarching, vertical panopticon, the abandon released (Figures 8.1a and 8.1b).[26]

No park fete photograph that I have found captures these two kinds of experiences in a single image; they crash against each other most powerfully in the reader's mind's eye. Photos from Burchenal's textbooks, however, do show schoolgirls suffused with abandon as they figure the shapes of folk-dance choreographies: one's head turns rightward, another's body arches back, for instance, as all *Reap the Flax*. This composite of information about effort qualities that informed performances of folk-dance choreographies indexes, I believe, the possibilities for and the extent to which individual variation persisted within the group focus of park fete dancing. Folk-dancing didn't press little girls into uniform molds, in other words; it accommodated their individual agencies as they moved into and out of group forms. Embodied here were the very concerns that troubled economic relations, constructions of gender identities, and struggles about race in the early twentieth century. Park fetes proposed that solutions to the dilemma were inherently dynamic, unstable, possible in local situations but also full of contradictory impulses.[27]

The prose of Girls' Branch handbooks, the pleasures of the dancing field reproduced for newspaper consumption, these and other evidences of folk-dance practices privilege the utopian effects claimed for folk-dancing. They celebrate the kinesthetic joyfulness the girls exhibited, and they project a melioration of social interaction that promoters hoped would ensue. But historians should also ask: What was subordinated or concealed by these formulations? What gritty side of the practice lay unarticulated in grainy photographs and earnest texts?

To weigh the effects of change is, of course, a traditional charge that historians have endeavored to meet. And it is only prudent as a matter of method to take proponents' claims with a grain of salt. But the questions framed above are informed as well by deconstruction theory and the work of Michel Foucault on systems of punishment and a discourse of sexuality in post-seventeenth-century Western societies. Foucault's work asserts the salience of the body as a material of power, as a medium which can be mobilized through a variety of "disciplines," or systems for training the body, to instate relations of domination and subordination. Bodies are anything but unshaped, unconstrained, or lacking political valence, he argues. Applied to park fetes, this analysis promotes recognition of folk-dancing as a discipline. It presses us to ask what linkages folk-dancing creates between bodily and ethnic identifications and the political ordination or ranking of those ethnicities. Deconstruction in its turn proposes that every act of privileging some thing — be it a term, value, or group — proceeds by way of suppressing some other, at least in systems such as the Western one in which language (and processes of conception) are based in a binary logic of opposition. This argument reminds historians when assessing the effects of change to search for that which goes "unsaid" or is taken as customary. With park fetes, it impels us to unmask the naturalization of girls' dancing, that constructed "naturalness" attributed to girls' folk-dancing, and to scrutinize the instrumentalization of dancing – the purposeful linkage of dancing to gender issues. The effects produced by park fetes may be sought then in at least two arenas: that of sorting and appropriating the cultural practices of immigrant others; and the construction of gender.

A rare glimpse of folk-dancing from the participant's remembered perspective may be gleaned from the recollections of Helen Tamiris, a choreographer-dancer well known for her work in the 1920s' genre of modern dance. Her autobiographical writings make fleeting, fond reference to public school folk-dancing activities that must have been Girls' Branch work:

> All my spare time, often deliberately cutting a geometry or Latin class, I spent in the gymnasium with my instructor, who too loved dancing and was trying to incorporate it into the formal physical training required by the Board of Education. Both at the [Henry Street] settlement and here, I was now deeply engrossed in Folk Dancing – It was called Character dancing – and was based on steps taken from the peasant dances of various countries.[28]

Tamiris's recollection signals the period perception that Girls' Branch folk-dancing brought to the United States the peasant dances of foreign countries. Did Girls' Branch activity constitute another instance of American imperial reach, colonizing or appropriating the indigenous dance materials of other peasant (read inferior) cultures? Further, did Girls' Branch activity produce bowdlerized folk-dance?

Burchenal's activity as a folk-dance collector and teacher is material to answering this question. She began journeying abroad as early as 1902, traveling to countries in Western Europe, including Ireland and Scandinavia. By her own account, she attempted to live among the people in towns and festivals that she visited, learning dances first-hand and performing them with native people whenever possible. She frequently traveled in the company of her sister, whose musical expertise was pressed into service when Burchenal later published collected textual notations of the dance materials she gathered.[29]

PRODUCING BOWDLERIZED FOLK-DANCE?

Burchenal worked to immerse herself in contemporary practices of Western European traditional folk-dance materials. But, in many respects, Girls' Branch stagings of the materials she collected and taught seemed to make only limited reference to the originals. Girls' Branch guidelines strictly enjoined girls in participating clubs from wearing special costumes. Everyday school dress was the rule, with ribbons or perhaps a sash allowed to distinguish the clubs one from another. "Folk" or "ethnic" dress, however, was in no way attempted.[30] Acoustic matters were handled in a similar vein. The music for park fetes was supplied by brass bands and no effort was made to replicate the instrumentation or texture of the "native" accompaniment that served this dance material in its European context. Burchenal's published books of notated dances provide piano reduction scores for each dance; these music scores were certainly used for club work at the school level. Perhaps most significantly, the mixed-gender

ELIZABETH
BURCHENAL.
EXECUTIVE SEC'Y-
GIRLS BRANCH
PUBLIC SCHOOL
ATHLETIC LEAGUE.

"GUSTAFS
SKAAL"
DANCE...

SOME of the GIRLS in the HIGHLAND FLING...

performance of couple dances was not reproduced in Girls' Branch club work and park fete performances. Girls danced with girls – no heterosexual coupling took place. Further, linguistic evidence from Burchenal's texts published during her tenure with the Girls' Branch suggests that girls danced *as* girls. The instructions for each dance identify dancers by assigning numbers to each girl or to the spatial position each occupied in a group or "set" configuration. Or the directions refer to the two girls who form a couple as "partners." These strategies substituted gender-neutral references for mentions of a "man's" part or "woman's" position, effectively absenting male roles from the conception of Girls' Branch folk-dancing. From the lexicon of instructional terms to execution of the choreography, the heterosexual gendering of these dances, and the European model, was downplayed in park fete realizations. As these evidences confirm, the Girls' Branch clearly chose to adopt a revisionist practice of costume, music, and gendered performance in the years of Burchenal's association with it.

To be sure, the Girls' Branch utilized this revisionist practice – this bowdlerization – to achieve specific social and political goals. Reliance on everyday dress rather than "ethnic" costume sought to reinforce the sense of community and common purpose among the girls. It took into account as well the economic circumstances of working-class families that might not permit the annual purchase of a special dress for intra-school meets or park fetes. The decision not to replicate specific instrumentations for folk-dances was probably made for economic reasons, while the absenting of male performers and erasure of male roles in the conception of folk-dances indexes the Girls' Branch conscious effort to perform gender and to gender dance performance as female.

The promoters' goals aside, though, did Girls' Branch folk-dancing strike emigré people as bowdlerized? Correlation of schools participating in Girls' Branch folk-dancing with their geographic location on Manhattan Island shows, for example, that a good two-thirds of the schools involved from 1909 through 1913 were located on the lower East side, a locus for working-class, immigrant people who labored in several different sweated trades at the turn of the century.[31] Families in these neighborhoods arguably retained acquaintance with European dance practices, among first-generation adults if not their American-born children. According to Luther Gulick, spectators attending a 1908 Girls' Branch demonstration "shared in the fun, nodding delighted heads and tapping responsive feet to the familiar rhythms, and rapturous comments in nearly every language of Europe mingled with the frequent applause."[32] Whatever had been expurgated, something of a familiar original remained recognizable to immigrant parents of Girls' Branch participants. Put another way, parents made a meaning for the dancing they viewed that conceivably differed from the Girls' Branch meaning – parents grasped the Old World provenance of the dancing and assigned value to it. The interpretive community that viewed park fetes was itself multiple and heterogeneous; Girls' Branch renderings of European dance materials could at one and the same time

◐ **Figs 8.1a–8.1b** Newspaper photographs represented competing and simultaneous experiences of Girls' Branch park fetes: a long-shot distilled geometrizing and unifying effects; close-up shots captured the exuberant spirits of individual dancers. Although the print quality of the photographs looks poor by 1990s standards, the framing of the photos performed important ideological work.
Figure 8.1a Park fete seen at a distance, May 1913.
Figure 8.1b Park fete seen in close-up, May 1912.

reference, even sample, an "authentic" original and construct a new practice.

The revisionist features of Girls' Branch practice might also be seen as homogenizing or Americanizing the European dances taken as source material. At one level, the lack of variation in costume and instrumentation provisions would tend to make the dances look and sound more alike, leaving difference to be discerned primarily at the rhythmic and kinetic levels. Here, indeed, one form of "homogenization" can be seen at work. But to argue this point alone – that distinctive features were blurred and that European dances were dissolved through lack of difference into American dance as a means of managing or controlling the influx of immigrant peoples – neglects to consider the contemporary perception in many quarters that the United States *lacked* tradition, lacked a heritage of dance and other cultural forms with which Europe was replete. America was young, as nations go, and had acquired a reputation for emphasizing material acquisition. Settlement workers, who were daily brought into contact with the community and cultural practices of their immigrant neighbors, decried the situation. The pageantry movement responded to a felt lack of historic national identity by producing at the regional level community-based re-enactments of historical events. The arts and crafts movement and the museum movement responded in their different ways to the search for and constitution of an artistic and historical heritage.[33] Luther Gulick himself hopefully proclaimed the potential for folk-dancing to give the country "a national life far richer, deeper, and more beautiful than one where the main emphasis in education was upon bare intellectual training for the purposes of 'practical success.'"[34] Thus, folk-dance as taught by the Girls' Branch can be seen as constructing an American sense of tradition through the experiencing of dance materials unique to the floods of immigrants making new lives in America in the early twentieth century. Rather than simply assimilating European materials to an American tradition or dancing *urtext*, Girls' Branch folk-dancing may be seen as making an *urtext*, the making of Americans, as Gertrude Stein might have put it.

PRODUCING TRADITION?

There is no small irony in an approach that would construct the "American" heritage from materials and practices borne by and embodied in the outsiders, the immigrants, the newcomers to the country. The contemporary case of England, another country scrutinizing its heritage and seeking a distinctive national identity, supplies useful perspective on the American endeavor. England experienced its revivals of traditional music and traditional dance at the turn of the century, but for different reasons, and it turned to "indigenous" British materials such as sword, morris, and country dancing.[35] It is startling and important to understand in this light that the American privileging of European folk-dancing denied and left unrecognized the presence and cultural practices of African-Americans, long resident in the land. It left unremarked as well the more recent flows of Asian immigrants to the West Coast. Further, the bulk of the folk-dances presented in park fetes were drawn from Northern and Western Europe – not from Southern and Eastern Europe, the countries of origin for the so-called "new immigration" of the early twentieth century.[36] At the same time that folk-dancing constituted an American tradition through dancing, it sorted and ranked the ethnic heritages that comprised the newfound sense of history. Folk-dancing confirmed the political priority assigned to people and practices of Anglo-Saxon derivation, assigning only occasional place, and thus status, to dances from Italy, Bohemia, or Russia. And in failing to acknowledge black and

Asian peoples and practices as folk sources for the work of cultural construction, Girls' Branch dancing reinforced the contemporary social and political erasure of these people.

Park fetes turned the disciplinary powers of folk-dancing to the work of worrying and constructing Progressive-era gender roles as well. Throughout the Progressive era, women laid claim to a variety of activities in the supposedly male public sphere, thereby contesting the boundaries of gender roles assigned by separate spheres ideology. Girls' Branch park fetes participated in this laying claim to public space, but in a carefully delimited way: fetes were structured to assert female presence without dissolving into male modalities. Thus, as the culminating event of a year's work, park fetes were structured as celebrations rather than competitions. This was in decided contrast with boys' work, which featured competitive athletic meets as early as 1903. To be sure, the Girls' Branch did sanction limited competition in the form of intra-school folk dance and athletic meets. But it never permitted competition *between* schools. Further, the criteria used for judging in-school meets similarly constrained the nature of the competition that was permitted and placed emphasis on communal responsibility. Specifically, "memory" and "form" remained the two stable criteria through time. "Skill," a criterion articulated in 1908, had been dropped by 1914. Even the conditions for participating in PSAL activities contributed to a construction of public sphere dancing that carefully differentiated female and male behavior. Eligibility requirements stressed high grades in effort, deportment, and proficiency for boys' and girls' work alike in 1909–10, the year of the third annual fete. The Girls' Branch revised the requirements the following year, however, deciding that eligibility would be entirely at the discretion of school principals.[37] Thus, boys' participation continued to be predicated on their competitive standing in the categories of behavior and academic accomplishment. This validation of boys' competition was confirmed by the athletic work itself, which promoted fierce inter-school competition between clubs. Girls' participation hinged instead on a principal's subjective evaluation of their worthiness, further reinforcing the cooperative, conciliatory group spirit promoted by the competition-minimizing framework erected for folk-dancing.

Park fetes thus claimed a place for women in the public sphere, relinquishing the separateness of the domestic sphere but not the distinctive qualities assigned females by separate spheres ideology nor the practice of same-sex affiliation. Moving beyond the confines of schools and their physical plants, fetes brought girls into the vernal spaces of urban parks carved out of – and in opposition to – the surrounding commercial and industrial city. Here dancing girls held in tension the competing demands of individual and group agency in a *laissez-faire* society. As had a number of Progressive-era reform efforts, park fetes capitalized on women's presumed difference to direct attention to social and political problems. In addition, the pastoral settings reinforced connections between generativity in the natural world and women's reproductive roles in the social world. Folk-dancing, then, was deeply involved in both contesting and elaborating a taxonomy of female-appropriate activities at a time of climax, and impending crisis, for gender roles fashioned by separate spheres ideology.

Girls' Branch work exerted pressure on this taxonomy as well by making canny use of structural means. Park fete organizers fully appreciated the allure of public spectacles and they were equally sensitive to the commercialization that characterized contemporary professional sporting events. Thus they prepared park fetes carefully, trying to counter the commodification that attached to other forms of public female dancing such as burlesque performance and Broadway dancing.[38] They sought to resist commodification and commercialization by controlling the content of dances – no ballroom or exotic "Oriental" dances for schoolgirls – and by scheduling fetes during afternoon hours, which were working hours for most of the public. And they neither issued nor sold tickets to the event. In these efforts they proved fairly successful – contemporary photographs suggest that on-site viewers were relatively few, and that no single viewing position could take in the totality of the event.

Also, the very organization of the Girls' Branch as a teaching and producing enterprise asserted an enlarged framework and set of functions susceptible to women's agency and self-making. At the moment of its founding, the female organizers of the Girls' Branch resisted efforts to make them a ladies' auxiliary, or support group, for the male-focused Public Schools Athletic League. The women argued for, and succeeded in creating *and* funding, a woman-constituted voluntary organization promoting female activities. In this they eschewed earlier nineteenth-century structures for female public sphere activity, in which women raised money for group or community projects but wielded no decision-making power. They aligned themselves instead with models for postbellum voluntary organizations like the Women's Christian Temperance Union that pursued female-articulated goals while spending woman-raised monies. The Girls' Branch consistently obtained the cooperation of New York City's Park, Education, and Transportation Departments in conducting the fetes, combining private with municipal resources to provide a public service to city schoolchildren. By selecting Burchenal to develop the repertoire of dances and methods for transmitting it, this woman-centered structure also positioned Burchenal to constitute a professional identity as a folk-dance collector and teacher.[39] In operating annual folk-dancing programs and planning year-end park fetes, the Girls' Branch enterprise staked out public sphere territory as a bureaucracy relying in important part on the guidance of a folk-dance expert. Such bureaucracy formation and concession to specialists, characteristic of business management strategies as well as new electoral politics in the Progressive era, provided the structural means by which Girls' Branch patrons and producers constituted themselves as a public instrumentality, a force for social and cultural action.

Contesting and constituting a taxonomy of women's public sphere activities in this variety of ways, Girls' Branch work produced a feminization of dancing. Not only did females embody contending Progressive-era political and gender ideals as performers of folk-dances, they also imagined, formulated, and constructed the folk-dance practice. This feminization of folk-dancing empowered female teachers under Burchenal's direction to gain and claim expertise as folk-dance educators, thereby making inroads into the largely male-dominated enclave of dance pedagogy. Like Burchenal, numerous women writers found publishers for folk-dance, singing game, and rhythmic play instruction books gauged to children's needs. This too marked expansion of the primarily male-authored nineteenth-century dance manual market. The feminization of dancing that Girls' Branch work promoted thus perpetuated the body–woman cathexis and extended it to a body–woman–dance linkage. This linkage constituted a positive good for woman and dance in the Progressive era because folk-dancing had successfully asserted a social effectivity, an instrumentality for raising and

FEMINIZING DANCE?

worrying social and political concerns. This feminization of dancing even created conditions of possibility for some women to imagine and pursue careers as choreographers and performers rather than as collectors and teachers; Helen Tamiris, daughter of lower East side Russian immigrant parents, was signal in this regard.[40]

The positive valence accorded the woman–body–dance linkage would prove temporary and unstable. During the Progressive era, the constitution and gendering of folk-dance as a bodily discourse could simultaneously discipline female bodies to a status of subordinate difference and yet garner increased social effectivity for dancing bodies on the basis of that difference. The privileging of women's difference that separate spheres ideology spawned would decline in the 1920s, however, and with it the gender-specific rationale for women's intervention and claim to instrumentality in public social and political domains. The effectivity of women's dancing would come to be assessed differently; Tamiris and her modern dance peers Doris Humphrey, Martha Graham, and Hanya Holm, along with others, would have to negotiate new meanings for feminized dance practices in their time. Unlike the functionalization of dance for establishing Americans' sense of a national heritage, which has proven largely unique to the Progressive era, the gendering of dance as a female practice has had lasting effects.

The body–woman–dance linkage still operative in the 1990s confirms that which Progressive-era folk-dancing indexed: the salience of the body as a site for inscribing relations of power; and the potency of dance practices for troubling and negotiating meanings. Girls' Branch folk-dancing prospered, I believe, because it held in tension several oppositions in American culture. It offered an instrumentality for working through tensions about the nature of subjectivity – in the Progressive era these included questions about social identification as independent, individual agents or membership and action in groups. It supplied a means for addressing concerns about national identity – for questioning whether people should look to unmarked "American" or to richly marked "European" materials as the sources for identity as a country. And it provided a mode for performing gender – for worrying the circumscription and possibilities for autonomy in a gender role for women that disavowed self-assertion and competition. Performing gender, this Girls' Branch folk-dance work also contributed forcefully to the continued gendering of dance performance and instruction in twentieth-century America. And that development, dance historians should say, requires its own study of change through time, its own careful theorization of causes and effects.

NOTES

1   *"5,000 Schoolgirls Dance on the Green,"* Brooklyn Daily Eagle, *19 May 1915, Picture and Sporting section, p. 5.*

2   *See for example, Burchenal,* Folk-Dances and Singing Games *(1909) and Burchenal, ed.,* Official Handbook of the Girls' Branch of the Public Schools Athletic League of the City of New York, 1914–1915.

3   *"5,000 Schoolgirls Dance on the Green."*

4   *See, for example, Beaumont (1982), Schlundt (1962), Hilton (1981), Shelton (1981), and Warren (1991).*

5   *Works by Foster (1986) and Franko* (The Dancing Body) *develop several of these critical emphases, while not constituting themselves as studies of change through time. Recently published works by Manning (1993) and Franko* (Dance as Text) *achieve diachronic perspective.*

6   *Statistics for participation are developed in Tomko (1991, 243, 307–8).*

7   *Wells (1971, 272–82); Daniel Scott Smith (1979, 226); Woloch (1984, 271–6).*

8   *See Welter (1966, 131–75), for the classic statement on separate spheres ideology; also Cott (1977); and Woloch (1984, 113–26).*

9   *Chafe (1972, 55).*

10   *For women's work and suffrage activity see Pleck, "A Mother's Wages," 367–92; Kessler-Harris (1982); Dye (1980); Flexner (1959); Kraditor (1965); and Dubois (1978). On suffrage pageants see Prevots (1990).*

11   *See Russett,* Sexual Science; *Russet,* Darwin in America; *Verbrugge (1988); Thompson (1986, 172).*

12   *The sources for this synthesis may be found in Tomko (1991, 214–25).*

13   *See Clarke (1873); and Newcomer (1959, 28–9).*

14   *Hall (1905, 1: 132, 202–3, 211, 213).*

15   *Gulick and Smith, "Dancing as a Part of Education," 9445–52. While the date is not clear, evidence suggests that the Girls' Branch also adopted the questionnaire method utilized in Hallian child-study research, conducting a survey of physical training professionals around the country to determine those activities deemed most suitable for girls' work.*

16   *Gulick,* The Healthful Art of Dancing, *141; Gulick and Smith, "Dancing as a Part of Education," 9447.*

17   *Davis (1967, 60–71).*

18   *De Lauretis, "Feminist Studies/Critical Studies," 11.*

19   *Bancroft, "Contributions of Dr. Luther Halsey Gulick," 381.*

20   *Gulick,* The Healthful Art of Dancing, *102, 115, 131–2, 135–6; Gulick and Smith, "Dancing as a Part of Education," 9445, 9447–8.*

21   *Hall (1905, 1: 233).*

22   *Gulick and Smith, "Dancing as a Part of Education," 9446–7.*

23   *Linda Gordon, "What's New in Women's History," 25.*

24   *Burchenal, "A Dance Around the May-Pole," 5, 66. See also Girls' Branch handbooks for 1910–11 and for the years 1914–15 through 1917–18. The former was edited by Jessie Bancroft, the latter by Elizabeth Burchenal; all were published in New York by American Sports Publishing Co.*

25   *See, for example,* Folk-Dances and Singing Games. *By the 1920s and 1930s, photo subjects came to include adults as well as girls dancing, frequently captured in indoor settings or, when out of doors, adjacent to entrances or stairways.*

26   *See, for example, "When 7,000 School Girls Danced Around Eighty-Two May Poles in Central Park,"* New York Times, *25 May 1913, Picture section, part 1, pp. 4–5 and "Folk Dances by 6,000 City School Girls Turn the Lawn of Park into Fairyland,"* The World, *15 May 1912, p. 5.*

27   *Buker (1991, 218–44).*

28   Tamiris in Her Own Voice: Draft of an Autobiography, *9.*

29   *It is possible that Burchenal learned dances from immigrant people in New York City as well. See Tomko (1991, 231–2).*

30   *See* Folk-Dances and Singing Games. *Burchenal's publishing career was a substantial one, beginning in 1908 and continuing through the 1930s with revisions and reissues of earlier books. Photographic examples show that, while Girls' Branch dress consistently adhered to the standards mentioned above, other groups with whom Burchenal worked, in the 1910s as well as in the 1920s and 1930s, dressed in "ethnic" or European costumes, or facsimiles of them.*

31   *Schools were correlated with lower East side locations using* New York Directory 1909–1910, vol. Resh–Z; *and* Atlas of the City of New York, *vol. 1.*

32   *Gulick, "Teaching American Children to Play," 195–6. The demonstration was scheduled for conferees attending a Playground Association of America congress in New York City.*

33   *See Addams (1981); Boris (1986); Harris (1962); Prevots (1990).*

34   *Gulick and Smith, "Dance as a Part of Education," 9452.*

35   *Karpeles (1967) and* Traditional Dance, *vols 5|6, 1988, offer several perspectives on the English traditional dance revival.*

36   *See Higham (1988); Berrol, "In their Image," 417–33; Berrol, "Germans versus Russians: An Update," 142–56; Rischin (1962); Levine (1977).*

37   Bancroft, Girls' Athletics, *93; Jable (1984, 219–38).*

38   *On burlesque see Allen (1991); Dreiser offers a period view of Broadway dancing in*
     Sister Carrie.

39   *Burchenal's varied preparation and professional posts are detailed in Tomko (1991,*
     chapter 4, 214–313).

40   Tamiris in Her Own Voice: Draft of an Autobiography, *4.*

Overreading *The Promised Land*:
towards a narrative of context in dance

RANDY MARTIN

Is history over, or simply sleeping (or dreaming)? In asking this question, I echo a decade of attacks on social projects for change that are often negatively associated with the 1960s. Those who ask this question hope to prove in their answers that the need for a left has come to an end. There is certainly nothing new about the attempt by forces of dominance to dismiss as obsolete the visions of those who seek profound social alternatives. My concern with the present version of 1960s bashing as a means of devaluing a particular historical legacy is the extent to which the left has been tempted to assimilate this rightist idea. What I propose in this essay is to approach the analysis of dance through overreading as a means to dream on, to perpetuate and, at the same time, reconfigure, the invaluable aspirations for social change identified with the 1960s. Overreading draws on the social movement in dance to re-envision the context both for critical innovations in dance and for social movements beyond the stage.

Those working in U.S. concert dance today must contend with a mythology that a dance boom that blossomed in the 1960s had, by the 1980s, gone bust, and that this bust, in turn, prognosticated the aesthetic demise of the art form.[1] This myth for dance replicates the thesis that people are impoverished because of the inadequacies in their culture. The rhetoric circulated so vigorously by the right in the 1980s claimed that social programs (ranging from the arts to affirmative action) disseminated poisonous ideas that were killing the country and had to be exterminated by defunding. It is, no doubt, an absurdity to think that the right could stop dance — or history — in its tracks (especially considering the persistence of myriad forms of dancing). But revisiting the ideology of boom and bust as it is localized in concert dance, concentrates and displays the issues sufficiently to help unseat the belief that history has met its end. The idea that history has ended seeks to eliminate the contest over the future that has marked the whole process of modernization by busting the role of critical or adversarial culture in the present. The assertion that history has ended and, with it, the left has gone bust, is ultimately a form of self-fulfilling prophecy that attempts to replace an abundance of alternatives with an environment of scarcity that limits the imagination of what is possible in the present.

My strategy to develop a critique of the right that re-invents the left will be to focus on a single dance, one that is brimming with a history that disallows the demise of the left. That dance is an evening length's production by the Bill T. Jones/Arnie Zane Company of *The Last Supper at Uncle Tom's Cabin/The Promised Land* (1990), with Jones, Artistic Director.[2] While no single work of art can effect historical transformation, it can provide the occasion to reflect on such possibilities. Jones's piece assembles many narratives in such a way as to point out how they may move together in an artistic, but also a social totality. The very ambition of the dance breaks with the ideology of bust and the rhetoric of scarcity that can be traced to a rightist notion of history as a past flowering of the human condition that could abruptly come to a close in the present. While, as the title indicates, the piece draws from biblical, literary, and historical sources, it gives particular weight to materials and ideas associated with the 1960s (in particular, Martin Luther King and Amiri Baraka) in a way that rehistoricizes that moment's effects on the present. The abundant reflexivity and ample physicality displayed in the dance offer a means to join theory and practice in a manner that resists the idea of history coming to an end.

Overreading rests on the assumption that the subtext displayed in dancing accounts for more than that particular aesthetic activity and points instead to the very contours through which a given horizon for social activity is possible. Hence overreading has a double significance, to read more in the dance than its dancing can bear and to read through and past the dance to the point where it meets its own exterior or context. Overreading departs from those critical practices such as formalism, that relies on a stable demarcation between a piece's interiority and its exteriority and that considers a discussion of context as an interference with the veracity of the work. Instead, overreading attempts to appropriate the internal movement of dance to the ordering of context, rather than simply addressing ever-widening horizons of a somehow static work.

But in order to accomplish an overreading, the structure of the dance must be enlisted to organize the present writing. This essay, therefore, begins with a narration of the dance. It then seeks to join the artistic with the social conjuncture by a critique of the logic of boom and bust. Finally, it attempts to theorize the context of apparently disparate or seemingly discrete contemporary political expressions. The central conceit of this tripartite analytic structure is that it corresponds to the principal sections of the dance work itself and can be used to indicate both contrasting temporalities (dynamics of change structured in a given time frame) generative of the dance and the narrative of context. A narrative of events which simulates the sequential movement of real time, is employed by both the dance (in its telling of *Uncle Tom's Cabin*), and the paper which gives an account of the work, as an initial staging device. Dance and essay then operate on what could be called a time of levels of effectivities where local effects (from the aesthetic to the institutional) play off one another without being reducible to the same linear time. Finally, dance and writing entertain a utopia of the real which, by identifying how context is inscribed in the work, raises a time of totalizations, of generative principles for rendering complex wholes (a context composed of effectivities), that allows for a conception of art and society as problem and project beyond the presumed scarcities of a history and politics gone bust.

DANCING PARTICULAR TALES

"The Last Supper" begins in the midst of the Civil War. The somber tones of Abraham Lincoln's second inaugural address precede the visibility of any dance movement.... "One eighth of the whole population were colored slaves, not distributed generally over the Union, but localized in the Southern part of it. These slaves constituted a peculiar and powerful interest." The stage is bathed in a deep blue light that casts the figures upon it in the negative. What emerges from the darkness of this overdetermined past of revolution and apocalypse are dancers in V-formation, simulating the prow of a slaver. The darkness of their own history forcibly severed from its root, they stamp out a march in place. They bear long oars that evoke their own movement towards another's promise of their emancipation. Given that they remain within the "territorial" confines of the performing arena (in this case, the Brooklyn Academy of Music, or BAM), freedom and the peculiarity of the "powerful interest" will have to be sought and found somewhere within this circumscribed space.

R. Justice Allen, an actor I had initially misrecognized as Jones himself, appears in front of a painted flat of Uncle Tom's Cabin, which has the look of an enlarged movable theater for marionettes, or, more to the point a minstrel show, complete with curtain and racialized faces that conceal the race of their bearer.[3] Here the set serves as a narrative frame for the dancing, connecting Jones's choreography with Stowe's story. By reducing the actual area of performance, the set keys the eye to foreground movement in that concentrated space as something virtuosic, against the larger field of scenic space that remains open around the edges of the larger BAM stage, and it also constructs a kind of human picture book at moments in the choreography when movement is arrested in illustrative friezes. Already virtuoso dancing is construed as a genre of spectacle requiring scenic support. Already we feel an ironic probing of the very conventions upon which danced narration has traditionally been based. At the same time, the alternation of the synchronic (frieze) and the diachronic (movement) within the same frame could itself be a metonym for the dilemma of historical representation more broadly. The dilemma itself is, as it were, overrepresented in the very historical content of what is being framed, the textualizing of a foundation for the antinomies of blackness.

If my misrecognition of Allen for Jones was attributable to more than my own (in)discrimination or absence of vision, it could be explained by the position Allen assumes as the character who interrupts the historical authorial representation of black by white. Allen, as choreographer and also narrator, introduces the audience to that author, Sage Cowles, the actress who plays Harriet Beecher Stowe. Given that Stowe, the author, only appears in the "Concluding Remarks" of her novel to give account of its message, her presence here is something of a reversal. Her appearance signals both a backward glance through her text, for the epic is greatly compressed here, and an indication that the dance which follows comes after the text. She begins to spin her yarn but Allen, the choreographic narrator, starts to yawn.

His success in quieting the author, textualizing her so that he can resume narration, begins the dancing in earnest. If virtuosity foregrounds the dancing, it also privileges Tom in the narrative. His virtue, as is here retold, rests on his standing as a "spiritual leader" who is a "man of principle" the principle in question being slavery which in upholding his end of the Hegelian bargain, forbids him from betraying his master, even as others, like Eliza, escape to "freedom." In Tom's interest we are asked, "What is there for those who are left behind? Freedom." Since slavery is a system of exchange, Tom circulates among many masters, who, despite their varied dispositions, do not alter his status, until he becomes the property of Simon Legree. This last whips him to death for refusing to whip or betray others.

Except for Tom, all of the other dancers are masked, leaving their gender, among other identities, concealed, but making possible a reassignment of identity on the basis of race. The masks are worn in reverse. This permits a disorientation of the dancers' bodies onto which are grafted the multiple dance forms from jigs to ballet to gravity-friendly floor movement that here suggest a certain affinity between choreography and slavery. The parade of styles displayed by each body as so many mastered techniques marks an accomplishment in dance (talent) homologous to the appropriation of a body whose relation of production gets stamped with a falsely singular identity (African). The emergence of modern dance out of the conjuncture between the naturalizing narratives of talent and race as bodily a(/in)scriptions is established early enough in "The Last Supper" to become an object of the work's own critical activity.[4]

In his re-presentation of certain sequences, Jones permits the audience to reflect on what catches their eye. For example, Tom in a dance-as-video sequence is resurrected, and the whipping scene played in reverse, with Legree now peeling the blows off Tom's body, then in forward motion again, and, ultimately forced to confront an endless stream of slaves whose very return demands further repression. Denied the value in exchange, it is now Legree's mastery that is effaced. It is in this opening scene with its masking of faces, confusing of genders, citations of multiple dance traditions, and video-like replay, that narrative conventions are most intact and most critically confronted. As Stowe's tale ends, it seems to spawn others less coherent, that together form a narrative of narratives.

In subsequent sections, chronology is eschewed for an abstraction of what might be the persistent presence of the historical, the traces of an authority that will not relinquish their command over the body. In a men's septet that genders the relation of slave-catcher and prey, "The Dogs," we are treated to the full fleshiness of uncovered flanks with boots and a gasmask-like facial garb that is suggestive perhaps more of a boar's than a dog's snout. This stomping surfeit of the masculine moves only to the verbal command of two upstage figures. With martial precision these loyal pets are taken through a rigorous but unattached semiosis of gesture until they get their final marching orders and depart the stage. The more they display their affinity for discipline, the more the frailties of sustaining this vision of masculinism are revealed. For it is precisely the exuberant pursuit of command that maintains the flaccidity of the men's buttocks, hinting perhaps that in strength there is weakness.

Next, in "Eliza on the Ice," four women pass the mask of a black female face, first among themselves then to Sage Cowles, who, still attired as Harriet Beecher Stowe, now assumes the voice of yet another personage, Sojourner Truth. This ventriloquy mirrors that of suffragette Frances D. Gage, to Sojourner herself in recounting the famous speech at the Akron Convention of 28–29 May 1851. Gage was entreated by "timorous and trembling ones" not to let Truth speak due to the presumed havoc it would bring in the representation of their movement. "Every newspaper in the land will have our cause mixed up with abolition and niggers, and we shall be utterly denounced."[5] The speech that so effectively "mixed up" race and gender was here being used to accompany a series of solos, that pass the word, initially among women and then across gender. For the first, Cowles incants "Ain't I A Woman?" while Andrea Woods, a woman whose physiognomy conjures up that of Sojourner Truth's, braids balletic and folk movement in a manner evocative of the scene at the Cabin. But that legacy seems quickly foreclosed as "The Dogs," newly trained from the prior scene, cross the stage and take her with them delivering the soloist who follows.

Next, Cowles pursues Heidi Latsky with a wireless microphone. Latsky recites a text of her own about trust, abuse, and betrayal, allowing the sharp gestures of Cowles's probing pursuit to evince stinging words that then send her spiraling down and across the floor, apparently set in motion by what she says. "I believed my father. My father told me to turn the other cheek." The microphone effects the pre-alienation of voice so that when it finally finds Latsky's lips, she is given the word, a moment that also arrests her movement and then, in a condition of auto-narration, enables it. For the solo by Betsy McCracken that follows, that phallic little stub that gave the word is now displaced by an oar from the opening of the piece. Affixed to the dancer's white unitard is a slender chain suggestive of an improbable bondage. The men, constantly intervening as they did from the gallery and pulpit where Truth herself spoke, are momentarily kept in check with the oar. But the leggy men return with their snout masks and jackboots, to insinuate a partnership into the final solo that effects the dancer's own motive force as the men pass her among themselves. They appear to serve as her agency, a collective exterior, until the other women enter to save her, not escaping, but dancing away the uninvited partners. Then Stowe returns twisting Sojourner's "Truth" through reversed recitations like, "?from come Christ did Where. woman a wasn't Christ because men as rights much as have can't women says he, there black in man little that. . . . woman a I Ain't."

The women who have soloed whip their own bodies in a figuration of the curvaceous that has been ascribed to the feminine. As they exit, Gregg Hubbard rises from upstage and as he does, begins to emulate their movement, while pulling a tube of material down over his buttocks to a point midway down his thigh where it creates that illusion of leg associated with the broadcasting of female sexuality. Shod in high heels, he hops and caresses his breasts and crotch, then follows the path and motion through Sojourner's now de-ontologized question regarding womanhood. He reverses the orders that had made the men move as men while upholding the Truth of that final reversed line, "woman a I Ain't." This concludes the first act.

The opening of the second act, "The Prayer" finds Bill T. Jones in a black suit and white shirt, standing a dozen feet away from his seventy-five-year-old mother, Estella Jones, herself a preacher and gospel singer. She speaks while he remains in silence. "I have a chance to sing for you again tonight and y'all better sit quiet and listen." In her melodious prayer, she thanks Jesus and asks that the dancers be given strength. Of her tenth of twelve children, born into their family of migrant farmworkers and now HIV positive, she asks, "Look down on my son, Lord, I feel that he needs you." She generates a gospel medley, beginning with "Wade in the Water," and Jones, at first impassive, is moved. His hand covers his mouth. The inertial residues of the pedestrian appeared contained in one hand that remains in his pocket until this too is freed to the service of Jones's kineticization of his mother's words, treating her phrases as if he were an oscilloscope, he dances in the same plane as she until coming to rest at her side, monitoring her as it were. Yet in Jones's body, we clearly have an instance of multiple waves that can be set in motion in different directions simultaneously. Jones, in a later interview, remarked upon the transgressive significance of his mother's agreement to allow him to dance to her prayer. This acceptance was also "a kind of sacrilege" because such dancing would not be allowed in their church.[6]

When his mother departs, her evocation of Jesus is transmitted upstage to a frieze of the Last Supper complete with its long table. Allen (in a further suggestion of his placement as Jones's double) faces the (dinner) company, and to the recorded sound of a basketball dribble, shoots an imaginary ball through the frieze image's metaphysical hoop – but the score of a ball, softly bouncing off into the distance, indicates that he missed. He then joins what he has just faced. The frieze itself breaks up into activities that explore the opposition and effacement of sport and dance, game and play suggested by that prior face-off. Dancing is used to block shots, or is interrupted with chair games. It accompanies itself as an activity, then is juxtaposed to a dialogue of Lamentations (chapter 3, verses 1–29) spoken between Allen and Andre Smith, who had played Tom. The decomposition and recomposition of a work of art whose form and content are considered canonical renders problematic the generally implicit authority that frames both art and history.

The cast returns to their march formation of the first act and narrates participation in their own civil war as they sing against the "masters" in a version of the Battle Hymn of the Republic, "We mean to show Jeff Davis that the Africans can fight." They have gained in agency and illumination since that first voyage across the Middle Passage. They reach a line of chairs down-stage which they proceed to reorganize into that familiar musical game, but this time there are a surplus of places over persons. As they scramble and sit, there is an evocation of the earlier question of "those who are left behind," now, not only in life, but in death. The motifs of gaming slide between more martial authorizations as they move to commands that they parody in the strictness of their execution. They take farther what "The Dogs" had only intimated, that the disciplining of the body never seems to exhaust what either discipline or a body can do. In the spaces created between the commands, necessary if they are to maintain their discrete instrumentality, dancers find time to slip into embrace. The embrace is here figured as a moment of volition rather than intrinsically volitional, as what opens up against the impossibility of the fullness of authority.

In this section, the simpler commands, numerical, monosyllabic, that had elicited their direct and indirect responses, find their way to that most contemporary form of call and response. The company settles back into their "Supper" while R. Justice Allen offers an auto-historical rap called "Somethin' Ta Think About":

> *Young gifted and black was my identity, but I was blind, no I couldn't see, from Vietnam came dope in body bags, I started hangin' and bangin' and got hooked on skag. . . . I lost regard for life through my forgotten tears, picked up a gun, stick 'em up cost me fifteen years, hardtime is whatyacallit, a ward of the state in a legal slave system full of death and hate.*

Once in jail he is now "rocking 'round the world with Bill T. Jones." Such forms of lateral mobility are rarely mentioned in dance, and the movement from street to stage scarcely done in a way where art does not suffer for its implication in mimesis. BAM is indeed amidst the streets where rap is commonly heard. But that proximity is drawn upon in a different manner in the section that follows.

At BAM, and all other locations where the piece is performed, a local cleric here, Catholic priest Michael Perry, is invited on-stage to recite the story of Job, a biblical test case for faith of a wealthy and "blameless" man. Satan ("a Hebrew word meaning 'adversary' or 'accuser' not the devil of New Testament thought"),[7] when asked by God what he thinks of His exemplary follower, suggests that Job's adherence is based on material interest. Rising to the challenge, God permits Satan to strip Job of wealth, and inflicts "loathsome sores" on him. Job's suffering is the body upon which his faith is tested, but it is a dialogic examination in which Job can challenge the principles of the test and in the strength of his intercession achieve the restoration of wealth and faith, body and soul.

This scene opens to the lush strains of "Round Midnight," played live by a saxophone-only sextet led by Julius Hemphill who has also provided the musical score for the entire evening. That a piece so devoted to the elaboration of difference would find its musical accompaniment in a unity of instrumentation works to suggest the very conditions upon which difference rests. That from these horns comes not only the functional differentiation associated with a jazz "combo" but a musical combination of styles – in this case from blues to free jazz – is certainly consonant with what Jones's own company can produce in movement. In this instance, however, it is Jones's own dancing that is featured.

He is initially flanked by Arthur Aviles and Sean Curran who effect hieroglyphic shapes and then rip Jones's shirt with a knife as the biblical commandment is handed down. Jones takes on his punishment in dance, but does so in a way that appears to divide his body against itself. With bare back to the audience, his feet weave rapidly in finely articulated locomotion. They seem almost weakened and intoxicated by the strength of his back arched in the contortion of pain but displaying in its stolidity its capacities to bear the weight of his sentence. Fluidity below, elegant carving above, he embodies the dualism of the fable while mobilizing the evidence of faithful suffering to the ends of kinetic "sacrilege." Having used dance once again to transgress the space of the sacred in the act of displaying it, Jones then steps outside of dance altogether to engage in a sort of occupational discussion, allowing his dancing to serve as the referent for a foray back into the sacred. His self-emancipation from adherence to the principle that had just governed him draws the problematic of slavery into yet another setting.

After dancing, Jones sits down with the father at the table of the Last Supper and engages the priest in a reflection on evil and anger. The good father answers in the negative when queried as to the evilness of homosexuality, a response suddenly secularized in light of Perry's own referentiality in this context where one's presence is meant to represent another. But he could be speaking equally about the demands of representation when in analogy between dancing and preaching, he says "we are all inadequate . . . there is no way that either you or I in either of our forms can catch the fullness." This most explicit articulation of the relation between the theological and the secular, an historical materialism as Cornel West would argue that is particularly constitutive of the African-American experience,[8] is twinned throughout the piece. The former is joined with the latter precisely in the desire (what Perry calls faith) that emerges in the difference between the demands of authority (the impossible fullness) and the drive that makes activity itself possible.

For the final act, the cast is enlarged by the addition of forty-five dancers, drawn from whatever community the piece is performed in (twenty-two cities in the USA alone).[9] This mass, not commonly associated with North American modern dance since the large-group works of the 1930s, displaces the intimacy of a group of dancers that, in the last two hours, have begun to impart a certain familiarity. The larger group undermines the feeling of scarcity wrought by AIDS, defunding, and ideological attack, that had descended upon the dance world by the mid-1980s and instantly assumes the role of a raucous cheering public brought directly on stage in an effacement of the conventions of dance-viewing etiquette. They also, in effect, occupy the space outside the frame of the initial set for Uncle Tom's Cabin, constituting a sort of human landscape for that promised land into which those first dehumanized character-izations had sought to escape. This public, however, is available for a display of mobilization in a manner unavailable to the paying audience. They are less a chorus offering commentary than a body that collects the desire for dancing. They are mobilized as witness, as movable props (as an antidote to the harried spearholder), and ultimately as that very excess of movement from which dance itself springs.

As props, they hold large, flat, painted masks that resemble African deities and cover the dancers' heads and chests. For Jones, the masks as tokens of memory mark a problem of historical narrative.

> I read Uncle Tom's Cabin *in the same way that I collect black memorabilia – it's a testament to where we have been. The question is, were we ever there, or is that where Stowe, a well meaning white liberal Christian woman, said we were? When you look at it as a contemporary person, white or black, the memorabilia shouts, "This is a lie," The question remains, what is the truth.*[10]

As prop, therefore, the expanded cast takes on this task of forcing contemporaries to look at the memorabilia and see the lie of representation within it. Even after they shed these masks, the corps effected gestures that resembled the African icons – as if to make of themselves a fetish. This links them to the physical memorabilia and allows them to serve as an object lesson, albeit initially at their own (dancing) expense. Yet while the initial choreographic device relies upon hierarchy (hence retaining the frame-implicated set of the first act – now as a virtual space – that had marked virtuosity in these dancers), by the end of the piece, as will shortly become evident, the division of dancers will yield to shared conditions for the recognition of their difference.

This final act, like those that precede it, begins with an alluded opposition of sacred and profane, but here the positions are situated within the black community and the words are Martin Luther King's and Amiri Baraka's. Baraka's words retain their original form. King's final words of his "I have a dream" speech (delivered at the March on Washington demonstration of 28 August 1963) are reordered in a manner suggestive of their own historical profanation to proclaim "last at free are we." This oft-repeated phrase sends the public back into King's text kinesthetically rather than verbally. This section contains some of the most spirited individual dancing in the piece with Sean Curran striking a barefoot tap that appears to send sparks flying through his head and upper torso, while his companions file somberly by. Arthur Aviles, who can affect a heliocentrism at any altitude, spirals his way around Lawrence Goldhubber, a man considerably larger than any other in the company.

As is common in pieces of this magnitude we get to see phrases of movement more than once. Within the choreographic structure, however, repetition plays with the movement of time internal to the piece to create the sense of recurrence as an effect of memory.[11] The referents of the historical past are localized in the work and the selectiveness of what recurs given the full weight of a discovery without the apparatus to privilege what is now revealed. Upon Aviles's return to the aforementioned duet only moments after it first happened, his naked body is offered for revelation. Jones himself remarks, "Whom I choose to show naked first sets up the pariah syndrome."[12] It becomes apparent that this particular state of difference has less effect on his ability to move than on our condition of watching him. But then there is some recapitulation of whippings from the first act (while the crowd chants "Dream a have I") and a series of falls from the supper table into the arms of the clothed mass. Now in this singular nakedness there seems to be some sacrifice afoot.

In the *Dutchman*'s (1964) final seduction scene that follows, (here staged with the woman who had played Harriet Beecher Stowe on the table of the Last Supper), there is, as well, the implied sacrifice of race to sexuality – as if these identifications could be subtracted from one another. Yet the apparent exclusivity of identities is established only to be undermined through the operation of the dance piece. In Baraka's play, set in a subway car, a young, well-dressed black man, "Clay," is first amused by "Lula," an older white woman's sexual taunts until she brands him an Uncle Tom. Her reverie makes explicit that it depends on an appropriation of a blackness Lula seeks in Clay. He is incited to warn her of what may be appropriated from her people, who had never imagined their black objects, what Baraka calls "all these fantasy people, all these blues people," capable of such activity, including murder.[13]

But it is Clay who is murdered instead by Lula with the complicity of the public that has amassed around them. Now this public in question is composed of the enlarged cast who begin to carry on their own kinetic business in various states of undress, seemingly indifferent to the textualizing in their midst. But their indifference leaves the other public in something of a bind over where to place their attention, given that the progressive nudity down-stage has the potential to up-stage the tragic act. The audience is being asked to make a visual decision that rests upon Jones's division of stage and identities, that could be consequential for commitments beyond the theater.

After Clay's body is removed, the stage is reunified in the development of undress that is sustained over the final thirty minutes of the piece. Indifference alternates with involvement. There are exchanges of kisses and embrace and selective rejection but without any immediate principle. Sage Cowles and her husband, John, give "go" commands to the throng who run through each other in a realization of the worst fears of those with an antipathy to crowds. In the density of lifts and tricks that this circulating economy of dancers makes possible, there is, over time, a loss of the ability of movement in its individual instances to serve as a punctuation for experience by producing in the audience that transcendental gasp, the "ah." There are enough dancers so that one mass can constantly replace another in the stage space. The audience gets acclimatized both to the exceptionality of risky movement and the evanescence of human surplus.

These dancers taunt those who fear losing art to the popular, that familiar neo-conservative complaint, as they efface the intentionality of choreographic form with shapeless mass and emit raucous whoops and heys in a simulation of a sporting event that conflates players and spectators. This is a kind of wilding without victims. It celebrates the survivability of the transgressive. Towards the very end of the piece bodily difference is most exposed, and the nudity that had earlier marked the deficient pariah for sacrifice has now become an available surplus. Unison increasingly serves as a mobilizing principle. Hand-slaps on the floor propelled by a series of rolls, distribute to another part of the body the marching to bondage through freedom that had opened the work when the cast first sails from Africa. The slaps soon yield to spinning waves of bodies that disperse themselves through one another. This formation itself breaks down as the dancers file through one another. Exuberance alternates with a rhapsodic calm sermon that finds the performers in various associations until they are all in the same condition of gentle exposure passing by one another, stepping back so that others may be foregrounded, and singing a few hymnal tones, until they face the audience in stillness.

By now they have made the strange familiar, and normalized what might once have been claimed to be so threatening, for in 1990 the piece was performed in the midst of state-administered anti-obscenity pledges. The refamiliarization of the body in its manifest difference displayed on the BAM stage, here encountered that conjuncture which had sought to render all of its various productions intolerably strange.

In the very sweep of this dance, recognition of the shared grounds for identity are joined with several streams of a narrative of emancipation. The freeing of the slaves to choreographer-employer Jones's slavery of a different sort that occurs between the first and third acts finds its reversal by the finale in a liberation from the labors (of dancing) altogether. The "we" who are "last at free" that remains strongly identified with African-American history, retains a certain ambiguity of identification at a different level in the light of the work's epistemology of labor. Coterminous with this emancipation from labor, the cast in its fullness presents a socialization of nudity, slipping out of costume, mask, characterization, role as an escape from narrative altogether. In practice, they offer a resistance to all of the devices employed over the course of the evening to singularize dancers' identities or divide the cast against itself, whether visually or functionally. There is no speculation of what this promised land would look like, clearly any attempt to do so would reinscribe the piece in some further narrative. Rather, the ending suggests a dialectic between narrative and its other as what is constitutive of the historicity shared by dance and other social activities. The rhetorical strategy of shifting among narrative ploys to suggest the possibility for an internal movement, could be seen as the terrain promised in Marx's unfulfilled account of capital.

On the other hand, it could be argued that Jones does present a particular vision of what lies beyond history (which for Marx meant within history given that everything up to this point had only been pre-history). His comment in one interview about wanting to "elevate the struggle" so "that out of the fighting we will triumph, that something great and beautiful will come out of it," is consonant with The Last Supper's own historical narrative that evokes that particularly class-bound 1960s' utopian form on stage, the commune, as the beginning of the beyond of the present.[14] Even with the association of nudity with the primitive (whether taken to mean uncivilized or communally self-sufficient) such references in contemporary political discourse have often become a code word for the very unruliness of opposition produced by the 1960s. At the time of this performance the initiative of cultural representation could be said to have passed into the hands of the enemies of what the 1960s might have produced. At least saying so made it possible for the right to picture the left as forces of reaction to those imagined to be politically unaffiliated.

In this complex conjuncture, The Last Supper was an instance of what the right feared most, a good (and therefore politically ungovernable) example. Because of the magnitude of the piece, different sections were commissioned separately. The final section was developed in

Minneapolis but the university forbade students to dance without clothes. The uneasiness of presenters was met by special sessions of the Association of Performing Arts Presenters. The president of this organization, Jackie Davis, referred to the piece in testimony before Congress about the NEA's social impact. "Ironically, The Last Supper, so susceptible to criticism from NEA bashers, came to epitomize the positive social influence of the Arts Endowment before Congress."[15]

Jones's *The Last Supper*, assimilated something of a larger historical sensibility which it applied to narrative, although the movement of this narrative proceeds in dance terms through the continual effacement of each instance of authorization (from the displacement of Harriet Beecher Stowe to initiate choreographic authority, to the lusty pursuit of command that disappoints it) that gives rise to narration. This relentless eclipsing of narrator and narration could only lead us to hypothesize about the conjuncture in which a piece such as *The Last Supper* becomes possible, appreciating all the while the indeterminacy "in the last instance" between the moment of art and that of the world. To contour such a conjuncture entails figuring the choreography's own internal breaches and transgressions with those crossings of the line(s) – economic, political, and cultural (what gets articulated more concretely in terms of race, class, gender, sexuality) – that have provoked such anxiety in the world. In the final section of this essay, I will address the social context for this anxiety more directly as one where the right has sought to privatize and depoliticize all manner of social and cultural activities that, like Jones's work, have crossed the line into the public domain.

CONTEXTUALIZING EFFECTS OF BOOM AND BUST

Hopefully, enough has been said of the work of Bill T. Jones and his company to suggest that dance practice can still boom in the 1990s. Yet it should also be apparent that *The Last Supper at Uncle Tom's Cabin/The Promised Land* operated actively against the ideology of a decline in dance and of the political imaginary by the manner in which it set a range of dancing and of politics into play within the same work, thereby narrating a more expansive view of what both could be. At the same time, Jones's own choreographic assent represents a negotiation within the political economy of art that was emblematic of a concentration of productive resources among fewer companies (not just dance) that characterized a globalizing capitalist economy during the 1980s that left so many facing the very conditions of scarcity that his work opposes. After eleven years working as a duo, Jones and Zane formed their company in 1982, a time when the contraction in arts funding began to be felt and arts management assumed an increasingly significant role in career success. Twelve years later, the group had performed in thirty states and twenty-two countries, working not only in major dance venues, but in opera houses and on television. Its operation on this scale has become inseparable from certain conceptions of success strongly associated with the 1980s themselves.

It is the contradiction between the control of resources for accomplishing social needs (aesthetic or otherwise) and the proliferating articulation of those needs by those who demand resources that Jones himself confronts and that urges a reappraisal of the rhetoric of boom and bust. For, contrary to the impulses of standard dance criticism, overreading assumes that what is critical in art is displayed most forcefully when it can reflect on its own exterior – which is what links the institutional materiality of art to that of society generally.

The classic study on the economics of the performing arts isolates dance from theater and concert music, as experiencing the only genuine expansion during the 1960s.[16] A more recent study documents the expansion of the number of dance companies during the 1970s not just in New York but nationally, irrespective of the size of the urban center.[17] But the boom has been more than numerical, although its aesthetic dimensions and cultural significance are more difficult to measure. Arguably, the possibilities and occasion for human movement have been explored with an intensity unprecedented in the United States, yielding a dramatic expansion of the dance lexicon.

Yet, as it has become increasingly specified and specialized in terms of human movement, dance activity has also pushed the boundaries between dance and other performance idioms. The different solutions to the problem of minimalism associated with the explorations of pedestrian movement by the dancers at Judson Church and of Grand Union on the one hand and the subtle modulations of a Laura Dean on the other, joined dance with developments in music and theater, such as those of Robert Wilson, both conceptually and practically. The Tanztheater of Pina Bausch and a host of other Europeans pushed dance past expressionism in the direction of self-representation that had been largely absent from the generally mute medium so that the dancer appeared as more than a body laboring under choreographic authority. The presentation of self in much contemporary concert dance initially emphasized relations of gender but soon came to embrace matters of sexual preference, race, the political economy of dance. The dancing body was now placed in tension with its confinement to movement as something that specified it but also kept it sequestered from other issues. It was not simply that dance took on subject matter, for that had never been foreign to the first dance modernists. Rather, subject was unbounded by media and reached for social and historical context in a manner that had probably no parallel since the political works of the 1930s.

The juxtaposition between the ordinary and the epic, between affect drawn through movement and drama achieved through the address of audience, amplified the tension between the space of the dancer's body and that of performance in a manner that sought to join social spaces beyond the stage. The presence of this kind of material in so many pieces was indicative of how dance had reframed questions of the relation of structure and process in artistic work more generally. The interest, intended to be shared by the audience, in how the work was generated in the process of performance, alluded to the forms of sociality that made dancing possible. Process was allowed constantly to abut structure just as personal reminiscence increasingly found use in connection with historical reckoning.

That so many small venues which were able to sustain dance performance had once been public spaces (churches, schools, sites of abandoned industry) rather than unused theaters (of which there is no scarcity) was indicative of how the vitality of the performing arts could contribute to a very determined project of urban renewal. At the same time, outdoor festivals, environmental pieces and site-specific works not only served to congregate groups of people but also to interrogate the conditions under which art was made available to its public. Surely this was not the first time that modern dance had raised such issues – one need only think of Isadora Duncan and Loie Fuller – but they were now being raised with respect to a different set of concerns about access to urban space as a newly problematic feature of society. Nor could it be said that current dance output has lost touch with these concerns or its ability to touch them.

Clearly, the most dynamic initiatives in dance were part of a broader cultural phenomenon, the extension of public life promulgated by the demands of various social movements. The specificity of the dance boom would have to be located in terms of the ways in which this context animated the relation between form and content in dance. But the clear expansion of dance activity also needs to be explained in terms of an infrastructure of support. Given the uniqueness of dance economics, that increases in productivity do not translate into the reduced unit costs characteristic of other industries, growth comes at the expense of a growing gap between revenues and expenditures. The solution, agreed upon in the literature, is to find some mechanism other than the market to sustain growth.[18] But social investment within the framework of a capitalist economy scarcely occurs without struggle and mobilization. The initiation of the National Endowment for the Arts (NEA) in 1965, prompted no doubt by an immediate sense of preserving the national patrimony, of which modern dance was undervalued kin, had its broader context in the implications for civility demanded by, among others, the movement for civil rights in this country.

These demands met a response in the establishment of an entire apparatus of state funding. The Great Society programs, while prompted by social movements, were the glimmer of decency in the apex of U.S. imperium fevered by wars hot and cold. The NEA was but one small part of a social hypothesis that claimed culture as necessary to a just society. With respect to dance, the efforts to institutionalize social justice made possible the creation and expansion of academic departments and performance venues, seen broadly as features of a more democratic culture. The democracy here had to do not merely with allocation of resources for the development of social institutions, but that those institutions could be shaped by and through participation.

As we are all well aware, this dramatic expansion has now become a draconian contraction. The contraction has been as much ideological (in the sense of an idea outside of dance that is opposed to it) as financial, and ultimately constitutes an effort to reform the polity to limit public participation. For while it is true that many social programs have been reduced, the federal budget and its accumulated deficit expanded yearly during the 1980s. Those who called for "less government" responded with greater state expenditures – but of a certain sort – simply put, to free economy from the demands of its public. Capital, the putative means and ends of that economy, increasingly restless with the social costs of democracy, was looking for pastures beyond our shores and the government was serving as combined realtor and travel agent. At issue for partisans of democracy was how a massive redirection of resources was politically managed and ideologically legitimated.

The redirection of resources can be traced to the policies generated in the service of a highly mobile capital (deregulation, tax cuts, free trade, deficit monetarism, in short the odd assortment of initiatives dubbed Reaganomics) and a countercultural assault from the right that sought to pin social decay on cultural difference. Clearly it has not been the case that every or even most dance works have aesthetically addressed this social situation. Rather, the main impact that rightist ideology had on dance was to create a national climate for its reception that robbed performances of their own immediate context. The significance of the hateful pronouncements of Jesse Helms, Dana Rohrabacher, William Dannemeyer and the like lay in their ability to bring the subject of dance and art generally from the specialized discourse of a criticism already predisposed to decontextualize aesthetic expression, into a nationally public arena with a highly simplistic view of how context operates within an aesthetic. Hence, critic and conservative politician were complicit in maintaining the static divide between what is interior and exterior to the art work that both *The Last Supper* and overreading seek to undermine.

By claiming to value work exclusively in terms of its content, the very voices who brought the matter to the public made it impossible to discuss whether such work could be considered art, presumably their very question, by denying the ways in which art brings content into tension with form. The ability of those espousing rightist ideology to trade on the effacement of high and popular, the critique of specialized knowledge, and invocation of the public, signalled an abuse of the very principles of democratization embodied in the social gains that supported the dance boom. Most importantly, the assault on public funding for the arts that took the explicit form of vows of self-censorship to grant recipients, was part of an effort to redraw the boundaries between public and private life and draw art within the domain of the latter.[19] Surely the NEA gets more credit than it deserves for actually funding art (federal funds constitute only 5 per cent of the total of public and private support)[20] but, as a mechanism for legitimating forms of art and as an object of public discussion, its influence is far more extensive.

In the early 1980s, when Jones and Zane were coming to prominence, cultural policy expressed through the agency of federal funding signaled a turn from supporting emerging choreographers to established artists. Then director of the NEA Frank Hodsoll defended deep cuts to his agency by denying that anything of the vitality in the arts would be lost.[21] By the end of the 1980s, appropriation levels had barely crept up to what they were at the start of the decade before declining again. For dance, specifically, both money and number of grants declined (particularly given cumulative inflation of over 50 per cent over the decade), from $9,122,202 and 398 grants, to $8,964,738 and 355.[22] While the amount of money given to individual choreographers more than tripled, this has to be factored against the impact of a decade of inflation and real-estate speculation on the dance community, especially its ability to appropriate space – the very premise of its activity – for habitation, rehearsal, and performance.[23]

More significantly, something with the look of a national cultural aesthetic was appearing in politicians' pronouncements about what could be considered appropriate form and content in the arts. This of course had its very concrete manifestations in the anti-obscenity riders attached to choreography grants, and the overriding of panel-approved grants by NEA head, Frohnmayer. These acts did not go unanswered. In 1990, $750,000 worth of NEA money was rejected by artists and organizations who refused to sign the pledge and some of those who were denied, like Bella Lewitsky and Tim Miller, sued the NEA.[24] The pledge was rescinded. The integration achieved between dance and performance art gave strong identification to performers like Holly Hughes and Karen Finley, the latter chosen and rejecting to co-host the 1990 Bessies, the New York dance awards held at BAM, in light of the fateful triangle it had formed with the likes of Philip Morris and R. J. Reynolds–Nabisco, and the art police (RJR–N being the largest corporate donor to the arts at $15 million, and to Jesse Helms). While arts activists from Get Smart passed out leaflets rolled as cigarettes on these connections outside the theater, speeches advocating further activism were made about them from within. Two months after the Bessies (12 September 1990), *The Last Supper at Uncle Tom's Cabin/The Promised Land* opened on the same stage, drawing into its midst the politics of the dance community's own occasion for celebration and self-recognition.

A UTOPIA OF THE REAL

The "promised land" referenced in Bill T. Jones's title has a double meaning. It joins the Reconstruction promise of "Forty Acres and a Mule" meant to provide the means of subsistence that would offer the material conditions to break decisively with slavery's exploitation and the historical aspiration (with both sacred and secular expressions) for a world transformed, a promise that rests on a very different system for the allocation of surplus. While the first promise was broken and the second remains presently unfulfilled, the joining together of a politics of subsistence and surplus has much to recommend it, as does recognizing the persistence of the conditions of enslavement under putative emancipation, especially the virulence of racism itself. Jones's powerful synthesis hints at how production and reproduction, public and private, might be located in the same dance. Here I want to import some of those dance insights into an exploration of the staging of theory and practice in contemporary politics.

One of the contributions to emerge out of feminist theory has been to demonstrate that the relation between public and private spheres is itself a political construct. This has made it possible to problematize the presumed identification of women with the private and the private with the apolitical.[25] While the fundamental distinction between socialized production (where the resources and capacities for making society lie) and social reproduction (the renewal of those capacities) retains logical and structural significance, politics that emerge during the 1980s undermine any simple binary opposition that would differentiate public and private spaces and politics. The ideological thrust of the rightist movements that emerged during the 1980s was to maintain the binary of private and public so as to deny political claims on the basis of race, gender, and sexuality as purely private matters inappropriate to politics. At the same time, the right attacked the very privacy that it saw as harboring identities that deviate from some putative norm. The attack on these other bodies occurred in the same conjuncture that a highly mobile capital was fleeing its own sites of socialization, an economic formation also known variously as deregulation, privatization, and free trade. One consequence of capital flight is a decline in real wages, which, in a consumer-driven economy can promote long-term recession.

If the deflation of labor's means to rescue capitalist overproduction (the excess capacity of supply over commodifiable demand) through consumption declines in the first world, it also reconfigures labor in/as the third world. If the third world is where capital has newly (again) landed to appropriate surplus which that labor will never use, this newly mobilized capital has the effect of driving a wedge between the category of labor and that of population as such. Typically, third world labor in a global economy is labor whose wages are insufficient to purchase the commodities it produces (and often those commodities are not even marketed to that labor). The *maquiladora*, the free enterprise zone, North American Free Trade Agreement (NAFTA), all represent capital's ability to penetrate the geography of the third world in order to establish an internal boundary of production against reproduction.

For the freedom alluded to in these highly fluid economic formations is none other than the freedom of capital from the demands of its prior situation, either in terms of taxes, organizations on behalf of labor, or political institutions (like the national state) where that labor could redress these economic disruptions. The more dramatic impact, however, rests upon those whose bodies are not the object of multinational capital's desire, that population already expropriated from the land and its means of subsistence that constitute the aggregations of population found in the globally urban (where urbanization now ranges between 70 and 80 per cent throughout the world). If forced migration to the cities had once fueled industrial capital, such migration is now an effect of deindustrialization on a global scale. The chief consequence is a surplus population reflected in unemployment figures of 40–70 per cent not uncommon in third world cities and precisely within the range of unemployment experienced by African-American males aged eighteen to twenty-five in US cities and within the range of workers laid off in those industries of the former USSR considered to have made the transition to the market. If slavery had once been a means to appropriate populations into the global circuits of capital, more insidious forms now operate to exclude people from them. It is these permutations of slavery and the sacrifices they bring that are exposed so effectively in *The Last Supper*.

If the market had been figured once as the site of the simulacra for the body's universal desire (universal in the sense of assimilating every instance of a body, no matter how different that desire might be), it is now constructed to exclude whole universes of bodies. Against its real dependence on cheapened labor, the third world is figured in first world political discourse as a trap, a place that forces of modernization can get stuck in. What seems to join the logic of the timing of intervention in Somalia with that of Bosnia is not so much the belated admission of oil interests in the former place, but that the disposal of (surplus) bodies in the latter place had not fully run its course. In the fiery Los Angeles spring of 1992, we could similarly ask how the found innocence in the abuse of one body occasioned the desire for the abuse of many – namely the narrative (which was shared by all of the presidential candidates at the time, and echoed by defense attorneys and police chiefs a year later) of necessary coercion as a solution to the problem that the uprising displayed.

Despite the formulation of a term like New World Order, and the intensification of myriad forms of racism upon which it relies, this enthusiasm for coercion has yet to find an ideological expression anywhere near as pointed as anti-communism had been. What is more apparent is that the divide between labor and population introduces the grounds for a new episteme of bodily discipline, where surplus bodies encounter a rhetoric of deficits. This rhetoric can be introduced to cleave race, gender, and most recently age over who will get more of less. The scarcity effect that this produces justifies no end of auto-limitations on desire, precisely what Jones – by refusing the cleavage of identities against themselves through their shared display of a common capacity for movement – seeks to counter by transforming a condition of scarcity (such as nudity) to one of surplus.

All this is to say that the body gets privileged in this political conjuncture of surplus desire unleashed from the boundaries of market, and in the coercive strategies meant to recontain them. These body politics (on stage and off) migrate across that oversimplified divide of class/state (or old) and new social movements/identity politics.[26] The migrating body as a globally socialized condition is the counterpoint to the mobility of capital. It is a body constituted in the crossing of borders (like *The Last Supper*'s migrations into and from slavery, the interruption of speech and movement, and the prolonged passing into the communal of Jones's last act) and hence made sentient of its loss of a locational specificity and its spatial dispersion.

I have no doubt labored a point, not only to show the labor of politics where so much force has been expended to disappear it, but also to hint, as Jones's dancers do, at a labor that emerges against the grain of the market. For while emergent politics associated with the 1960s that continue to develop in the 1980s and 1990s, make demands for material resources (for control over both conditions of production (jobs and labor mobility) and reproduction (from health to sex and healthy sex)), they do so in a manner that does not rest easily within the prevailing language of consumption. The array of social movements that cause the right such anxiety imagine a politics of the body where desire cannot be contained by the simple transit between markets for labor and for commodities, rather, as *The Last Supper* ultimately insists, where desire is generated in transit. At the same time, these deterritorialized flows are themselves generated out of a socialization process that takes group formation rather than individuation as its object. The proliferation of asserted group identities is wholly consistent with the segmentation of markets (greater aggregate sales through the constitution of target groups rather than mass markets) practiced by the most recently capitalized sectors of the technoculture. Yet with all these politics what we see is the organizational effect of socialization without the commodified focus of that effect. Hence through the political economy of representation, it is possible to appropriate the imaginary lives of those very subcultures which are then excluded from economy altogether in the hyperactive and destructive mobility of capital. Jones's staging of the re-inclusion of these masses, performs against this edifice of representation.

This disarticulation of socialization and circulation may turn out to be the most profound contradiction of what the decade of privatization produced. It is a product, however, that is less surprising than its own rhetoric would have allowed if we recall that the freeing of capital (getting government off our (its) back) was and remains a statist project. It is the very centrality of the state that leaves the depletion of the material supports of the public sphere confronting the parched bones of that state's repressive apparatus. For this reason the supposed disappearance of the state as an apparatus of social regulation generates its own narrative of the return of the repressed. That what returns is precisely repression is amply evident to all of those engaged in a politics of deprivatization, of decensoring or, to return to the dance, of necessary exposures. These various body politics face the dilemma of demanding that the dogs be called off (once, like Jones's slave-catchers, we notice the foibles of their relation to authority).[27]

Among social movements, the body is not always represented as the subject of the politics under consideration. Yet dance that is full of these politics offers not only the reflexive display of the body as a site of politics but something of the methodology of the social through which a political site is produced. The question that dance figures most forcefully for the debate is what becomes of the status of the body when the divide between coercion and consent, public and private, state and identity politics is complicated? This question does not assume that dance could be generative of a politics elsewhere but that it might provide a more comprehensive grasp of those conditions under which politics is already inscribed but scarcely legible through existing figures of analysis. Let me return to *The Last Supper* to rehearse how some of these connections in a given work could be made available as a more general narrative for the reading of history.

The Last Supper at Uncle Tom's Cabin/The Promised Land moves, like this essay, through a range of narratives that suggest a complex array of temporalities for theory and practice (sited/cited/sighted in the same textualized event – essay and dance – but dependent on different scales and sequences of time). Three moments can be discerned very schematically (to avoid overstating their separation), that are ordered sequentially but that in practice permeate both dance and essay as a movement. To begin, both dance and essay use a particularized narrative (that of Uncle Tom's Cabin and the descriptive account of the dance itself). Each then moves to a contextualization of the grounds and constituent features of that narrative. This intertextualization of a sacred–profane/slavery–emancipation opposition becomes problema-tized when its normativity is dislodged as with the presumed opposition of representation and practice in dance, and correspondingly in politics from the 1960s to the 1990s. Dance and essay then undertake a reflection on the possibility for theory itself with a renewed appreciation of the context for practice. The final act of the choreography questions the possibility of dancing beyond the dance into the promised land, a certain utopia of the real, and the essay speculates about the politics that might emerge beyond the conceptual division of old and new social movements. Hopefully, the cumulative effect of these moments would point towards the possibility and promise for overreading dance.

Like self-critical theory, Jones's piece arrives at the point of grasping its own conditions of possibility in the display of the social body as the very product of the evening's work. In it, a virtual inventory of crossings was signalled – from slavery as private property (under the whip of Legree or the jail cell of Allen's rap) to freedom (of and from dancing) in the publicity of the social body; from the profanation of the sacred (the ready appropriation of a private religious language in Jones's duet with his mother or the local cleric) to the deprofanation of the secular (in the reverie of communal nudity);[28] from cross-gendering to de-gendering, racial transgression to deracialization, dance-labor that circulates across style to the end of that labor; from masking, with its intimation of something private to the loss of that ground for split-representation. Each of these crossings or transgressive elements is foregrounded during certain times in the piece but they all circulate throughout it, indicating a complex and differential economy of narrative temporalities where stories that reference different scales of historical time and experience can be told and exchanged. And yet if the piece managed to locate each of these positions and trace through their politics as an account of transformation, it also demonstrated the totalization of context (i.e., the process by which the contours of the whole social formation are made legible) that made these various specificities possible. That is, the dance itself provides a context within which to imagine the social and historical horizons where apparently disparate politics emerge and the conditions under which such politics might coalesce without disappearing into one another. The dance narrates together the times of many historical tales that span different scales of time (Christianity, slavery, civil rights, sexual liberation, rightist triumphalism) that suggests a means to narrate the historical context for the dance and for contemporary politics as well. Yet even in a work as strongly narrative as *The Last Supper*, the work's refusal to be only narrative points both through what stories conventionally get told about the present and beyond those common tales as well.

The particular move towards social and historical context signaled in the dance medium that in so many critical formulations, had been most resistant to such contexts, winds up mapping the traces of its own possibility. This is why it may be worth the effort to fight the rhetoric of bust that signals lowered expectations for everything from the dance world to the American dream, even while struggling against the displacement of material resources that make the production of dances and dreams so challenging. If, even in its own excesses, a given work of dance generates a larger fund of aspiration than it actually offers, it retains the capacity to bail itself out of the arresting strictures of the bust or breakdown in its own system. It can thereby serve to join the figuration of diverse social mobilizations in a dance before they can fuse in practice.

The process that figures the context within which diverse political impulses are combined is what I am here terming totalization. Totalization is but one gesture within *The Promised Land*, but one with the capacity to amplify the shared context for social transformation that may be scarcely legible from within a given political expression. This gesture, one could say, is the utopia that winds up being particularized momentarily but concretely in performance. Performance is utopian precisely in its intimation of an entirely different world that flashes through this one. This is not a utopia that one could move into, but a passing state that takes the fleeting movement towards it as its own. While the archetypal utopian community had to retire someplace where no others could see it, the politicality of dance (which is surely not all of it) places utopia on display with all its possibilities and limitations. By making more of each instance of dance (or any other activity) than it could possibly claim for itself, the desire is expressed for an economy other than the one productive of endlessly regressive cycles of scarcity and deficit. It is this desire, this promised land, that partners theory and practice.

NOTES

1   *The economic rhetoric of boom and bust that generally refers to oscillations in rates of growth that constitute the so-called business cycle is particularly slippery when applied to cultural phenomenon, given its tendency to conflate quantity and quality. It is precisely the attribution of numerical variation in the amount of dance generated*

or consumed to the latter's cultural value that indicates the bad faith of the analogy. In practice, even the relation between art and its economy is more complex. Although recession and Reagan had taken hold in 1982, one piece in the New York Daily News (17 February 1982) declared, "Triumph for the City Ballet and the Dance World Booms." The article provided the following figures: between 1975 and 1982 the number of companies in New York City grew from eighty to some 500, involving over 10,000 dancers. Writing a few years later, one critic, Roger Copeland, suggested that Baryshnikov's appearance in the film The Turning Point signalled the end of the boom that began in the 1970s. For him the antinomy of the boom was not economic but cultural: "the rising fortunes of American dance are directly, statistically proportional to the declining standards of American literacy." Dance, an object that can be consumed visually, without reflection is most like television and in that regard, "a respectable form of anti-intellectualism," Copeland (1986, 10–13). See also, Leila Sussmann's (1984) study of the boom in dance companies.

2   At least part of this departure from my earlier work that had sought to bracket dance off from representation can be accounted for methodologically. While that work all bore some relation to ethnography, the present study is indeed readerly in the sense that it appropriates an already textualized account of dancing. I have never seen an actual performance of The Last Supper at Uncle Tom's Cabin/The Promised Land but have relied on multiple viewings of a video of a performance screened at Lincoln Center's Dance Library. The piece was viewed several times before I wrote my own narrative of it and several times after I had produced an initial account. This is not to suggest that ethnographic observation is further from theory or closer to the aesthetic than historicizing narrative based on extant representational materials, such as video. Rather, the two approaches are constitutive of a theoretical project for dance in a way that criticism has yet to demonstrate. My work on dance ethnography appears in Performance as Political Act: The Embodied Self; "Dance Ethnography and the Limits of Representation," Social Text; and "Agency and History: The Demands of Dance Ethnography."

3   For a rich discussion of the minstrelization of Uncle Tom's Cabin in the 1850s as placing on display the entire social unconscious of antebellum USA, see Eric Lott (1993), especially chapter 8, "Uncle Tomitudes: Racial Melodrama and Modes of Production," 211–33.

4   This moment in the dance is also one of the literalizations of the Stowe text where the whole series of disruptions that generate the flight and return are initiated when the slave-trader Haley sees Eliza's son Harry dancing through myriad characterizations of the times. See Stowe (1981, 44).

5   This of course is Gage's own account, quoted in Mari Jo and Paul Buhle (1978, 103).

6   See Maya Wallace (1991, 58).

7   The New Oxford Annotated Bible, Bruce M. Metzger and Roland E. Murphy, 625.

8   *See* Prophesy Deliverance! An Afro-American Revolutionary Christianity *and* Prophetic Fragments.

9   *For accounts of the tour and the casting, see Allison Sarnoff, "Getting into the Promised Land" and "The Presenter's Challenge," and Elizabeth Zimmer "Ten Hours at Uncle Tom's Cabin."*

10   *Elizabeth Zimmer, "Moving Truths," 221.*

11   *See James Snead, "Repetition as a Figure of Black Culture."*

12   *Quoted in* Dance Magazine, *November 1990, "Nudity in Promised Land Causes a Stir," 13.*

13   *In Baraka,* Dutchman, *36.*

14   *Quoted in Bill Bissell (1991, 36–9).*

15   *Sarnoff, "The Presenter's Challenge," 26.*

16   *William Baumol and William Bowen (1968 [1966]).*

17   *Judith Blau (1989).*

18   *See, for example, Baumol and Bowen (1968); Douglas C. Dillon, (1970); and Dick Netzer (1978). Note that these studies were all published before the putative "bust."*

19   *Here the two frequently used meanings of the term private were intentionally blurred, private in the economic sense of market driven and in the philosophical and anthropological significance of the sphere of domesticity – presumably where all issues of sexuality belong. Hence the public funding of art was being reconceived as a matter for the private domain of the market in order to reprivatize issues recently politicized by social movements away from the domain that could guarantee them recognition and resources.*

20   *See the introduction to the National Endowment for the Arts (1986).*

21   *Reported in "An Interview with Frank Hodsoll," with William Keens (1982, 8).*

22   *See NEA Annual Reports for 1981 and 1991.*

23   *The relevant frame of reference for assessing these spending levels is the federal budget as a whole, which doubled over the course of the decade. Hence it was certainly not the case that the arts funding was experiencing a discipline reflective simply of fiscal trends in the budgetary process. Rather, funding was subject to an anti-economy. The only appreciable increases in the last three years were to the NEA's own administrative budget (the numbers are 11.3 million in 1982 and 14.9 million in 1987, according to NEA annual reports).*

24   *Steven Dubin (1992) tracks these controversies rather closely.*

25   *See, for example, Janet Siltanen and Michelle Stanworth (1984); Joan B. Landes (1988); Frances Bonner et al. (1992).*

26   *For a useful discussion, see Juan Flores and George Yúdice (1990).*

27   *All this is not to suggest that what Stuart Hall (1988) identified in the late 1980s as "the exhaustion of consent," assumes some heyday free of coercion; see his* Hard Road to Renewal. *Stanley Aronowitz (1973), in an early revisionist impulse,* False Promises, *reminded us of the "unsilent fifties" marked by repression of dissent and labor tumult. Yet even if we were to momentarily segregate the US exterior from its interior markets, and somehow bracket the forces marshaled in the repression of anti-capitalism from Cuba to Vietnam, it remains a quandary why so many troops were needed to put down dissent in the streets and universities of this country, if consent were so firmly intact. Instead, what can be said about the 1980s is that the discourse of consent collapses so that repression finds its way into those spaces thought able to police their own desires, especially family, domesticity, sexuality, and corporeality per se (bodies that, so to speak, stick to themselves). What renders this all the more complex is that the discourse of coercion properly effected through the state apparatus was ventriloquized by putatively private interests formally outside it, what could be called the New Right. In practice, the New Right's own confusion of public and private facilitated the circulation of their influence in the corridors of state power. With their formal ejection from those halls, however, the scope of their ambition to regulate political economy through culture has not diminished, and remains perhaps the most forcefully articulated idea in U.S. politics.*

28   *This deprofanation itself constitutes a countermovement to that of Howe's own text. In her introduction to* Uncle Tom's Cabin, *Ann Douglas remarks, "There is the gradually varied narrative turn from the profane to the sacred, from the common to the uncanny" (1981, 29).*

Fragments for a story of tango bodies (on Choreocritics and the memory of power)

MARTA E. SAVIGLIANO

LIBRETTO

Part I

Prelude

The Operetta begins with a musical prelude performed by a tango sextet. Near the end of the prelude, the Choreocritic (narrator) provides an introduction to the operetta in the form of three parallel proposals and a refrain. She moves from one proposal to the next performing a transformist act: first, she enacts a poetic, apologizing persona; second, an aggressive, avant-garde scholar; and finally, an exotic, intellectual tanguera. Unsatisfied with the results of her different approaches, she continues with her introductory recitations into Scene One.

While reciting her first proposal, the Choreocritic's hands, alternately, hide and reveal her face from/to the audience, in slow cascading gestures. She is loosely wrapped in a light-blue, gauze scarf and wears a blonde, curly wig.

Choreocritic's spoken text:

Poetic Proposal: I cannot think. I cannot think of a time. I cannot think of a time when things happened without me, without me being there. To tell you the story, I must rely on my imagination.

I can only do stories, not histories, no matter how much I research. And no matter how many fragments I collect, I can neither leave them alone nor bring them back dead. I can only imagine them alive, moving, breathing between my sweaty hands.

I can only imagine peopled things, not necessarily "inhabited" but certainly, somehow animated. Things, whether subjects or objects, with intentions although not necessarily clear ones. I fear fears without memory, sadness without wounds, ideas like lost souls without bodies and finally, for the time being, I fear bodies colonized by words especially when conjured, dancing, from the past – since they cannot move/talk back.

Choreocritics is, for me, an invitation to imagine stories about people who move for and against each other, articulating webs of power. No rigid hierarchies or boundaries between facts and fictions, the weight of the storyteller's presence and of her present is acknowledged – although we frequently forget to tell that part of the story since we are more fascinated by the past we are enticed to imagine.

While forgetting, I imagine I remember these Fragments For A Story Of Tango Bodies.

In reciting her second programmatic proposal, the Choreocritic removes the scarf and the wig revealing a designer robe-manteau and dark hair, neatly coiffed and fastened up at the back. She draws her prescription glasses out from a pocket as she changes positions. She performs clear-cut movements with her feet that follow the displacements in theoretical perspective. She travels from center-stage left to right, up-stage, down-stage, and so on.

Scholarly Proposal: Choreocritics, the approach I am proposing to pursue here, comprises: a critical take on choreography; a choreographic reading of theories and their writing; a critical stance towards theorizing choreographical undertakings; and a choreographic theorization of criticism.

Choreocritics can advance only through specificity and, thus, the dance form will be the main ingredient or organizing tool in any such analysis. The dance itself and the sociohistorical conditions it expresses and produces through a complex cultural performance situate both the analysis and the analyst.

The Choreocritic removes her designer dress revealing a black, tangoesque evening gown. She discards her glasses and lets down her hair, clips on monumental earrings and struggles to attach a big red rose to the lower back of her tango dress. Performing timid tango steps she recites:

These Fragments For A Story Of Tango Bodies are an attempt to practice choreocriticism, reading tango's fragmented history through the memory of power it evokes in its very movements. The memory of power, in turn, is read in those fragments of tango actually or fictively danced by bodies who left traces of their movements/displacements, which are the movements/displacements of power itself. Tangos read power and power reads tangos, shaping each other in the choreocritic's writings, as they are set to perform choreocriticism. The choreocritic's subject positions and those of the audience generate different tango-power connections in each reading/staging, bringing the libretto into the politics of interpretation.

Choreocritic's Refrain:

A tango story begins in the middle because its origins inhabit the total margins of memory, pushed aside and away by the powers that delineate legitimate space and time, geographies and chronologies.

Scene One: tangoland, tanguage and tangomanners

Duet of an androgynous, declassé, dark solo dancer and his shadow.

Bare stage. Dancers anticipate the movement instructions and descriptions recited by the Choreocritic, who stands down-stage (center). Two dancers are located center-stage, one on the left, the other (a shadow) on the right. There is a triangular illumination effect from down-stage to up-stage.

Choreocritic's spoken text:

South of the South of the world, always just about to fall off it, there is a flat, flat land so evenly spread out that its people inadvertently live in a latent state of horizontal vertigo.[1] This strange malaise only manifests itself in the presence of someone else, provoking an irresistible drive to firmly grab and stare at the other without a smile, and step on his or her foot. These manners should not be confused with a greeting although it is a practice of recognition, of acknowledging of existence. A profound sense of vacuum takes hold of the left foot: too much air, not enough ground despite the immensity. Legs grow longer and stronger attempting to control gravity if not history. It is a game of minds or, to be more precise, of bodies pushing mind boundaries; a somewhat repressed desire that began circulating before the turn of the last century, where the *pampas* meet the wide brown river.

Once you feel that the horizon should be empty and open, at your total disposition, that nothing or no one should get in your way – not because you wish this but rather because this is the way things are – that no matter what, you are always in the wrong place doing the wrong thing because you cannot remember what you were supposed to do or where, and there is no sign erected against the flatness to remind you, you have fallen into horizontal vertigo. Too much air, not enough ground despite the immensity, because of the flatness. Lying down is not an option; you cannot afford to let anything drop. Your ears start buzzing and the whizzing in your hairs stretches your spine, tail heavily held down to the ground, weak knees but a strong pulling, curving your neck at the top, lifting your shoulders in upheaval. If this is the case, and you clearly feel that unless your feet start moving you have lost your balance, you are ready for it. Arrogant and defiant, burdened and ready to tango. Step after step, the outer edge of the ball of each foot sliding as close as possible to the ground, leaving clouds of dust behind you; knee against knee as in making fire; a slight torsion at the waist turning shoulders and hips into opposite alignments and a casual but definite grave thrust. Always that restless drive to grab, to stare shamelessly and stumbling to step on someone. Effortless. Embracing yourself does not help. The encounter has to be dealt with. It is right in the middle.

Dancer and "shadow" face each other without moving towards each other.
Choreocritic sings (falsetto, in lunfardo[2]) the following text, while the dancers perform a frantic, fast-paced tango-milonga:

Qué saben los pitucos, lamidos y shushetas;	*What do those classy, pretentious, high-brows know;*
qué saben lo que es tango, qué saben de compás.	*what do they know about tango, what do they know about rhythm.*
Aquí está la elegancia. ¡Qué pinta! ¡Qué silueta!	*Here is elegance. What a look! What a figure!*
¡Qué porte, qué arrogancia, qué clase pa'bailar!	*What posture, what arrogance, what classy dancing!*
Así se corta el césped mientras dibujo el ocho,	*This is how the grass is cut while drawing the figure eight,*
para estas filigranas yo soy como un pintor.	*to make these filigrees, I am like a painter.*
Ahora una corrida, una vuelta, una sentada;	*Now a run, a turn, a "sitting down" figure*
así se baila el tango . . . ¡un tango de mi flor!	*This is how one dances tango . . . a tango worthy of me!*

Así Se Baila el Tango (This is How One Dances Tango) tango-milonga, 1942.
Lyrics by Elizardo Martínez Vilas.
Music by Elías Randal.

Choreocritic's spoken text continues as the dancers anticipate the recited movements. They improvise on "sad thoughts" and "absent-mindedness":

Since its inception, tango has always played on rivalry in search of identification – a specific rivalry, arrogantly antagonizing the usurper. Out of this solid tension that pretends casualness a monster is created: no head, one torso, four legs. It moves rhythmically, with no hint of the grotesque, following the uneven times of fate. Nothing can describe it better than the tanguage that says: "Tango is a sad thought that can be danced."[3] And it should be performed absentmindedly.

Black-out

Chorus canon (all characters who have appeared so far).
Chorus stands on stage, in the dark. Text sung (a capella) as in murmuring, spreading rumors, and finally gossiping:
Power is thick, dense, heavy; its nature is viscous ... it's sticky. It hides from itself as if it would always be somewhere else and in someone else's hands, arrested, ready to be overtaken. It lures, it fascinates because of its absent presence. Permanently fretted, rubbed by/against it, unable to take it, a grasp.
Choreocritic's refrain:
To be repeated and continued.

Scene Two: tango embrace

Multiple confrontational duets.
Cast: Choreocritic; Dancers: Mulattos, Soldaderas and Criollo Soldiers, Compadrito and Milonguita, Immigrants, Elite Men.
Choreocritic and Dancers' refrain: Tango started as a dance, a tense dance.
The dancers repeat the refrain while the Choreocritic recites the text. The Choreocritic is located center-stage left. Each group of dancers initiates its steps as the Choreocritic makes reference to that group's intervention in the making of tango. They interrupt their movements each time the Choreocritic asks a question about the nature of the tango "embrace." As the recitation unfolds, the dancing couples move towards center-stage, closer to each other, interfering with each other's trajectories and exchanging partners, displaying confrontation. As the dancers accumulate center-stage, there are always more men than women. The men must compete to dance the tango.
Choreocritic's spoken text:
Tango started as a dance, a tense dance, in which a male/female embrace tried to heal the racial and class displacement provoked by urbanization and war.[4] But the seductive, sensual healing was never to be complete, and the tensions resurfaced and reproduced. Tango encounters were a catalyst for further racial and class tensions augmented by the avalanche of the European immigrants. Tango helped to provoke these encounters and, at the same time, expressed their occurrence.

Black men and women probably initiated the first tango steps in the Río de la Plata: flirtatious *ombligadas* and *culeadas*,[5] bodies alternately coming close to each other and moving apart. Their displays of eroticism scandalized and created distance/difference, racial and class difference with their masters and exploiters,[6] but they did not embrace. They did not need to hold tight; their color held them together.

The tango embrace was created, perhaps, in the midst of the internal wars that persisted for more than forty years following the independence from Spain: The tight and failed embraces of prostitutes (*soldaderas* and *cuarteleras*[7]) following the armies of poor *mestizos* and *pardos*.[8]

After the unification of the country, which forced Argentina into a new national identity that focused on the interests of Buenos Aires – the harbor city, looking at Europe – tango's embrace became a must.[9] Racial and class displacements were intersected by rural–urban movements. The harbor city demanded new laboring flesh to get the beef ready for export.

Buenos Aires was changing from a big village into a city; the *criollos*[10] and *mulatos* herding cattle to the city and working at the slaughterhouses and the *saladeros*[11] were lonely, angry, and frustrated men. Their immediate world was changing at a pace for which their nomadism as former *gauchos*[12] and soldiers was unsuited. They needed to embrace even tighter; no matter whom or where. And they would fight for the opportunity to do so.

This is the story of the *guapo* or *compadrito*,[13] those men of different skin shades but the same dark fate who cultivated courage – courage as a skill and as a value. In Borges's words, these *guapos* were specialists in progressive intimidation, "veterans in winning without having to fight." With a few knife-fights over questions of honor behind them, few words but plenty of bad attitude, they established a reputation and territory for themselves on the outskirts of the city.

Guapos struggled for some maleness, fighting over women who were scarce in fact as well as in imagination.[14] Urbanization and industrialization had left their women behind, and these civilizing projects were being instigated by other men. Urbanization and industrialization wore a face, that of the wealthy men who looked lasciviously at their poor women. These wealthy men paid to embrace poor women, being unable to touch the women of their own kind without commitment.

Whether the *guapos* cared or not about their women it is hard to tell; they learned to look tough, to despise life, and to disdain women. Perhaps they disdained women defensively, because women were unattainable or difficult to keep. Perhaps they came to despise life from fighting over women in order to keep on being men despite their class. The *macho* identity was born out of this contradiction, and women's identities were born out of the competition among men: *macho* men of different colors and classes pulling at women from different directions shaped their nameless identities.

None of these tensions were resolved when the European immigrants, a new army of laborers, arrived. No time for healing. More exiles, more distress, and again, few women. How tight could tango's embrace get? The stiff torsos of the black dances became stiffer; the swaying hips (*quebradas*) and the sharp interruptions of the dancing marches (*cortes*) lost their joyful fluidity and became grave, and so did the faces, concentrated in displaying filigrees of footwork (*figuras*) for an attentive audience of *pardas* and *chinas*,[15] themselves escaped from domestic service to become near-prostitutes.

Whose embrace was the tango embrace? Tango's choreography emerged out of mutual admiration and scornful disdain among the different races, classes, and ethnicities lumped together in the city. The lighter colored ones imitated the skillful movements of the blacks and, self-conscious of their shortcomings, ended up caricaturing them. The darker ones, in trying to rub on some fashionable white elegance but knowing that this would bring them no more respect, mocked the loose embrace of the quadrilles, mazurkas, habaneras, and waltzes, tingeing it with bodily proximity and sweat.[16] The tango dance emerged from these racial and class conflicts and competed for a place of its own among the dances that were already being danced, pending, as always, benediction in the cultural empires of the world. Men's and women's bodies displayed tensions of the "correct" and the "incorrect," of the "civilized" and the "primitive," of the "authentic" and the "parody," and all these tensions were sexualized so as to render the conflicts natural, universal, and unavoidable.

Black-out

Chorus canon (all characters who have appeared so far).
Chorus stands on stage, in the dark. Text sung (a capella) as in murmuring, spreading rumors, and finally gossiping:
Power is thick, dense, heavy; its nature is viscous . . . it's sticky. It hides from itself as if it would always be somewhere else and in someone else's hands, arrested, ready to be overtaken. It lures, it fascinates because of its absent presence. Permanently fretted, rubbed by/against it, unable to take it, a grasp.
Power melts when held in hands. It transports with its animal smell, promising to finally shape unspoken, unthought desires. Power is a movement, a displacement as such. When thought of as a thing, it is one that can only be sensed by tracing its social life.
Choreocritic's refrain:
To be repeated and continued.

Scene Three: "El Cívico y La Moreira"

Three tango tableaux-vivants.
Cast: Tango Historian, El Cívico and La Moreira (dancers), Choreocritic.
Music: La Morocha, tango (1905), played by an organ-grinder.[17]
Buenos Aires. A room in a tenement house, tidy and shiny "like a jewelry shop." Louis XIV furniture, dolls and bows, and cushions decorated by malevos at the prison. A bed with a knife under the pillow. A dresser on top of which there is a great collection of perfumes and make-up utensils, mostly for a man's hair and moustache.
El Cívico and La Moreira compose the first tableau-vivant as the Tango Historian, standing down-stage left, recites the text.
The Tango Historian's spoken text:
In the years [190]5, 6, 7, and 8, *El Cívico*, between twenty-five and twenty-eight years old, lived in room number 15 of *El Sarandí*, a tenement house located on the street of the same name. His profession was that of exploiting his woman, *La Moreira*. . . . He was of south Italian

ancestry (Albanian); she was the daughter of Andalusian gypsies. It is unnecessary to depict *El Cívico* as an extremely good-looking guy, because the key to his success, as we all know, lay in his seductive ways.... The second key was his acute cleverness, his hidden criminal coldness, his art with the dagger, his courage. The third key was his "congeniality," his wealthy manners, his refined sociability, his skill at dance and his skill at talk....

At dusk, *La Moreira* would go with other women to the "bar" of *La Pichona* ... where she "worked" as a prostitute, as a *lancera*, as a go-between for clients and other prostitutes, and as a dancer. As a *lancera* because she stole wallets from the drunk distracted clients and from the immigrants who had money; as a go-between because she was associated with her "husband" in that business of deceiving poor souls and selling them as "novelties"; as a dancer, because she was a great one and because *La Pichona*'s "bar" was one of the places that helped to give the tango its fame and its association with prostitution. At night, she was a tango-woman. Brave gypsy blood ran through her veins, and, even though she was apparently very feminine and quite beautiful, in her dark endeavors she showed great "courage" in throwing the dagger, and that is where her name comes from. She usually carried a knife; but when she had to wander alone at night in the outskirts or in dealing with "difficult" business – just think of the resentment of the less successful ruffians, lazy and cowardly, but nonetheless dangerous, whose women she took away – she wore high boots, almost up to her knee, and in the right one she carried a dagger or saber. Do not forget that the outskirts of the city saw times of violent madness and lust. Her looks: Not too tall, perfect forms, sensual voice, like her face; like her walk.... Blue or red silk blouse with white polka-dots.... She closed her blouse from the neck to the bosom with silk ribbon.... The lace collar completely covered her neck. Her waist was held by a contoured corset, armed with whalebone. The skirt was pleated and of a gray or light green color, and its exaggerated width displayed the *frou-frou* of her starched petticoats.... Her hairdo, a roundlet at the nape of her neck, held by turtle-shell clips and combs, big golden earrings – the size of a glass rim – and from the necklace dangled a locket. Well, the locket carried a portrait of *El Cívico*.... And he loved his woman. The most dreadful thing about this arrogant subject was his love for his woman. That professional prostitute who every afternoon kissed him goodbye on her way to the brothel. *El Cívico* loved her. *La Moreira* was truly his beloved, his everlasting companion.... His political indifference, among many other indifferences, gives evidence of that obsession.... The endurance of their relationship was dependent in this case not on the marriage contract but on his morbid loving, on his continuously renewed attractiveness, on his being a consecrated artist of sex. Free of bourgeois commitments, without distractions, without physical or mental absences, in private life all of him was a refined and continuous caress, attuned to the sensitivity of his woman, and even asleep he knew how to be her sorcerer.... When he hit her, she would let him do it, even though she was able to fight back like a *guapo*, because he did not punish her with the brutality of those who could not master their whores, but with the demands of a handsome master or jealous lover. If she would have left him, he would have tracked her down to kill her; or perhaps he would have sought forgetfulness in alcohol.... Tango lyrics do not lie when they insist, since Contursi, on moving Argentinean people with the laments of the abandoned *canfinflero* (ruffian/pimp).[18]

El Cívico and La Moreira compose the second tableau-vivant as the Choreocritic recites the text, standing down-stage right. They display discomfort with the Choreocritic's analysis, turn their backs to the audience and perform grotesque movements. They challenge and question the Choreocritic's words with gestures, comments, and hissing.

Choreocritic's spoken text:

Tangos frequently portray characters with complex, troublesome gender identities when seen under the scrutiny of bourgeois patriarchal eyes. This perspective, in turn, opens up a space for the proliferation of worrisome "perversions." What could be expected of a couple such as the one made up of an unmanly although very male (*macho*) man like *El Cívico* and a woman like *La Moreira*, feminine in excess and yet aggressively masculine? Nothing but more transgression. *La Moreira* seduces women, taking them away from other men, competitors in the business of prostitution. She provides *El Cívico* with an income combining the gains of the women that she seduces with that earned through her own sexual dealings with male clients. *El Cívico* lies at home or hangs out at the bar, drinking with his male friends, comfortable to be provided for. He fights with other men when necessary, that is, when *La Moreira*'s dagger is not enough. What kind of heterosexual relationship is this? – Tallón asks himself in providing this portrait to his readers in 1959, as an eye-witness of troubling times past. *El Cívico* pathetically monogamous, effeminately in love with *La Moreira*, "knowing how to be her sorcerer even asleep." *La Moreira* more pragmatic in sexual matters, always threatening to leave him and still carrying his portrait in a locket. One a pimp/gigolo, the other a prostitute/entrepreneur; each performing excess and lack, both genderwise and in their fragile monogamous heterosexual duties. Their relationship entails a doubled masquerade in which each edge of the male–female compound is exploited and recombined, eclectically: He performs a dependent sentimental ruffian, she a self-made, treacherous broad. They are locked in yet another parody: that of heterosexual bourgeois mores.[19]

Tallón's transgressive "great dancers" of the tango are threatening in their exuberantly shaped yet ambivalent, unstable genders and sexuality: *El Cívico* is a cruel, even violent ruffian, but he is sensual, loving, and coquettish, although exploitative and courageous, even when economically and emotionally dependent; *La Moreira* is an astute and merciless broad, ambitious and potentially treacherous but submissive and condemned. There is no doubt that he leads and she follows, but she can foresee his next move even before he thinks of it. This is the tension of the tango *malevo*, the dance of a whiny ruffian and a rebellious broad.

El Cívico and La Moreira compose the third tableau-vivant, finally seduced by the Choreocritic's "theory," which offers a portrait of a "whiny ruffian" and a "rebellious broad."

Black-out

Chorus canon (all of the characters who have appeared so far).
Chorus stands on stage, in the dark. Text sung (a capella) as in murmuring, spreading rumors, and finally gossiping:
Power is thick, dense, heavy; its nature is viscous ... it's sticky. It hides from itself as if it would always be somewhere else and in someone else's hands, arrested, ready to be

overtaken. It transports with its animal smell, promising to finally shape unspoken, unthought desires.

Power is a movement, a displacement as such. No clear point of departure, no clean line of trajectory, no constant thrust, no final aim except for the potentialization of itself. Its majestic, outworldly looks are tied to hyper-grounded occurrences of struggle. Power moves in a dominion of pure specificity and total pragmatism.

Choreocritic's refrain:

To be repeated and continued.

Scene Four: Plumette's diary – from cancan to tango

Solo.

At center-stage: a big door, two steps at the threshold, white papers on a step. Plumette's Impersonator picks up the diary fragments and reads aloud. She is dressed awkwardly as a cancan dancer and strips into a tight tango costume of black satin as she advances through the text. She signals the parts of the body referred to in the diary entries, unable to perform the movements or to recreate the ambience.

Music: Cancan, tango, and ragtime played on "old" records.

Plumette's spoken text:

Montmartre. A knock on a door. On the steps, at the threshold, she left only her rush and this:

August 1897: I woke up this morning knowing that I would kick high, higher than ever, higher than anyone has ever kicked before. And then, every man will hold his breath, and I will do the deep split. All hearts in Paris will pound to the beat of my kicks. My rowdiness will nurture the revolt of pleasure. My skirts, up and down, up and down, will cut the air and choke the audience. Everyone will toast to the liberation of the senses. Wine and beer will spill on my ruffles attempting to wet me down, to soak my feathers, to prevent my flight. But no one can stop my cascade of lace. *Mesdames et messieurs! Je suis Plumette!* Boots and sticks cannot arrest the rising and falling of my long striped legs. I am the queen of *Le Chahut*. Each kick of mine is a gust of encouragement and an inspiration to rebellion.

March 1898: I twisted my ankle, I tore my petticoat. This drunken painter is making me sick, visiting every night with the same excuse. That roaring bunch of bums is leaving me deaf. I wish I could stop playing the revolutionary *danseuse*. . . . My wings are aching!

July 1911: No obscene gestures, no scandalous remarks; no one was shouting at me tonight. Perhaps my age is finally showing. Or maybe, this time, the audience could easily tell that I would not be listening. I would not even be looking at them, raptured, as I was, in following my partner's will. My soul, though, was reaching at them with every step, asking for reassurance. Remember me, *Plumette*? My kicks of freedom, my ruffles of provocation? My body is now confined to a tight satin dress, confined in a tarnished embrace, confined to a varnished stage. Everyone seems relieved after the kicking rowdiness of my former cancan, myself included.

It must be this music. "It's good business," he said. "*Le Tango* attracts our best clients, those who can afford to drown their nights in champagne." And as if by some magic trick, I was wrapped up in black; my rage, hopes, tenderness, all. Wrapped up. My legs have been put back to earth. Trapped in his legs, they have lost their flight. No more *frou-frous* to play, display concealment. My legs, permanently denuded under the tight, slit skirt and my power contained. But my arrest seems to fuel silent, expectant passions. Deplumed *Plumette*. Nocturnal shackles around my waist. Indecently following a man, in public. His presence on stage is my embarrassment. He leads me. His steps prevent my kicks from spreading in unfettered arousal. How could I have come to accept this? It must be this dark music that promises bitterness and feeds on my surrender.

October 1915: They came to the club tonight, a whole bunch of them, their uniforms dishevelled, drunken moustaches crawling out from under their forward-tilted caps. They want to believe that the splashing blood is a bad dream and that this scene is real. The fact is that the maps are changing and the world trembles with expansionist roars. Bodies are restless. They want to move to the rhythm of exotic musics, they are ready to hear orders for advancing over foreign lands. Skirts will be short tonight. Our clients have no time to spend wondering about legs hidden in drapery. Animal dances, they call them. They are right for our times.

(It seems that soon after the last entry, *Plumette* gave up dancing and became a cook. In any case, the back of the last page of the diary contains a recipe for frog legs with garlic and peppercorns.)

Black-out

Chorus canon (all characters who have appeared so far).
Chorus enters onto the stage, in the dark, with audible steps. Text sung (a capella) as in murmuring, spreading rumors, and finally gossiping:
Power is thick, dense, heavy; its nature is viscous . . . it's sticky. Permanently fretted, rubbed by/against it, unable to take it, a grasp.
Power melts when held in hands. It transports with its animal smell. It is a movement, a displacement as such. Power moves in a dominion of pure specificity and total pragmatism. Power seems to belong to a universe of full intentionality: It defies representation except for the one of a "source" while endlessly pulling in resistant resources. Positionless and yet ubiquitous, power takes up faces and operates in a time and place it defines for itself.
Choreocritic's refrain:
To be repeated and continued.

Scene Five: desire, passion, and fate

Tango-ronda on a slippery stage.
Cast: Desire, Passion, and Fate – three dancers, hardly distinguishable from one another.
Desire, Passion, and Fate perform ronda variations on a slippery stage, chasing each other to the point of exhaustion, following the taped voice of the Choreocritic, who pronounces ruminations as if the steps are choreographed in her mind. The dancers giggle and address short phrases to each other while dancing, as in a childlish ronda.

Choreocritic's voice:

Desire generates Passion in a different space, the space of alterity, as it longs for it. In the desiring imagination – informed by a philosophy of conquest and consumption – Passion is a vital resource lost when, driven by the ambitions of civilization, Desire abandons the paradise of wildness. Hence, Desire stands restless at the threshold of the rational world, keeping the memory of and the connection to the magical world of Passion. Desire's memory, however, is fragile and in locating Passion always somewhere else (in the past, in remote places and cultures, in bodies marked by a different race, class, religion, sexuality, and/or gender), it forgets that Passion is a power of Desire's own creation. For free of its ontological ties to Desire, Passion becomes empowered, although this freedom rather than precluding bondage will justify innumerable violent episodes of conquest and articulation. Passion takes hold of those bodies, places, and times imputed as Others, who then, empowered, alternately resist and succumb to that extractive operation by which Desire nourishes itself while multiplying its bottomless dissatisfaction.

Passion and Desire do not move in plain opposition to each other. They circle one another in an ambivalent but unbalanced dualism in terms of power. Desire is invested with legitimacy, the authority enjoyed by those in power; Passion's power lies in its illegitimate nature precisely because it is imputed to nature, to the primitive, to the irrational. Hence, Passion's power resides in "empowerment," in seeking to partake of some crumbs of the power held in legitimate hands. Passion's power is akin to a terrorist maneuver that asks for containment. It is wild, inhuman, beyond conquerable nature – that is, supernatural – and must be subjected to the workings of the civilizing/humanizing Desire. Passion's doings are outside the realm of History; they belong to the universe of Fate. Desire gives rise to subjectivity: desiring subjects who master Passion by making of Passion artifacts and objects of Desire, which is permanently displaced, disembodied, and re-incorporated into someone/somewhere else – hence the Lacanian riddle "desire of Other's desire, desire for the desiring Other." Desire follows and replicates the avatars of conquest, civilization, and progress. Contrarily, Passion resides right at the dead-end of survival. Passion mobilizes agents, not subjects but messengers inscribed with the indecipherable muteness of Fate.

Desire sets Passion into circulation and not itself, as we often hear. Desire moves like a hunter who creates his own prey. Passion, the hunted, shows itself and hides away, lures Desire into existence so that it can attain existence itself, so that it can be recognized, identified, if nothing else, in the shape of the provoking Other, inhabiting the space of those anti-selves whose own mesmerized desires belong to the realm of Fate. Passion is created as that inexhaustible reservoir of deep, strong, irrational drives, a treasure that naturally fell into the hands of those Others awaiting the needy pirates' discovery and pillage. Passion: that immense wealth, so overwhelming that it seems to exceed all theories of value, that turns the powerful into have-nots, re-arranging the world order so as to reverse the allocation of guilt at stake in every colonizing episode. Desire, Passion, and Fate endlessly repeat a narrative of inscrutable bondage, a tango *à trois*: immoral in its doings, prudish in its careful justifications and unable to repent.

Dancers end by defiantly facing the audience.

The Choreocritic mutters the tango "La Mariposa" (in lunfardo):

No es que esté arrepentido	*It's not that I repent*
de haberte querido tanto,	*having loved you so much,*
lo que me apena es tu olvido	*what saddens me is your forgetfulness*
y tu traición,	*and your betrayal,*
me sume en amargo llanto.	*it immerses me in bitter tears.*

"*La Mariposa*" (The Butterfly) tango, 1926.
Lyrics by Celedonio E. Flores.
Music by Pedro Maffia.

Black-out

Chorus canon (all characters who have appeared so far).
Chorus enters onto the stage, in the dark, with audible steps. Text sung (a capella) as in wondering, suspecting, and finally confessing:
Power seems to belong to a universe of full intentionality: it defies representation except for when it takes up faces. Cutting off patterns directly from embodied textures, stitching bureaucratically misfitting parts, one after another, with invisible thread, stepping relentlessly on the pedal like a mad, expert seamstress driven by ambitions of seamlessness, power fabricates. Evoking power produces in me nightmarish chronicles:
It would be easier to confess a crime. I would be handcuffed and put away to rot in the dark, free to plead guilty without feeling guilt. Convinced of my own righteousness, I would be proud of doing wrong . . . after all, justice has never been just to me.
If it were perfect, I wouldn't be able to do anything about it. I wouldn't be allowed to go back to the scene. I would remain perfectly cut-off from it. It would be a crime of full responsibility, full complicity, full consequences. Some remorse but no regrets. No trial, no courtrooms. For me, plain confession; straight culpability. A perfect crime in that any possible hesitation to confess would be irrelevant. Actually, no confession would be needed. Their finger pointing straight at me would be enough. The crime itself could perfectly be non-existent. Under their wishful authority, it would just come true.
Choreocritic's words and refrain:
I used to engage in such fictional conversations with *El General* (1976). (Pause.)
To be repeated and continued.

Scene Six: Doña Divina's tango (the one she never danced)

Screening.
Movie screen replaces stage. Projection and sound effects.
At 2:35 sharp, every afternoon, Doña Divina slips back into her dreams. It cannot wait. It happens right on time. It is about to start any minute now. Clarita takes off her shoes and sits

on the small rug by the big bed, ready to watch her grandmother's memories flicker against the window, like old movies on a yellow screen.

Doña Divina, young. (Were you about nineteen?) She walks down the steps holding her skirt. She sneaks out into the *siesta* heat. (Where is your hat?) He smiles, invitingly, all tailored in blue. The Model A Ford trumbles away from the family's summer residence. A cloud of dust.

The chauffeur follows short directions. The Lieutenant, impeccable, tries to place hands on his beloved, now kidnapped and transformed into a victim. The smell of betrayal widens her nostrils and brightens her eyes. (Love or lust, Grandma?) The car door swings open on her side. She rolls out. A cloud of dust.

Great grandfather Raimundo paces up and down the corridor, knotting his hands. A lawyer must be hired to defend the family's honor. Newspaper headlines. At the courthouse, Horacio writes up the case while fighting unappeasable thoughts. (Mamá never tired of mentioning Divina's legs: so agile, hairless, colored by two drops of native blood.) A cloud of dust.

Horacio wins the case and petitions for Divina's hand. Family relief. Church. Divina in a cloud of lace. Beautiful. (My mother never tired of mentioning Divina's posture, like a gypsy, the pride in her spine.)

Dorita, Mamá, and Ramón: Three children born in low, earthy clouds. Divina cooked soap and beer – stinky bitterness that kept the household fermenting, alive – except on national holidays. (Didn't your *pasteles* ever harmonize your home?) Mamá and Ramón played *casita* in the yard. Dorita was the fairest and prettiest, the favorite, but she was always ill. Mamá slurped angel-hair noodles wishing she would turn blonde and pink like a cherub. Ramón was punished for walking to the dinner table on his hands, getting ready to flee with the next visiting circus. The air in the house was stuffy, a dusty mixture of unfulfilment and anger.

One day they were off to Paris, Grandpa attempting a second rescue. He could not speak or play outside of politics. Divina saw the tango for the first time that summer, before the Big War, on board *La France*. That evening, the waves rocked her scandal from the past into the present. There he was, on the third deck, that degraded lieutenant rhythmically entangled in her life. He remained impeccable, embracing a woman who looked just like herself. Divina stuck in her dusty cloud, now clinging, feignedly, from the rim of her hat. For once, her choked sensuality ran red down her throat.

"Child," says Doña Divina interrupting her own tango, "I feel so much like dying that I can hardly wait anymore."

"Are you afraid?" Clarita whispers.

"No. It's not fear, *querida*. It's madness. I've gone crazy with age."[20]

"Is madness hopeless, *abuela*?"

"Yes. I had three hopes in my life, and those same hopes were the three things that bring *bandidos* to their ruin; but I did not get to be a bandit, so my three hopes are still around, running, on their own."

"Should I go out there and look for them?" asks Clarita, excited.

"Be modest, Clarita. Just talk about yourself. That's the only thing we can honestly hope to know."[21]

Clarita noticed that, when dreaming, Doña Divina's eyes never closed. They showed dry sadness or malicious joy through a dignified cloud of Córdoba dust.

Black-out

Chorus canon (all characters who have appeared so far).
Chorus enters onto the stage, in the dark, with audible steps. Text sung (a capella) as in wondering, suspecting, and finally confessing:
Power is sticky; power fabricates. It produces in me nightmarish chronicles: It would be easier to confess a crime. If it were perfect, I would remain perfectly cut-off from it. Plain confession. Actually, no confession. The crime itself could be perfectly non-existent. Under their wishful authority, it would just come true.

I used to engage in such fictional conversations with *El General* (1976). He was so confident in his mental powers that conspiracies would take flesh and be repressed in a single imaginative blow (1977). He would do as if . . . and, it would happen (1978). He was one of the magicians who ruled my country and made friends "disappear" (1979). His powers were so strong that, once it was all over, he wouldn't remember he had done it (1980). When the young dead came back haunting, he would reprimand his subalterns for not doing a good enough job of termination (1981). When the young alive congregated at *La Plaza* demanding human rights, he would dismiss us under the slogan that "Argentineans **are** human **and** right" (1982).

In those days, we also tried out tricks on him. For example, how to shrink and fit in that invisible space between the sink and the cupboard (so that he wouldn't find us); where to hide the political literature (so that he wouldn't burn it and us); where to put away thoughts and fears (so that he wouldn't sniff down to us).
Choreocritic's words and refrain:
El General had three faces at a time, and every so often, he would change them all at once. (Pause.) To be repeated and continued.

Scene Seven: El General and the music-box

El General enters the stage, disoriented. Stumbling, kicks open a red music-box. The music-box sings to a tango tune:
Confession makes you stronger,
it will keep you alive much longer.

Black-out

End of Part I

Part II
Scene One: eroticism, exoticism, and the colonizing gaze

Tango à trois.
Cast: Choreocritic, El General, Colonizer, Chorus.
The Choreocritic (center-stage left) sits at her desk writing. She pauses periodically to think or

to browse through books, note cards, and the pages of a manuscript. As she writes, her tape-recorded voice "reads" the text; her voice adopts the fretful tone of a milonguita. El General (an authoritarian compadrito) and the Colonizer (a foreign spectacle impresario) repeatedly interrupt the Choreocritic's work. At first, they try to drag her onto the dance floor to dance a tango. She resists, and El General and the Colonizer end up dancing with one another.

Meanwhile, as the tape recording of the Choreocritic's voice advances, the Chorus highlights some of her words by repetition and mockery.

Choreocritic's voice on tape, "reading" her text:	*Chorus:*

Tango expresses, performs, and produces Otherness erotically through exoticism, and in doing so, it plays seductively into the game of identification – an attempt at "selving" by creating anti-selves. Tango is simultaneously a ritual and a spectacle of traumatic encounters, and of course "it takes two": two parties to generate Otherness, two places to produce the exotic, two people to dance.

Of course it takes two . . . *(nodding their heads).*

In thinking about two and tango it is the male/female couple who rush in, dancing Otherness and exoticism, but it actually takes three to tango: a male to master the dance and confess his sorrows; a female to seduce, resist seduction, and be seduced; and a gaze to watch these occurrences. The male/female couple performs the ritual, and the gaze constitutes the spectacle. Two performers, but three participants, make a tango. However, the gaze is not aloof and static; rather, it is expectant, engaged in that particular detachment that creators have towards the objects of their imagination. The gaze can substitute for the male dancer; the gaze can double itself and dance instead of the tango couple. The gaze and the tango performers can change places, but they cannot exchange roles. The tango couple, whether dancing or looking back at the gaze that usurps their

Actually, it takes three . . . *(consult with one another through the exchange of skeptical glances).*

The gaze can double itself . . but, they will not exchange their roles *(shaking their heads strongly).*

steps, is fixed in a "down–up" relationship with the gaze, a position from which, in Eduardo Galeano's words, one can see only giants.[22] Conversely, the gaze – a spectator by nature – will always be placed "up–down," a location from which everything's importance is reduced to miniature dimensions.

When tango performers and spectators no longer shared a common race, class, and/or culture, tango became exotic for the ones "up" who were looking "down." When those situated "up" in the power hierarchy were drawn, for a variety of reasons, to perform the tango themselves, tango became exoticized; its choreography, lyrics, and music split and changed. Within the analytic (artificially drawn) boundaries of the national – as opposed to international – context, that is, within the domestic dynamics of the political economy of passion in Argentina, the gaze, the third participant in the tango, was mostly that of the male elite intruding in and transforming the underworld of Buenos Aires. When the elite men, fighting the *compadritos* for an active place in the dance, started to tango with the *milonguitas*, the tango saddened and slowed down. When middle-class dancers took the place of the ruffianesque ones, the tango became so bland as to be hardly recognizable. But the lyrics, romanticized ruffianesque stories, were there to remind them that they could look "up–down" at the barbaric past and "down–up" at social mobility and civilization. These elite and middle-class Argentinean gazes, however, did not have the power to exoticize on their own. They were dependent looks, and they carried dependent hopes and desires. The gaze with the power to exoticize is the colonial

"Down-up," all giants *(grave tone voices; bodies stretch, mimicking gigantic proportions).*

"Up-down," miniatures! *(giggles; bodies contract, mimicking miniaturesque proportions).*

When the elite. *(Chorus anticipates tape. They adopt rigid, snobbish postures.)*

When the middle-class dancers. *(Chorus anticipates tape. They perform bland tango steps.)*
But, but . . . *(enjoying the sound of the world).*

Dependent looks . . . *(looking at each other, puzzled).*

gaze, and this is the lens through which
local admirers would see the tango.

Exoticism and auto-exoticism are
interrelated outcomes of the colonial
encounter, an encounter asymmetric in
terms of power. And they contribute to the
further establishment of imperialism.
Perhaps exoticism is one of the most
pervasive imperialist maneuvers. The
promises of incorporation into
Civilization through Progress can produce
a stumbling development filled with
economic fits and starts. Previously
non-existent middle classes can emerge
from massive pits of poverty, and enjoy,
now and then, crumbs of wealth. The
promise of development is a bourgeois,
modern, imperialist drug. But without
exoticism, the hooking-up would not be
complete. Exoticism creates the need for
Identity and assures that it cannot be
attained: It is the imperialist hook that
cannot be unhooked. Exoticism creates
the abstract, unfulfillable desire for
completeness in the colonized while
extracting his or her bodily passion.
Exoticism is a colonial erotic game played
between unequal partners.

In tango, the *latina* or *latina*-like
couple dances for the bourgeois colonizing
gaze. French, British, U.S. colonizers,
and their local allies have been key in
shaping the scandalous meaning of the
tango steps. Fascinated with what he
interprets as the erotic male/female plays
of *compadritos* and *milonguitas*, the
colonizer sees a spectacle in miniature of
his own plays with the colonized: the
colonized female dancing in
cooperative/resistant movements with the
colonizing male, held tightly in his
imperial arms, following his lead. The
reverse, however, is probably even more

Exoticism! *(first, fascinated and then,
following the text word by word with
extreme attentiveness).*

Unfulfillable *(shaking their heads in
despair, sighing, and finally chatting
distractedly in a low voice until their next
intervention).*

The colonizer and the colonized . . .,
extract. *(At first, the reference to "the
colonizer and the colonized" recaptures
the Chorus's attention. They are soon
taken, however, by the sound of the word
"extract." They repeat "ct" and play with
the making of the sounds in their mouths.)*

true. The colonizer dumps on the tango his own representation of the imperial erotic relationship with the colonized. In addition, the colonizing gaze extracts tango's passion to nurture its bourgeois, respectable but voracious desire – the colonizer's male, insatiable desire for conquest and domination. The colonizer dominates with desire; the colonized resists with passion. Furthermore, this subversive, struggling condition is not a choice; throughout history the colonized have been driven to resist by the imposition of imperial fate and its fatalist rulings. Tango scandalously fits the secret, dark, exploitative side of the imperial promises of civility and civilization.

Dark, dark *(repeating and playing with the sound of the "k").*

Tango's erotic and exotic steps are hard to distinguish in this colonial context. For the purpose of drawing a parallel between the role of the colonized in the imperial dance and the female role in tango, I will briefly isolate the erotic component of the tango steps. It should be clearly understood, however, that the erotic and the exotic moves are performed at the same time and in unison, and that the exotic component ultimately gives full meaning to the erotic.

Hard, hard, hard *(repeating and playing with the sound of the "d," until the Choreocritic's taped voice pronounces "however" in a warning tone).*

However ... *(looking at each other meekly. They remain silent and still until their next intervention).*

As the tape continues with "The Erotic Step," the Choreocritic and the Chorus pay attention to the movements performed by El General and the Colonizer, which follow the rhythm of a languid tango.

The Erotic Step: Just walk. Walk together. Walk as close as necessary. So close that, at a certain point, the differences between the two of you will become essential. The need to master the other is irresistible. The resistance to being engulfed is hysterical. Keep on walking. You cannot give up. It is beyond your control. Just try to make it beautiful. Perform. Do not hide your fear, just give it some style. Move together but split. Split your roles. Split them once and for all. One should master, the other should resist. And forget that you know what the other is going through.

No matter how hard I try to isolate the tango couple from the gaze, the colonizer's viewpoint (either performed by himself or by his admirers) slips into the dancers' intimate scene. The sexual politics of tango cannot be split from the presence of the spectator, a male/colonizing spectator (even when the audience is a mixed male/female one), but I will try again.

In the tango-dancing couple, the role of the Other is performed by *la Otra* (the female Other). This *Otra* is guilty of Otherness or, to put it differently, is accused of being an *Otra* in that she lacks and exceeds in "something" compared to the male. Her excessive passion and her lack of control over it beg for the male's embrace and leadership.

Hard, hard *(dragging the sounds of the letters)*.

Intimate . . . hmmm *(extremely interested)*.

La Otra! *(joyfully clapping and cheering at the mention of their heroine)*.

The Choreocritic, unsatisfied with the Colonizer's performance, takes his place in the dancing couple. The Chorus and the Colonizer now watch attentively as the Choreocritic dances with El General. The tango music accelerates as they perform complex footwork and figures.

She will be dragged into the dance, be led through it, and be held while performing unstable/excessive footwork. Her "instinctive" passion can never be totally subdued, and she passionately resists and is comforted by the male embrace/control. But her passion is aroused by the male desire. He instigates her passionate outbursts by that thigh of his, insistently seeking to slip in between her legs throughout the whole musical piece. She resists with her hips, disjointedly moving them back and forth, her smooth satiny skirt easing both his way in and her way out. Her high heels unbalance her own resistance; or it could be – and usually is – interpreted the other way around: it is precisely her suggestive hips and footwork that provoke his desire for sexual conquest. The dancing couple will not clarify the issue. Ambiguity in these erotic matters is the key to perpetuating the ritual. Their torsos show agreement, their faces, fatalism, tied up in their tightly held hairs. But from their waists down, struggle. The erotic step is developed in this context, heavily focused in the presence – the body – of *la Otra*. The male imposes his reassurance, confirming his Identity by sitting her, albeit briefly, on his lap (*la sentada* is the name given to this figure). She, *la Otra*, has helped him to define his masculine self: The movements of *la Otra*, her display of resistance/difference, provokes and constantly reshapes his Identity. Her own identity, as she falls back on her feet, remains unsettled, incomplete, on the move in those transitions between accepting and resisting subordination to his Identity. Hers is a colonized identity born to be unfulfilled. Although this is the knot in which she is caught, it is not a problem rooted in her "essence" or in female "nature." Her incompleteness is rooted in the erotic power game that establishes as a rule the search for a stable, totalizing Identity.

In the intimacy of tango's erotic step the male dancer and the colonizing spectator become allies, almost 0/one and the same, hiding from each other their asymmetries in power and hiding their power over her altogether. *La Otra* should repeatedly resist, give in and resist,

Ambiguity in these matters . . . (*resigned at first and then, enacting "torsos show agreement," "faces fatalism," and so on, as in following choreographic instructions*).

Yes! *La sentada!* (*performing grotesque sentada figures*).

Knot and . . . caught (*playing with the sounds of the words*).

confirming simultaneously his Identity
and the colonizer's supremacy. The
female dancer's role is one of legitimizing
the need for external intervention and
leadership.[23] A phrase to keep in mind:
"One's sense of self is always mediated by
the image one has of the other. (I have
asked myself at times whether a
superficial knowledge of the other, in
terms of some stereotype, is not a way of
preserving a superficial image of
oneself)."[24]

Keep in mind *(wondering where "the
mind" is: they look into each others'
pockets, ears, shoes, buttons).*

The Exotic Step: In the exotic
component of the Tango dance, the *latina*
couple, a heterosexual couple, is the focus
of Otherness (difference, distance, and
inequality). The male/female erotic
tensions (intimate sexual politics) are
consumed by the expectant desire of the
colonizer's gaze. The couple, not the
female alone, is the passionate source for
the reassurance of the colonizer's
Identity. The *latina* "nature," primitive
and close to human instincts, demands a
civilized control while providing
passionate defiance. The gaze of the
colonizing spectator is now the single
interpreter of the scene. The struggle
between femaleness and maleness has
moved a step down on the social
evolutionary scale on which bourgeois
imperial civilization reigns at the top. The
latina couple has been exoticized. It
stands there, before the colonizer's eyes,
as a symbol of a primitive past. And the
distance, the difference attained, is
pleasurable.

Latina couple! *(celebrating at first and
then, confused as they try to "establish
distance" and "consume" each other).*

Latina "nature" . . . *(thrilled at first and
then, worried about the latina couple as
they learn that it "has moved a step down
on the social evolutionary scale." They
take measuring tapes and rulers, notepads
and pencils out of their clothes. They
record each other's measurements and
attempt to figure out a scale. They discuss
their resulting positions on the scale until
the Choreocritic's taped voice pronounces
the word "excess").*

In the performance of the exotic step,
another dimension of Otherness is
exploited: The ambivalent attraction and
repulsion that the Other provokes in the
One. Fascination. The exotic threatens the
colonizer (the One) through her displays

of excess. The exotic is the passionate haunting past at the margins of the imperial civilized world. For the Other to become an Exotic, this threat needs to be tamed, tilted towards the side of the pleasurable, the disturbingly enjoyable: the erotic. The dangerousness, however, should be retained, evoked again and again, as a proof of the necessity of colonial civilized domination.[25] Exotic places, persons, and things often display the amiable side of the Other: plants, perfumes, clothing, jewelry, food and spices, art, courtship, songs and dances. The threatening side, equally exoticized, remains in the background, a haunting violence: dictators, volcanos, diseases, polygamy, poverty. The femaleness of the exotic is identified precisely in this ambivalence. The exuberance, sumptuousness, danger, and sensuality of the exotic are, again, a result of measuring the Other (as she is constituted) with the imperial bourgeois morality of the colonizer's stick. The exotic Other always comes out of this operation as an oddity: lacking something – rationality, control, decorum, propriety – and exceeding in something else – violence, sensuality, passion.

    The exotic tango steps are yet the immoral steps of a *latina* couple as seen by the colonizer's gaze on the stages or the screens of the theater of Civilization. Western imperial stages and screens are set up to pass judgment, to frame, and to present the exotic as such. These imperial bourgeois settings constitute the exotic. "Civilized" theaters (Western and bourgeois in their moral standards), whether actually located in the West or in the Rest of the World, stage and project exoticism as the return of the colonially repressed.

Excess ... hmmm *(relieved)*.

Exotic Other .. *(exuberantly seducing one another)*.

Exotic tango ... *(improvising "exotic" tango steps)*.

The *latina* couple of the exotic tango performs passion in the imperial or imperialized courts of the world without compassion, compatibility, empathy, or any other sort of reciprocal passionate response on the part of the colonizing gaze. The tango couple falls into the abyss of the colonizer's Desire. Exotic Otherness is precisely this condition of incompatibility (no shared pathos, no passion in common, no feeling together) that opens the necessary space for exploitation to develop.

(In unison with the voice on tape) Exotic Otherness is precisely this condition of incompatibility (no shared pathos, no passion in common, no feeling together) that opens the necessary space for exploitation.
Turn, turn, turn *(gyrating dizzily)*.

At the turn of the century, tango brought novelty into the exotic genre; it performed a "distinguished" and *demi-monde*, urbane exoticism from the recently independent colonial world. Tango was an Exotic suited to the complex modern imperial bourgeois ordering of the world. All contradictory alignments were played out through the tango in terms of the erotic.

The tango was originally poor but moving upwards, urban with some traces of ruralness, white with some traces of color, colonized with some traces of native barbarian in the process of being civilized. It was a perfect candidate for the modern capitalist condition of the exotic. It was an exotic on the move, unlike previous versions of crystallized exoticism. It also displayed a new kind of eroticism. In tango, eroticism was controlled and suggestive. Tango did not perform "instinctive" sensuality like the dances of the "primitives"; it did not perform rowdy excitement like the dances of the peasants; it did not perform overt lack of decorum, cynicism, and defiant aggression towards the upper classes, like the dances of the urban marginals; and it did not focus solely on the erotic powers of

Poor but, white but, native but . . .
(bumping into each other every time they pronounce "but").

No, not, not *(emphatically shaking their whole bodies)*.

the female body, like other "traditional" exotic dances. Tango's sexual politics were centered in the process of seduction. A fatal man and a *femme fatale* who, despite their proximity, kept their erotic impulses under control, measuring each other's powers. Their mutual attraction and repulsion were prolonged into an unbearable, endless tension. And everything took place under male control.

In addition, the tango couple did not exhibit a clear-cut class, nor a clean race. At times, the fatal man would resemble a distinguished dandy and suddenly he would behave like a ruffian/pimp. The *femme fatale* would alternately seduce and reject her partner, and it was hard to tell if she was a skillful prostitute or a sensual lady. Tango was a newly developed exotic/erotic hybrid. As such, it had entrenched in itself the capacity to perform through a dancing couple the major characteristics of the bourgeois colonizer's Desire. And this prolonged, unfulfillable, male-controlled Desire was performed passionately. Tango was a mirror representation of the bourgeois colonizer's Desire, performed with the passion of the neo-colonized. In tango, the gaze of the colonizer could take a look at itself, through the tense, passionate, dramatic steps of the colonized molded in the colonizer's cast. Tango understood the colonizer's Desire from within. Tango could be clothed in tails and satins. But it could also be put in its place: The place of the colonized in the process of being civilized. Tango then would wear its *gaucho* costumes: the robes of exotic passion, of the freedom and loose wilderness of the *pampas sudamericanas*. Tango was a versatile, hybrid, new kind of exotic that could adopt the manners of the

Fatal, *fatale (exaggerating the French pronunciation),* attraction and repulsion, endless . . . *(showing uneasiness, checking their watches, wary at the length of the scene).*

Hybrid, hermaphrodite dancing *(excited at their discovery).*

Mirror, mirror . . . neo? *(feeding "passion" into each other's desiring, devouring, mouths).*

Within. Tails and satins. *(They briefly perform elegant, Frenchified, tango steps. Some dancers show enthusiasm and others, boredom). Without (their steps evolve into a tango arrabalero – rough and energetic).*

colonizer while retaining the passion of the colonized, both at heart and on the surface. *Tangueros* were offered the most "distinguished" positions among the exotic at the time and performing tango was one of the few sources of income available to them. In this triangular paradox, auto-exoticism was probably a (colonially) loaded choice.

> *Chorus exits in disarray as the voice on tape ends. El General, the Colonizer and the Choreocritic bow for the audience, proud, arrogant, "distinguished."*

> *Black-out*

Chorus canon (all characters who have appeared so far).
Chorus enters the stage, in the dark, with audible steps. Text sung (a capella) as in story-telling:
In those days, we also tried out tricks on him. For example, how to shrink and fit, where to hide the literature and put away thoughts and fears (so that he wouldn't sniff down to us). But *El General* had three faces at a time, and every so often he would change them all at once.
Lonely and frequently drunk, one day *El General* made a decision, on his own and clean. He had the suspicion that, no matter what, dirty wars were not sufficiently honorable. And the Queen of England surprisingly received the proclamation: *"Las Malvinas son Argentinas."*
Brief spotlight on El General, dizzily strategizing, bent over maps and globes.
For a week or so, his dreams of national popularity came true. Many men played the bombing and bullets game, and laughed with excitement at the idea of confronting an angry Prince Andrew in the South Atlantic. The world could hardly believe it: an unknown British colony in Argentinean waters was being contested.
Choreocritic's words and refrain:
In those days, we also tried out tricks on him. For example . . . (Pause.) To be repeated and continued.

Scene Two: the postcolonial encounter[26]

Tango parade.
Cast: Choreocritic, Postmodern Academics, Postcolonial Intellectuals, Subalterns, Immigration Officer.
The Choreocritic reads her essay at a conference for an audience of Postmodern Academics. They sit, listen, take notes. The Postcolonial Intellectuals arrive late. The Immigration Officer, sitting in a booth, stops each of them at the entrance and glances at their documents. The Postcolonial Intellectuals leave their suitcases at the edge of the conference setting and

find a seat, perturbing the general attention. Subalterns start walking into the scene, some alone, others in small groups, tired and carrying heavy bags, oblivious to the conference. They interfere with the audience's view of the "conference" setting. The Immigration Officer steps nervously out of his booth and attempts to impose order by asking them for their documentation, resident status, return tickets, and so on.

Choreocritic's "essay" (spoken text):

Others are pure bodies, nothing but flesh, unspeakable. They are always waiting, out there, in a long line, to be interpreted, represented, and translated.[27] Postcolonial intellectuals are Others who attempt to represent and position themselves in a world constituted as such by a long history of colonialism.[28] As a perspective, postcoloniality emerges in postmodern times: times of reordering the world and of redefining (re-organizing?) imperialism without many philosophical clues but with plenty of experience in exerting power.[29] Postcolonial intellectuals are particularly interested in the possibilities that this crack opens for a reconceptualization of the margins and peripheries of a world globalized by imperialism and transculturation; margins so intensely articulated to the center, so entrenched at its very core, that those very entities (cores/peripheries) become dislocated. These confusions announce changes, and changes entertain promises, again soaked in confusion. Postmodernism performs a confession of exhaustion while claiming control over the confusion through its very consciousness – that is, the confession. Postcolonial cultural workers build-up in the cracks exposed by postmodernism as fast and surprisingly as possible. Moving theoretically as if postmodernism were a reality, beyond discussions of factual or virtual truth, "postcolonials," as the Others of postmodernism, confirm the breakdown of modernity. In so doing, postcoloniality embraces postmodernity, positioned from an outside that lies in the middle.

In the postcolonial encounter, postcolonial critics are the internalized Other now impersonated and politicized, pushing postmodernity to take the necessary steps into post-imperialism. In order to do so, postcolonial intellectuals must part-take of postmodern myths and realities from an/Other dimension, the one of postcoloniality. Already an Other, asserting the historical import of colonialism in the making and collapse of modernity now displaced into postmodernity, the postcolonial intellectual becomes an ex-colonial re-colonized under postmodernity, struggling for decolonization.

Postcoloniality evokes at once postmodernism and colonialism, and conjures the image of the postcolonial space as postmodern colony, bringing in the presence of the resistant and subversive Other, so indispensable in these colonial and postmodern matters. Alterity is internalized, assimilated (where it should have always been), saturated by the embodiment of the imagination or the fantasy of total fusion: The postcolonial encounter. An encounter provoked, this time, by the displacement of the ex-colonized, who are still searching for decolonization. Identity fragmentations proliferate at the dissolution of the radical border of imperialism. Mobility, nomadism, transmutedness. Homelessness, nostalgia. Exile, uprootedness. Diaspora. Migration, invasion of the territories of former invaders. Exploitation turned into cannibalization, reversed, returned against itself since paramount alterity does not acknowledge difference in clusters. Hybridity.

As I think about the postcolonial encounter, these questions prompt my tango parade: If postmodernism were, among other things, a newly situated colonial attitude, how does it

subject postcolonials? What do postcolonials come to represent in the postmodern imagination? Are the politics of postcoloniality engulfed by the postmodern logic?

It might be helpful to go back to Anthony Kwame Appiah's (1991) question: "Is the Post-
in Postmodernism the Post- in Postcolonial?"[30] The "post" in postcoloniality cannot be
severed from that other "post" of the postmodern condition that made it think of itself,
simultaneously, in the past and future tenses. Postcolonial intellectuals inhabit postmodernity
clinging to a "post" that talks back as a parody of postmodernism in several ways.
Postcoloniality performs the pendular gesture of shoving colonialism towards the past and
bringing it back into the future implicated in the "post," while not forgetting to sweep by the
omitted "modern" that it replaces with "colonial," as a reminder that modern and colonial
enterprises have historically gone hand in hand. Postcolonial intellectuals use a variety of
modern and postmodern analytical tools, frequently displacing them from the theoretical
narratives, intellectual histories and political contexts in which they were originally elaborated,
purposefully combining them in anarchic ways.[31] In so doing, the postcolonial critic mimics
postmodern messiness and introduces an ambivalent suspicion regarding abandonment to this
condition and ironic control over it: Is the postcolonial colonized into postmodern disorientation or is he or she doubling and subverting the colonizing logic that persists in modern
rationality, which is disavowed and continued through postmodernism?

Hybridity, for example, while overtly calling attention to the complexities embedded in the
colonizer/colonized plays of identification – often addressed at pinpointing the pitfalls of
decolonization projects that rely on the recovery of roots and the authentic – also brings to mind
the hybrid position of the postcolonial *vis-à-vis* postmodernity.[32] Postcolonials, knowing
postmodernism from within, implode the nostalgic side of nihilistic postmodernity and promise
some (political) action from the margins of the overall decentered world by retracing the lost
memories of colonialism, that is, the memory of power ... the memory of change? The hybrid
postcolonial critic juggles the memories of colonialism and the learnings of postmodernism into
an expectant, rarefied air. The postmodern spectator watches and awaits, ambivalent, the
postcolonial performance of unlearning colonial teachings while suspecting or announcing that
it is too late. Too late for decolonization. For decolonization already took place in a dramatic
although unglamorous way, self-fulfilling the prophecies on the colonizer rather than the
colonized side.

Perhaps postcolonial intellectuals' decolonization entails unlearning the privilege of representing the unrepresentable, those whose marginality is unimaginable. "The postcolonial
intellectuals learn that their privilege is their loss. In this they are a paradigm of the
intellectuals."[33] In looking for clues on how to address the decolonization of our colonized
thirdworldean minds, I read in this phrase an invitation to learn that our words cannot take hold of
those bodies, purposes, and fates towards which we merely point by naming the subalterns.[34]

> Outside (though not completely) the circuit of the international division of labor, there
> are people whose consciousness we cannot grasp. . . . Here are subsistence workers, the
> tribals, and the communities of zero workers on the street or in the countryside. To
> confront them is not to represent (vertreten) them but to represent (darstellen)
> ourselves.[35]

As we speak, the theoretical carnival parades the avatars of the postcolonial encounter – that is, the encounter between postmodern and postcolonial intellectuals that occurs in a U.S. conference room. Meanwhile, at home the once literally decolonized now long for recoloniza- tion. De-linking has now turned from a revolutionary strategy into a nightmarish reality. Exploit me! Extract my surplus! Give me a chance!, say politely the ex-colonized as they attempt to move to those still titillating, shifting centers they skilfully detect in a world that pronounces itself as decentered and thoroughly marginalized. The memory of power, in its full ambivalence as exploitative and enabling, repressive and productive, is kept in the bodies of the ex-colonials and performed through the body politics of migration, exile, self-exile, diaspora, on the one hand, and, on the other, through soliciting of foreign investments, international tourism and the privatization of formerly state-administered industries and services. The once national bodies are thus exposed to transnational fates. Under these conditions, subalterns from the former colony, once decolonized, work and hustle. What else can I say? Unable to represent them, I see ourselves, intellectuals, longing for a re-colonization on our own terms. Do we know any other version of freedom?

> Chorus (all characters in the scene) recite together with the Choreocritic the last line of her "essay": "Do we know any other version of freedom?" (Pause.)
>
> As the lights go down, the chorus repeats the refrain: "Memory of Power, Memory of Power, Memory of Power," as in conjuring the final scene.

Black-out

Scene Three: tango on power

> Complete cast of characters, some reading, some listening, some reciting, some sleeping, most of them sitting on the floor and a few walking. All of them deal, in some way, with the following text.

Chorus's spoken text:

Power is thick, dense, heavy; its nature is viscous . . . it's sticky. It hides from itself as if it would always be somewhere else and in someone else's hands, arrested, ready to be overtaken. It lures, it fascinates because of its absent presence. Permanently fretted, rubbed by/against it, unable to take it, a grasp.

Power melts when held in hands. It transports with its animal smell, promising to shape at last unspoken, unthought desires. Power is a movement, a displacement as such. When thought of as a thing, it can only be sensed by tracing its social life.

No clear point of departure, no clean line of trajectory, no constant thrust, no final aim except for the potentialization of itself. Its majestic, outworldly looks are tied to hyper-grounded occurrences of struggle. Power moves in a dominion of pure specificity and total pragmatism.

Power seems to belong to a universe of full intentionality: It defies representation except for the one of a "source" while endlessly pulling in resistant resources. Positionless and yet ubiquitous, power takes up faces and operates in a time and place it defines for itself.

Cutting off patterns directly from embodied textures, stitching bureaucratically misfitting parts, one after another, with invisible thread, stepping relentlessly on the pedal like a mad, expert seamstress driven by ambitions of seamlessness, power fabricates.

Choreocritic's aria:

Evoking power produces in me nightmarish chronicles: It would be easier to confess a crime. I would be handcuffed and put away to rot in the dark, free to plead guilty without feeling guilt. Convinced of my own righteousness, I would be proud of doing wrong ... after all, justice has never been just to me.

If it were perfect, I wouldn't be able to do anything about it. I wouldn't be allowed to go back to the scene. I would remain perfectly cut-off from it. It would be a crime of full responsibility, full complicity, full consequences. Some remorse but no regrets. No trial, no courtrooms. For me, plain confession; straight culpability. A perfect crime in that any possible hesitation to confess would be irrelevant. Actually, no confession would be needed. Their fingers pointing straight at me would be enough. The crime itself could perfectly be non-existent. Under their wishful authority, it would just come true.

I used to engage in such fictional conversations with *El General* (1976). He was so confident in his mental powers that conspiracies would take flesh and be repressed in a single imaginative blow (1977). He would do as if ... and, it would happen (1978). He was one of the magicians who ruled my country and made friends "disappear" (1979). His powers were so strong that, after it was all over, he wouldn't remember he had done it (1980). When the young dead came back haunting, he would reprimand his subalterns for not doing a good enough job of termination (1981). When the young alive congregated at *La Plaza* demanding human rights, he would dismiss us under the slogan that "Argentinians **are** human **and** right" (1982).

In those days, we also tried out tricks on him. For example, how to shrink and fit in that invisible space between the sink and the cupboard (so that he wouldn't find us); where to hide the political literature (so that he wouldn't burn it and us); where to put away thoughts and fears (so that he wouldn't sniff down to us).

El General had three faces at a time, and every so often, he would change them all at once. Despite his cleverness, we could always tell who he was by the looks of his *Ministro* who would never leave him alone. Those weird ears ... always attuned to Washington and to the bureaucrats of the IMF. Sacrifice and austerity were demanded from those arrogant, unrealistic people. *El General* was promised unpopular but historical glory.

Lonely and frequently drunk, one day *El General* made a real decision, on his own and clean. He had the suspicion that, no matter what, dirty wars were not sufficiently honorable. And the Queen of England surprisingly received the proclamation: "*Las Malvinas son Argentinas.*"

For a week or so, his dreams of national popularity came true. Many men played the bombing and bullets game, and laughed with excitement at the idea of confronting an angry Prince Andrew in the South Atlantic. The world could hardly believe it: an unknown British colony in Argentinian waters was being contested. *El General* was immersed in a delirium of blood and fire. He needn't fear hell any longer; he had created it on earth. The young dead kept on piling-up, but they wouldn't remain inert. And he also found that betrayal occurs even in hell. "Surrender – ordered Washington – you have abused our confidence and goodwill." *El General* was promised a comfortable cell and the people were promised democracy (1983).

General! I saw you at your trial frantically reading the bible while the young dead lined up accusations of torture, rape, and murder (1984). The next time I saw you, you were strolling with your wife at the recently inaugurated luxurious mall where, democratically, clear consciences were on sale (1990). And you could afford one while we, democratically, kept on paying our national debt.

General! You **imagine** our crimes and we automatically become shadows, exiles, and corpses. We **know** your crimes, and you live happily ever after.

General! Now, your close collaborators populate our regained democratic ballots (1993).

The whole cast faces the audience, in full attention, reciting the final lines:

Is this the way in which power "circulates"? If so, General, I gather that in our country, somehow, power has become stagnant, locked-up and arrested. (Pause.)

Perhaps my powers have been sentenced to exhaustion in w-i-s-h-i-n-g y-o-u t-h-e w-o-r-s-t of all deaths.

The Choreocritic closes the piece with the refrain:

To be **remembered** and continued.

FIN

NOTES

1   *Alicia Dujovne Ortiz, in "Buenos Aires," borrows the concept* horizontal vertigo *from Drieu La Rochelle and uses it to describe the* pampas*'s "ideal metaphysical space": a baroque space of too much emptiness. See Alicia Dujovne Ortiz "Buenos Aires" in* Critical Fictions: The Politics of Imaginative Writing, *edited by P. Manani (Seattle: Bay Press, 1991), 117.*

2   Lunfardo *is the name given to the slang of Buenos Aires.*

3   "El tango es un pensamiento triste que se puede bailar," *a popular saying usually attributed to Enrique Santos Discépolo.*

4   *For a comprehensive description of the hectic, convulsive times lived at the Río de la Plata when the "birth" of tango occurred, see Fernando Assunção,* El Tango y Sus Circunstancias (1880–1920) *(Buenos Aires: Librería El Ateneo Editorial, 1984).*

5   Ombligadas *and* culeadas*: Pronounced pelvic movements while walking back and forth in the course of a dance.* Ombligadas *("navelings") describe the displacements by which the dancers approximate each other with their abdomen and* culeadas *("rumpings"), with their rears.*

6   *See Fernando Assunção,* El Tango y Sus Circunstancias (1880–1920) *(Buenos Aires: Librería El Ateneo Editorial, 1984); Oscar Natale,* Buenos Aires, Negros y Tango *(Buenos Aires: Peña Lillo Editor, 1984); and Horacio Salas,* El Tango *(Buenos Aires: Planeta, 1986).*

7   Soldaderas *and* cuarteleras: *Women who followed soldiers in battle as logistic support. Among other services they acted as prostitutes.*

8   Pardos: *Dark-skinned men, usually descendants of African slaves.*

9   *After gaining independence from Spain, Argentineans engaged in more than forty years of inter-provincial wars; the unification of the country was established in 1852. The federal alliance of provinces was brought into the hegemony of Buenos Aires (declared the federal capital) in the 1880s, under the pressure of political leaders allied to British economic interests. See Liborio Justo,* Nuestra Patria Vasalla: Historia del Coloniaje Argentino. Tomo IV *(Buenos Aires: Editorial Grito Sagrado, 1989); and José Luis Romero,* La Experiencia Argentina y Otros Ensayos *(Mexico, D.F.: Fondo de Cultura Económica, 1989).*

10   Criollos: *Persons born in the South American colonies of European parents (often extended to mixed Spanish/Amerindian ancestry). Also, people of the "land" – that is, the interior and rural areas.*

11   Saladeros: *Meat-packers.*

12   Gauchos: *Rural characters associated with the Argentinean* pampas *(plains).*

13   Guapos, compadritos: *Defiant, street-wise, courageous male characters of the tango environment.*

14   *In defining scarcity one is always faced with the problem of how needs are created, conceptualized, and assessed. Horacio Salas reports that during this period (1860s to 1890s), the city of Buenos Aires had 60,000 to 100,000 fewer women than men. This demographic imbalance might have allocated a precious value to women and turned them into a "scarce resource," since these men felt that they could not hope to hold on to ("embrace") anything other than women. See Horacio Salas,* El Tango *(Buenos Aires: Planeta, 1986).*

15   Chinas: *Women from the "interior" of the country, usually* mestizas *(mixed Spanish/Amerindian ancestry). The female partner of the gaucho.*

16   *For an exhaustive compilation of the debates on "who" (by race and class) introduced "what" into the tango choreography, see Oscar Natale,* Buenos Aires, Negros y Tango *(Buenos Aires: Peña Lillo Editor, 1984); and Fernando Guibert,* Los Argentinos y El Tango *(Buenos Aires: Ediciones Culturales Argentinas, 1973).*

17   La Morocha *(1905), music by Enrique Saborido and lyrics by Angel G. Villoldo, was one of the first tangos to achieve great popularity both in Argentina and abroad (more than 390,000 copies of the sheet music were sold over several editions). The lyrics of* La Morocha *evoke an image of an Argentinean woman who is very different from* La Moreira. *The refrain of* La Morocha *reads: "Soy la morocha argentina / la que no siente penares. . . . / Soy la gentil compañera / del noble gaucho porteño, / la que conserva el cariño / para su dueño" (I am the Argentinean morocha / the one who* *feels no sadness.... | I am the gentle companion | of the* gaucho porteño, *| the one who keeps her love | for her owner). The two popular images of Argentinean women's femininity coexisted conflictively at the time.*

18   *Excerpted from José S. Tallón,* El Tango en sus Etapas de Música Prohibida *(Buenos Aires: Instituto Amigos del Libro Argentino, 1964).*

19   *These thoughts on the performance of masquerade as opposed to the spectacle of masquerade have been triggered by my reading of Sue-Ellen Case, "Toward a Butch-Femme Aesthetic," in* The Lesbian and Gay Studies Reader, *ed. Henry Abelove, Michele Aina Barale, and David M. Halperin (New York: Routledge, 1993), 294–306.*

20   *Lines from an interview with Aníbal Troilo, a famous Argentinian composer and bandoneonist, by María Esther Gilio,* EmerGentes *(Buenos Aires: Ediciones de la Flor, 1986).*

21   *Lines from an interview with Silvina Ocampo, a contemporary Argentinian fiction writer, by María Ester Gilio,* EmerGentes *(Buenos Aires: Ediciones de la Flor, 1986).*

22   *Eduardo Galeano,* El Descubrimiento De América Que Todavía No Fue y Ostros Escritos *(Barcelona: Editorial Laia, 1986), 117.*

23   *In this analysis I have been following loosely as well as confronting unorthodoxically the Lacanian findings of Laura Mulvey, "Visual Pleasure and Narrative Cinema," in* Feminism and Film Theory, *ed. Constance Penley (New York: Routledge, Chapman and Hall, 1988), 57–68; Mary Ann Doane,* The Desire to Desire: The Woman's Film of the 1940s *(Bloomington: Indiana University Press, 1987); Mary Ann Doane, "Woman's Stake: Filming the Female Body," in* Feminism and Film Theory, *ed. Constance Penley (New York: Routledge, Chapman and Hall, 1988), 196–215; Kaja Silverman, "Fassbinder and Lacan: A Reconsideration of Gaze, Look and Image,"* Camera Obscura *19 (1989), 54–84; Craig Owens, "The Discourse of Others: Feminists and Postmodernism," in* The Anti-Aesthetic: Essays on Postmodern Culture, *ed. Hal Foster (Port Townsend, Washington: Bay Press, 1983), 57–82.*

24   *Vincent Crapanzano [1985] quoted in Trinh, T. Minh-ha,* Women, Native, Other: Writing Postcoloniality and Feminism *(Bloomington: Indiana University Press, 1989), 144.*

25   *For a similar understanding of the "exotic" see George Rousseau and Roy Porter, eds,* Exoticism in the Enlightenment *(Manchester: Manchester University Press, 1990). Michael Taussig, in* Shamanism, Colonialism and the Wild Man. A Study in Terror and Healing *(Chicago: Chicago University Press, 1986), has followed a so-called "surrealist" path in analyzing the constitution of "wildness" with a complexity and fluidity I have been incapable of developing in this description of the "exotic" tango. I thank Peggy Phelan for calling my attention to this text.*

26 *I thank Gayatri Spivak and Parama Roy for reading and commenting on this scene in the context of a seminar held at the Center for Ideas and Society at the University of California, Riverside, in the spring of 1994. I cannot, however, implicate them in the results. Their criticisms have been incorporated imperfectly and are still haunting the Choreocritic's text and my desire for decolonization.*

27 *See, for example, Gayatri Spivak, "Three Women's Texts and a Critique of Imperialism,"* Critical Inquiry *12(1) (1985), 243–61; and Gayatri Spivak, "Can the Subaltern Speak? Speculations on Widow Sacrifice," in* Marxism and the Interpretation of Culture, *ed. Cary Nelson and Lawrence Grossberg (Urbana: University of Illinois Press, 1988), 271–313.*

28 *See Gayatri Spivak,* The Postcolonial Critic: Interviews, Strategies, Dialogues, *ed. Sarah Harasym (New York: Routledge, 1990); and Gayatri Spivak, "Gayatri Spivak on the Politics of the Subaltern. Interview by Howard Winant," Socialist Review 20(3) (1990), 81–97.*

29 *See Ella Shohat, "Notes on the 'Post-Colonial,'"* Social Text *31/32 (1992), 99–113; and Robert Young,* White Mythologies: Writing History and the West *(London: Routledge, 1990).*

30 *Kwame Anthony Appiah, "Is the Post-in Postmodernism the Post- in Postcolonial?"* Critical Inquiry, *17 (Winter 1991), 336–357.*

31 *On "theoreticist anarchism," see Homi Bhabha, "Signs Taken for Wonders: Questions of Ambivalence and Authority under a Tree Outside Delhi, May 1817,"* Critical Inquiry *12(1) (1985), 144–65.*

32 *See Homi Bhabha, "Of Mimicry and Man. The Ambivalence of Colonial Discourse,"* October *28 (1984): 125–33; and Homi Bhabha, "The Other Question: Difference, Discrimination and the Discourse of Colonialism," in* Literary Politics and Theory: Papers from the Essex Conference 1976–1984, *ed. Francis Barker (London: Methuen, 1986), 148–72.*

33 *Spivak, "Can the Subaltern Speak?" 287.*

34 *I am tentatively following here Gayatri Spivak's elaborations on postcolonial intellectuals and their attempts to represent the subaltern (Spivak, "Can the Subaltern Speak?" 287–9). I have appropriated, stretched, and run away with her concepts. I assume that postcolonial intellectuals are scholars like her who have made the field of colonial studies known in the U.S. academy from a postcolonial perspective. I also recognize a common ground between these "postcolonial" intellectuals originally from India and other third world intellectuals who were raised in settler colonies like Argentina and are now teaching at U.S. universities. Thus, I picture the Choreocritic (and myself) as "postcolonial" intellectuals. Through the character of the Choreocritic I attempt to represent the conflations and misrepresentations that are present and vibrant in the U.S. academy vulgarizations of* *postmodern and postcolonial intellectual positions. The theatricalization of a postcolonial encounter is thus a parody of the colonial encounter – an encounter between so-called postmodern intellectuals and so-called postcolonial intellectuals in the U.S. academic conference setting. My intention is to represent this encounter broadly and to learn from it rather than to pursue a careful textual analysis for which other scholars are better qualified.*

35 *Spivak, "Can the Subaltern Speak?" 288–9.*

BIBLIOGRAPHY

"5,000 Schoolgirls Dance on the Green." *Brooklyn Daily Eagle,* 19 May 1915. Picture and Sporting section, 5.

Addams, Jane. *Twenty Years at Hull-House.* 1910. Reprint, New York: New American Library, 1981.

Akhmatova, Anna. "Requiem, 1935–1940." Trans. Stanley Kunitz and Max Hayward. In *Against Forgetting: Twentieth Century Poetry of Witness.* Ed. Carolyn Forché. New York and London: W. W. Norton, 1993, 101.

Alderson, Evan. "Metaphor in Dance: The Example of Graham." *Dance History Scholars Proceedings.* Riverside, CA: Dance History Scholars, 1983, 111–18.

Alejandro, Reynaldo G. *Sayaw Silingan; The Dance in the Philippines.* New York: Dance Perspectives Foundation, 1972.

Allen, Robert. *Horrible Prettiness; Burlesque and American Culture.* Chapel Hill: University of North Carolina Press, 1991.

Anon., *Le Foyer de l'opéra.* Paris: Hippolyte Souverain, 1842.

Anon., *Le Monde d'amour.* Geneva: Lepondvil, 1842.

Anon., *Les Filles d'opéra et les vertus de table d'hôte.* Paris: J. Labitte, 1846.

Appadurai, Arjun. "Disjuncture and Difference in the Global Cultural Economy." *Public Culture* 2(2), 1990, 1–24.

Appiah, Anthony Kwame. "Is the Post- in Postmodernism the Post- in Postcolonial?" *Critical Inquiry* 17 (Winter 1991), 336–57.

Aquino, Francisca Reyes. *Philippine Folk Dances.* Manila: n.p., 1983.

Aragon, Louis. *Le Fou d'Elsa.* Paris: Editions Gallimard, 1963.

Aronowitz, Stanley. *False Promises.* New York: McGraw-Hill, 1973.

Artaud, Antonin. "Le théâtre de la cruauté." *84,* nos. 5–6 (1948), 11–135.

Aschengren, Eric. "The Beautiful Danger: Facets of the Romantic Ballet." *Dance Perspectives* 58 (Summer 1974).

Asplund, Gunnar *et al. Acceptera* (Arlöv: Berlings, 1980), facsimile of the 1931 edition.

Assunção, Fernando O. *El Tango y Sus Circunstancias (1880–1920).* Buenos Aires: Librería El Ateneo Editorial, 1984.

Atlas of the City of New York, Borough of Manhattan, vol. 1, Battery to 14th Street to 1906. Corrected to May 1909. Philadelphia: G. W. Bromley & Co., 1909.

B***, A. and J. Ball. *Histoire pittoresque des passions chez l'homme et chez la femme, et particulièrement de l'amour.* Paris: Chez les Principaux Libraries Imprimeur d'Alexandre Baily, 1846.

Bancroft, Jessie H. *Girls' Athletics for Elementary, High and Collegiate Grade being the Official Handbook of the Girls' Branch of the Public Schools Athletic League of the City of New York 1910–1911.* New York: American Sports Publishing Co., 1910.

Bancroft, Jessie H. "Contributions of Dr. Luther Halsey Gulick to the Public Schools of New York City (Concluded)." *American Physical Education Review* 28 (October 1928), 378, 380–2.

Baraka, Amiri (Leroi Jones). *Dutchman.* New York: William Morrow & Co., 1964.

Bartenieff, Irmgard, with Dori Lewis. *Body Movement; Coping with the Environment.* New York: Gordon & Breach, 1980.

Barthes, Roland. *Camera Lucida: Reflections on Photography.* Trans. by Richard Howard. New York: Farrar, Straus & Giroux, 1981.

Bateson, Gregory. **"Bali: The Value System of a Steady State."** In *Steps to an Ecology of Mind*. New York: Ballantine Books, 1972, 107–27.

Bateson, Gregory and Claire Holt. **"Form and Function of the Dance in Bali."** In *Traditional Balinese Culture*. Ed. Jane Belo. New York: Columbia University Press, 1970, 322–30.

Baty-Smith, Gregoria. **"*Tinikling* in Labanotation: A Search for Transcribing a Non-Western Dance."** Paper presented at the Fifth International Dance Conference, Hong Kong, 1990.

Baumol, William and William Bowen. ***Performing Arts: The Economic Dilemma,*** Cambridge, MA: MIT, 1968 [1966].

Beaumont, Cyril. ***The Ballet Called Swan Lake.*** 1952. Reprint, New York: Dance Horizons, 1982.

Benjamin, Walter. ***Illuminations.*** Ed. H. Arendt. New York: Schocken Books, 1969a.

Benjamin, Walter. **"The Work of Art in the Age of Mechnical Reproduction."** In *Illuminations*. Ed. with an introduction by Hannah Arendt. Trans. by Harry Zohn. New York: Schocken Books, 1969b, 217–51.

Berman, Marshall. ***All That Is Solid Melts Into Air.*** New York: Simon & Schuster, 1982.

Bernheimer, Charles. **"Penile Reference in Phallic Theory."** *Differences* 4(1) (Spring 1992), 116–32.

Berrol, Selma. **"In their Image: German Jews and the Americanization of the *Ost Juden* in New York City."** *New York History* 63 (October 1982), 417–33.

Berrol, Selma. **"Germans versus Russians: An Update."** *American Jewish History* 73 (December 1983), 142–56.

Bhabha, Homi. **"Of Mimicry and Man: The Ambivalence of Colonial Discourse."** *October* 28, 1984, 125–33.

Bhabha, Homi. **"Signs Taken for Wonders: Questions of Ambivalence and Authority under a Tree Outside Delhi, May 1817."** *Critical Inquiry* 12(1) (1985), 144–65.

Bhabha, Homi. **"The Other Question: Difference, Discrimination and the Discourse of Colonialism."** In *Literary Politics and Theory: Papers from the Essex Conference 1976–1984*. Ed. Francis Barker. London: Methuen, 1986, 148–72.

"Bibliography: Tadeusz Kantor." A bibliography of writings by and about Tadeusz Kantor, compiled by Michal Kobialka. *The Drama Review* 30(3) (Fall 1986), 184–98.

Bissell, Bill. **"Faith in the Larger Sense."** *High Performance* (Fall 1991), 36–9.

Blasis, Carlo. *Traité elementaire, theorique et pratique de l'art de la danse....* Milan: Chez Beati et A. Teneti, 1820.

Blau, Herbert. **"Look What Thy Memory Cannot Contain."** In *Blooded Thought: Occasions of Theatre*. New York: Performing Art Journal, 1982, 72–94.

Blau, Herbert. **"The Thought of Performance: Value, Vanishing, Dream, and Brain Damage."** In *Blooded Thought: Occasions of Theatre*. New York: Performing Art Journal, 1982, 25–48.

Blau, Herbert. **"Universals of Performance; or Amortizing Play,"** and **"Shadowing Representation."** In *The Eye of Prey: Subversions of the Postmodern*. Bloomington and Indianapolis: Indiana University Press, 1987, 161–88, 189–206.

Blau, Judith. *The Shape of Culture: A Study of Contemporary Cultural Patterns in the United States.* Cambridge: Cambridge University Press, 1989.

Blum, Judy. **"Reconstructions."** *Women and Performance* 5(2) (1992).

Boigne, Charles de. *Petits mémoires de l'opéra.* Paris, 1857.

Bonner, Frances *et al.*, eds. *Imaging Women: Cultural Representations and Gender.* London: Polity Press, 1992.

Boris, Eileen. *Art and Labor: Ruskin, Morris, and the Craftsman Ideal in America.* Philadelphia: Temple University Press, 1986.

Bourdieu, Pierre. *Outline of a Theory of Practice.* Cambridge: Cambridge University Press, 1977.

Bowlby, Rachel. "The Happy Event." *Paragraph* 14(1) (March 1991), 126–32.

Bowlby, Rachel. "A Happy Event: The Births of Psychoanalysis." In *Shopping with Freud.* London: Routledge, 1993, 72–81.

Breuer, Josef and Sigmund Freud. "Studies on Hysteria." In *The Standard Edition of the Complete Psychological Works of Sigmund Freud.* Trans. by James Strachey, Anna Freud, and Alix Strachey. London: The Hogarth Press, vol. II, 1985.

Bruner, Edward. "Introduction: The Ethnographic Self and the Personal Self." In *Anthropology and Literature.* Ed. Paul Benson. Chicago: University of Illinois Press, 1993, 1–26.

Bryson, Norman. *Looking at the Overlooked: Four Essays on Still Life Painting.* Cambridge, MA: Harvard University Press, 1990.

Buck-Morss, Susan. "The *Flâneur*, The Sandwichman and the Whore." *New German Critique* 39 (1986), 99–140.

Buhle, Mari Jo and Paul Buhle, eds. *The Concise History of Woman's Suffrage.* Urbana: University of Illinois Press, 1978.

Buker, Eloise A. "Rhetoric in Postmodern Feminism: Put-offs, Put-ons, and Political Plays." In *The Interpretative Turn: Philosophy, Science, Culture.* Ed. D. R. Hiley, J. F. Bohman, and R. Shusterman. Ithaca: Cornell University Press, 1991, 218–44.

Burchenal, Elizabeth. *Folk-Dances and Singing Games.* New York: G. Schirmer, 1909.

Burchenal, Elizabeth. "A Dance Around the May-Pole." *Woman's Home Companion* 37 (April 1910), 5, 66.

Burchenal, Elizabeth, ed. *Official Handbook of the Girls' Branch of the Public Schools Athletic League of the City of New York, 1914–1915.* New York: American Sports Publishing Co., 1914. Burchenal-edited *Handbooks* for the 1915–16 through the 1917–18 years were issued by the same publisher.

Butler, Judith. *Gender Trouble: Feminism and the Subversion of Identity.* New York/London: Routledge, 1990.

Calvino, Italo. *Invisible Cities.* Trans. by William Weaver. New York and London: Harcourt Brace Jovanovich, 1974.

Caruth, Cathy. "Unclaimed Experience: Trauma and the Possibility of History." *Yale French Studies 79, Literature and the Ethical Question.* Ed. Claire Nouvet, 1991.

Case, Sue-Ellen. "Toward a Butch-Femme Aesthetic." In *The Lesbian and Gay Studies Reader.* Ed. Henry Abelove, Michele Aina Barale, and David M. Halperin. New York: Routledge, 1993, 294–306.

Case, Sue-Ellen. "Meditations on the Patriarchal Pythagorean Pratfall and the Lesbian Siamese Two-Step." In *Choreographing History.* Ed. Susan L. Foster. Bloomington: University of Indiana Press, 1995.

Castle, Terry. "In Praise of Brigitte Fassbaender (A Musical Emanation)." In *The Apparitional Lesbian: Female Homosexuality in Modern Culture.* New York: Columbia University Press, 1993, 200–38.

Chafe, William H. *The American Woman: Her Changing Social, Economic, and Political Roles, 1920–1970.* New York: Oxford University Press, 1972.

Clarke, Edward. *Sex in Education.* Boston, MA: James R. Osgood, 1873.

Clément, Catherine. *Opera, or the Undoing of Women.* Trans. by Betsy Wing. Minneapolis: University of Minnesota Press, 1988.

Clifford, James. **"On Ethnographic Surrealism."** *Comparative Studies in Society and History* 23(1) (1981), 539–64.

Clifford, James. **"Introduction: Partial Truths."** In *Writing Culture; The Poetics and Politics of Ethnography.* Ed. James Clifford and George E. Marcus. Berkeley: University of California Press, 1986.

Colomina, Beatriz. **"The Split Wall: Domestic Voyeurism."** In *Sexuality and Space.* Ed. B. Colomina. New York: Princeton Papers on Architecture, 1992, 73–128.

Copeland, Roger. **"A Curmudgeonly View of the American Dance Boom."** *Dance Theatre Journal* 4(1) (1986), 10–13.

Cordova, Sarah Penelope Davies. **"Poetics of Dance: Narrative Designs from Staël to Maupassant."** Ph.D. dissertation, University of California, Los Angeles, 1993.

Cott, Nancy. *The Bonds of Womanhood: "Woman's Sphere" in New England, 1780–1835.* New Haven: Yale University Press, 1977.

Cranefield, Paul. **"Josef Breuer's Evaluation of his Contribution to Psychoanalysis."** *International Journal of Psychoanalysis* XXXIX, part V (September–October 1958), 319–22.

Croce, Arlene. **"The Spelling of Agon."** *The New Yorker* (12 July 1993), 84.

Daly, Ann. **"The Balanchine Woman: Of Hummingbirds and Channel Swimmers."** *Drama Review* 31(1) (Spring 1987), 8–21.

David-Menard, Monique. *Hysteria from Freud to Lacan. Body and Language in Psychoanalysis.* Trans. by Catherine Porter. Ithaca: Cornell University Press, 1989.

Davis, Allen F. *Spearheads for Reform: The Social Settlements and the Progressive Movement 1890–1914.* New York: Oxford University Press, 1967.

Davis, Tracy C. **"Questions for a Feminist Methodology in Theatre**

History." In *Interpreting the Theatrical Past; Essays in the Historiography of Performance.* Ed. Thomas Postlewait and Bruce A. McConachie. Iowa: University of Iowa Press, 1989.

De Certeau, Michel. *The Practice of Everyday Life.* Berkeley: University of California Press, 1984.

De Certeau, Michel. *The Writing of History.* Trans. by Tom Conley. New York: Columbia University Press, 1988.

De Lauretis, Teresa. *Alice Doesn't: Feminism, Semiotics, Cinema.* Bloomington: University of Indiana Press, 1984.

De Lauretis, Teresa. "Feminist Studies/Critical Studies: Issues, Terms, and Contexts." In *Feminist Studies/Critical Studies.* Ed. Teresa de Lauretis. Bloomington: Indiana University Press, 1986, 1–19.

Deleuze, Gilles. "Ethology: Spinoza and Us." In *Zone 6: Incorporations.* Ed. Jonathan Crary and Sanford Kwinter. New York: Urzone Inc., 1992, 625–33.

Deleuze, Gilles and Félix Guattari. *A Thousand Plateaus: Capitalism and Schizophrenia.* Trans. and foreword by Brian Massumi. Minneapolis: University of Minnesota Press, 1987. Original French edition: *Mille plateaux,* vol. 2 of *Capitalisme et schizophrénie.* Paris: Les Editions de Minuit, 1980.

Dell, Cecily. *A Primer for Movement Description.* New York: Dance Notation Bureau, 1970.

Denby, Edwin. *Dance Writings.* New York: Alfred A. Knopf, 1986.

Derrida, Jacques. "Structure, Sign, and Play in the Discourse of the Human Sciences." In *Writing and Difference.* Trans. by Alan Bass. Chicago: University of Chicago Press, 1978. Original French edition: *L'écriture et la différence.* Paris: Seuil, 1967, 278–93 (English ed.).

Derrida, Jacques. "The Theater of Cruelty and the Closure of Representation." In *Writing and Difference.* Trans. by Alan Bass. Chicago: University of Chicago Press, 1978. Original French edition: *L'écriture et la différence.* Paris: Seuil, 1967, 232–50 (English ed.).

Derrida, Jacques. *Speech and Phenomena and Other Essays on Husserl's Theory of Signs.* Trans. by David B. Allison. Evanston: Northwestern University Press, 1973.

Derrida, Jacques. **"Fors."** *The Georgia Review* 31, no. 1 (Spring 1977).

Derrida, Jacques. *Positions.* Trans. and annotated by Alan Bass. Chicago: University of Chicago Press, 1981.

Dillon, Douglas C. **"The Economic Crisis in the Arts."** *Business in the Arts.* Ed. Gideon Chagy. New York: Paul Ericksson, 1970.

Doane, Mary Ann. *The Desire to Desire: The Woman's Film of the 1940s.* Bloomington: Indiana University Press, 1987.

Doane, Mary Ann. **"Woman's Stake: Filming the Female Body."** In *Feminism and Film Theory.* Ed. Constance Penley. New York: Routledge, Chapman and Hall, 1988, 196–215.

Douglas, Ann. **"Introduction."** In *Uncle Tom's Cabin.* New York: Viking, 1981.

Dreiser, Theodore. *Sister Carrie: A Novel.* New York: Harper, 1912.

Dubin, Steven. *Arresting Images: Impolitic Art and Uncivil Actions.* New York: Routledge, 1992.

Dubois, Ellen Carol. *Feminism and Suffrage: The Emergence of an Independent Women's Movement in America 1848–1869.* Ithaca, NY: Cornell University Press, 1978.

Dujovne Ortiz, Alicia. **"Buenos Aires."** In *Critical Fictions. The Politics of Imaginative Writing.* Ed. Philomena Mariani. Seattle: Bay Press, 1991, 115–30.

Dumont, Jean-Paul. *Visayan Vignettes; Ethnographic Traces of a Philippine Island.* Chicago: University of Chicago Press, 1992.

Duras, Marguerite. **"The Atlantic Man."** In *Two by Duras.* Trans. by Alberto Manguel. Toronto: Coach House Press, 1993. Original French edition: *L'Homme atlantique.* Paris: Les Editions de Minuit, 1982.

Dye, Nancy Schrom. *As Equals and as Sisters: The Labor Movement and the Women's Trade Union League of New York.* Columbia, MO: University of Missouri Press, 1980.

Fajardo, Libertad. *Visayan Folk Dances.* Manila: n.p., 1979.

Fardon, Richard, ed. "General Introduction." In *Localising Strategies.* Edinburgh: Scottish Academic Press; Washington: Smithsonian Institution Press, 1990.

Felman, Shoshana. "Education and Crisis, or the Vicissitudes of Teaching." In *Testimony: Crises of Witnessing in Literature, Psychoanalysis, and History.* Ed. by Shoshana Felman and Dori Laub. New York and London: Routledge, 1992, 1–56.

Flexner, Eleanor. *Century of Struggle: The Women's Rights Movement in the United States.* Cambridge, MA: Harvard University Press, 1959.

Flores, Juan and George Yúdice. "Living Borders/Buscando America: Languages of Latino Self-Formation." *Social Text* 24 (1990), 57–84.

Forché, Carolyn. "Introduction." In *Against Forgetting: Twentieth Century Poetry of Witness.* Ed. Carolyn Forché. New York and London: W. W. Norton, 1993, 42–3.

Foster, Susan. *Reading Dancing: Bodies and Subjects in Contemporary American Choreography.* Berkeley: University of California Press, 1986.

Foucault, Michel. *The Order of Things.* New York: Vintage Books, 1973.

Foucault, Michel. *The History of Sexuality.* Trans. by Robert Hurley. New York: Pantheon Books, 1978.

Foucault, Michel. "What is an Author?" In *Language, Counter-Memory, Practice: Selected Essays and Writings.* Ed. D. F. Bouchard. Ithaca: Cornell University Press, 1992, 113–38.

Frank, Arthur W. "For a Sociology of the Body: An Analytical Review." *The Body: Social Process and Cultural Theory.* Ed. M. Featherstone, M. Hepworth, and B. S. Turner. London: Sage Publications, 1991, 36–102.

Franko, Mark. *The Dancing Body in Renaissance Choreography (c. 1416–1589).* Birmingham, AL: Summa Publications, 1986.

Franko, Mark. "Emotivist Movement and Histories of Modernism: The Case of Martha Graham." *Discourse* 13(1) (Fall/Winter 1990–1), 111–28.

Franko, Mark. *Dance as Text: Ideologies of the Baroque Body.* Cambridge: Cambridge University Press, 1993.

Franko, Mark. *Dancing Modernism/Performing Politics.* Bloomington: Indiana University Press, 1995.

Freeman, Lucy. *The Story of Anna O.* New York: Walker & Co., 1972.

Freud, Sigmund. "From the History of an Infantile Neurosis." *The Standard Edition of the Complete Psychological Works of Sigmund Freud.* Trans. by James Strachey, Anna Freud, and Alix Strachey. London: The Hogarth Press, vol. XVII, 1918.

Freud, Sigmund. *Beyond the Pleasure Principle.* Trans. and ed. by James Strachey. Introduction and notes by Gregory Zilboorg. New York and London: W. W. Norton & Co., 1961.

Freud, Sigmund. "Further Recommendations in the Technique of Psychoanalysis: Recollection, Repetition and Working Through (1914)." First published in *Zeitschrift*, Bd. II, 1914. Cited in the translation by Joan Riviere in *Therapy and Technique*. Ed. and with an introduction by Philip Rieff. New York: Collier Books, Macmillan Publishing Co., 1963, 157–66.

Freud, Sigmund. *Moses and Monotheism.* Trans. by Katherine Jones. New York: Vintage Books, 1967 edition.

Freud, Sigmund. *Standard Edition.* Vol. 5. London: The Hogarth Press, 1971.

Freud, Sigmund. *Standard Edition.* Vol. 6. London: The Hogarth Press, 1971.

Freud, Sigmund. *Standard Edition.* Vol. 9. London: The Hogarth Press, 1978.

Freud, Sigmund. *Standard Edition.* Vol. 23. London: The Hogarth Press, 1978.

Frykman, Jonas. "I Rörelse: Kropp och Modernitet i Mellankrigstidens Sverige." *Kulturella Perspektiv* 1 (1992), 30–42.

Fuss, Diana. "Freud's Fallen Women: Identification, Desire, and 'A Case of Homosexuality in a Woman.'" *Yale Journal of Criticism* 6(1) (Spring 1993), 1–23.

Galeano, Eduardo. *El Descubrimiento De América Que Todavía No Fue y Otros Escritos.* Barcelona: Editorial Laia, 1986.

Garafola, Lynn. "The Travesty Dancer in Nineteenth Century Ballet." *Dance Research Journal* 17(2) & 18(1) (Fall–Spring 1985–86), 35–40.

Gasché, Rodolphe. "*Ecce Homo* or the Written Body." *Oxford Literary Review* 7(1–2), 1985, 3–24.

Gautier, Théophile. *Gautier on Dance.* Trans. by Ivor Guest. London: Dance Books, 1986.

Gerould, Daniel C. "Tadeusz Kantor: A Visual Artist Works Magic on the Polish Stage." *Performing Arts Journal* 12, vol. IV, no. 3 (1980), 27–38.

Gilio, María Esther. *EmerGentes.* Buenos Aires: Ediciones de la Flor, 1986.

Gilpin, Heidi. "Failure, Repetition, Amputation, and Disappearance; Issues of Composition in Contemporary European Movement Performance." Ph.D. dissertation, Harvard University, 1993a.

Gilpin, Heidi. "Static and Uncertain Bodies; Invisibility and Instability in Movement Performance." *Assaph; Studies in the Theatre* 8 (1993b), 99–121.

Gilpin, Heidi. "Aberrations of Gravity." *ANY (Architecture New York)* 5: Lightness (March/April 1994), 50–5.

Gilpin, Heidi. "Amputation and Dismembered Identities: Pina Bausch's Film *Die Klage der Kaiserin/The Lament of the Empress.*" In *Other*

Germanies: Cultural Diversity and Women's Art. Ed. Karen Jankowsky, Carla Love, and Thomas Jung, forthcoming.

Gordon, Linda. "What's New in Women's History?" In *Feminist Studies/Critical Studies.* Ed. Teresa de Lauretis. Bloomington: Indiana University Press, 1986, 20–30.

Goux, Jean-Joseph. "The Phallus: Masculine Identity and the 'Exchange of Women.'" *Differences* 4(1) (Spring 1992), 40–75.

Graham, Martha. "A Modern Dancer's Primer for Action." In *Dance as a Theatre Art.* Ed. Selma-Jeanne Cohen (1941). New York: Dodd, Mead, 1974, 135–43.

Graham, Martha. "Dancer's Focus." In *Martha Graham. Sixteen Dances in Photographs,* by Barbara Morgan. 1941. Reprint. Dobbs Ferry, New York: Morgan & Morgan, 1980, 11.

Grand-Carteret, John. *XIXe Siècle: classes, mœurs, usages, costumes, inventions.* Paris: Librarie de Firmin-Didot et Cie, 1893.

Greenlee, Ralph Stebbins and Robert Lemuel Greenlee. *The Stebbins Genealogy.* Chicago: McDonohue & Co., 1904.

Guest, Ivor. *The Romantic Ballet in Paris.* London: Pitman, 1966.

Guibert, Fernando. *Los Argentinos y El Tango.* Buenos Aires: Ediciones Culturales Argentinas, 1973.

Guilcher, Jean-Michel. *La Contredanse et les renouvellements de la danse française.* Paris: Mouton, 1969.

Gulick, Luther Halsey. "Teaching American Children to Play: Significance of the Revival of Folk Dances, Games and Festivals by the Playground Association." *The Craftsman* 15 (November 1908), 192–9.

Gulick, Luther H. *The Healthful Art of Dancing.* New York: Doubleday, Page & Co., 1910.

Gulick, Luther H. and Harry J. Smith. "Dancing as a Part of Education;

Happy Results of Rhythmic Play by New York School Children." *The World's Work* 14 (October 1907), 9445–52.

Hall, G. Stanley. *Adolescence: Its Psychology and Its Relations to Physiology, Anthropology, Sociology, Sex, Crime, Religion and Education,* 2 vols. New York: D. Appleton & Co., 1905.

Hall, Stuart. *Hard Road to Renewal.* London: Verso, 1988.

Halperin, David. *One Hundred Years of Homosexuality: And Other Essays on Greek Love.* New York: Routledge, 1990.

Haraway, Donna. "Manifesto for Cyborgs: Science, Technology, and Socialist Feminism in the 1980's." *Socialist Review* 15(2) (1985), 65–108.

Haraway, Donna. "The Promises of Monsters." In *Cultural Studies.* Ed. Lawrence Grossberg, Cary Nelson, and Paula Treichler. New York: Routledge, 1992, 295–337.

Harris, Neil. "The Gilded Age Revisited: Boston and the Museum Movement." *American Quarterly* (Winter 1962), 545–66.

Harris, Neil. *The Artist in American Society: The Formative Years, 1790–1860.* New York: Braziller, 1966.

Harrison, Robert Pogue. "Heresy and the Question of Repetition. Reading Kierkegaard's *Repetition.*" In *Textual Analysis. Some Readers Reading.* Ed. Mary Ann Caws. New York: The Modern Language Association of America, 1986.

Hastrup, Kirsten. "Writing Ethnography; State of the Art." In *Anthropology and Autobiography.* Ed. Judith Okley and Helen Calloway. London: Routledge, 1992, 116–33.

Hegel, Georg Wilhelm Friedrich. *Phenomenology of Mind.* Trans. by J. B. Baillie. New York: Macmillan, 1961.

Heimannsberg, Barbara and Christoph J. Schmidt, eds. *The Collective Silence: German Identity and the Legacy of Shame.* Trans. by Cynthia Oudejans Harris and Gordon Wheeler. San Francisco: Jossey-Bass, 1993.

Higham, John. *Strangers in the Land; Patterns of American Nativism, 1860–1924,* 2nd ed. New Brunswick: Rutgers University Press, 1988.

Hillman, James. *The Dream and the Underworld.* New York: Harper & Row, 1979.

Hilton, Wendy. *Dance of Court & Theatre; The French Noble Style, 1690–1725.* Princeton, NJ: Princeton Book Co., 1981.

Hirschmuller, Albrecht. *The Life and Work of Josef Breuer: Physiology and Psychoanalysis.* New York and London: New York University Press, 1989.

Hölmstrom, Kirsten Gram. *Monodramas, Attitudes, Tableaux Vivants: Studies on Some Trends of Theatrical Fashion, 1770–1815.* Stockholm: Almqvist & Wiksell, 1967.

Humphrey, Doris. *The Art of Making Dances.* New York: Grove Press, 1959.

Jable, J. Thomas. *"The Public Schools Athletic League of New York City: Organized Athletics for City School Children, 1903–1914."* In *The American Sporting Experience: A Historical Anthology of Sport in America.* Ed. Steven A. Riess. New York: Leisure Press, 1984, 219–38.

Jackson, Jean. *"'I am a Fieldnote'; Fieldnotes as a Symbol of Professional Identity."* In *Fieldnotes; The Makings of Anthropology.* Ed. Roger Sanjek. Ithaca: Cornell University Press, 1990, 3–33.

Jackson, Michael. *Paths Toward a Clearing.* Bloomington: University of Indiana Press, 1989.

Jameson, Fredric. *The Ideologies of Theory: Essays 1971–86.* Minneapolis: University of Minnesota Press, 1990.

Jardine, Alice. *Gynesis: Configurations of Woman and Modernity.* Ithaca: Cornell University Press, 1985.

Jones, Ernest. *Sigmund Freud: Life and Work.* London: The Hogarth Press, vol. 1, 1954.

Jung, Carl Gustav. *Memories, Dreams, Reflections.* Ed. Aniela Jaffé. New York: Vintage Books, 1963.

Jung, Carl Gustav. *Man and his Symbols.* New York: Anchor Books, 1964.

Jung, Carl Gustav. *The Archetypes and the Collective Unconscious.* Trans. by R. F. C. Hull. Princeton: Princeton University Press, 1980.

Justo, Liborio. *Nuestra Patria Vasalla: Historia del Coloniaje Argentino. Tomo IV.* Buenos Aires: Editorial Grito Sagrado, 1989.

Kantor, Tadeusz. "Le Théâtre impossible." *Les Lettres françaises,* 12 July 1972.

Kantor, Tadeusz. "Characters in *The Dead Class.*" Trans. by Karol Jakubowicz. *Gambit: International Theatre Review* 9(33–4) (1979), 137–40.

Kantor, Tadeusz. "The Theatre of Death. 1975." *The Drama Review* 30(3) (Fall 1986), 137–8. Trans. by Voy T. and Margaret Stelmaszynski, reprinted from *Canadian Theatre Review* 16 (Fall 1977).

Kantor, Tadeusz. "The Writings of Tadeusz Kantor, 1956–1985." Includes manifestoes on the Autonomous and Informel Theatres and the Theatre of Death, and other texts. Trans. by Michal Kobialka. *The Drama Review* 30(3) (Fall 1986), 114–76.

Kantor, Tadeusz. "The Zero Theatre *or* The Theatre of Nullification, 1963." Trans. by Michal Kobialka. *The Drama Review* 30(3) (Fall 1986).

Kantor, Tadeusz. *Today is My Birthday.* La MaMa E.T.C. Theater, New York, program. 18–23 June 1991.

Kaplan, Marion. *The Jewish Feminist Movement in Germany: The Campaigns of Judischer Frauenbund, 1904–1938.* Westport, CT: Greenwood Press, 1979.

Karpeles, Maud. *Cecil Sharp: His Life and Work.* London: Routledge & Kegan Paul, 1967.

Keens, William. "An Interview with Frank Hodsoll." *American Arts* (January 1982), 8.

Kessler-Harris, Alice. *Out to Work: A History of Wage-Earning Women in America.* New York: Oxford University Press, 1982.

Kierkegaard, Søren. "Repetition: A Venture in Experimenting Psychology." In *Fear and Trembling/Repetition. Kierkegaard's Writings, VI.* Ed. and trans. by Howard and Edna Hong. Princeton: Princeton University Press, 1983.

Kirstein, Lincoln. *The Book of the Dance: A Short History of Dancing.* Garden City: Garden City Publishing Co., 1942.

Klassowicz, Jan. "*The Dead Class* Scene by Scene." Trans. by Karol Jakubowicz. *Gambit: International Theatre Review* 9(33–4) (1979), 107–35.

Klassowicz, Jan. "Tadeusz Kantor's Journey." Trans. by Michal Kobialka. *The Drama Review* 30(3) (Fall 1986), 98–113.

Kleist, Heinrich von. "Über das Marionettentheater." *Berliner Abendblätter* (12–14 December 1810).

Kobialka, Michal. "Let the Artists Die?: An Interview with Tadeusz Kantor." *The Drama Review* 30(3) (Fall 1986), 177–83.

Kobialka, Michal. *A Journey Through Other Spaces: Essays & Manifestos, 1944–1990, by Tadeusz Kantor.* Berkeley and Los Angeles: University of California Press, 1993.

Koestenbaum, Wayne. *The Queen's Throat: Opera, Homosexuality, and the Mystery of Desire.* New York: Poseidon Press, 1993.

Kraditor, Aileen. *The Ideas of the Woman Suffrage Movement 1890–1920.* New York: Columbia University Press, 1965.

Laban, Rudolf and F. C. Lawrence. *Effort.* Estover, Plymouth, England: Macdonald & Evans Ltd, 1974.

Lacan, Jacques. "The Freudian Unconscious and Ours." In *The Four Fundamental Concepts of Psycho-Analysis.* Ed. Jacques-Alain Miller. Trans. by Alan Sheridan. New York: Norton, 1981. Original French edition: *Le Seminaire de Jacques Lacan, livre XI: les quatre concepts fondamentaux de la psychanalyse.* Paris: Editions du Seuil, 1973.

Lacan, Jacques. "The Subversion of the Subject and the Dialectic of Desire in the Freudian Unconscious." In *Ecrits.* Trans. by Alan Sheridan. New York: W. W. Norton & Co., 1977, 292–325.

Landes, Joan B. *Women and the Public Sphere in the Age of the French Revolution.* Ithaca, NY: Cornell University Press, 1988.

Laplanche, Jean. *Life and Death in Psychoanalysis.* Trans. by Jeffrey Mehlman. Baltimore and London: Johns Hopkins University Press, 1976.

Laqueur, Thomas. *Making Sex: Body and Gender from the Greeks to Freud.* Cambridge, MA: Harvard University Press, 1990.

Levine, Lawrence. *Black Culture and Black Consciousness: Afro-American Folk Thought from Slavery to Freedom.* New York: Oxford University Press, 1977.

Lo-Johansson, Ivar. *Författaren.* Stockholm: Bonniers, 1976.

Lott, Eric. *Love and Theft: Black Face Minstrelsy and the American Working Class.* New York: Oxford University Press, 1993.

Lyotard, Jean-François. *Phenomenology.* Trans. by Brian Beakley. Albany: State University of New York Press, 1991.

Maletic, Vera. *Body–Space–Expression. The Development of Rudolf Laban's Movement and Dance Concepts.* New York: Mouton de Gruyter, 1987.

Manning, Susan A. *Ecstasy and the Demon: Feminism and Nationalism in the Dance of Mary Wigman.* Berkeley: University of California Press, 1993.

Martin, John. "Final Dance Recital by Martha Graham." *New York Times,* 20 April 1931, 15.

Martin, John. *America Dancing: The Background and Personalities of the Modern Dance.* New York: Dodge, 1936.

Martin, John. **"A World Premiere Danced by Graham."** *New York Times,* 24 January 1946, 31.

Martin, John. **"The Dance: 'Dark Meadow.'"** *New York Times,* 27 January 1946, 2.

Martin, John. ***Introduction to the Dance*** (1939). Reprint. New York: Dance Horizons, 1965.

Martin, John. ***Reflections of John Joseph Martin.*** Los Angeles: UCLA Oral History Program, 1967.

Martin, John. ***The Modern Dance*** (1933). New York: Dance Horizons, 1972.

Martin, John. **"Dance as a Means of Communication."** In *What is Dance?* Ed. Roger Copeland and Marshall Cohen. Oxford: Oxford University Press, 1983, 22–3.

Martin, Randy. ***Performance as Political Act: The Embodied Self.*** New York: Bergin & Garvey, 1990.

Martin, Randy. **"Dance Ethnography and the Limits of Representation."** *Social Text* 33 (Winter 1992), 102–22.

Martin, Randy. **"Overreading Dance: Addressing the Narrative of Context through Bill T. Jones' Promised Land."** Irvine, 10 May 1993, manuscript.

Martin, Randy. **"Agency and History: The Demands of Dance Ethnography."** In *Choreographing History.* Ed. Susan Foster. Indianapolis: University of Indiana Press, 1995.

Martins, Robert. **"'World Music' and the Global Cultural Economy."** *Diaspora* 2(2) (1992), 229–42.

McClary, Susan. **"Music, the Pythagoreans, and the Body."** In *Choreographing History.* Ed. Susan Foster. Bloomington: University of Indiana Press, 1995.

McCullough, Jack W. ***Living Pictures on the New York State.*** Ann Arbor:

UMI Research Press, 1981.

Metzger, Bruce M. and Roland E. Murphy, eds. *The New Oxford Annotated Bible.* New York: Oxford University Press, 1991.

Miklaszewski, Krzysztof. "Tadeusz Kantor: Exegi monumentum ... or 'The Love and Death Machine.'" Interview with Krzysztof Miklaszewski. *Le Théâtre en Pologne/The Theatre in Poland* 11–12(351–2) (November–December 1987), 3–8.

Moon, Michael. "Flaming Closets." *October* 51 (Winter 1989), 19–54.

"Mrs. Clara Power Edgerly." *Werner's Magazine* 19/1 (1897), 80.

Mulvey, Laura. "Visual Pleasure and Narrative Cinema." In *Feminism and Film Theory.* Ed. Constance Penley. New York: Routledge, Chapman and Hall, 1988, 57–68.

Natale, Oscar. *Buenos Aires, Negros y Tango.* Buenos Aires: Peña Lillo Editor, 1984.

National Endowment for the Arts Annual Report, Washington DC: NEA, 1986.

Ness, Sally A. *Body, Movement, and Culture; Kinesthetic and Visual Symbolism in a Philippine Community.* Philadelphia: University of Pennsylvania Press, 1992.

Netzer, Dick. *The Subsidized Muse.* Cambridge: Cambridge University Press, 1978.

New Cassell's German/English Dictionary. New York: Funk & Wagnalls, 1962.

New York Directory, 1909–10, vol. Resh–Z. New York: Trow Directory, Printing & Book Binding Co., 1909.

Newcomer, Mabel. *A Century of Higher Education for Women.* New York: Harper, 1959.

Nilsson, Jan-Olof. "Modernt, Alltför Modernt: Speglingar." *Nationella Identiteter i Norden – Ett Fullbordat Projekt?* Ed. by A. Linde-Laursen and J.-O. Nilsson. Stockholm: Nordiska Rådet, 1991.

Novack, Cynthia. *Sharing the Dance: Contact Improvisation and American Culture.* Madison: University of Wisconsin Press, 1990.

Ocko, Edna. "Books in Review." In *New Theatre and Film* (April 1937), 34–5.

Okley, Judith, ed. "Anthropology and Autobiography; Participatory Experience and Embodied Knowledge." In *Anthropology and Autobiography.* Ed. Judith Okley and Helen Calloway. London: Routledge, 1993, 1–28.

Ottenberg, Simon. "Thirty Years of Fieldnotes; Changing Relationships to the Text." In *Fieldnotes; The Makings of Anthropology.* Ed. Roger Sanjek. Ithaca: Cornell University Press, 1990, 139–60.

Owens, Craig. "The Discourse of Others: Feminists and Postmodernism." In *The Anti-Aesthetic: Essays on Postmodern Culture.* Ed. Hal Foster. Port Townsend, Washington: Bay Press, 1983, 57–82.

Oxford English Dictionary. Oxford: Oxford University Press, 1985.

Phelan, Peggy. *Unmarked: The Politics of Performance.* New York and London: Routledge, 1993.

Pleck, Elizabeth H. "A Mother's Wages: Income Earning among Married Italian and Black Women, 1896–1914." In *A Heritage of Her Own: Toward a New Social History of American Women.* Ed. Nancy F. Cott and Elizabeth H. Pleck. New York: Simon & Schuster, 1979, 367–92.

Prevots, Naima. *American Pageantry: A Movement for Art and Democracy.* Ann Arbor, MI: UMI Research Press, 1990.

Råberg, Per G. *Stockholmsutställningen 1930: Debatt och Kritik.* Dissertation, Stockholm University, 1964.

Rignall, John. *Realist Fiction and the Strolling Spectator.* London and New York: Routledge, 1992.

Rischin, Moses. *The Promised City; New York's Jews 1870–1940.*
Cambridge, MA: Harvard University Press, 1962.

Ritchie, Andrew Carnduff. *Abstract Painting and Sculpture in America.*
New York: The Museum of Modern Art, 1951.

Robin-Challan, Louise. **"Danse et danseuses l'envers du décor,
1830–1850."** Dissertation, University of Paris, 1983. (Bibliothèque de Cité
Universitaire: G.3848.)

Romero, José Luis. *La Experiencia Argentina y Otros Ensayos.* Mexico,
D.F.: Fondo de Cultura Económica, 1989.

Rose, Dan. **"Ethnography as a Form of Life: The Written Word and the
Work of the World."** In *Anthropology and Literature.* Ed. Paul Benson.
Chicago: University of Illinois Press, 1993, 192–224.

Rousseau, George S. and Roy Porter, eds. *Exoticism in the
Enlightenment.* Manchester: Manchester University Press, 1990.

Rubin, Gayle. **"The Traffic in Women."** In *Toward an Anthropology of
Women.* Ed. Rayna R. Reiter. New York: Monthly Review Press, 1975,
157–210.

Russet, Cynthia Eagle. *Darwin in America: The Intellectual Response
1865–1912.* San Francisco: W. H. Freeman, 1976.

Russett, Cynthia Eagle. *Sexual Science: The Victorian Construction of
Womanhood.* Cambridge, MA: Harvard University Press, 1989.

Ruyter, Nancy Lee Chalfa. *Reformers and Visionaries; The
Americanization of the Art of Dance.* New York: Dance Horizons, 1979.

Saint-Georges, Vernoy de, Théophile Gautier, and Jean Coraly. *Giselle ou
les wilis, ballet fantastique en 2 actes.* Paris: Mme Ve Jonas, Libraire de
l'Opéra, 1841.

Salas, Horacio. *El Tango.* Buenos Aires: Planeta, 1986.

Sarnoff, Allison. **"Getting into the Promised Land."** *Dance/USA*

Journal (May/June 1991), 24–6.

Sarnoff, Allison. **"The Presenter's Challenge."** *Dance/USA Journal* (May/June 1991), 24–6.

Schlundt, Christena L. *The Professional Appearances of Ruth St Denis & Ted Shawn: A Chronology and an Index of Dances 1906–1932.* New York: New York Public Library, 1962.

Schwartz, Hillel, **"Torque: The New Kinaesthetic of the Twentieth Century."** In *Incorporations – Zone 6.* Ed. J. Crary and S. Kwinter. New York: Urzone, 1992, 71–126.

Sears, David. **"Graham Masterworks in Revival."** *Ballet Review* 25 (Summer 1982), 25–34.

Shapiro, Meyer. **"Nature of Abstract Art."** *Marxist Quarterly* 1 (January–March 1987), 77–98.

Shawn, Ted. *Every Little Movement; A Book about Delsarte.* Reprint of second revised and enlarged edition of 1963. New York: Dance Horizons, 1974.

Sheets-Johnstone, Maxine. **"Phenomenology as a Way of Illuminating Dance."** In *Illuminating Dance: Philosophical Explorations.* Ed. Maxine Sheets-Johnstone. Cranbury, NJ: Associated University Presses, 1984, 124–45.

Shelton, Suzanne. **"The Influence of Genevieve Stebbins on the Early Career of Ruth St. Denis."** In *Essays in Dance Research: Dance Research Annual IX.* New York: CORD, 1978.

Shelton, Suzanne. *Divine Dancer: A Biography of Ruth St. Denis.* Garden City, NY: Doubleday, 1981.

Shelton, Suzanne. **"Jungian Roots of Martha Graham's Dance Imagery."** *Dance History Scholars Proceedings.* Riverside, CA: Dance History Scholars, 1983, 119–32.

Shohat, Ella. **"Notes on the 'Post-Colonial.'"** *Social Text* 31/32 (1992), 99–113.

Siegel, Marcia B. *The Shapes of Change. Images of American Dance.* Boston, MA: Houghton Mifflin Co., 1979.

Siltanen, Janet and Michelle Stanworth, eds. *Women and the Public Sphere: A Critique of Sociology and Politics.* London: Hutchinson, 1984.

Silverman, Kaja. "Fassbinder and Lacan: A Reconsideration of Gaze, Look and Image." *Camera Obscura* 19 (1989), 54–84.

Smith, Daniel Scott. "Family Limitation, Sexual Control, and Domestic Feminism in Victorian America." In *A Heritage of Her Own: Toward a New Social History of American Women.* Ed. Nancy F. Cott and Elizabeth H. Pleck. New York: Simon & Schuster, 1979, 222–45.

Snead, James A. "Repetition as a Figure of Black Culture." In *Out There: Marginalization and Contemporary Cultures.* Ed. Russell Ferguson, Martha Gever, Trinh T. Minh-ha, and Cornel West, with foreword by Marcia Tucker. New York: The New Museum of Contemporary Art, and Cambridge, MA, and London: MIT Press, 1990, 213–30.

Solomon-Godeau, Abigail. "The Legs of the Countess." *October* 39 (Winter 1986), 65–108.

Sorell, Walter. *The Dance Through the Ages.* New York: Grosset & Dunlap, 1967.

Spingarn, Joel Elias. *Creative Criticism, and Other Essays.* Port Washington, NY: Kennikot Press, 1964.

Spivak, Gayatri Chakravorty. "Three Women's Texts and a Critique of Imperialism." *Critical Inquiry* 12(1) (1985), 243–61.

Spivak, Gayatri Chakravorty. "Can the Subaltern Speak? Speculations on Widow Sacrifice." In *Marxism and the Interpretation of Culture.* Ed. Cary Nelson and Lawrence Grossberg. Urbana: University of Illinois Press, 1988, 271–313.

Spivak, Gayatri Chakravorty. *In Other Worlds: Essays in Cultural Politics.* New York: Methuen, 1988.

Spivak, Gayatri Chakravorty. "Gayatri Spivak on the Politics of the Subaltern. Interview by Howard Winant." *Socialist Review* 20(3) (1990), 81–97.

Spivak, Gayatri Chakravorty. *The Postcolonial Critic. Interviews, Strategies, Dialogues.* Ed. Sarah Harasym. New York: Routledge, 1990.

Spivak, Gayatri Chakravorty. "Acting Bits; Identity Talk." *Critical Inquiry* 18 (1992), 770–803.

St. Denis, Ruth. *An Unfinished Life; An Autobiography.* New York: Harper & Brothers, 1939.

Stebbins, Genevieve. *Society Gymnastics and Voice Culture; Adapted from the Delsarte System.* Fourth ed. New York: Edgar S. Werner, 1893.

Stebbins, Genevieve. *The Genevieve Stebbins System of Physical Training.* New York: Edgar S. Werner, 1913.

Stebbins, Genevieve. *Delsarte System of Expression.* Sixth revised and enlarged ed. New York: Edgar S. Werner, 1902. Republished New York: Dance Horizons, 1977.

Stevens, Wallace. "The Snow Man." In *The Palm at the End of the Mind: Selected Poems and a Play*. Ed. Holly Stevens. New York: Vintage Books, 1972.

Stowe, Harriet Beecher. *Uncle Tom's Cabin.* New York: Viking Penguin, 1981 [1852].

Straub, Kristina. "The Guilty Pleasures of Female Theatrical Cross-Dressing and the Autobiography of Charlotte Charke." In *Body Guards*. Ed. Julia Epstein and Kristina Straub. New York: Routledge, 1991, 142–66.

Suleiman, Susan Rubin. *Subversive Intent: Gender, Politics and the Avant-Garde.* Cambridge, MA, and London: Harvard University Press, 1990.

Sussmann, Leila. "Anatomy of the Dance Company Boom, 1958–1980." *Dance Research Journal* 16(2) (1984), 23–8.

Swales, Peter. "Freud, His Teacher and the Birth of Psychoanalysis." In *Freud: Appraisals and Reappraisals*. Ed. Paul Stepansky. Hillsdale, NJ: Analytic Press, 1986.

Tallón, José S. *El Tango en sus Etapas de Música Prohibida.* Buenos Aires: Instituto Amigos del Libro Argentino, 1964.

Tamiris in Her Own Voice: Draft of an Autobiography. Transcr., ed., annot. by Daniel Nagrin. *Studies in Dance History* 1(1) (Fall/Winter 1989–90), 1–64.

Taussig, Michael. *Shamanism, Colonialism and the Wild Man. A Study in Terror and Healing.* Chicago: University of Chicago Press, 1986.

Taussig, Michael. "*Maleficium*: State Fetishism." In *Fetishism as Cultural Discourse*. Ed. Emily Apter and William Pietz. Ithaca and London: Cornell University Press, 1993, 217–47.

Tedlock, Dennis. *The Spoken Word and the Work of Interpretation.* Philadelphia: University of Pennsylvania Press, 1983.

The Drama Review 30(3) (Fall 1986): Special Issue on Tadeusz Kantor.

Thompson, Leslie. "People as Machines and the Body as Property." *The Midwest Quarterly* 27(2) (Winter 1986), 163–80.

Tomko, Linda J. "Women, Artistic Dance Practices, and Social Change in the United States, 1890–1920. Ph.D. dissertation, University of California, Los Angeles, 1991.

Touchard-LaFosse, Georges. *Chroniques Secrètes et Galantes de l'Opéra, 1665–1845.* Paris: Gabriel Pioux et Cassanet, 1846.

Traditional Dance 5/6 (1988).

Trinh, T. Minh-ha. "Outside In Inside Out." In *Questions on Third Cinema*. Ed. Jim Pines and Paul Willemen. London: British Film Institute, 1989, 133–49.

Trinh, T. Minh-h. *Women, Native: Other: Writing Postcoloniality and Feminism.* Bloomington: Indiana University Press, 1989.

Verbrugge, Martha. *Able-Bodied Womanhood: Personal Health and Social Change in Nineteenth-Century Boston.* New York: Oxford University Press, 1988.

Véron, Louis. *Mémoires d'un bourgeois de Paris....* Paris: G. de Gonet, [1853]–1855.

Vigarello, Georges. *Le corps redressé: histoire d'un pouvoir pedagogique.* Paris: J. P. Delarge [1978].

Wallace, Maya. "In Search of the Promised Land." *Dance Magazine* (October 1991), 56–9.

Warren, Larry. *Anna Sokolow: The Rebellious Spirit.* Princeton, NJ: Princeton Book Co., 1991.

Weber, Samuel. *Institution and Interpretation.* Minneapolis: University of Minnesota Press, 1987.

Webster's Dictionary. Ninth ed. Springfield, MA: Merriam-Webster.

Wells, Robert V. "Demographic Change and the Life Cycle of American Families." *Journal of Interdisciplinary History* 2 (Autumn 1971), 272–82.

Welter, Barbara. "The Cult of True Womanhood, 1820–1860." *American Quarterly* 18 (Summer 1966), 131–75.

Werner's Directory of Elocutionists, Readers, Lecturers and Other Public Instructors and Entertainers. New York: Edgar S. Werner, 1887.

West, Cornel. *Prophesy Deliverance! An Afro-American Revolutionary Christianity.* Philadelphia: Westminster Press, 1982.

West, Cornel. *Prophetic Fragments.* Trenton: Africa World Press, 1988.

"When 7,000 School Girls Danced Around Eighty-Two May Poles in Central Park." *New York Times,* Picture section, part 1 (25 May 1913), 4–5.

White, Deborah Elise. "Studies on Hysteria: Case Histories and the Case

Against History." *MLN (Modern Language Notes)* 104(5) (December 1989), 1034–49.

Williams, Linda. **"Film Body: An Implantation of Perversions."** *Ciné-Tracts* 12 (Winter 1981), 19–35.

Willingham, John R. **"The New Criticism: Then and Now."** In *Contemporary Literary Theory*. Ed. Douglas Atkins and Laura Morrow. Amherst: University of Massachusetts Press, 1989.

Wolff, Janet. **"The Invisible Flâneuse: Women and the Literature of Modernity."** *Theory, Culture & Society* 2(3) (1985), 37–46.

Woloch, Nancy. *Women and the American Experience.* New York: Alfred A. Knopf, 1984.

Wood, Elizabeth. **"Saphonics."** In *Queering the Pitch: The New Gay and Lesbian Musicology.* Ed. Philip Brett, Elizabeth Wood, and Gary C. Thomas. New York and London: Routledge, 1994, 26–7.

Yates, Frances A. *The Art of Memory.* Chicago: University of Chicago Press, 1966.

Young, Robert. *White Mythologies. Writing History and the West.* London: Routledge, 1990.

Zimmer, Elizabeth. **"Moving Truths."** *Elle* (November 1990), 221.

Zimmer, Elizabeth. **"Ten Hours at Uncle Tom's Cabin."** *Dance/USA Journal* (May/June 1991), 24–6.

INDEX

absolute dance 35–6, 37, 39

architecture: bodily memories and 53 *ff*

arms: ballet, in 1; Indonesian dance, in 131–2

autoeroticism 11, 16

ballerina: commodification of 6, 9, 12, 14, 16; phallus, as 1 *ff*

ballet: contemporary 2–3, 7–8; gendered bodies in 1, 3, 7–8, 10; global visibility of 2, 3; plots 2, 4, 6–7, 9, 11, 14; Romantic 3 *ff*, 70; vocabulary of 4, 7

bodily memories 53 *ff*

body parts: coding of 8; psychoanalysis and 90 *ff*; representations of states of being, as 9

Breuer, Josef: psychoanalysis and the body 90 *ff*

buildings: bodily memories of 53 *ff*

capitalism: boom and bust and dance 177 *ff*; commodified female dancer and 6, 9, 12, 14, 16; effect

on bodies 163–4

Choreocriticism 199 *ff*

choreography: aeriality of 14; ballet plots and 6–7; nationalism, expressing 27; phallic inheritance of ballerina and 15; psychoanalysis, conversing with 100; subjectivity of 42; vocabulary of 7

colonization: ballet dancers' bodies and 2

courtship: ballet and 7

criticism: disappearance and 106 *ff*; John Martin and 28 *ff*; limitations of language in 35–6, 37, 39, 42, 44–6, 108–9

cross-cultural encounters 129 *ff*

cultural difference: ballet as expression of 2

Dark Meadow: John Martin and 26, 27, 28 *ff*, 41–6; Jung and 42–4

Dead Class 116 *ff*

death: Tadeusz Kantor and 116 *ff*

decline of dance: right-wing ideology and 177 *ff*

Delsartean performance: dance and 72, 74, 76, 82; drills 70, 72, 73, 76, 81–2, 85; expression and 71–2; female body and 72, 85–6; female direction of 76; gender and 84–6; generally 71–2; Genevieve Stebbins and 72, 74 *ff*; living pictures 73; male body and 72; male roles 79, 81; nudity and 79, 85; pantomimes 72, 73, 85; sexuality and 84–6; sources of 70–1; statue posing 70, 72, 73, 76–81, 83, 84–5; tableaux 73, 81

disappearance in performance 106 *ff*

displacement in performance 106 *ff*

eating: politics of 58–9

economics and dance 177 *ff*

expressional dance: John Martin's concept of 30 *ff*

eyes: ballet, in 1, 2; flâneuse, of 53 *ff*; Indonesian dance, in 131; Philippino dance, in 136